NEW PERSPECTIVES ON THE HOLOCAUST

NEW PERSPECTIVES ON THE HOLOCAUST

A Guide for Teachers and Scholars

EDITED BY ROCHELLE L. MILLEN

with TIMOTHY A. BENNETT, JACK D. MANN,
JOSEPH E. O'CONNOR, *and* ROBERT P. WELKER

NEW YORK UNIVERSITY PRESS
New York and London

NEW YORK UNIVERSITY PRESS
New York and London

© 1996 by New York University

Library of Congress Cataloging-in-Publication Data
New perspectives on the Holocaust : a guide for teachers and scholars
/ edited by Rochelle L. Millen with Timothy Bennett . . . [et al.].
       p.   cm.
    Includes bibliographical references and index.
    ISBN 0-8147-5539-9 (alk. paper).—ISBN 0-8147-5540-2 (pbk. :
alk. paper)
    1. Holocaust, Jewish (1939–1945)—Study and teaching.
2. Holocaust, Jewish (1939–1945)—Causes. Holocaust (Jewish
theology)   4. Holocaust (Christian theology)   I. Millen, Rochelle
L.,   1943–   .
D804.33.N49   1996   96-10023
                            CIP

New York University Press books are printed on acid-free paper,
and their binding materials are chosen for strength and durability.

Manufactured in the United States of America
10   9   8   7   6   5   4   3   2   1

Dedicated to the memory of Siegfried Sander (1907–1933), refugee from Nazi Germany, esteemed member of the Springfield, Ohio, community, friend of Wittenberg University. The generosity of his wife, Mrs. Ilse B. Sander, has made possible the publication of this volume.

CONTENTS

III. TEACHING TOWARD DIALOGUE: SPIRITUAL AND MORAL ISSUES

ILLUSTRATIONS

CONTRIBUTORS

MICHAEL F. BASSMAN is Assistant Chair and Associate Professor in the Department of Foreign Languages and Literatures at East Carolina University. He was a founding member of the program in Ethnic Studies and currently serves as Director.

TIMOTHY A. BENNETT is Associate Professor of German, Wittenberg University, where he teaches courses in German language, literature, and culture. He has published on Heinrich Mann and Isolde Kurz. Along with Rochelle L. Millen, he has worked to develop a learning community at Wittenberg entitled "Germans and Jews: Culture, Identity and Difference."

JACQUELINE BERKE is Professor Emerita of English and Co-Director, Center for Holocaust Study, Drew University, and is on the Advisory Board of the National Catholic Center for Holocaust Education. She is the author of *Twenty Questions for the Writer.*

FRANKLIN BIALYSTOK is the author of works on Holocaust pedagogy, remembrance, and history, and materials dealing with anti-racist education. Currently he is a doctoral candidate in the Department of History, York University, Toronto.

GAY BLOCK, a portrait photographer since 1974, began her career by creating the series "Portraits of Jews in America, 1974–85," which included images of her own community in Houston, the Jews of Miami's South Beach, and a girls' summer camp. Her books include *Fifty Texas*

Artists, and, with Malka Drucker, *Rescuers: Portraits of Moral Courage in the Holocaust.* This work was shown at the Museum of Modern Art, N.Y., and now travels the United States and Europe. She is a recipient of NEA grants and her work is in many museum collections.

RICHARD BREITMAN is Professor of History, American University. He has written three books on various aspects of the Holocaust, the most recent being *The Architect of Genocide: Himmler and the Final Solution* and an expanded edition of *Breaking the Silence,* coauthored with Walter Laqueur.

ANDREW CHARLESWORTH is Reader in Human Geography at Cheltenham and Gloucester College of Higher Education in Great Britain. Previous to that he lectured at the University of Liverpool. He is an internationally recognized scholar on rural protest in Britain 1750–1850. He is now actively publishing and researching in the areas of Holocaust education and landscapes of Holocaust memorialization.

CHARLES R. CLARKE is Chairperson, Department of Psychology, Monroe Community College.

SHARON L. DOBKIN is Associate Professor of Psychology, Monroe Community College.

MALKA DRUCKER has written sixteen books for young people, including the acclaimed Jewish Holiday Series, *Grandma's Latkes,* and *Jacob's Rescue.* She collaborated with photographer Gay Block to create *Rescuers: Portraits of Moral Courage in the Holocaust.* A frequent lecturer to groups of all ages and backgrounds, Drucker believes that the rescuers offer a role model to inspire and goad each of us to reach the highest moral behavior of which we are capable.

CAROLE FINK is Professor of European International History at Ohio State University. She is the author of *Marc Bloch: A Life in History* and *The Genoa Conference: European Diplomacy,* which was awarded the George Louis Beer Prize of the American Historical Association. Her current research in Jewish history, politics, and diplomacy includes studies of the Polish Minority Treaty of 1919 and of the murder of Walther Rathenau in 1922.

HENRY GONSHAK is Associate Professor of English, Montana Tech, of the University of Montana. He teaches a course on the Holocaust—the first such class to be offered at Montana Tech.

STEPHEN R. HAYNES, Associate Professor of Religious Studies, Rhodes College, Memphis, has published articles related to the Holocaust and Jewish-Christian relations in various scholarly journals. Other publications include *Prospects for Post-Holocaust Theology* and *Reluctant Witnesses: Jews and the Christian Imagination*.

MATTHIAS HEYL is a historian and lecturer in the Department of Education, University of Hamburg, Germany. He is currently completing his dissertation, a comparative study on Holocaust Education in Germany, the Netherlands, the United States, and Israel. He is coeditor of *Das Echo des Holocaust: Paedagogische Aspekte des Erinnerns,* Hamburg 1992 (with Helmut Schreier) and *Die Gegenwart der Schoah: Zur Aktualitaet des Mordes an den europaeischen Juden,* Hamburg 1994 (with Helmut Schreier).

CHAPLAIN (CAPTAIN) CARLOS C. HUERTA is presently an active duty chaplain in the United States Army. He is currently assigned as Battalion Chaplain for the 1st Battalion, 33rd Field Artillery, United States Army Field Artillery Training Center, Fort Sill, Oklahoma. Rabbi Huerta has numerous publications in Holocaust Revisionism/Denialism. He is presently working on a book in this area.

STEVEN L. JACOBS, Rabbi of Temple B'nai Shalom of Huntsville, Alabama, teaches Jewish and Shoah Studies at several colleges and universities. The author of many articles and reviews, he serves on the Alabama State Holocaust Advisory Council. His books include *Rethinking Jewish Faith: The Child of a Survivor Responds, Contemporary Jewish Religious Responses to the Shoah,* and *Contemporary Christian Religious Responses to the Shoah*.

ELISABETH I. KALAU is Associate Professor, Rehabilitation Services Program, Department of Health and Rehabilitation, at the University of Maine at Farmington and a member of the Board of Directors of the Holocaust Human Rights Center of Maine. Aged fourteen in 1945, she was a member of the Hitler Youth while her mother volunteered for the

German Red Cross and her father, a Nazi army officer, was in France, Poland, and Russia.

STEVEN T. KATZ is director of the Center for Jewish Studies and Professor of Religion at Boston University. He is the editor of the journal *Modern Judaism* and the author, among other works, of *The Holocaust in Historical Context.*

SHARON LEDER is Assistant Professor of English, Nassau Community College, Garden City, New York. She is coeditor of *Truth and Lamentation: Stories and Poems in the Holocaust.* She is also author of *The Language of Exclusion: The Poetry of Emily Dickinson and Christina Rossetti.*

DAGMAR C. G. LORENZ is Professor of German, Ohio State University. Her books include *Ilse Aichinger, Franz Grillparzer: Dichter des sozialen Konflikts, Verfolgung bis zum Massenmord, Diskurse zum Holocaust in deutscher Sprache,* and *Insiders and Outsiders.*

YAACOV LOZOWICK is Director of the Yad Vashem Archives in Jerusalem. He is the author of articles in English, German, and Hebrew on Eichmann, the Einsatzgruppen, and other aspects of Holocaust history.

JACK D. MANN is Associate Professor of Art, Wittenberg University, and director of the Ann Miller Gallery. He has recently completed a Holocaust memorial sculpture for Rockdale Temple in Cincinnati, Ohio.

MARSHA CAROW MARKMAN is Associate Professor of English, California Lutheran University. She is currently conducting research for a book on Holocaust diaries.

RAFAEL MEDOFF is Visiting Scholar, Jewish Studies Program, at Purchase College, State University of New York. He is the author of *The Deafening Silence: American Jewish Leaders and the Holocaust,* as well as of numerous essays and reviews.

ALAN MILCHMAN teaches in the Department of Political Science, Queens College of the City University of New York.

ROCHELLE L. MILLEN is Associate Professor of Religion, Wittenberg University. She has published articles relating to the Holocaust, modern Jewish intellectual history, and women and Jewish law. A contributing editor of the *Menorah Journal,* she is a member of the Board of the Ohio Council of Holocaust Education.

JOSEPH E. O'CONNOR, Professor of History, Wittenberg University, teaches courses on modern Europe, the Tsarist Empire and the former Soviet Union. He has published articles on Russian history and the history of the former Yugoslavia.

THE REVEREND JOHN T. PAWLIKOWSKI is Professor of Social Ethics, Catholic Theological Union, Chicago. He has authored ten books and numerous articles, many in the area of Christian-Jewish relations and the Holocaust. *Christ in the Light of the Christian Jewish Dialogue* and *The Holocaust and Christian Theology* are among his most important works. He is a member of the Bishops' Committee for Catholic-Jewish Relations. A member of the U.S. Holocaust Memorial Council since 1980, he was recently honored as "Person of the Year" for Interreligious Reconciliation by the Polish Council of Christians and Jews at a state ceremony in Warsaw.

ALAN ROSENBERG is Assistant Professor of Philosophy, Queens College of the City University of New York.

ANN L. SALTZMAN is Associate Professor of Psychology and Co-Director, Center for Holocaust Study, Drew University.

DONALD G. SCHILLING is Professor of History, Denison University, where he teaches courses on Germany history and the history of the Holocaust. In February 1994, *German Studies Review* published his most recent article, "Politics in a New Key: The Late Nineteenth-Century Transformation of Politics in Northern Bavaria."

WILLIAM E. SEIDELMAN, M.D. is Professor, Department of Family and Community Medicine, University of Toronto. Medical Director of the Ambulatory HIV Program at the Wellesley Hospital, Toronto, Ontario, he is an internationally recognized expert on the history of medicine in Nazi Germany and the continuing ethical challenges arising from that legacy.

DAFNA SHIFFMAN-HUERTA, M.D., a former officer in the Israel Defense Forces and a graduate of Ben Gurion University of the Negev Medical School, collaborated extensively on the organization and preparation of "Holocaust Denial Literature: Its Place in Teaching the Holocaust"; Dr. Shiffman-Huerta died in Jerusalem prior to its completion. Her gentle but insistent probing for truth will be missed.

MILTON TEICHMAN is Professor of English and Coordinator of Jewish Studies at Marist College, Poughkeepsie, New York. He has written on the poetry of Wordsworth and Coleridge, the teaching of the Holocaust, and the teaching of writing. He is coeditor of *Truth and Lamentation: Stories and Poems on the Holocaust.*

ROBERT P. WELKER is Associate Professor of Education and Director of Common Learning, Wittenberg University. Dr. Welker is the author of *The Teacher as Expert* and is currently working on a book about how professional self-perceptions are influenced by stories.

SARA LEUCHTER WILKINS is Senior Communications Specialist at Ashland Coal, Inc., in Huntington, West Virginia, and Adjunct Professor of History at Marshall University. She co-conducted the Wisconsin Survivors of the Holocaust Oral History Project under the auspices of the State Historical Society of Wisconsin. She also wrote and edited an extensive guide to the oral history collection and has lectured and published widely on the uses of oral history to document the Holocaust experience.

FOREWORD

ROCHELLE L. MILLEN

Memory is the basis of individual personality, just as tradition is the basis of the collective personality of a people. We live in memory and by memory, and our spiritual life is at bottom simply the effort of our memory to persist, to transform itself into hope, the effort of our past to transform itself into our future.

— MIGUEL DE UNAMUNO, *Tragic Sense of Life*

Myth and memory condition action. There are myths that are life-sustaining and deserve to be reinterpreted for our age. There are some that lead astray and must be redefined. Others are dangerous and must be exposed.

— YOSEF HAYIM YERUSHALMI, *Zachor: Jewish History and Jewish Memory*

This volume is the outgrowth of an international conference "Teaching the Holocaust: Issues and Dilemmas" held at Wittenberg University, in cooperation with Yad Vashem in October, 1993.

Acutely aware of our inability to master the unmasterable[1] and of the need to find words to help understand the fundamentally unspeakable horror of the Holocaust, several of us at Wittenberg University felt compelled to create a forum where the pressing questions of Holocaust education could be explored. As scholars and teachers of the humanities, we wished to plan a conference which would speak against silence while grappling for words and images; to open a conversation which might move toward mastering the incomprehensible; and to gather together scholars and teachers who struggle with how to teach the Holocaust.

This task had several sources of inspiration. In July 1991, I attended the Yad Vashem Educators' Summer Seminar, which influenced me to organize a similar type of gathering here in the United States. My parents, of blessed memory, immigrants from Poland to the United States in 1936, lost many members of their families to the onslaughts of the

Einsatzgruppen in 1943. Growing up in a family shadowed by this loss made even more powerful all that Yad Vashem offered its seminar participants. In addition, teaching Jewish Studies at a church-related university has served as an impetus for exploring central issues of Christian-Jewish relations and their connection to the Holocaust. Colleagues in several departments expressed interest in working on an international meeting. Thus the October 1993 conference, organized by Wittenberg University in cooperation with Yad Vashem, the Holocaust Martyrs' and Heroes' Remembrance Authority in Jerusalem, Israel, came to be.

The papers in this volume, culled from conference presentations, represent a diversity of approaches and suggest how profoundly educators are engaged by the moral dilemmas posed by the Holocaust. They demonstrate the search for language that is both personal and discipline-based and the pondering of the problem not only of what to teach, but also of how to transmit and to what ends. They acknowledge the need for an interdisciplinary approach, one which accesses our variegated ways of knowing. Thus, the essays are interspersed with photographs and abbreviated versions of the stories behind the photographs, making us aware, through visual and narrative means, of the complexity of events that was the Shoah. The axiological uncertainties emanating out of Holocaust-related events remain unresolved; nevertheless, they demand we attempt to deal with them.

The conference, of course, had its own context and was especially effective in the many conversations and interactions it spawned among presenters, students, faculty, and the general public. The papers in this volume also manifest a dialogue among different aspects of Holocaust studies. In the give-and-take presented here lies an important contribution, a series of tentative but forward-moving steps toward expressing and dealing with the methodological and substantive problems facing committed teachers and academics.

The five essays in part 1, "Viewing the Holocaust in Context," confront issues of history and interpretation of historical events. As such, part 1 places us within the parameters of the incidents themselves and compels us to consider their complexity. Part 2, "Considering Issues of Teaching and Curriculum," moves beyond issues of interpretation of historical controversies to emphasize methodological and conceptual complexities. As the central focus of this volume, it offers concrete suggestions, carefully constructed curricula, unusual projects and per-

spectives, and selected bibliographies. It continues the important, ongoing conversations among humanities scholars and middle/high school
teachers about the Holocaust and the unique pedagogical challenges it
presents. Essays on the general theme of "Teaching toward Dialogue:
Spiritual and Moral Issues" constitute part 3. These six essays, drawing
upon the emphasis on historical substance and the teaching of methodology in parts 1 and 2, confront specific dilemmas of dialogue between
diverse groups and conceptions: Israelis and Germans; post-war Germans with their history; Jews and Christians; post-Holocaust Jewish and
Christian theology; and medical ethics and Nazi doctors. The volume
thus concludes by thickening, yet clarifying, the moral and religious web
of issues generated by the Holocaust.

The authors, all actively involved in teaching about the Shoah, reflect
upon questions that teachers at many levels face in the classroom. They
add complexity to the multidisciplinary aspect of Holocaust studies and
the issues surrounding the teaching of the Holocaust, particularly the
issue of Jewish-Christian relations. Indeed, both the 1993 conference
and this collection of papers deriving from it represent a significant
instance of Jewish-Christian cooperation in facilitating Holocaust education.

The support, encouragement, and advice of the Wittenberg academic
administration, especially then-President Dr. William A. Kinnison, Pro-
vost Dr. Sammye Greer, and Vice-President Dr. Charles Dominick, are
related not only to their genuine interest in a most worthy academic
and educational enterprise, but also—and perhaps essentially—to the
forward movements within the Evangelical Lutheran Church in America
in regard to Jewish-Christian relations. It appears not to be a coincidence
that Wittenberg's support for the conference and this volume came at a
time when the agenda of the 1993 Churchwide Assembly of the Evangelical Lutheran Church in America was to consider a statement on Lu-
theran-Jewish relations. Indeed, that Assembly overwhelmingly passed a
recommendation condemning the "ugly, poisonous words—words
which proved to be seeds for a deadly harvest"[2] in Luther's 1543 tract,
"On the Jews and Their Lies." This collection, then, is testimony to the
willingness of certain individuals and groups to enter into dialogue; to
listen respectfully to each other; to face the immeasurable pain and
shame—legacies of the Shoah; and to move from the "deadly harvest"
to the planting of new seeds.

All of the editors, Timothy A. Bennett, Jack D. Mann, Joseph E. O'Connor, Robert P. Welker, and myself, extend deepest thanks to Mrs. Rosemarie Burley, Faculty Secretary at Wittenberg, for her astuteness, efficiency, and capacity for laughter. We greatly value her professionalism and wish to acknowledge her contributions to bringing this volume to fruition. Our thanks to Ms. Jennifer Hammer, Associate Editor at New York University Press, for her encouragement and guidance, to Gene U. Harvey, Director of Academic Computing at Wittenberg for his technical assistance, and to the Wittenberg Faculty Research Fund Board for underwriting the index.

We are indebted to Gay Block, photographer, and Malka Drucker, author, for permission to use photographs and paraphrase captions from their extraordinary book *Rescuers: Portraits of Moral Courage in the Holocaust* (New York: Holmes and Meier, 1992).

We would like to thank the *Journal of Ecumenical Studies* for permission to use a revised version of Stephen R. Haynes's essay "Christianity, Anti-Semitism and Post-holocaust Theology: Old questions, Changing Paradigms" (32:1, Winter 95).

Finally, we wish to express our sincere appreciation to Mrs. Ilse B. Sander for her generosity in making possible the publication of this volume. It is dedicated to the memory of her late husband, Siegfried.

As a focal event of modern Western history, the Holocaust demands that we explore ways to draw from its awe-fullness, to learn to educate toward goodness and moral responsibility. This work is one response to that demand.

NOTES

1. Charles Maier, *The Unmasterable Past: History, Holocaust, and German National Identity* (Cambridge: Harvard University Press, 1988). Gershom Scholem, in his 1966 essay "Jews and Germans" (reprinted in *On Jews and Judaism in Crisis: Selected Essays* (New York: Schocken, 1978) concludes his reflections by stating, "Only by remembering a past that we will *never completely master* can we generate hope in the resumption of communication between German and Jews, and in the reconciliation of those who have been separated" (92, emphasis mine).

2. Statement of the Rev. John K. Stendahl as quoted in *Reports and Records*, vol. 2; Assembly Minutes, 1993 Churchwide Assembly, *ELCA*, 463.

PART I

VIEWING THE HOLOCAUST IN CONTEXT

INTRODUCTION

JOSEPH E. O'CONNOR

The twentieth century is becoming inured to catastrophes. The Armenian atrocities, the bombing of Hiroshima, tribal vengeance in Rwanda, and ethnic cleansing in Bosnia—these and innumerable other acts of modern barbarism threaten to scar our collective conscience so severely that we no longer feel compassion. We grow numb; we are tempted to feign ignorance. Yet those who teach the history of the Holocaust cannot afford to turn away. In the words of Leni Yahil, "The catastrophe was not of the Jews alone. It was a general human catastrophe: Europe's culture and civilization, forged through centuries, was ravaged during the days of Hitler's rule, and the human condition in the modern, technological world was illuminated by the fires of the crematoria of Auschwitz." [1]

In the first selection presented in this section, Alan Milchman and Alan Rosenberg suggest that our views of the Holocaust are traditionally caught in a series of binary opposites. "The uniqueness of the Shoah is counterposed to its historicization, the one excluding the other. Similarly, the singularity of the Holocaust is counterposed to its universality—and once again, the one excludes the other." Thus, from a historical perspective, the most fundamental question that teachers of the Holocaust must concern themselves with impinges on the nature of history itself. Was the Shoah a singularity, an event of such unprecedented evil that it transcends history, or was it thoroughly imbedded in the political and cultural tradition of the West? This question has been debated among historians for more than a decade and echoes to one degree or another in all the selections of this section.

Milchman and Rosenberg themselves reject the argument that the

3

Holocaust was either unique or universal, singular or historical. They insist that it was both, a "caesura," an interruption in history, but linked to what they believe is a particularly Western notion of "truth as representation," a notion that lends itself to the reduction of all to manipulable and dispensable entities. They regard the Holocaust as a singular combination of modern technology and mechanical mentality — Heidegger's "planetary technics" — yet universal, for its constituent elements remain with us, awaiting only a propitious occasion to be revived again.

Steven T. Katz likewise rejects the binary opposites that Milchman and Rosenberg describe. In our second selection, he decries what he calls the "mystification of the Shoah." It is not, he insists, "in some mysterious ontological manner outside of time"; it is rather "an immanent historical event that is, and must be, fully subject to the rigorous canons of historical research." That said, Katz argues that the Holocaust was unique, without historical parallels. In particular, he rejects the notion that Stalin's Gulag was equivalently horrific. He supports his case by examining, on the basis of recollections of Alexander Solzhenitsyn, Pyotr Yakir, and others, the treatment of children in the Gulag and in the camps of the Holocaust. In the former, he argues, Soviet children, while treated brutally, were in many cases kept alive. They were not, on principle, to be annihilated, for they ultimately represented the future of the Soviet state. There was no such protection for Jewish children in the Shoah. They were the "carriers of that cosmic contagion that threatened death to us all" and therefore had to be put to death along with their elders. Katz has no wish to diminish the terror of the Gulag. But he insists that its parameters were different; it was not a parallel system to the Holocaust.

Carole Fink, author of our third selection, is similarly convinced that the Holocaust is woven into the warp and woof of history but draws our attention to another historical controversy. She distinguishes between historians who view the Holocaust as the inevitable outgrowth of centuries of European anti-Semitism and those, not merely German, historians who would direct our attention to contingent factors and disconnect the Holocaust from the tradition of German and Western culture. Renouncing both determinism and the view that the Holocaust was utterly contingent, she focuses on what she believes was a prophetic moment in German history, the assassination of the talented Jewish Foreign Minister, Walther Rathenau, in 1922: "This was the first time in German history that a Jew in a prominent position was killed because he was a Jew in a prominent position." As such, she believes, it presaged the calamity that was to begin eleven years later.

While rejecting the notion that the Holocaust was inevitable—"only in hindsight can it be interpreted as the sum total of its pre-history"—Dagmar C. G. Lorenz, the author of our fourth selection, insists that the Shoah was more than just another stage in the history of the persecution of the Jews. It was, she believes, the consequence of centuries of anti-Semitic discourse so pervasive that it calls into question Western culture itself. Beginning with Luther and continuing through the Enlightenment and the obsession with race in the nineteenth century, she offers examples of cultural prejudice in language and literature which easily provided fuel for the fires of Auschwitz. In the darkness of this tradition, she finds the source of the Shoah, and in turn suggests that the Holocaust is of such terrible significance that it requires a reevaluation of all of Western discourse.

Perhaps the most productive controversy among historians of the Holocaust has been the long-term debate between "intentionalists," who emphasize Hitler's role in determining the Final Solution, and "functionalists," who see the Final Solution not as the result of a specific and premeditated decision but emerging from the chaotic radicalization of Nazi policy in the wake of military failure in Russia. Richard Breitman, a contributor to this debate, is author of the final selection of this section. To those who have noted the paucity of documents directly connecting Hitler to the decision to annihilate the Jews of Europe, Breitman argues that "Hitler and Himmler were addicted to secrecy," and offers as evidence a fascinating analysis of a cleverly deceitful letter from Himmler to Heinrich Müller, head of the Gestapo, concerning the treatment of corpses of deceased Jews.

Breitman also pleads, in a sentiment shared by all five contributors to this section, for historians whatever their viewpoint to be careful in their research and precise in their writing. "Mistakes and misinformation," he fears, "may be exploited by those who wish to create new, destructive myths." His plea is well timed in light of increasing efforts to perpetuate the most destructive historical myth of all, the myth of denial.

NOTE

1. Leni Yahil, *The Holocaust: The Fate of European Jewry, 1932–1945* (New York: Oxford University Press, 1990), 9.

CHAPTER 1

Two Kinds of Uniqueness: The Universal

Aspects of the Holocaust

ALAN MILCHMAN AND ALAN ROSENBERG

Of all the dilemmas, paradoxes, and enigmas facing those who study the Holocaust, the question of its uniqueness or singularity is perhaps the most vexing and divisive, the one issue most likely to generate partisan debate, and to provoke emotional heat in discussion.[1] Quite apart from the intensity with which the question of the uniqueness of the Shoah is often propounded or rejected, those involved in this debate, with some notable exceptions, are in agreement on at least one fundamental point: the issue of the singularity of the Holocaust is embedded in a series of binary oppositions. Thus, the uniqueness of the Shoah is counterposed to its historicization, the one excluding the other. Similarly, the singularity of the Holocaust is counterposed to its universality—and once again, the one excludes the other.[2]

The historicization of the Holocaust, with its insistence on the need for contextualization and by its use of comparative methods to explore the similarities as well as differences between the Holocaust and other manifestations of human-made mass-death, seems to challenge any claims for its singularity. Thus Ernst Nolte's insistence that Stalin's Gulag is comparable to the Holocaust, and that the Extermination was itself provoked by Hitler's fear of the Gulag, to which it was a desperate reaction, points to the danger of the historicization of the Holocaust becoming the occasion for its relativization, and normalization, which can even—as it does in Nolte's hands—degenerate into apologetics.[3]

Though representing a very different political perspective than Nolte's, because it involves not even the least hint of apologetics but rather insists on the extreme horror of Auschwitz, André Glucksmann's writ-

ings manifest the same binary opposition between uniqueness and historicization in their treatment of the Holocaust. For Glucksmann, the singularity of the Holocaust is elided as it is submerged in a train of
barbarism, and human-made mass-death, that have punctuated the history of the West, and of modernity in particular: "at Buchenwald and
Auschwitz the Germans did indeed act in the European way, exempli-
fying a European (even Western, modern, revolutionary) manner of
imposing 'final solutions,' a manner which was illustrated equally well
at Pulo-Condor in Vietnam, under French and then American occupation, and, through half a century, in the Soviet Union's Kolyma." [4] What
we want to highlight here is not Glucksmann's insistence that Auschwitz
was a product of European or Western civilization, nor his use of
comparisons with other cases of modern barbarism, both of which seem
to us to be sound, but rather the ease with which the uniqueness of the
Shoah simply vanishes in a discourse which historicizes. [5]

The recourse to binary oppositions is no less evident when the question of the singularity of the Holocaust encounters the claims for its
universality. Thus, Elie Wiesel has passionately argued that the uniqueness of the Holocaust is such that it cannot even be designated an event
in history: "the universe of concentration camps, by its design, lies
outside if not beyond history. Its vocabulary belongs to it alone." [6] Such
a view sees the Shoah as a transcendent event, unconnected to the
trajectory of our techno-scientific civilization sprung from the sociocultural matrix of the West; its singularity is such that it exceeds the power
of language to express it: the Holocaust is finally ineffable.

Even where the Holocaust is not judged to be transcendent, or ineffable, but is conceived as having an exclusively or essentially anti-Jewish
character, its possible universality is effectively precluded. That is the
thrust of the questions rhetorically raised by David Vital, with respect to
the Holocaust:

> Was it then in some crucial and decisive sense not only an event in
> but also peculiar to Jewish history, and comprehensible ultimately
> only in its terms? . . . is it amenable to being rendered intelligible
> only in terms that are specific to the Jews? [7]

Indeed, it would seem that a claim for the universality of the Holocaust must involve a rejection of its uniqueness. That, at least, is how
Yehuda Bauer has formulated the question:

If what happens to the Jews is unique, then by definition it doesn't concern us, beyond our pity and commiseration for the victims. If the Holocaust is not a universal problem, then why should a public school system in Philadelphia, New York or Timbuktu teach it? Well, the answer is that there is no uniqueness, not even of a unique event. Anything that happens once, can happen again: not quite in the same way, perhaps, but in an equivalent form.[8]

In this paper, we intend to argue for the uniqueness of the Shoah. However, our own conception of that uniqueness seeks to explode the binary oppositions in which this question has been entangled. For us, the very singularity of the Holocaust must be integrally linked to its historicization, and contextualization, which perforce will involve comparisons, aimed at elucidating similarities as well as distinctions between different manifestations of human-made mass-death. Contextualization, and the comparative method, far from eliminating the unique elements of the Holocaust, in our view can highlight its singularity, even as they focus our attention on its similarities to other exterminatory events. In much the same fashion, we will insist that the singularity of the Extermination is inextricably bound to its universality. The Holocaust world that emerged in all its singularity, albeit in an incipient form at Auschwitz, and the other Nazi death camps, has now become an objective-real possibility on the front of history.

In elaborating a conception of the uniqueness of the Holocaust that explodes the binary oppositions that have made such a claim incompatible with the historicization, or universality, of the Shoah, we intend to proceed in two steps. First, we will take up some issues of an ontological and epistemological nature concerning the meaning of uniqueness, and its application to historical events. Second, we will articulate our own conception of the singularity of the Holocaust, one based on its rigorous contextualization and its awesome universality.

The ontological-epistemological question that arises when one designates an historical event as unique is twofold: what is the ontological status of that which we commonly designate as an "event"; and when one claims that one cluster of "events" is radically different from another, is the ascription of "different" or "unique" placed upon the event, or is it inherent in it?

The very term "event," by virtue of its ontological fixity, seems to belie the social construction of reality and its processual character. That events are constructed, in an ongoing process by historical actors and by those who theorize them, that there is no event without interpretation, is obscured by a nomenclature that rigidly compartmentalizes and separates past, present, and future, and segments reality into discrete events, which seemingly exist apart from the process of interpretation and reinterpretation through which they arise. Given the overwhelming linguistic presence of traditional ontology, it is extremely difficult even to find the language to evoke the character of reality as socially constructed and processual. The use of the gerund form, eventing, would best capture the fact that history is an ongoing process, but its very linguistic awkwardness constitutes a formidable obstacle to such usage. Putting the term *event* in quotation marks might alert the reader to the danger of seeing events as finished once and for all, or viewing them as having an existence separate from the process of interpretation itself, but that too is an awkward procedure. We should be sensitive to these linguistic issues, even as we provisionally continue to the use a language which normally speaks of historical events as if they were fixed and discrete.

To speak of the uniqueness of an event is to ascribe meaning to it. Is this meaning applied to the event, or is it already inscribed in it? What is at issue here is our concept of truth. The Western tradition has in one way or another been shaped by a conception of truth as representation, in which our mental picture correctly represents what is "out there," in this case the historical event, and in which our words "correspond" to the things that they designate or represent. This is the epistemological corollary to a static ontology which sees discrete events rather than an ongoing process.

We reject the idea that meaning already inheres in events, and that it is the task of the historian, the social theorist, or the philosopher to discover that meaning, and to articulate it in words that correspond to the events that they designate. This is not to say that the ascription by the historian or philosopher arbitrarily "creates" the meaning of events. Such meaning is socially or culturally constructed by the actors in the historical process, then enshrined in the theorization of those selfsame events, which is the activity of the historian or philosopher. On this view, truth is a function of our way of being-in-the-world; events, and their meaning, are "carved out" of the flow of our being-in-the-world, and socially constructed. This means that any historical event can always be redescribed, or reconstructed, from a different cultural or social perspective, thereby giving rise to what Jean-François Lyotard has termed "differends."[9] Nonetheless, the designation of an historical event as unique or singular is culturally meaningful insofar as it enables us to construct, and act in, the world. And it is on this basis that a designation of the Holocaust as unique can be made.

The ontological-epistemological questions raised above are especially pertinent to the Holocaust because the very Western conception of truth as representation, and the metaphysics that is linked to it, may itself be a factor that led to the death-world that emerged at Auschwitz. Truth as representation, and the metaphysics of the subject in which it is embedded, is linked to the universal mathesis, and the reduction of all entities, including human beings, to standing reserve, that the German philosopher Martin Heidegger saw as the basis of planetary technics, and which he designated as the reign of *das Ge-stell* or enframing. With enframing, everything, including humans, shows up as raw material to be manipulated, controlled, processed, or dispensed with, by the imperative of a boundless will-to-power. The technological understanding of beings, which Heidegger saw as the hallmark of our Western, now increasingly global, civilization, including its conception of truth as representation, is a part of the sociocultural matrix that produced the death-world constructed by the Nazis at Auschwitz.[10] Of course, this is not to draw a straight line from truth as representation to the death camps. However, it can alert us to the manifold of intersecting lines out of which the possibility of the Holocaust became actuality.

We now want to turn to the complex of factors that lead us to insist on the uniqueness of the Holocaust, even as we argue for both its historicization and its universality. The claim of "uniqueness" is intended to set apart from other historical events, to distinguish in the flow of history, just that singular event that has the potential of transforming a culture, or altering the course of history, in a profound or decisive way. We believe that the Holocaust was just such a transformational event. Indeed, following Phillipe Lacoue-Labarthe, we can best describe the Holocaust—or to use Lacoue-Labarthe's terminology, "the Extermination"—as a caesura in global history.[11] For Lacoue-Labarthe, a "caesura would be that which, within history, interrupts history and opens up another possibility of history, or else closes off all possibility of history."[12] The German-Jewish historian and social theorist, Dan Diner, has expressed the transformational character of Auschwitz by his designation of it as a Zivilisationsbruch, or break or rupture in civilization.[13] Tropes such as a caesura, or Zivilisationsbruch, are intended to make manifest the starkness of the transformation wrought by the Extermination, to emphasize the uniqueness of the event, which rent the very fabric of civilization. The Holocaust, of which Auschwitz is emblematic, opened a door into a world in which human-made mass-death can become constitutive of the sociocultural matrix.

While constituting the novum that opened a door into a possible Holocaust world, Auschwitz also closed a door on another world, the world shaped by the dream of the imminent dawn of perpetual peace, and the idea of inevitable and continuous progress, that had been one strand of the Enlightenment project. That project of modernity at the least had to face the formidable challenge of those forces incarnating the dark side of modernity, of the will-to-power that Heidegger saw as inseparable from the reign of planetary technics. It is this conundrum that has led Lyotard to "argue that the project of modernity (the realization of universality) has not been forsaken or forgotten but destroyed, 'liquidated.' There are several modes of destruction, several names that are symbols for them. 'Auschwitz' can be taken as a paradigmatic name for the tragic 'incompletion' of modernity." [14]

Yet the caesura that was Auschwitz did not appear out of nowhere. As Claude Lanzmann has insisted,

> To say that the Holocaust is unique and incommensurable does not imply that it is an aberration that eludes all intellectual and conceptual comprehension, which falls outside history and is denied the dignity of being a historical event. On the contrary, we consider the Holocaust to be a completely historical event, the legitimate, albeit monstrous, product of the entire history of the Western world.[15]

Linking the Holocaust, and its uniqueness, to the history of the West, however, raises several crucial questions. It is important to avoid the trap of a teleological reading of the history of the West, in which the Holocaust becomes fate, the preordained outcome of the flow of history. While Lanzmann's formulation may be open to such a reading, Lacoue-Labarthe seems to us to have fallen clearly into just that trap when he asserts that "in the Auschwitz apocalypse, it was nothing less than the West, in its essence, that revealed itself." [16] History is not the revelation of essences; indeed, the whole vocabulary of essence, and its revelation, must be suspect. Teleology apart, Lanzmann's formulation is questionable because it totalizes, and demonizes, the history of the West. We too believe that the Holocaust is the outcome of profound tendencies integral to the project of the West, but that project, that history, cannot be reduced to an antechamber to Auschwitz.

In contextualizing the Holocaust firmly within the history of the West, we must be clear as to just which facets of its project could have produced the Shoah, and warrant its designation as unique. The Israeli historian, Otto Dov Kulka, expanding on the pathbreaking work of Shmuel Ettinger, has argued that the singularity of the Holocaust derives from the centrality of anti-Semitism to the Nazi project. However, in a bold move, Kulka links this anti-Semitism to the whole trajectory of the West, where it constitutes a leitmotiv of its cultural history. For Kulka, anti-Semitism is not merely an expression of conservative or reactionary trends which have opposed the project of modernity, which is where most historians locate the phenomenon, but of the very "progressive" tendencies arising in the Enlightenment and providing the cultural dynamic for the project of modernity.[17] Far from making the anti-Semitism that he finds central to the Shoah the occasion for interpreting it as a transcendent event, Kulka's argument for the singularity of the Holocaust rests on its historicization; for Kulka, "the 'Jewish Question' was placed at the heart of an historical event [the Holocaust] that can be regarded as the gravest and most menacing crisis of Western civilization: an attempt to revolt against the roots of its very existence."[18]

Where Kulka sees in the Holocaust a revolt against the cultural roots of the West, French postmodernist thinkers, such as Phillipe Lacoue-Labarthe, Jean-François Lyotard, Jacques Derrida, and Maurice Blanchot insist that in its choice of the Jew as the "other" to be exterminated, the West manifested its essence, or at the least profound tendencies at the heart of its project.[19] Thus, Lacoue-Labarthe has argued that "it was not at all by chance that the victims of that annihilation attempt [the Extermination] were the witnesses in the West of another origin of the God who was venerated and thought there—if not indeed, perhaps, of another God—one who had evaded capture by the Hellenistic and Roman traditions and who thereby stood in the way of the programme of accomplishment."[20]

While the understanding of the role of anti-Semitism in the singularity of the Holocaust cannot be separated from its contextualization in the history of the West, we cannot reduce the uniqueness of the Extermination to its choice of victim. Hannah Arendt's strictures in this regard cannot be ignored: "Anti-Semitism by itself has such a long and bloody history that the very fact that the death factories were chiefly fed with Jewish 'material' has somewhat obliterated the uniqueness of this operation."[21] It is not only that anti-Semitism has been a constant in the history of the West, whereas the exterminatory project, and its actualization in the death camps, was a novum, that led Arendt to look beyond the Jewish question for the bases of the uniqueness of the Holocaust. It was the "nonutilitarian character" of the camps, their senselessness in terms of instrumental reason, that seemed to her one of the bases for distinguishing the death camps from earlier orgies of bloodletting, whatever the nature of their victims.[22]

Nonetheless, we want to insist on two other factors firmly ensconced within the project of modernity which seem to us to be integral to designating the Holocaust as unique: the reign of planetary technics and the rage against alterity.

In the Shoah, the practice of mass-murder and genocide, which had previously occurred in history, was inextricably linked to the very development of science and modern technology. One of the crucial distinctions between the death-world created by the Nazis, and orgies of mass-murder before and even after (as in Bosnia today), was the technical efficiency and organization of the Holocaust. The Shoah was made possible by the ruthless application of the prodigious creations of twentieth-century science and technology. This is not simply a matter of the actual instruments of death, for as Steven T. Katz has pointed out, "death by gas was not a major technological advance as compared with, say, the jet engine, radar, and sonar, the Nazis' own V1 and V2 rockets, or, above all else as a qualitative breakthrough, the atomic bomb."[23] Nonetheless, Zyklon B, and the crematoria, as instruments of death, were far more technically sophisticated than the guns of the Einsatzgruppen, or the deliberate torture, starvation, or working to death of millions in the Gulag. Indeed, they were the fruits of the same nexus of technological and scientific productivity that resulted in the atomic bomb, and upon which our late-twentieth-century civilization now rests. More pertinent, perhaps, is the fact that the direct instruments of death were themselves inserted into a matrix that was the culmination of the West's technological development—transport, record-keeping, surveillance—which made possible the industrialization of mass-death that was a unique characteristic of the Holocaust.

However, the link between technology and the event of Extermination will elude us if we limit ourselves to conceiving technology in purely instrumental terms, to seeing it merely as a collection of machines, technical instruments, and procedures. Such a definition of technology overlooks the mentality on which technology as instrumentality is based. To avoid confusion, we will distinguish between "technology" in the instrumental sense, and "technics," which underlies it and constitutes the mode by which humans disclose and relate to entities—other humans, their products, and nature. In the reign of planetary technics, as Heidegger has indicated, all entities are conceived, and treated as mere "standing reserve," to be manipulated and utilized in the service of an insatiable will-to-power. It is this manner of disclosing entities, this reign of planetary technics, that provided the framework in which technology as instrument could be utilized in the mass production of death.

In the Holocaust, perhaps for the first time in human history, science and technology, together with their bases in planetary technics, were joined in the effort to totally exterminate the Other, alterity itself—in that instance in the form of the Jews. The more the inexorable "progress" of techno-scientific civilization atomizes human beings, and shatters the bonds of communities, the more the modern state is compelled to fabricate a "pseudo-community" based on a mass mobilization around populist-nationalist ideologies. Such "pseudo-communities" are less an effort to return to a premodern world, than an adaptation of techno-scientific civilization to a situation that its basic conditions of existence may have rendered irreversible. Absolute rage at the Other, at alterity itself, is the counterpart to the effort to create "pseudo-communities" within the shell of modernity. The Other is a nonperson in a "pseudo-community" which demonizes him, victimizes her—and then erases them from its collective memory. In Hitler's Germany, the Jews were the embodiment of alterity, the Other, a scourge to be exterminated.

If the Holocaust was, to use Blanchot's words, "the absolute event of history,"[24] then its uniqueness, we believe, lies in its unprecedented combination of the utilization of all the fruits of planetary technics, and its science and technology, in the service of the total elimination of the Other. It is precisely this singularity that confers universality on the

Holocaust. The elements out of which the Holocaust emerged remain features integral to our modernity. Planetary technics and the rage against alterity await a political movement which can recombine them, perhaps with a lethality comparable to that of the Nazis. Hannah Arendt recognized this potential for a repetition of the horrors of the Extermination:

> It is in the very nature of things human that every act that has once made its appearance and has been recorded in the history of mankind stays with mankind as a potentiality long after its actuality has become a thing of the past . . . the particular reasons that speak for a possibility of repetition of the crime committed by the Nazis are even more plausible. The frightening coincidence of the modern population explosion with the discovery of technical devices that, through automation, will make large sections of the population "superfluous" even in terms of labor, and that, through nuclear energy, make it possible to deal with this twofold threat by use of instruments beside which Hitler's gassing installations look like an evil child's fumbling toys should be enough to make us tremble.[25]

If we add to Arendt's grim scenario the rage at alterity which haunts our late modern world, the existence within each of our societies of an Other, scorned and hated, then the danger that we again may cross the threshold into a Holocaust world looms especially large.

The universality of the Holocaust lies precisely in the fact that its constituent elements, those that stamped it with its singularity, are over-ripe in our techno-scientific civilization, and that the cry that arose from the ashes at Auschwitz, "never again!", may prove to have been futile.

NOTES

1. For an overview of the intense debate over the singularity of the Holocaust and an annotated bibliography of some of the most important literature see Alan Rosenberg and Evelyn Silverman, "The Issue of the Holocaust as a Unique Event" in Michael N. Dobkowski and Isidore Wallimann, *Genocide in Our Time: An Annotated Bibliography with Analytical Introductions* (Ann Arbor, Mich.: Pierian Press, 1992).

2. Though our own view is quite different from his, among scholars of the Holocaust, Steven T. Katz is one of the few who insists on viewing its uniqueness in a historical, and comparative, perspective. See the essays collected in his *Historicism, the Holocaust, and Zionism: Critical Studies in Modern Jewish*

Thought and History (New York: New York University Press, 1992), as well as his *The Holocaust in Historical Context,* vol. 1 (Oxford: Oxford University Press, 1994), the first of three volumes.

3. See Ernst Nolte, "Between Historical Legend and Revisionism? The Third Reich in the Perspective of 1980," and "The Past that Will Not Pass: A Speech that Could Be Written but Not Delivered," both in James Knowlton and Truett Cates, trans., *Forever in the Shadow of Hitler? Original Documents of the Historikerstreit: The Controversy concerning the Singularity of the Holocaust* (Atlantic Highlands, N.J.: Humanities Press, 1993). It is important to note that Nolte, in contrast to Paul Rassinier or Robert Faurisson, is no "denier" who controverts the existence of the death camps, but a relativizer, or "trivializer," for whom the Holocaust loses its uniqueness in the midst of the many other examples of human-made mass-death which have made the twentieth century so bloody.

4. André Glucksmann, *The Master Thinkers* (New York: Harper and Row, 1980), 44. In his most recent work, *Le XIe Commandement,* Glucksmann extends his analysis of "final solutions" to include the butcheries perpetrated by Third World dictators such as Khomeini and Saddam Hussein, subsuming the human-made mass-death inflicted on its subjects by the state under a kind of "fundamentalism" or ideological will-to-mastery that originated in European civilization, but which has now become global.

5. Two other examples of the binary opposition between singularity and historicization are apposite here. William V. Spanos has argued that insisting on the uniqueness of the Holocaust will make us insensitive to other cases of human-made mass-death that punctuate the history of the West to the present day, for example the horrors inflicted on the Vietnamese by the United States, "a violence that was also racist and genocidal and thus in some fundamental sense commensurate in its horrible consequences for the Vietnamese people with the horror of the Nazi project to exterminate the Jews." See William V. Spanos, *Heidegger and Criticism: Retrieving the Cultural Politics of Destruction* (Minneapolis: University of Minnesota Press, 1993), 220. Detlev J. K. Peukert has contended that the insistence on the singularity of the Shoah and its Jewish victims obscures the fate of other victims of the Nazi terror: "The thesis of the 'singularity' of the Holocaust is to be rejected because, consciously or not, it hierarchizes the victims of the National Socialist machinery of destruction." See Detlev J. K. Peukert, "Alltag und Barbarei: Zur Normalität des Dritten Reiches" in Dan Diner, *Ist der Nationalsozialismus Geschichte? Zur Historisierung und Historikerstreit* (Frankfurt am Main: Fischer Taschenbuch Verlag, 1987), 54. As long as singularity and historicization are viewed in terms of binary oppositions, either the specificity of the fate of the Jews or the agonizing cries of the other victims of mass-death are bound to be slighted.

6. Elie Wiesel, "Now We Know" in Richard Arens, ed., *Genocide in Paraguay* (Philadelphia: Temple University Press, 1976), 165.

7. David Vital, "After the Catastrophe: Aspects of Contemporary Jewry" in Peter Hayes, ed., *Lessons and Legacies: The Meaning of the Holocaust in a Changing World* (Evanston, Ill.: Northwestern University Press, 1991), 132. In his account of the understanding of the Holocaust in Israel, Tom Segev has pointed out that at the time of the Eichmann trial the Israeli establishment "rejected efforts to categorize the Holocaust as a universal crime, seeing them as attempts to diminish the significance of the Final Solution and to deny the Jewish people's unique right to demand the support of other nations." See Tom Segev, *The Seventh Million: The Israelis and the Holocaust* (New York: Hill and Wang, 1993), 358.

8. Yehuda Bauer, "Right and Wrong Teaching of the Holocaust" in Josephine Z. Knopp, ed., *The International Conference on Lessons of the Holocaust* (Philadelphia: National Institute on the Holocaust), 5.

9. For Lyotard, events must be "phrased" or put into meaningful conceptual frameworks. A differend arises where alternative or competing phrasings exist, where the very language of one phrasing excludes the meaning of the other, rendering them incommensurable. See Jean-François Lyotard, *The Differend: Phrases in Dispute* (Minneapolis: University of Minnesota Press, 1988).

10. For an analysis of the ways in which Heidegger's thinking can help illuminate the Holocaust, see Alan Milchman and Alan Rosenberg, "Heidegger, Planetary Technics, and the Holocaust" in Alan Milchman and Alan Rosenberg, eds., *Martin Heidegger and the Holocaust* (Atlantic Highlands, N.J.: Humanities Press, 1995). Heidegger's own indisputable entanglement with Nazism, as well as the profound ambiguities that characterized his thinking in the early 1930s, are treated in Alan Milchman and Alan Rosenberg, "Resoluteness and Ambiguity: Martin Heidegger's Ontological Politics, 1933–1935" in *The Philosophical Forum*, vol. xxv, no. 1 (Fall 1993).

11. Lacoue-Labarthe speaks of the history of the West. In fact, the expansion of the West and its techno-scientific civilization, encompassing virtually the whole planet in the course of the twentieth century, is tending to create an effectively global history.

12. Philippe Lacoue-Labarthe, *Heidegger, Art, and Politics: The Fiction of the Political* (Oxford: Basil Blackwell, 1990), 45.

13. Dan Diner, "Between Aporia and Apology: On the Limits of Historicizing National Socialism" in Peter Baldwin, ed., *Reworking the Past: Hitler, the Holocaust, and the Historians' Debate* (Boston: Beacon Press, 1990), 143, translation modified. For a collection of essays devoted to German-Jewish thinkers who viewed the Holocaust as a Zivilisationsbruch, including Theodor W. Adorno, Max Horkheimer, Leo Löwenthal, Hannah Arendt, Günther Anders,

and Ernst Bloch, see Dan Diner, ed., *Zivilisationsbruch: Denken nach Auschwitz* (Frankfurt am Main: Fischer Taschenbuch Verlag, 1988).

14. Jean-François Lyotard, *The Postmodern Explained: Correspondence 1982–1985* (Minneapolis: University of Minnesota Press, 1993), 18.

15. Claude Lanzmann, "From the Holocaust to the *Holocaust*" in *Telos,* no. 42 (Winter 1979–80): 137–38. In the same essay, Lanzmann describes the Holocaust as "the expression of the deepest tendencies of western civilization." Ibid., 140.

16. Lacoue-Labarthe, *Heidegger, Art, and Politics,* 35.

17. Otto Dov Kulka, "Critique of Judaism in European Thought: On the Historical Meaning of Modern Anti-Semitism" in *The Jerusalem Quarterly,* no. 52 (Fall 1989): 141–44.

18. Ibid., 141. For Kulka, this revolt, fueled by the Enlightenment's idealization of the Greco-Roman world which had been shattered and destroyed by the Judeo-Christian project that has shaped the West, was indeed a revolt against its roots.

19. See Lacoue-Labarthe, *Heidegger, Art, and Politics;* Jean-François Lyotard, *Heidegger and "the Jews"* (Minneapolis: University of Minnesota Press, 1990); Jacques Derrida, "Force of Law: The 'Mystical Foundations of Authority' " in Drucilla Cornell, Michael Rosenfeld, and David Gray Carlson, eds., *Deconstruction and the Possibility of Justice* (New York: Routledge, 1992); and Maurice Blanchot, *The Writing of the Disaster* (Lincoln: University of Nebraska Press, 1986).

20. Lacoue-Labarthe, *Heidegger, Art, and Politics,* 37. For Lacoue-Labarthe, the project that has shaped the West in its modernity is neither of Greek nor Jewish provenance, but rather Hellenistic and Roman, and it was that Latin tradition that has shaped Christianity in the West.

21. Hannah Arendt, "Social Science Techniques and the Study of Concentration Camps" in Alan Rosenberg and Gerald E. Myers, eds., *Echoes from the Holocaust: Philosophical Reflections on a Dark Time* (Philadelphia: Temple University Press, 1988), 367.

22. Ibid., 366. Dan Diner also points to the "antirationality" and negation of instrumental reason as the conceptual key to the uniqueness of the Holocaust. See Diner, "Between Aporia and Apology," 143–44.

23. Steven T. Katz, "Technology and Genocide: Technology as a 'Form of Life' " in Katz, *Historicism, the Holocaust, and Zionism,* 195.

24. Blanchot, *The Writing of the Disaster,* 47. Derrida echoes Blanchot when he designates the Holocaust as a "limit experience." See Derrida, "Force of Law," 61.

25. Hannah Arendt, *Eichmann in Jerusalem: A Report on the Banality of Evil* (Harmondsworth, Eng.: Penguin Books, 1977), 273.

CHAPTER 2

Children in Auschwitz and the Gulag:

Alternative Realities

STEVEN T. KATZ

Contrary to the widespread tendency to relativize the Holocaust and to employ it as a universal metaphor for evil, I would insist that the destruction of European Jewry is an unprecedented and phenomenologically—not morally—singular form of evil. Though many have sought, in various ways, to deny the uniqueness of the Shoah, the closer one examines its detailed structure, and the intentionality of its creators, the more obvious it becomes that Auschwitz and Treblinka have no real historic parallels.

In this chapter, I support this conclusion through a close and careful comparative analysis of the treatment, the fate, of children (not infants) in the Gulag and the Nazi Death Camps. In contradistinction to those who would assimilate these two environments and treat both as if they represented one common mode of oppression and destruction, it will be seen that based on the relevant historical evidence and the testimony of survivors of both systems, Auschwitz and the Gulag were radically dissimilar.

"THOU SHALT NOT KILL CHILDREN"

What happened to children in the Gulag and at Auschwitz? In order to answer this question, we must first recall an important distinction that operated within Soviet culture vis-à-vis young people, between those who were orphans and those who were juvenile criminals. The lot of the former has been described as follows:

The waifs were taken from the streets—not from their families— into the colonies for juvenile delinquents (there was one attached to

19

the People's Commissariat of Education as early as 1920; it would
be interesting to know, too, how things went with juvenile offenders
before the Revolution), into workhouses for juveniles (which existed from 1921 to 1930 and had bars, bolts, and jailers, so that in
the outworn bourgeois terminology they would have been called
prisons), and also into the "Labor Communes of the OGPU" from
1924 on. They had been orphaned by the Civil War, by its famine,
by social disorganization, the execution of their parents, or the
death of the latter at the front, and at that time justice really did try
to return these children to the mainstream of life, removing them
from their street apprenticeship as thieves. Factory apprenticeship
began in the labor communes. And this was a privileged situation
in the context of those years of unemployment, and many of the
lads there learned with a will.[1]

Such juveniles were not part of the criminal population of the Gulag.

By comparison, the latter's presence in the Gulag was the harsh product of a developing view in Soviet law[2] that made children twelve and
over subject to exile and slave labor and which after 1935 did so
without any allowance for their age.[3] As Solzhenitsyn sums it up: "The
conclusion we draw is that from 1935 to 1948 children *were* sentenced
for taking apples."[4] The myriad abuses, the uncamouflaged exploitation, present in the numerous penal institutions established for such
youthful inmates, from beatings to sexual exploitation, can all too easily
be imagined. This was no place for children! Yet, in disentangling the
governing principles that operated in these brutal and brutalizing penal
environments, we discover one constraining moral rule that was in
force and generally respected: *the children were to be kept alive.*[5] They
received, for example, as mandated by the system that had imprisoned
them, *additional* rations[6]—though, inevitably, in a manner subject, like
all else in the Gulag, to corruption.[7] All allowances for corruption made,
with all necessary skepticism, the inescapable fact of the extra rations
remains. National requirements and fundamental morality—*permitted
by the regnant doctrine*—conspired to moderate the rigid social organization and the resultant existential experience of these youngsters.
Though alienated and violated in many ways, these young criminals
were *not* murdered:

> The kids knew their strength very well. The first element in their
> strength was unity, and the second impunity. It was only on the

outside that they had been driven into here on the basis of the law for adults. But once in here, in the Archipelago, they were under the protection of a sacred taboo. "Milk, chief! Give us our milk!" they would howl, and beat on the door of the cell and break up their bunks and break all the glass in sight—all of which would have been termed armed rebellion or economic sabotage among adults. They had nothing to fear! Their milk would be brought them right away!

Or say that they were marching a column of kids under armed guard through a city, and it seems even shameful to guard children so strictly. Far from it! They had worked out a plan. A whistle—and all who wanted to scattered in different directions! And what were the guards to do? Shoot? At whom? At children? . . . And so their prison terms came to an end. In one fell swoop 150 years ran away from the state. You don't enjoy looking silly? Then don't arrest children! [8]

They do not shoot children in the Gulag, even youthful criminals, even while these juvenile offenders contravene the system, abuse its overseers, and finally flee from its incarcerative embrace. The victimization of teenagers has real limits, at least one real limit: the requirement that, in almost any circumstance, their life be preserved.

Pay close attention to the key clause in Solzhenitsyn's text: "they were under the protection of a sacred taboo," in other words, thou shalt not kill children. This singular moral law applies even in the Gulag, restrains even Stalinist behavior,[9] and is acknowledged as a binding ethical imperative even when it is confronted by the meta-historical truth embodied in the proletarian revolution. A "future novelist (one who spent his childhood among the kids) will describe to us a multitude of kids' tricks"—our own great chronicler of the Stalinist nightmare records. He will tell us, how the kids "ran riot in the colonies, how they got back at and played nasty tricks on their instructors. Despite the seeming severity of the terms meted out to them and the camp regimen, the kids developed a great insolence out of impunity." [10] Thou shalt not kill children.

Just how far this animating impunity extended is attested to, for example, in this precise report of a gang rape of a camp nurse:

Some excited and frightened children ran to the nurse of a children's colony and summoned her to help one of their comrades who was seriously ill. Forgetting caution, she quickly accompanied them to their big cell for forty. And as soon as she was inside, the whole anthill went into action! Some of them barricaded the door and kept watch. Dozens of hands tore everything off her, all the clothes she had on, and toppled her over; and then some sat on her hands and on her legs; and then, everyone doing what he could and where, they raped her, kissed her, bit her. It was against orders to shoot them, and no one could rescue her until they themselves let her go, profaned and weeping.[11]

To fully comprehend the immediacy of this sexual assault, the kisses, the bites, the perversion, it is necessary to understand that it is preceded by a substantive understanding on the part of these youngsters that, however violative their collective behavior, they possess an irreplaceable value to the state that transcends any consideration of their murder by the state. And after such an unbridled assault there may or may not be some punitive response, but this too occurred within ethico-political bounds that at least implicitly acknowledged their ontic primacy, the unsurpassed worth of their being, whatever utilitarian or societal ends the Stalinist regime envisioned for them in their adulthood.

Such unrestricted behavioral latitude created young monsters who equated "good" with self-interest and "bad" with all that obfuscated or thwarted it. Their uninhibited conduct, their quasi-solipsistic ethical comportment, was an added torment to the rest of the camp population, as the offended memory of many a camp inmate makes plain. Aino Kuusinen remembers her journey from Moscow to Kotlas:

> The "Stolypin" carriage was hitched to a train and in pitch darkness we set out for an unknown destination. The worst feature of the journey was the juveniles, who were given the upper berths and perpetrated all kinds of indecencies—spitting, uttering obscene abuse and even urinating on the adult prisoners.[12]

Yet, for all their bestiality, for all their anarchic miscreance, the youthful humanity of these urinators was respected by the system. They were neither harmed nor hung, but lived above the law while they proceeded to injure and kill others.[13] And they did so consciously, as *zoon logon archon* in Aristotle's formulation,[14] for they knew the curious, outrageous rules under which they lived. Rules which they could lavishly manipulate in light of the constitutive ethical relationship, grounded not least in self-interest, that existed between themselves and those in control of the political order. Put another way, they insisted that insofar as they represented the future of the Soviet polity they possessed, despite the brutal daily circumstances of their existence, some real power that, in its turn, was able to modify the determinate immoral-statist assault against them. The *need*(s) of the rulers, the very needful character of their opposition, empowered—however peculiarly and within limited parameters—these youngsters.

Things, however, were vastly different under the Nazi occupation as one of the Gulag's smarter fifteen-year-old kids tells Solzhenitsyn in the course of a revealing conversation:

> Before the war, at the age of nine, Slava began to steal. He also stole "when our army came," and after the war, and, with a sad, thoughtful smile which was so old for fifteen, he explained to me that in the future, too, he intended to live only by thievery. "You know," he explained to me very reasonably, "that as a worker you can earn only bread and water. And my childhood was bad so I want to live well."
>
> "What did you do during the German occupation?" I asked, trying to fill in the two years he had bypassed without describing them—the two years of the occupation of Kiev. He shook his head.
>
> "Under the Germans I worked. What do you think—that I could have gone on stealing under the Germans? They shot you on the spot for that." [15]

This alert teenage boy knew the "secret" that those who liken the Gulag and Auschwitz too casually dare not face: "The Nazis shot you on the spot," or worse. [16]

The technical dichotomy between waifs or orphans and criminals did not exist for Nazism where Jewish children were at issue. There was no categorical distinction between "unfortunates" to be cared for by the State, to whom the State had an obligation, and juvenile delinquents who needed incarceration, and who, despite their crimes the state still had an interest in. All Jewish children of whatever age, sex, background, and personal virtues were incorrigible criminals of the worst sort— racial criminals. All stood "legally" condemned to the severest punishments decreeable by the omnipotent Aryan state. No Jewish children either separately or together had any meaningful impunity, any delineated protection juridical or moral, from anything[17]—not least from a violation of the elemental taboo: *thou shalt not kill children.* Being Jews, if still immature ones, they too were carriers of that cosmic contagion that threatened death to all. As such they had to be "cleansed"[18] not only out of the body-politic, but out of history and nature as well. "The baby's mother went up to one of the friends and implored him: 'Let the child go. He hasn't done anything: he's only a baby!' But the heart of stone was not moved. He replied, 'He's a baby now but he'll grow up to be a Jewish man. That's why we have to kill him.' "[19]

In support of this stringent argument for differentiation I cite the following symptomatic incidents, among a vast array of homicidal occurrences that challenge the limits of our imagining. Begin first with the *regular* use of Jewish children in medical experiments at the Neuengamme and other camps that specialized in "scientific" research.

In November 1944, the SS brought a transport from Auschwitz to Neuengamme containing twenty-five children between six and twelve years of age. Dr. Heissmeyer in Berlin had previously selected those children for experiments for the "benefits of progress in medicine." The doctors placed the children in an isolated block under the care of prisoner professors and Dutch orderlies. All the children showed some evidence of tuberculosis.

The researchers started the experiment three weeks after the arrival of the children. The project's originator, Dr. Heissmeyer, came from Berlin every ten days to work with the children. He made incisions in the skin and rubbed cultures of tubercular bacilli into the skin of the left or right arm. After a few days redness and swelling appeared on the arm and the auxiliary glands enlarged; the child's temperature rose sharply for a few days, and then returned to normal in a week. The process was repeated several times. After administering a local anesthetic such as novocaine, a doctor made a long incision under the armpit to remove the lymphatic nodes of each child, an operation lasting about fifteen minutes. He then plugged and dressed the wound and sent the sterile test tubes, numbered and named, to Berlin. There, technicians bred new cultures of tubercular bacilli, made an emulsion, and sent the mixture back to the camp. Every two weeks each child was given an injection of the vaccine from his own lymphatic node. After four or five months the majority of the children ran high temperatures. In the third month, enlarged lymph nodes appeared in 80 percent of the children. The doctors noted serious lung changes in almost every child.

While secretly giving sweets and toys to the children, adult prisoners had an opportunity to observe the experiment. Dr. Kowalski, one of those prisoners, provides us with descriptions of the disposition of the tubercular children. In April, when the allies were nearly at the gates of Neuengamme, Dr. Heissmeyer proposed that the children be transferred to a subcamp of Neuengamme called Bullenhausendamm. He wanted all traces of the experiment eliminated, including the children. General Pohl gave the order and the doctors moved the children to Bullenhausendamm, where they were taken down into the basement. After administering morphine, the doctors put ropes around the children's necks and hanged them, as one prisoner observed, "like pictures hung up on a wall on hooks." [20] Such experiments, including Mengele's infernal activities at Auschwitz, assume the complete absence of inherent value in these youngsters. Answering to a "higher" racial law, these physicians were able, in the name of the Aryan people, to violate every inherited cultural decency, to mock every law of natural morality, to perpetuate absolute evil, against the living bodies of these Jewish children.

Then there is the fate of the Jewish children of Zhitomir:

> Children up to the age of twelve were brought to the execution place in wagons, naked and unshod. The air shook from the wails of the children. I met one man who was witness to the executions. He had once been a stevedore of the Baranovka cooperative. He told me that he saw many Jewish children thrown into the ditches and buried alive. In the town of Lubar, Zhitomir region, we were shown graves of Jews murdered in the Peshchana field. At the order of the chief of the Zhitomir Gestapo, children up to the age of twelve were not shot, but were thrown into ditches and buried alive. For several days the earth trembled above the infants. Their blood seeped up to the surface.[21]

The senseless terror of this merciless scene is overwhelming—and every elemental question, the impotence of really understanding such an infernal ritual of death, emerges anew over against it. Why did they need to bury the children alive? Why? Was it to economize? Though offered as an explanation, it is an absurd suggestion. Such utilitarian justifications could only suggest themselves, and even then not convincingly, as crude rationalizations to a mind, to a spirit, so corrupt that the suffering of a child—not to speak of the life of a child—would not be felt to be worth a penny (more or less). Was it for the sake of "convenience?" But surely it is more convenient to kill someone, even a child, cleanly than to force it into an open grave and bury it alive. For conscience's sake? Obviously not. Then why?[22] Any explanation that meets even the minimal demands of conceptual adequacy will have to include a profound awareness of such happenings as chthonic ministrations, as solemnities of Aryan consecration, in which the murder of such Jewish children is the sacrificial act par excellence. For the Gestapo chieftain who orchestrated this monstrous rite, these young deaths were an exaltation, a confirmation of his (the Third Reich's) deepest pieties. They affirmed his Aryan manhood: he was no shirker, the Jews, Jewish children, must suffer, must die, and he was willing to participate, without pity and without evasion, directly in their annihilation.

Or consider the different meaning of child's play, of sport, in the Gulag and in the Nazi Death Camps. In the former,

> The kids' actions were unpremeditated, and they didn't mean to cause hurt or offense. They weren't pretending; *they simply did not consider anyone a human being* except themselves and the older thieves. That is how they came to perceive the world, and how they clung to that view. At the end of work they would break into a column of adult zeks who were utterly fagged out, hardly able to stand, sunk in a kind of trance or reverie. The kids would jostle the column, not because they had to be first—this meant nothing—but just for the fun of it. They used to talk noisily, taking the name of Pushkin in vain. ("Pushkin took it!" "Pushkin ate it!") They used to direct obscene curses at God, Christ, and the Holy Virgin, and they would shout out all sorts of obscenity about sexual deviations and perversions, not even shamed by the presence of elderly women standing there—let alone the younger ones.
>
> During their short camp stay they attained the peak, the summit, of freedom from society! During the periods of long roll calls in the camp compound the kids used to chase each other around, torpedoing the crowd, knocking people into one another. ("Well, peasant, why were you in the way?") Or they would run around a person, one after the other, as they might around a tree—and the person was even more useful than a tree, because you could shield yourself with him, jerk him, make him totter, tug him in different directions.[23]

What different sport the children of the Janowski Camp were part of:

> *Obersturmführer* Wilhaus especially enjoyed this form of sport. He was in the habit of standing on the balcony of his camp office and taking pot-shots at the prisoners working below to amuse his wife and nine-year-old daughter. Sometimes Wilhaus would order someone to throw three- or four-year-old children into the air while he shot at them. His daughter would clap her hands and cry: "Do it again, Papa, do it again." And he would go on shooting.[24]

Again, and still more brutal, if any measures still apply, was the following incident:

> "Cover the accursed Jewish blood!" the officer ordered. Several days later, they took us to the Golosayev woods. The woods were brightly lit up with huge bonfires. We saw sumptuously set tables. At the tables sat officers in parade uniforms. Near the bonfires were many small children trembling with fear. . . . I heard one German officer explain to the soldiers how the game was to be played. From a distance of twelve meters, they were to toss the children in such a manner that their heads would strike a trunk of the tree. For every cracked skull they would receive a glass of schnapps.
>
> This gruesome pastime lasted for several hours. The woods were filled with the cries of the children.
>
> "Now there isn't a Jew left in all of Kiev!" the German officers yelled, as they tossed the children into the ditch. "We will do the same all over the world. We will annihilate all the Jews."[25]

It cannot be believed though it did happen. And it happened because the humanity, the justifying ethical claim, of the Jewish three- or four-year-old, unlike that of the Soviet youngster, had been nullified altogether. The defining conditions of the "relationship" between Obersturmführer Wilhaus and his Jewish wards, or again, that between the German soldiers and the Jewish children whose heads would be crushed for fun in the Golosayev woods, was so alienated, so distorted, so untouched by either ethical or utilitarian constraints, by even the most minimal ties of interpersonal reciprocity, that everything and anything was possible.

Children in the Gulag received an extra food ration—it was a demand of the system. These children were the future of the Soviet regime. In

Kharkov, the Germans issued no food, for the Jewish children had no future.

Little children were dying. They looked emaciated; they begged for bread in thin, weak voices. The mothers appealed to the officers, but loud laughter was their only answer. The commandant promised to help the children. He fulfilled his promise very soon. In the dim lantern light the Gestapo searched out the children and smeared their lips with some kind of liquid. Shortly after, the barracks resounded with dreadful cries. The children were in agony, threw themselves on the earthen floor. In the morning mountains of children's bodies were loaded onto wagons.[26] And if, by some quirk of fate, they did have something to eat, this too only meant death:

[a] witness recalled seeing a little boy jump off an incoming truck of Jewish children. He held an apple in his hand. Boger, one of the SS terrors, and another officer were talking nearby: the child was standing next to the car with his apple and was enjoying himself. Suddenly Boger went over to the boy, grabbed his legs, and smashed his head against the wall. Then he calmly picked up the apple. And Draser told me to wipe "that" off the wall. About an hour later I was called to Boger to interpret in an interrogation and I saw him eating the child's apple.[27]

Three incidents further illustrate the brutality:

"With my own eyes," continued Magidov, "I saw Germans kill Jewish children. One cold rainy night the children were dragged out of their homes, their clothes torn off their bodies and chased around the settlement. The Germans flogged their naked bodies with rubber knouts. At the hospital a fearful scene took place: a German held a child by its feet, shouted: "One!" A second German struck the child on the head with an iron rod. Covered with blood, the child was thrown into the pit. No one knew whether he was alive or dead. Most of the children drew their last breath on the damp earth, saturated with their own blood."[28]

After a young woman gave birth [SS officer Gustav Franz Wagner ordered] the baby to be thrown into the latrine. Later prisoners found the baby floating in excrement.[29]

Eugenia Glushkina took along her two children aged twelve and seven. The third, who was a one-year-old infant, she left behind in his cradle, thinking that perhaps the beasts would spare him. But after the shooting, the Germans returned to the ghetto to pick up the rags. They saw little Alek in his cradle. One German dragged the child out into the street and smashed his head against the ice. The chief of the detachment ordered the body of the infant cut into pieces and given to his dogs.[30]

What is one to make of such *regular* and *regulative* happenings? A newborn infant drowned in excrement. A child cut to pieces and served up as dog food. *All* children sentenced to death by poison, shootings, drownings, beatings, starvation, torture, medical experimentation, overwork, hunger, burial while still alive, immolation, hangings, and gassing. A sentence of death so universal that it included every fetus, every newborn, every infant. "The particular bestiality [of the Nazis]," the villagers of Tartarsk reported in 1943, "was reserved for the children, whom they seized, blackjacked and, dead or half dead, threw into the pits."[31] And why? Because of the inexorable, noncontradictable racial necessities that the Führer, in his transcendental uniqueness, had discerned at the center of the law of historical and meta-historical being. Unless these biocentric laws were respected, society, even civilization as a universal norm, would be undone and communal anarchy—and with it the (Aryan) individual's descent into servitude and despair—would ensue. Killing all Jewish fetuses, murdering Jewish children by every means available is the prophylactic nonmetaphorical sacrifice, the propitiative nonsymbolic offering that will keep this individual and social chaos at bay. This is not the world of the Gulag, even when the devouring demands of ruthless class warfare is fully factored in—it is a world apart.[32]

Of the Jewish child, of the million Jewish children, whose lives were snuffed out we shall say no more—can one ever say enough—but with regard to the killers the recognition of a further, onto-psychic[33] dimension harboring within the barbaric act is required. For the slayers, to the extent that such outrages flowed not from bureaucratic-technological dispassion but from a sense of self, of commitment, of basic values shared with the regime, as a true believer, as confirmation of his or her Nazi beliefs and credentials, this murder was not murder alone, but an act of becoming.[34]

SS Sergeant Moll tore a child away from his mother, took him over to the crematorium, and threw him into the boiling fat of recently cremated victims. Then he turned to a colleague and said, "I have done my duty. I am satisfied." [35]

This self-authenticating "(pseudo) ethicization" of homicide, this sense that what one had done was not evil after all, was achieved through the sacramentalization of the outrage. The *Endlösung* in its totality, and all specific abusive and destructive acts within it, no matter how scandalous when judged by inherited moral categories, are transubstantiated by the racial mystery whose depth the Führer alone has plumbed. All ethical language of reproach, all juridical categories that define the act as murder, as a criminal deed, are altogether inappropriate; they need be replaced by the semiotics of Aryan mythography and the meta-legal biocentric axiology of Nazi ritual. Accordingly, Hitler, in his *Last Will and Testament,* speaks in the vocabulary of religion when he talks of Jews "atoning" for their "guilt," just as Sergeant Moll does when, after immolating the living child in the bubbling remains of other Jews, he lionizes his act in the prescriptive, Kantian sounding pronouncement: "I have done my duty." [36]

CONCLUSION

The fate, the alternate fate, of children in Auschwitz and the Gulag eloquently, if tragically, testifies against those who would relativize, and thereby reduce, the Holocaust. This is not to deny or misrepresent the horrors of the Stalinist camps, but to insist that both Auschwitz and the Gulag be accurately deciphered so that the evil that each represents can be understood properly. Moral outrage must be accompanied by conceptual precision and hermeneutical exactitude if the enterprise of comparative scholarship on the literature and phenomenology of mass death is not to degenerate into incorrect banalities.

NOTES

1. Aleksandr Solzhenitsyn, *Gulag Archipelago* (New York, 1975), part 3, 447–48. Stefan Knapp describes a similar situation in 1941:

We were building a children's village: these villages were called Children's Corners and they are important party inventions. A great many children are in the care of the state, either because they are illegitimate and their mothers have abandoned them . . . or because their parents were killed or imprisoned for political or other reasons. So the children were taken to these special villages—outsize orphanages, in a sense—which are run as a combination of boarding school and military camp. They work half the day and are given their schooling in the other half. In a great many ways they are well looked after—decently fed, for instance—on strictly military lines. These Arctic regions were uninhabited, apart from the camps. The idea was to accustom the children to the climate from their early youth and make them the nucleus of a new population. (*The Square Sun,* [London, 1965], 75–76)

The representative accounts of Solzhenitsyn and Knapp relating to the state care of orphan children find corroboration even in the evidence pertaining to the terrible years 1938–1940, supplied by E. Lipper, *Eleven Years* (London, 1951), 121–22. See also E. Ginzburg:

The children's home was also part of the camp compound. It had its own guardhouse, its own gates, its own huts, and its own barbed wire. But on the doors of what were otherwise standard camp hutments there were unusual inscriptions: "Infants' Group," "Toddlers' Group," and "Senior Group." After a day or two I found myself with the senior group. The very fact of being there restored to me the long-lost faculty of weeping. For more than three years my eyes had smarted from tearless despair. But now, in July 1940, I sat on a low bench in a corner of this strange building and cried. I cried without stopping, sobbing like our old nurse Fima, sniffing and snuffing like a country girl. I was in a state of shock. The shock jerked me out of a paralysis that had lasted for some months. Yes, this undoubtedly was a penal camp hut. But it smelled of warm semolina and wet pants. Someone's bizarre imagination had combined the trappings of the prison world with simple, human, and touchingly familiar things now so far out of reach, that they seemed more than a dream.

Some thirty small children, about the age my Vasya was when we were separated, were tumbling and toddling about the hut, squealing, gurgling with laughter, bursting into tears. Each of them was upholding his right to a place under the Kolyma sun in a perpetual struggle with his fellows. They bashed each other's heads unmercifully, pulled each other's hair, bit each other. (*Within the Whirlwind* [New York, 1967], 3)

This is not to subtract or detract from the intense misery and terror of the Gulag, but to recognize that within its crushing, hegemonic parameters there were postrevolutionary countervailing sociopolitical and ideological valences that contravened an all-inclusive genocidal criminality. The sustenance and protection of children were among these contrapuntal values.

2. The 1926 Penal Code, article 12, sentenced children twelve years and older to exile and prison but made certain allowances for their age. These mitigating reservations were removed by the Decree covering youthful offenders issued on April 7, 1935. And even this law was stiffened to include "carelessness" rather than only intentionally criminal acts according to the Decree of July 7, 1941. This latter decree was finally softened and some sentences commuted by the Decree of April 24, 1954.

3. Every commentator, both first and third person, remarks on the shame that the entire nation experienced when the age of imprisonment was unconscionably lowered by Stalin so that children under twelve could be *exiled* if found guilty of political crime under Article 58 of the Criminal Code. And who can wonder at this? See, for details, Robert Conquest, *The Great Terror* (New York, 1968), 86–87. He makes the important observation that though this law was actually enforced, as we know from Solzhenitsyn and others, the real purpose of the legislation was to allow Stalin to "threaten oppositionists quite 'legally' with the death of their children as accomplices if they did not carry out his wishes" (87). Orlov's *Secret History* reveals how often and effectively this strategy was employed and with what success.

4. A. Solzhenitsyn, *Gulag*, vol. 2, 450.

5. There were exceptions, e.g., the fourteen-year-old son of Nestor Lakoba, the Georgian Communist, was executed. Robert Conquest, "Introduction," to Pyotr Yakir, *A Childhood in Prison* (New York, 1973), 11.

6. P. Yakir reports: "At eight o'clock in the morning rations [in jail] were brought round. At that time adults got 600 grammes of bread, but I was brought a larger ration, as juveniles were entitled to 800 grammes" (*A Childhood in Prison*, 36–37). Yakir's position might have been somewhat anomalous, i.e., his treatment more benign, given the fame of his father, Army Commander Iona Yakir. However, there is nothing said explicitly in this remark or as regards its context that would suggest this, and he specifically speaks not only of himself but of "juveniles"—apparently meaning all juveniles—in this passage. Moreover, Eugenia Ginzburg, writing of the younger children, tells us that:

> It would be wrong to say that the children were kept on a starvation diet. They were given as much to eat as they could manage, and by my standards at the time the food seemed quite appetizing. For some reason, though, they all eat like little convicts: hastily, with no thought for anything else, carefully, wiping their tin bowls with a piece of bread, or licking them clean. (*Within the Whirlwind*, 4)

7. As A. Solzhenitsyn writes:

And what did he see in the children's colony? "There was even more injustice than in freedom. The chiefs and jailers lived off the state, shielded by the correctional system. Part of the kid's ration went from the kitchen into the bellies of the instructors. The kids were beaten with boots, kept in fear so that they would be silent and obedient." (Here it is necessary to explain that the ration of the youngest juveniles was not the ordinary camp ration. Though it sentenced kids to long years of imprisonment, the government did not cease to be humane. It did not forget that these same children were the future masters of Communism. Therefore they added milk and butter and real meat to their rations. So how could the *instructors* resist the temptation of dipping their ladle into the kids' pot? And how could they compel the kids to keep silent, except by beating them with boots? Perhaps one of these kids who grew up in this way will someday relate to us a story more dismal than *Oliver Twist? (Gulag,* vol. 2, 453)

8. A. Solzhenitsyn, *Gulag,* vol. 2, 454.

9. P. Yakir, e.g., tells of a hunger strike of juveniles in prison and its outcome:

Having organised ourselves into an egalitarian commune, we quickly came to the conclusion that a hunger strike should be declared in defence of our rights. So one morning we refused to take any food and set forth our demands as follows:

1. That we should be permitted to receive parcels and to use the prison shop.

2. That we should be allowed to send for the interrogators to have our cases explained to us.

After we had issued this statement, the duty warden and the block chief came running up every few minutes. At first they tried to use persuasion, then they began to shout and threaten us. Towards evening on the first day, the prison governor arrived and began shouting: "We'll have you wretches in court! What are you on about? Have you got something against the authorities? Aren't you getting enough kasha? Isn't the boiling water hot enough for you? I'll show you which side your bread's buttered!"

We were unmoved. The next morning when we were brought our bread ration, we refused to accept it. Apart from water nothing passed our lips. Forty-eight hours passed without anyone coming to call. The hunger strike was going perfectly. I argued with my cousin, who said that everything that was being done was right and proper. It was right and proper that we should be in prison. Our parents had been rightly and properly arrested and shot, and Stalin was a genius. I was against what was happening and saw the root of the evil in the sadist who was sitting on the throne.

On the fourth day everyone began to grow weak. To help keep all their spirits up I danced the "Tsyganochka" in one of my father's shirts, which came down to my knees. At lunch time on that same day the door to the cell opened and a group of bigwigs came in. The duty warder, the block chief, the prison governor and a man in civilian clothes who introduced himself as the city procurator. The procurator did the talking. He asked us to repeat our demands. We repeated them. He replied that the interrogators would come to see us without delay, that we could use the prison shop, but as far as parcels were concerned there was nothing he could do, as they had been instructed in a circular from Moscow that persons under investigation were not to have parcels.

I was the spokesman for the cell in these talks. I said that we would not call off the hunger strike, because Moscow could not have forbidden parcels to juvenile prisoners, and eventually Moscow would have to deal with people who had no respect for the law.

"All right, go ahead, starve yourselves to death," the prison governor erupted.

They left. On the following day the block chief came to see us and said that our demands had been accepted. Our relations had already been informed and would bring parcels that very day. (*A Childhood in Prison,* 51–52)

A second hunger strike, Yakir reports, brings forced feeding and a five year sentence in a corrective labor colony (ibid., 59–61), but even for this second serious offense, this collective organization against camp authority, Yakir is not murdered.

10. P. Yakir, *A Childhood in Prison,* 455.

11. Ibid., 455. Emphasis added.

12. Aino Kuusinen, *Before and after Stalin: A Personal Account of Soviet Russia from the 1920s to the 1960s,* trans. Paul Stevenson (London, 1974), 150.

13. Johan Wigmans writes of the teenagers in Karabas:

A completely separate problem in Karabas was that of the *maloletki,* the younger people aged between twelve and seventeen. Before they were finally sent to this camp, these children had hung around the city streets in bands of varying size and from an early age the boys had lived by theft and the girls by prostitution. . . .

In Karabas two hundred boys were housed in hut 4 and one hundred and fifty girls in the adjacent hut 5. Two Russian guards, both of them convicts, were under orders to see to it that the division between the two groups was strictly enforced; but they did not take too much notice of that and for a piece of bread or a handful of tobacco they would close their eyes to everything. The barbed-wire between the two huts presented even less of an obstacle and the inevitable result was a lively traffic, especially towards the evening.

The majority of these youngsters probably did not really mind having to live in these camps. Officially they were supposed to work but in practice that was the last thing they ever did. At the same time they had the benefit of regular meals and ample opportunity of learning from their cronies much that would come in useful once they were let loose. (*Ten Years* [London, 1964] 90–91)

14. Things (animals) capable of reason (logos).

15. *Gulag*, vol. 2, 457.

16. E. Ginzburg, who was so profoundly moved by the children of the Gulag that she wrote,

When one calls to mind Elgen's gray, featureless landscape, shrouded in the melancholy of nonexistence, the most fantastic, the most satanic invention of all seems to be those huts with signs saying "Infant's Group," "Toddler's Group," and "Senior Group." (*Within the Whirlwind*, 11)

still had the keen sense, the deep honesty, to recognize that:

They are never to be forgotten, those Elgen children. I'm not saying that there is any comparison between them and, say, the Jewish children in Hitler's empire. Not only were the Elgen children spared extermination in gas chambers, they were even given medical attention. They received all they needed by way of food. It is my duty to emphasize this so as not to depart from the truth by one jot or tittle. (*Within the Whirlwind*, 10–11)

17. The eternal witness to the truth to which I here refer were the biopsies, castrations, sterilizations, and other medical "experiments" carried out on Jewish children.

18. The term "ethnic cleansing" so much in the news recently (1993–1994) due to the savage situation in the former Yugoslavia should not be confused with my use of the term "cleansing" vis-à-vis the Nazi *Weltanschauung*. In the Bosnian case, fully recognizing the hideous indecency of Serbian behavior, and the thousands killed in this ethnic conflict, the Serbs have as their primary objective political and territorial ambitions related to the exchange of populations and the conquest of Muslim territory. In the case of the Third Reich, the ends desired were metaphysical and entailed not the exchange or the expulsion of the resident Jewish Community of Europe (and elsewhere) but its complete physical annihilation.

19. This testimony of a young girl of fifteen who was eight when these incidents occurred is recorded in Benjamin Tennenbaum, *Ehad Ba'eer U'Sh-*

nayim Ba'Mishpacha (in Hebrew), translated into English in A. Eizenberg, *Witness to the Holocaust* (New York, 1981), 310.

20. Konnilyn Feig, *Hitler's Death Camps* (New York, 1981), 212.

21. *Black Book: The Nazi Crime against the Jewish People* (New York, 1981; reprint of 1946 edition), 355–56.

22. Yitzchak Greenberg has called our attention to an analogous situation regarding young children thrown into open crematorium furnaces or fiery pits at Auschwitz in 1944, as testified to during the Nuremberg trials:

> WITNESS: . . . women carrying children were (always) sent with them to the crematorium. (Children were of no labor value so they were killed. The mothers were sent along, too, because separation might lead to panic, hysteria—which might slow up the destruction process, and this could not be afforded. It was simpler to condemn the mothers too and keep things quiet and smooth.) The children were then torn from their parents outside the crematorium and sent to the gas chambers separately. (At that point, crowding more people into the gas chambers became the most urgent consideration. Separating meant that more children could be packed in separately, or they could be thrown in over the heads of adults once the chamber was packed.) When the extermination of the Jews in the gas chambers was at its height, orders were issued that children were to be thrown straight into the crematorium furnaces, or into a pit near the crematorium, without being gassed first.
>
> SMIRNOV (Russian prosecutor): How am I to understand this? Did they throw them into the fire alive, or did they kill them first?
>
> WITNESS: They threw them in alive. Their screams could be heard at the camp. It is difficult to say how many children were destroyed in this way.
>
> SMIRNOV: Why did they do this?
>
> WITNESS: It's very difficult to say. We don't know whether they wanted to economize on gas, or if it was because there was not enough room in the gas chambers. (Yitzchak Greenberg, in Eva Fleischer, ed., *Auschwitz: Beginning of a New Era* [New York, 1977], 9–10)

Emil Fackenheim doubts, as do I, the economic explanation offered by the Polish guard. "Much evidence," he writes, "could be adduced to the effect that the Pole's opinion should not be taken as authoritative. Doubtless, in the new way of murdering children, utilitarian considerations played a role. But utility, in this case, was synthesized with idealism—[as Jean Amery has remarked regarding the ideal SS man] 'becoming great in enduring the suffering of others' " (*To Mend the World: Foundations of Future Jewish Thought* [New York, 1982], 132).

23. A. Solzhenitsyn, *Gulag*, vol. 2, 460. Italics in original.

24. *Black Book,* 246, citing the Soviet Extraordinary State Committee Report of 1944. Another use of Jewish children as targets is reported in Lvov as well. "Little children were condemned to a horrible death. They were turned over to the Hitler Youth, who used them as live targets during rifle practice" (*Black Book,* 310).

25. *Black Book,* 364–65.

26. *Black Book,* 369.

27. K. Feig, *Hitler's Death Camps,* 346.

28. *Black Book,* 338–39.

29. This incident occurred at Sobibor and is reported in K. Feig, *Hitler's Death Camps,* 289.

30. *Black Book,* 343.

31. *Black Book,* 340.

32. In advancing this strong conclusion, I am not simultaneously making the erroneous claim that the Gulag belongs to history and can be judged by usual ethical categories while the Holocaust, in some mysterious ontological manner, stands outside of time and defies all standard ethical judgments. As made clear in my discussion in *The Holocaust in Historical Context,* vol. 1 (New York, 1994), especially in my unqualified endorsement of the "historicization of the Shoah," 25–26, and in my detailed criticism of what I have called the mystification of the Shoah, 42–51, I hold that the destruction of European Jewry was an immanent historical event that is, and must be, fully subject to the rigorous canons of historical research, and the exacting rules of linguistic and moral description and decipherment. Moreover, it is this very insistence on the historical character of the Shoah that sustains my entire comparative enterprise, of which this extended analysis of the Gulag is an important part. Then again, my historicized understanding of the Death Camps is precisely what makes them relevant to succeeding generations. Though they are "a world apart" from the Gulag, both belong within our capacious human experience. Alternatively, to repeat a cardinal point made at length elsewhere (see, e.g., *The Holocaust in Historical Context,* vol. 1, 1–2 and 28–31), in advancing a claim for the uniqueness of the Shoah, in this case for the uniqueness of the Shoah vis-à-vis the Gulag, I am not proposing any theological claims. The uniqueness of the "Final Solution" does not derive from the uniqueness of its victims (i.e., the classical theological claim made on behalf of the Jewish people) but rather from the unprecedented and unparalleled genocidal ideology of those who perpetrated it.

33. I use this hybrid term to indicate that the act of killing as understood by the Nazi killers was not, in their own self-construction, merely a subjective, psychological act. Rather, for them, it also carried a fundamental ontological significance that had epic meaning both for the Aryan collective and for their own personal lives.

34. This comment raises basic issues as regards the differing forms that the self-consciousness of the Nazi murderers took. It is a question of major importance that, however, is beyond the scope of this essay.

35. Cited in K. Feig, *Hitler's Death Camps,* 346.

36. Interestingly, Adolf Eichmann used a similar idiom at his trial.

CHAPTER 3

Prelude to the Holocaust?

The Murder of Walther Rathenau

CAROLE FINK

Historians of the Holocaust have not agreed over its origins, its immediate antecedents, or even over its implementation. Was it the inevitable result of millennia of hatred of the Jews and/or ten centuries of specifically Christian Europe's anti-Semitism? Did it grow ineluctably out of the new, virulent nationalism of the nineteenth century and/or the cataclysm of World War I? Was it the product of Hitler's unrelenting racism and/or the German people's resentment and misery which found resonance almost everywhere under the Third Reich? Do we thus place the Holocaust in the category of an inevitable occurrence—like a tornado or an earthquake—unpredictable in its arrival but inherent within the context of the twentieth-century German and European history? [1]

Many historians—and not all of them German—say no. For at least a quarter of a century, many serious and reputable scholars have insisted on the noninevitability *as well as* the nonpredictability of the Holocaust. [2] Without minimizing the horrors that occurred between 1933 and 1945, or even those that came before, they have tried to loosen the chain linking all German, and a good deal of European, history with the Holocaust. Stressing the human agency on the one hand and institutional factors and contingency on the other, they have combatted the inevitabilists with documentation of roads not taken, orders not followed, and signals not received; of structural disorder and distorted forms of "modernization"; of *discontinuities* over conscious and intentional continuity on the twisted road from historic Jew-baiting and anti-Semitism to the gas chambers. [3]

In studying the Holocaust we come face to face with this dilemma, as we do in trying to comprehend other calamities of the past such as civil wars, world wars, and other forms of genocide. Indeed, the very word "calamity"—or perhaps catastrophe, or disaster, or tragedy, instead of event, occurrence, or even misfortune—reveals a great deal about our bias. After all, professional history—one of the great, if somewhat flawed creations, of modern times—is a human invention designed and sustained for a civic and moral purpose as well as for knowledge and fascinating recreation. As professionals, our goal is to *understand* in the deepest sense of the word.[4]

Faced with a subject like the Holocaust, our task is made all the more difficult by the welter and unevenness of the evidence, the continuing gaps and the perhaps eternal mysteries as well as by the theories that seem to multiply as the distance from the event grows—not to mention the ever-present public and political dimension of a subject whose code word is simply "Auschwitz."[5] The assignment demands the insight and skill to identify the related, and separate the unconnected—what good historians and discerning individuals have always tried to do—and to engage in the indispensable, hopefully informed, and alas! perpetual discussion of the meaning of the past: our connections with it, its connection to us.

Even if we renounce all forms of historical determinism—religious and racial, nationalist and Marxist, Freudian and feminist, and also reject a total sense of contingency in human affairs, we may still admit that there are pivotal moments in human history. They may either be obscure or conspicuous incidents; it is their gravity that counts. Such emblematic and prophetic events, with their deep roots and significant repercussions, invite serious historical examination. They tend to connect opposites and combine elements of continuity and discontinuity, predictability and unpredictability, inevitability and avoidability. Like a mimesis, they expose a literal and a profound reality.

On June 24, 1922, Germany's first (and only) Jewish foreign minister, Walther Rathenau, was shot and murdered by two young former German officers of professed right-wing leanings. The assassination, less than six months after Rathenau's appointment, was shocking in both its brutality and its expectedness. Albert Einstein was stunned. Heeding his friends' warnings of "widespread anti-Semitism," he canceled all his lectures; although refusing to escape from Berlin, he was "officially absent."[6] A few hundred miles away in Prague, Franz Kafka observed, "Incredible that he lived as long as he did; already two months ago we heard rumors of his murder."[7] In London, *The Spectator*'s obituary began: "as little a surprise as a murder can well be."[8]

Who was Walther Rathenau? One of Germany and Jewry's most exotic, complex, and tragic figures, his life and work encompassed powerful opposites.[9] An industrialist, social philosopher, and statesman, he attained the highest government office ever reached by a German Jew. As foreign minister, he steered the wobbly Weimar Republic in two directions—towards reconciliation with the Entente and rapprochement with Soviet Russia. As a marked victim of political and racial assassins and the subject of numerous biographies, he is a challenging figure of contemporary history.[10]

Born in 1867, Walther Rathenau was a true child of imperial Germany and its emancipated Jews. His father, Emil Rathenau, founded the huge centralized conglomerate, AEG, the German General Electric Company. Following his dutiful study of engineering, Walther Rathenau did his business apprenticeship in various AEG subsidiaries before returning to Berlin at age thirty-two; he continued to travel throughout Europe and to South America and Africa. Within the next decade he succeeded his father at the helm of AEG, also served on numerous boards, and became one of Europe's major economic leaders.[11]

The other Walther Rathenau sought an influential position in the German intellectual firmament. He was a talented musician and painter, an avid art collector and raconteur, a brilliant linguist and man of letters who produced five volumes on contemporary and philosophical issues. Like Friedrich Nietzsche, the dominant figure of his age, Rathenau lauded the creative spirit who labored to win things eternal and divine. A latter day utopian socialist, Rathenau called for state regulation to subordinate personal interest to the needs of the community and an international organization to control trade, finance, and raw materials.[12]

Like many Jews of his generation who had attained wealth and held intellectual and social pretensions, Rathenau subordinated his Jewishness to his Germandom—perhaps with more vehemence than most. In 1897, he characterized his people as "a separate and alien race," and asserted his complete devotion to Germany and to the German people. When he called his people "the salt of the earth," he added that too much salt produced an unsavory diet.[13] Rathenau argued vehemently against Zionism on ideological and practical grounds.[14] Nevertheless, he refused to follow his contemporaries Karl Kraus, Franz Werfel, and Kurt Tucholsky into conversion. If as a Jew he had to live as a second-class citizen — failing, for example, to obtain the socially indispensable officer's commission in the imperial army — he nonetheless refused to renounce his ancestral faith. Was it out of loyalty to his parents, respect for an ancient tradition, or his dogged attachment to outsiderness? This man who loved to bring simplicity to technical problems and complexity to human ones sustained a Jewish identity which reinforced the extremes of his externality from, and adherence to, the German people.[15]

The outbreak of World War I gave Walther Rathenau the opportunity to serve the German people in their hour of need. Like the ardent nationalist Fritz Haber, but unlike his pacifist countryman Albert Einstein, he rallied to the war effort. During the first nine months, Rathenau personally organized and directed the army unit set up to procure the raw materials and labor which were indispensable for the Reich's survival.[16] Eased out of office by the military, Rathenau turned to philosophy and writing, and even to a brief study of Chassidism under Martin Buber's guidance.[17] His German patriotism was sorely tested by the arrogance of the General Staff, by the kaiser's equivocations, and by Germany's political and military blunders. He opposed the imperialist treaty of Brest-Litovsk. When the western front collapsed in 1918, Rathenau vainly, and virtually alone, called for armed civilian resistance; he also opposed signing the Treaty of Versailles.[18]

Rathenau, the quintessential outsider, held a special vision of, and distance from, the German people. Well over six feet tall, with dark piercing eyes and a white goatee, he had a striking resemblance to Lenin. This brilliant, exotic looking bachelor was resented by the German upper classes for his "socialist tendencies," distrusted by the lower classes as a plutocrat, and a stranger to his own people whom he had mocked in print. (Einstein once remarked that Rathenau would be the Pope if he could!) When Rathenau moved among the literary, artistic, and business circles of middle-class Berlin he was invariably alone.[19] In February 1919, a telegram arrived at the Constituent Assembly in Weimar nominating Rathenau for the presidency of the new German republic which provoked uproarious laughter from the delegates on the Right and silence from the rest.[20]

Nevertheless, the beleaguered new Weimar Republic soon needed Rathenau's considerable financial and leadership talents. In 1920, he worked for the Socialization Commission and skillfully represented Germany at the Spa Conference on reparations. In July 1921, Rathenau accepted a Cabinet post as Minister of Reconstruction, swallowing his desire for the top job of foreign minister. During the next five months, he applied his skills and energy to the policy of "fulfillment," arranging compromises with France, Belgium, and England over Germany's huge reparations bill.[21]

Adept at bargaining with foreign statesmen and industrialists, Walther Rathenau was able to blunt the Allies' fears and suspicions of Germany and appeal for their generosity. He depicted a weak Germany, with tense industrial-labor relations and a fragile currency, menaced within by right- and left-wing radicalism and by regional divisions and threatened in the East by Soviet Russia, and thus incapable of paying reparations without immediate loans and moratoria. Despite the forcefulness of his message, or perhaps because his convictions seemed so solid, Rathenau came to be considered an "indispensable" figure in European politics. The more he succeeded abroad, however, the more his domestic enemies could label him the international Jew.[22]

On January 30, 1922 (exactly eleven years before Hitler's appointment to power), Walther Rathenau was finally placed at the helm of the foreign ministry. It was the eve of the world economic conference to be held at Genoa, the first meeting to which Germany and Soviet Russia were invited to participate as equals and whose agenda offered relief, reconstruction, and peace to Central and Eastern Europe. This offered Rathenau the great occasion of his life: the chance to represent Germany as a full partner of the West in the negotiations with Lenin's Russia.[23]

The world gave a mixed response to Rathenau's appointment. If British leaders hoped that Rathenau could "take even more courageous steps than before," the French feared that dialogues with the "clever" new foreign minister "would be interminable and lead nowhere." While the Belgians regarded him as a war criminal, responsible for the exploitation, deportations, and destruction of occupied countries during the war, the Italians were fascinated by Rathenau's exotic personality. And although the press seventy years ago was far more reticent over private matters than today, foreign journalists interpreted Rathenau's bachelorhood and solitary existence as testimony to his dedicated commitment to public service.[24]

Rathenau's political position was obviously delicate. He had to speak hard truths to his countrymen: Germany could not refuse to negotiate with its former enemies over reparations and it could not deny its liability. He also had to convince the Allies that their demands on Germany were economically, financially, and politically unfulfillable. He thus had to pursue highly intricate maneuvering among Britain, France, the United States, and Soviet Russia in the face of the unremitting opposition of hardline German nationalists. The August 1921 assassination of Matthias Erzberger—with whom Rathenau had devised this complex "fulfillment policy"—provided ample warning to his successor.[25]

Walther Rathenau, the ex-monarchist, the Jewish captain of industry with his spiritualist and socialist leanings, the amateur politician-statesman without a seat in the Reichstag, stood isolated in republican Germany. His support from the "good Germans," the "Weimar Germans," was noticeably tepid. The Democrats, the Center, and the Moderate Socialists kept their distance. Chancellor Wirth, who expected to control foreign policy, evidently intended to make Rathenau his court Jew, who was acceptable to British and Dutch bankers, tolerated by the French, and a useful signal to Moscow.[26]

Rathenau had powerful enemies among the Potsdamers, the monarchists, and the new right. In the *Wilhelmstrasse* he faced snobbish career diplomats who disliked his every move.[27] In the Reichstag, the brilliant hawkish Deutsche Volkspartei (DVP) leader Gustav Stresemann who chaired the Foreign Affairs Committee resented having been blocked from the *Wilhelmstrasse*. Hugo Stinnes, the right-wing industrialist, gave Rathenau a useful bogeyman for his diplomatic negotiations with the Allies; but at home Stinnes undermined Rathenau by attacking the foreign minister's patriotic credentials. The anti-Semitic press termed Rathenau's appointment the triumph of Jewish banking interests, Jewish socialism, and Jewish freemasonry as well as of the international, liberal banking conspiracy led by Lloyd George which aimed to dominate a prostrate Christian Germany. The lonely court Jew in a country of pan-German assassins, Rathenau seemed destined to sacrifice himself.[28]

On the eve of the Genoa Conference the foreign minister met for five hours with Albert Einstein and Kurt Blumenfeld to discuss Palestine, the Jewish problem, and his role as Germany's advocate before the entire world. Rathenau insisted on his right to speak for the entire German people just as Disraeli had represented England. But there were key differences. The baptized Disraeli was a more facile and clever actor; by enlarging the island kingdom's riches with the Suez Canal, by making Victoria the Empress of India, and by expanding British democracy, he had enhanced the pride and prestige of both his peoples. On the other hand, the aristocratic, unbaptized Rathenau, who was about to plead for a defeated, and largely unrepentant Germany, risked disappointment and danger for Germans, for Jews, and for himself. Late in the night Rathenau admitted to Einstein and Blumenfeld that he served a Germany which had never accepted him completely or unconditionally. The two Zionists walked the late night streets of Berlin vindicated, and frightened.[29]

And indeed, there was an unpleasant, if not unexpected surprise at the Genoa Conference: a stellar, thirty-four-nation summit gathering, the largest international conference until Helsinki in 1975.[30] After a brilliant opening, when Germany was welcomed virtually as an equal, Rathenau found himself excluded from the secret Allied-Russian negotiations. And so on Easter Sunday, April 16, 1922, he traveled the road to Rapallo and signed the notorious separate treaty with Soviet Russia. Overnight, the Rathenau esteemed abroad was transformed into another ruthless German, who had ruptured Western solidarity and signed with the barbaric Soviets. The would-be good European became the cunning Jew with his "underhanded tricks."[31]

His fulfillment policy in shambles, Rathenau's days in office appeared to be numbered, and his very life at stake. Indeed, there had been a four-year wave of murders in republican Germany, mainly of Jews and left-wing figures. Rathenau understood that by assuming the high post of foreign minister he too would be a target of assassins. Since January 1922, German students had chanted: "Strike down Walther Rathenau/ The God-damned Jewish sow!" Warned of an actual death threat by Chancellor Wirth, Rathenau had refused to retain a bodyguard.[32]

The actual murder reads like a powerful work of fiction. The plot began in April 1922 when a group of young men formed a conspiracy to kill Rathenau, claiming he was one of the three hundred Elders of Zion committed to taking over the world. The night before Rathenau was killed, he was bitterly attacked in the Reichstag by the demagogic Nationalist deputy Karl Helfferich, who charged: "The Calvary of fulfillment ... has ruined Germany, crushed our middle class, dragged countless persons into the depths of poverty and others into despair and suicide." Visibly shaken, Rathenau dined that night at the American Embassy then stayed up until 4 A.M. earnestly conferring with his rival Hugo Stinnes about reparations.[33]

The next morning at 10:45, Rathenau set out to work later than usual. About a mile and a half from his villa in Grunewald his open car was overtaken and stopped by an automobile with three handsome young men in spanking new leather jackets. When Rathenau's car was halted, one man shot the foreign minister with a submachine gun, while the second threw a hand grenade which lifted the victim from his seat; the driver of the assassins' vehicle then sped away. Rathenau had been shot five times; his jaw and backbone were completely shattered. He died almost at once. He was fifty-four years old.[34]

Not since the assassination of Abraham Lincoln did a nation make such a lavish display of mourning. The funeral service was held in the Reichstag with an oration delivered by the president of the Republic. The funeral cortege with an honor guard and the rolling of drums passed under the Brandenburg Gate on the way to the Rathenau family grave. Almost a half-million Berliners witnessed the solemn procession. The trade unions declared a day of mourning, and 200,000 workers assembled before the castle in Berlin; there were also workers' parades in Hamburg, Munich, Chemnitz, Eberfeld, Essen, and Breslau.[35] World leaders responded with an outpouring of sympathy for the fallen leader.[36]

Behind the public facade were less auspicious responses to Rathenau's murder. According to Stefan Zweig, "panic broke out" among the noisy vacationers bathing that June weekend on the North Sea. The pacifist Friedrich Wilhelm Foerster, who was on a speaking trip in Germany, warned that he too was on a "list," fled terrified back to Switzerland and never returned to Germany. On the streets of Berlin, the bourgeoisie decried the impact on the dollar-exchange. Because June 24 was the Saint's day of John the Baptist—one of the protectors of Prussian knighthood—and because on the day after a huge monarchist rally took place in Potsdam, rumors raced through Berlin's working-class districts of an impending St. Bartholomew's night. The director Fritz Lang claimed that he created his schizophrenic supercriminal Dr. Mabuse as a response to the senseless violence attached to Rathenau's murder.[37]

Privately, there was little sympathy for the victim. On the day after the murder, Friedrich Meinecke's fellow academics in Berlin raged over the communist menace to Germany. In Munich, Thomas Mann heard an eminent professor rejoice in "one less Jew!"[38] In Heidelberg, the Nobel-prize-winning physics professor Philip Lenard forbade his students to observe the day of Rathenau's burial and be "idle on account of a dead Jew." On his walks through the German capital, the Prague journalist Egon Erwin Kisch heard lawyers and government functionaries—still sporting their Wilhelmian mustaches—utter melodramatically "It's been done!"[39] And Kurt Tucholsky's newly-invented *Spiessbürger,* "Herr Wendriner," parodied the exasperation of solid German and Jewish businessmen with all the red flags, and the marching, and the huge and noisy lower-class demonstrations in Rathenau's name: Too much disorder over one pushy dead Jew![40]

Partisans of the Weimar Republic hoped that Rathenau's tragic death would represent a "defining moment" and produce a *ralliement* to the threatened regime. The liberal cosmopolitan Count Harry Kessler wrote in his diary "a new day of German history begins, or at least should begin."[41] Thomas Mann, a former ardent nationalist and monarchist, took his stand, uttering his incontrovertible "Yes" to the Republic.[42] Rathenau's archrival Stresemann, obviously next in line to head the *Wilhelmstrasse,* moved to distance himself from his rightist past and support the Weimar Republic.[43] On a signal from Moscow, communist leader Clara Zetkin called for a popular front against the enemies of the republic; and socialists Julius Leber and Paul Levi called for loyalty and toughness against Weimar's assassins.[44] In his poem "Rathenau," Kurt Tucholsky taunted, "Four years of murder: By God enough!" and demanded "old mother parliament" stomp its fist, dismiss the monarchist judges and disband secret groups, tame Ludendorff and contain the Reichswehr—"fight or die."[45]

But the political clarification sought by Kessler, and by Tucholsky, did not materialize. The timid Wirth pushed through a draconian "law for the protection of the republic" which neither tamed the right nor strengthened the center. He refused to call new elections or broaden his government. If no right- or left-wing putsch occurred after Rathenau's murder, neither Wirth nor any other Weimar leader seized the moment of his death to steer Germany away from the nationalist hatred and class cleavages which would ultimately destroy the republic.[46] But this was beyond Rathenau's capacity as well. The patrician Rathenau would not have been capable of achieving what another outsider, Willy Brandt, accomplished a half century later with his stunning combination of idealism and pragmatism, fineness and toughness—to steer an albeit smaller, stronger, better protected and reined-in West Germany through its perilous moments of violence and economic convulsions while also protecting its democracy.[47]

Walther Rathenau's assassination did have this repercussion: it greatly intensified the witches' sabbath of the German inflation, which actually began in 1914, speeded-up in 1920, and soared in 1922. The mark reached 401 to the dollar on July 1 and 1700 by the end of August; by then, a newspaper which cost 50,000 marks in the morning became a hundred thousand in the evening; people with things, with foreign currency, and with the ability to borrow made huge profits; salaried workers, the unemployed, savers, and retirees became impoverished. The inflation brought Germany a "madness of gigantic proportions," a profound destruction of values which had already been shattered by war and revolution; it exacerbated resentment and hatred—against rich foreigners and against the Jews.[48] Those who were responsible for the chaos—for the violence, and for the irresponsible economic and political policies—did not fear the chaos, and the damage to the republic, from which they would ultimately profit.

Walther Rathenau's murder also brought no relief from the Allies' reparations demands. When the shaky Wirth government was replaced by the unpolitical but equally obstinate Cuno cabinet, the German Republic moved rapidly towards default. With the United States calling in their loans, the Allies in January 1923 were forced to invade the Ruhr to collect coal instead of cash. Then followed eight violent months of civil strife and hyper-inflation, of communist uprisings and the first abortive Nazi putsch in November 1923. When the nadir had been reached, with U.S. help Stresemann and Germany's former enemies negotiated the Dawes Plan.[49] Rathenau had anticipated this solution in 1922, but he did not live to achieve it.

The short "golden twenties" of Dawes Plan years lasted only until the stock market crash of 1929. In the 1930 parliamentary elections, the Nationalist-Nazi bloc that had eulogized Rathenau's murderers emerged triumphant. After the Weimar Republic collapsed two-and-a-half years later, the Third Reich initiated the celebration of the day of Rathenau's murder.

In what sense was the assassination of Walther Rathenau a prelude to the Holocaust? Many historians have denied, or minimized, the aspect of anti-Semitism in Rathenau's murder, either stressing its *structural* and *political* causes (Weimar Germany's volatile mixture of anti-republicanism, anti-bolshevism, and anti-Westernism, its armed bands of militant right-wing youths, and its woefully disunited center and left) or the *personal* dimension (Rathenau's unpopularity among almost every segment of German opinion). In mirror image, the German and European left created a mythical Rathenau, transforming the industrialist-war leader into a "sacrifice" for the good Germany—as much a victim of the Allies' intransigence as of German right-wing bullets.[50] But these political Rathenaus—Rathenau as another martyr of Weimar's fragile democracy—disregard the flesh-and-blood reality of the time, which we must retrieve.

The virulent anti-Semitism of Imperial Germany—its exclusion and its scapegoating of the Jews—did not abate when the regime collapsed in 1918. Indeed, defeat and revolution, the Kapp Putsch, and the repeated reparations crises filled the anti-Semitic arsenal. The Right blamed every mistake of the Weimar government, every setback in the economy or in foreign affairs, on the Jews.[51]

Rathenau was the ideal embodiment of the Jew as a dominating and destructive figure. A racist pamphlet in January 1922 accused Wirth of delivering Germany over to "Jewish world control" and termed Rathenau's nomination "a bald provocation of the German people." The Nazi organ, the *Völkischer Beobachter,* headlined one of its articles "The resurrected Marx: Rathenau." The harassed Wirth government did not refute the attacks. Indeed, when the Right complained over the "disproportionate" number of Jews in Germany's delegation, it excluded one very talented non-Aryan from the Genoa Conference.[52]

To be sure, the climate of opinion in the German Republic was not all that uniform; not all Germans reduced their thinking to this level of stereotype or sought the reduction of "Jewish power," at least not in 1922. But during Rathenau's brief but eventful tenure, as the Republic's political and economic fortunes seemed to speed out of control, many Germans became frightened for themselves and their future. And for many of them, the lone and exotic Walther Rathenau represented a convenient scapegoat for everything that had gone wrong for Germany: reparations and unemployment; inflation and high prices; arrogant Frenchies and menacing bolshies. The world-turned-upside-down was represented by the fact that a vain, intellectual, cosmopolitan, left-leaning Jewish millionaire—especially one who resembled Lenin—was on top.[53]

Consequently, many contemporary observers, Jewish and non-Jewish, were convinced of the heightened danger exposed by Rathenau's murder. The Austrian-Jewish economist Gustav Stolper lamented the "anti-Semitic plague" that had attacked the German body politic;[54] and the playwright Carl Zuckmayer insisted, "He was murdered because he was a Jew."[55] The London *Jewish Chronicle* (June 30) reminded its readers that Rathenau had been "persecuted" since his appointment. *The Nation,* which termed Rathenau "one of the few statesmen whom Europe could not afford to lose" (July 5), also called him the victim of the Henry Fords who had preached against a "global Jewish conspiracy" (July 12). In August, *The Contemporary Review* called Rathenau a sacrifice to the "new anti-Semitism" wielding its new lethal weapons to exclude the Jews. The German-Jewish writer Emil Ludwig called Rathenau's "urge towards power" a fatal impulse in a land which had never permitted a Jew to hold the reins of State or had forgiven one who cherished that aspiration.[56] The Danish-Jewish literary critic Georg Brandes pinpointed the uniqueness of German anti-Semitism: in the Slavic lands there had been pogroms, mass killing, and mass plunder; while in the more "civilized" Reich single Jews were targeted for death.[57]

In August 1922, a Thuringian farmer assured his American train-mate that Rathenau had been killed simply "because he was a Jew." The trial of Rathenau's murderers confirmed that two of his assassins were fanatic anti-Semites who believed that they were eliminating a "pernicious influence," an "international Jew" who aimed to introduce bolshevism into Germany. Visitors to Germany in the summer of 1922 remarked that "everything but the weather was blamed on the Jews."[58]

Hence, Rathenau's death failed to kindle any spark of reconciliation between Germans and Jews. Brandes's caution about the peculiarity of German anti-Semitism remained valid. German Jewry, less than one percent of the population, more than ever feared to walk in Rathenau's footsteps and expose and endanger themselves. Walter Benjamin, in his anguished response to Rathenau's murder, wrote that the Jews could no longer hope to "speak" as Germans or even join the German "conversation."[59] And, just as important, the German people accepted, and in fact would expect, the Jews' almost total withdrawal from power. Walther Rathenau's great gamble—to join the opposites of Weimar and Potsdam and to stretch the German-Jewish relationship to its very extreme of acceptance—had been defeated.[60]

The contrast with other states is instructive. French Jews had endured the Dreyfus Affair and American Jews the Leo Frank Affair as disturbing anomalies that did not diminish their sense of belonging to, or acceptance by, their homeland.[61] But for German Jews there was no redemption. After five decades of nonacceptance and vilification, they could not avoid concluding that the circumstances surrounding Rathenau's murder provided the verdict of their compatriots' "hate, delusion, and ingratitude."[62]

Walther Rathenau was not the first victim of violence during the Weimar Republic; but this was the first time in German history that a Jew in a prominent position was killed because he was a Jew in a prominent position.[63] The small militant Nazi party lauded the killers, boycotted the commemorations, and maligned the victim. German Jews were cowed by an event which set a stark limit to their prospects, their acceptance, and their survival. And the world outside witnessed a murder which presaged the threat which materialized eleven years later not only to the Weimar Republic but to all the Jews of Germany and of Europe.

NOTES

1. See J. L. Talmon, "European History—Seedbed of the Holocaust," *Midstream* (May 1973): 7; Saul Friedländer, "From Anti-Semitism to Extermination: A Historiographical Study of Nazi Policies towards the Jews and an Essay in Interpretation," *Yad Vashem Studies* 16:4; Lucy Dawidowicz, *The Holocaust and the Historians* (Cambridge, Mass., 1981).

2. See, e.g., Peter Gay, "Introduction: German Questions," in his *Freud, Jews, and Other Germans* (New York, 1978), 3–28.

3. Todd Endelman, "Comparative Perspectives on Modern Anti-Semitism in the West" in *History and Hate: The Dimensions of Anti-Semitism,* ed. David Berger (Philadelphia, 1986), 95–114.

The debate between the intentionalists and functionalists is well summarized in Michael Marrus, *The Holocaust in History* (Hanover, N.H., 1987), chap. 3.

The modernization issue is covered in Michael Prinz and Rainer Zitelman, eds., *Nationalsozialismus und Modernizierung* (Darmstadt, 1990).

The totalitarian model is evaluated in Ian Kershaw, *The Nazi Dictatorship: Problems and Perspectives of Interpretation* (London, 1985).

Another omnipresent source of revisionism was "Germany was not the only country in which the evil penetrated," as the elderly Friedrich Meinecke contended in 1946: *The German Catastrophe,* trans. Sidney B. Fay (New York, 1963), 23.

4. Marc Bloch, *Apologie pour l'histoire ou métier d'historien* (Paris, 1974), 121. Bloch, a French Jew and notable historian, wrote this on the eve of his engagement in the French Resistance in 1943; a year later he was captured, tortured, and killed by the Germans on the eve of D-Day.

5. See the excellent discussion in Michael R. Marrus, "Reflections on the Historiography of the Holocaust," *Journal of Modern History* 66 (Mar. 1994): 92–116.

6. Einstein to Solovine, July 16, 1922, in Albert Einstein, *Lettres à Maurice Solovine* (Paris, 1956).

7. Letter to Max Brod, June 30, 1922, in Franz Kafka, *Briefe, 1902–1924* (Frankfurt am Main, 1975), 378.

8. "The Threat to the German Republic," *The Spectator,* July 1, 1922, 8.

9. Between December 9, 1993, and February 8, 1994, the largest exhibition on Rathenau was presented at the new German Historical Museum in Berlin; see the 455-page catalogue, with essays by an international group of nineteen historians: *Die Extreme berühren sich: Walther Rathenau, 1867–1922,* ed. Hans Wilderotter (Berlin, 1993).

10. The most important biographies include: Peter Berglar, *Walther Rathenau: Ein Leben zwischen Philosophie und Politik* (Graz, 1987); David Felix, *Walther Rathenau and the Weimar Republic* (Baltimore, 1971); James Joll, "Walther Rathenau: Prophet without a Cause," in *Intellectuals in Politics: Three Biographical Essays* (London, 1960), 59–129; Harry Count Kessler, *Walther Rathenau: His Life and Work* (New York, 1930); Peter Loewenberg, "Walther Rathenau and German Society," Ph.D. diss., University of California/Berkeley, 1966; Ernst Schulin, *Walther Rathenau: Repräsentant, Kritiker und Opfer seiner Zeit* (Göttingen, 1979); and Hartmut Pogge von Strandmann, ed., *Walther Rathenau: Industrialist, Banker, Intellectual and Politician: Notes and Diaries, 1907–1922* (Oxford, 1988).

Rathenau's private papers, which disappeared during World War II, were recently discovered in the former Special Government Archive in Russia: see Ernst Schulin, "Rathenau in Moskau," *Frankfurter Allgemeine Zeitung,* Sept. 29, 1992.

11. See Manfred Pohl, *Emil Rathenau und die AEG* (Mainz, 1988); Ursula Mader, *Walther Rathenau als Funktionär des Finanzkapitals: Beiträge zu einer politische Biographie (1867–1917),* Ph.D. diss., [East] Berlin, 1974; Peter Strunk, "Die Karriere Walther Rathenaus in der AEG," in *Die Extreme berühren sich,* 45–54.

12. Thomas P. Hughes, ed., *Ein Mann vieler Eigenschaften: Walther Rathenau und die Kultur der Moderne* (Berlin, 1990); Hubert W. Kran, *Die sozial— und gesellschaftspolitischen Vorstellungen Walther Rathenaus* (Bochum, 1975); James Joll, "Walther Rathenau—Intellectual or Industrialist?" in Volker Berghahn and Martin Kitchen, eds., *Germany in the Age of Total War* (London, 1981), 46–62.

13. "Höre Israel!" [written under the pseudonym W. Hartenau], *Die Zukunft* 18 (1897): 454–62.

14. Rudolf Kallner, *Herzl und Rathenau: Wege jüdischer Existenz an der Wende des 20. Jahrhunderts* (Stuttgart, 1976).

15. Ernst Schulin, "Walther Rathenau und sein Integrationsversuchals 'Deutscher jüdischer Stammes,' " in Walter Grab, ed., *Jüdische Integration und Identität in Deutschland, 1848–1918* (Tel Aviv, 1984), 13–38; Clemens Picht, " 'Er will der Messias der Juden werden': Walther Rathenau zwischen Antisemitismus und jüdischer Prophetie," in *Die Extreme berühren sich*, 117–28.

16. Lothar Burchardt, "Walther Rathenau und die Anfänge der deutschen Rohstoffbewirtschaftung im Ersten Weltkrieg," in *Tradition: Zeitschrift für Firmengeschichte und Unternehmerbiographie* 15 (1970): 169–96; Gerhard Hecker, *Walther Rathenau und sein Verhältnis zu Militär und Krieg* (Boppard, 1983).

17. Martin Buber, *Briefwechsel aus sieben Jahrzehnten*, vol. 2: 1918–1938 (Heidelberg, 1973), 299–301.

18. Wilhelm Herzog, *Menschen, denen ich begegnete* (Bern, 1959), 23–24.

19. Rathenau's "distinguished ambiguity," as depicted in the grandiose/impotent character of Paul Arnheim in Robert Musil's novel, *Der Mann ohne Eigenschaften,* included his uncertain sexuality: Alfred Kerr, *Walther Rathenau: Erinnerungen eines Freundes* (Amsterdam, 1935). He maintained an intimate, if chaste, lifelong relationship with his colleague's wife Lili Deutsch, as well as an apparently passionate tie *("eng befreundet")* with a racist writer and publisher, Wilhelm Schwaner (1863–1944): Martin Buber to Franz Rosenzweig, July 5, 1926, in Buber, *Briefwechsel,* vol. 2, 264–65.

20. Kessler, *Rathenau,* 272. See also Pierre Giraud, "L'image de Walther Rathenau dans la presse et la littérature allemandes," Ph.D. diss., University of Paris (Sorbonne), 1975.

21. Detailed in Felix, *Rathenau,* 41–104.

22. Hans von Raumer, "Walther Rathenau," *Deutsche Rundschau* 78 (July 1952): 664–69.

23. Carole Fink, *The Genoa Conference: European Diplomacy, 1921–1922* (Syracuse, 1993).

24. *Daily Telegraph* and *The Times,* Feb. 1, 1922; *Le Gaullois, Le Figaro, Le Temps, L'Oeuvre, Le Petit Journal,* Feb. 1, 1922; *L'Indépendance Belge,* Feb. 3, 1922; *Le Métropole,* Feb. 4, 1922; *Tribuna,* Feb. 3, 1922.

25. Klaus Epstein, *Matthias Erzberger and the Dilemma of German Democracy* (Princeton, 1959). In *Echo de Paris,* June 25, 1922, Louis Loucheur revealed Rathenau's premonition that he would be the next target of assassins.

26. Ernst Laubach, *Die Politik der Kabinette Wirth, 1921/22* (Lübeck, 1968); also Selma Stern-Täubler, *The Court Jew: A Contribution to the History of Absolutism in Europe* (New Brunswick, N.J., 1984).

27. Herbert von Dirksen, *Moscow, Tokyo, London: Twenty Years of German Foreign Policy* (Norman, Okla., 1952), 29–32, aptly summarizes the condescending view. On his personnel form for the foreign ministry, Rathenau gave his citizenship as "Prussian," acknowledged his untraditional bachelorhood, and left item #5, *"Konfession,"* blank, later adding in pencil "Diese Frage entspricht nicht der Verfassung." Facsimile in *Die Extreme berühren sich,* 200.

28. "My heart is heavy.... A man alone—knowing his limits and weaknesses—what can a man like that do in this paralyzed world, with enemies all around?" Rathenau to Lili Deutsch, quoted in Kessler, *Rathenau,* 323.

29. Blumenfeld, *Erlebte Judenfrage,* 142–45.

30. Details in Fink, *Genoa Conference,* 143–280.

31. Jacques Bainville, "Le coup de théâtre de Gênes," L.L.B., "L'accord de Rapallo," and Léon Daudet, "L'entrée en scène de M. Rathenau," all in *Action Française,* April 18, 1922.

32. Viscount Edward Vincent D'Abernon, *The Diary of an Ambassador: Versailles to Rapallo, 1920–1922* (New York, 1929), 323. The German text of the ditty was: "Knallt ab den Walther Rathenau/Die gottverdammte Judensau."

33. See report by U.S. Ambassador Houghton to Secretary of State Hughes, June 25, 1922, U.S. National Archives, Microfilmed Records of the State Department, M336, Reel 18.

34. A complete account of the murder is Martin Sabrow, "Märtyrer der Republik: Zu den Hintergründen des Mordanschlags vom 24. Juni 1922," in *Die Extreme berühren sich,* 221–36.

35. See reports by Addison to Balfour, June 26, 1922, British Foreign Office Records (FO 371)/7536 and U.S. Consul in Breslau to Hughes, June 28, 1922, Microfilmed Records of the U.S. State Dept., M336, Reel 18.

36. Carole Fink, "Ausländische Reaktionen auf den Mord an Walther Rathenau," in *Die Extreme berühren sich,* 237–46.

37. Paul M. Jensen, *The Cinema of Fritz Lang* (New York, 1969), 79–94; also Oscar Loerke, *Tagebücher, 1903–1939* (Heidelberg, 1955), 91–92, for the tense atmosphere after the murder.

38. Recalled in letter to Arthur Hübscher, June 27, 1928, in Thomas Mann, *Briefe, 1889–1936* (Berlin, 1961).

39. Egon Erwin Kisch, *Läuse auf dem Markt: Vermischte Prose,* vol. 10 (1985), 316.

40. Kaspar Hauser [Kurt Tucholsky], "Herr Wendriner telefoniert," *Die Weltbühne*, 18, no. 27 (July 6, 1922): 19.

41. Harry Graf Kessler, *Tagebücher, 1918–1937* (Frankfurt am Main, 1961), 323–24.

42. "Geist und Wesen der deutschen Republik: Dem Gedächtnis Walther Rathenaus," in Thomas Mann, *Gesammelte Werke,* vol. 11, (Frankfurt am Main, 1974), 853–60.

43. Gustav Stresemann, *Vermächtnis,* ed. Henry Bernhard, vol. I (Berlin, 1932), 21–22; cf. Henry A. Turner, *Stresemann and the Politics of the Weimar Republic* (Princeton, 1963). Historians still contest the extent of Stresemann's "conversion" but not his shock at Rathenau's murder.

44. Clara Zetkin, "Die proletarische Einheitsfront" (Aug. 1922) in *Ausgewählte Reden und Schriften,* vol. 2 (1918–1923) ([East] Berlin, 1960), 578–96; Paul Levi, *Zwischen Spartakus und Sozialdemokratie: Schriften, Aufsätze, Reden, und Briefe* (Frankfurt, 1969), 233–43; Julius Leber, *Schriften, Reden, Briefe* (Munich, 1976), 33–35.

45. "Rathenau," in Kurt Tucholsky, *Gesammelte Werke,* vol. 3 (1921–1924) (Reinbek bei Hamburg, 1975).

46. Stefan Zweig, "Zum Andenken Walther Rathenaus: Am Jahrestag seiner Ermordung, 24 Juni 1922," *Neue Freie Presse* (June 24, 1923); Georg Bernhard, *Die deutsche Tragödie: Der Selbstmord einer Republik* (Prague, 1933), 150–60.

47. After his own enforced retirement, Willy Brandt linked his ideas and values with Rathenau's: "What fascinated me about Rathenau, whose murder provided an early foretaste of the first republic's tragic fate, was that his undoubtedly upper middle class but liberal cast of mind forged a path to democracy and social responsibility. I also appreciated his recognition of the historical need for a harmonious compromise between Germany's politics towards West and East." *People and Politics: The Years 1960–1975* (Boston, 1976), 151.

48. Stefan Zweig, *The World of Yesterday* (New York, 1943), 310–12.

49. Stephen A. Schuker, *The End of French Predominance in Europe: The Financial Crisis of 1924 and the Adoption of the Dawes Plan* (Chapel Hill, 1976).

50. See *Manchester Guardian,* June 26, 1922; *Social Demokraten* [Stockholm], June 27, 1922.

51. Gustav Mayer, *Erinnerungen* (Vienna, 1949), 332.

52. Moritz Schlesinger, *Erinnerungen eines Aussenseiters im diplomatischen Dienst* (Cologne, 1977), 298.

53. There are intriguing parallels with other brilliant, solitary, and similarly vilified Jewish statesmen: Judah Benjamin, Leon Trotsky, Leon Blum, Maxim Litvinov, and even Henry Kissinger.

54. Toni Stolper, *Ein Leben in Brennpunkten unserer Zeit: Wien, Berlin, New York: Gustav Stolper, 1888–1947* (Tübingen, 1960), 158.

55. Carl Zuckmayer, *Als wär's ein Stück von mir* (Vienna, 1967), 309.

56. *Neue Zürcher Zeitung,* June 27, 1922.

57. *Politiken,* June 28, 1922.

58. Lowenthal, "Behind Rathenau," *Menorah Journal* (June 1923): 72–81.

59. Walter Benjamin to Florens Christian Rang, Nov. 18, 1923, in *Briefe* 1 (Frankfurt am Main-Suhrkamp, 1993), 309–13.

60. Arnold Brecht, *Aus Nächster Nahe: Lebenserinnerungen* (Stuttgart, 1966), 351–52. Cf. Fritz Stern, " 'Ich wunschte der Wagen möchte zerschellen': Zerissen wie das eigene Volk: Walther Rathenau als Unternehmer, Intellektueller und Staatsmann," *Die Zeit* 43, no. 49 (Dec. 2, 1988).

61. See Albert S. Lindemann, *The Jew Accused: Three Anti-Semitic Affairs (Dreyfus, Beilis, Frank, 1894–1915)* (Cambridge, 1991).

62. Albert Einstein, "In Memoriam Walther Rathenau," *Neue Rundschau* 33, no. 8 (1922): "I regretted that he became a Minister. Given the stance of most educated Germans against the Jews, I was convinced that the Jews' most natural reaction was to maintain a splendid isolation from the public arena. But I did not imagine that the hate, delusion, and ingratitude had extended so far. May I applaud those responsible for the ethical training of the German people for the past fifty years: By your fruits so shall you be known."

63. That Rathenau continues to be a lightning rod for racism is witnessed by the desecration of his grave during the wave of anti-Semitic and anti-foreign violence in Germany in 1993.

CHAPTER 4

Anti-Semitism in the Tradition of German

Discourse: The Path to the Holocaust

DAGMAR C. G. LORENZ

Most recent Holocaust scholarship emphasizes the uniqueness of the genocide perpetrated by the Nazis and the fact that it was more than simply another chapter in the century-long persecution of European Jews or anti-Semitism. Historical specificity at the exclusion of the larger context, however, encourages a no less slanted view than overgeneralization. The metaphorical use of the term "Holocaust" to describe the war in the Balkans, abortion, Aids, or rape, is inadmissible as is demonizing National Socialism as an evil empire, or sanctifying the topic of the Holocaust to such a degree that any discussion is stifled and writing about the event is made almost impossible. In this context, I refer to Theodor W. Adorno's much-debated statement that it is impossible to write poetry after Auschwitz[1] and the fact that this view contributed to the problem that Holocaust literature written by survivors in the German-speaking context has traditionally been measured by stricter standards than other literature.[2] Taken literally, Adorno's declaration could have silenced scores of Holocaust poets; however, they were the first to defy it.

Hannah Arendt's comment about the "banality of evil" toppled the Hollywood image of the Nazis as freaks or corrupt geniuses, as well as the exaggerations and distortions of the character traits of individual Nazis championed in personality-oriented studies.[3] Depicting National Socialism as diabolic, unprecedented, and monumental causes the image which Hitler and his followers had projected to the world to be perpetuated, but closer scrutiny shows Nazi ideology to be a product of its time. Embedded in Central European anti-Semitism, imperialism, and occultism, it added no fundamentally new ideas to early twentieth-century political discourse. As a mass movement, Nazism employed strategies similar to those of many other rivaling mass movements, including Communism. It is, in fact, the simplicity of Nazi thought rather than its complexity, its exploitation of widely discussed issues such race, gender, and the need to overcome decadence that ensured its overwhelming success.

This does not mean that the Holocaust was the only logical conclusion to earlier discourses, theories, and historical developments. Only in hindsight can it be interpreted as the sum total of its prehistory. Unprecedented phenomenona such as the mass or crowd dynamics, which distinguished the twentieth century from earlier epochs, were instrumental in bringing about the Holocaust, as Elias Canetti suggests in his study on mass psychology, *Masse und Macht*.[4] Without taking into account the specific conditions of the first third of this century, the Holocaust would elude interpretation. By the same token, the study of the Holocaust opens the road to the interpretation of important aspects of twentieth-century history that would otherwise remain incomprehensible.

Most Holocaust memoirs, literature, and criticism touch on the paradox of the Holocaust, the inseparable fusion of modern and archaic aspects. Yet most authors fail to unravel the enigma of the apparent regression into barbarism during the 1920s, a time of immense cultural and technological progress. Jewish intellectuals such as Lion Feuchtwanger, Wilhelm Reich, and Karl Kraus were convinced as early as 1933 that the weapons of the intellect were ineffective against the onslaught of this most primitive form of barbarism called National Socialism.[5] Progress and primitivism, technocratic organization and chaotic breakdowns where details were concerned were not mutually exclusive, but integral aspects of the same period. Both the ultimate control and the lack of control were encapsulated in that medium whose limits Ludwig Wittgenstein defined as the limits of his world, language.

Sander Gilman, in his study *Jewish Self-Hatred: Anti-Semitism and the Hidden Language of the Jews* (1986), explored Christian religious and secular discourse, in other words the discourse of Western civilization, as the medium of religious Jew-hatred and its secular variant, anti-Semitism. He showed that not even Jews as they assimilated themselves into European society and adopted the languages of their native countries could avoid absorbing the ideological constructs and stereotypes embedded in these languages, even if many of these concepts threatened their very existence.[6] If German-speaking Jews of exceptional intelligence such as Otto Weininger were defenseless against anti-Semitism, Gentiles were even more so, because they had no reason to resist the enemy images enclosed in their native language and religion. Quite the contrary, these enhanced their self-confidence by telling them that they were superior spiritual, intellectual, and physical beings. A brief review of German texts about Jews shows that German has been a vehicle for the proliferation of anti-Jewish discourses throughout the centuries, a language in which anti-Jewish views were not only reproduced, but radicalized at such important historical junctures as the Age of Reformation. Only in the last two centuries did an oppositional Jewish discourse arise.

Martin Luther's invectives against the Jews were written in German and, in contrast to earlier Catholic and Renaissance treatises, meant to inspire a public polemic rather than a scholarly debate. His "On the Jews and Their Lies" (Von den Juden und ihren Lügen) reads like a blueprint for the Nazi *Judenprogramm*.[7] Points four and five of the National Socialist Party Program state that no Jew could be a fellow German, a *Volksgenosse,* and that non-Germans were to be treated as aliens. This view corresponds with Luther's assertion that Jews were foreigners and thieves without any claim to the property they had acquired.[8] Not surprisingly, Nazi ideologues frequently referred to Luther as one of their precursors. With the intent to proselytize and in this way eliminate the segregated Jewish minority, Luther condemned the persecution of Jews in a treatise of 1523 (*Daß Jesus eingeborener Jude sei*). His efforts to make converts failed and in "Von den Juden und ihren Lügen" (1542–43) he discredited the Jews as the arch-enemies of Christians and Germans.[9] Among the measures to suppress the alleged anti-Christian and anti-German activities on the part of the Jews he recommended the burning of Jewish books, particularly the *Talmud,* forced labor for Jewish men and women, travel and residential restrictions, a teaching ban for Rabbis, the burning of the synagogues, the confiscation of property, and restricting the Jews' right to travel so that any Jewish individual met on highways outside the city could be killed with impunity. In a perversion of language that already foreshadows Nazi euphemisms, Luther maintained that his suggested measures were motivated by "tough compassion" and Christian charity. His attitude toward converts transpires from a remark in his Table Talks: "When I convince another pious Jew to take baptism, I will take him to the bridge across the Elbe river immediately after his baptism, tie a stone around his neck and throw him into the water." [10] The gypsies, Sinti and Roma, are the only other groups that Luther *expressis verbis* declared a threat to his fellow countrymen. Significantly, they were the only other ethnic groups whose total destruction was plotted by the Nazis.

Even the seemingly progressive programs promoting the improvement of the status of Jews during the Age of Enlightenment, including that of Christian von Dohm as well as the Toleration Edict issued under Emperor Joseph II, were geared toward making the most use of Jewish skills and talents and eventually eliminating the Jews by complete absorption into Gentile society: "Thus the preferential treatment accorded to the Jewish nation through the present amendment is due to the following: Our aim is to make them more useful and of greater service to the state, in particular through better education, instruction of their young people, and through the use of the sciences, arts, and crafts." [11] "Toleration," in other words, signified the opposite of Moses Mendelssohn's concept of tolerance which called for acceptance of and regard for the tradition and character of the other religion.

Without the scientific and technological advances of the last four centuries a wholesale genocide in Central Europe would be unimaginable. However, the Russian pogroms and the genocide of the Armenians perpetrated by the Turks under the guise of World War I between 1915 and 1922 prove that not every mass-murder requires advanced technology. [12] For Nazi ideology and practice, however, the language of nineteenth-century science plays an important role. It shaped the Nazi mentality as well as the planning and execution of the Holocaust. The proliferation of scientific theories whose merits the general public was unable to assess encouraged scientific research which served ideological goals. Hacks pilfering the works of Gregor Mendel and Charles Darwin declared race a scientific fact, Jew-hatred a scientific endeavor and a political necessity. [13] By the turn of the century, a veritable deluge of racist and Social Darwinist literature had sparked ethnocentric fanaticism in all of Europe. However, nowhere did the discourses of superstition, religion, and politics fuse so completely with those of modern medicine, science, and technology as they did in Central Europe. The boundaries between the traditionally separate discourses were dissolved in an almost Wagnerian fashion and a "totalitarian" mass discourse was created, of which the speeches of Josef Goebbels and the orations in *The Triumph of the Will* are paradigmatic. Characteristic of this all-inclusive discourse accessible to readers and listeners of the most divergent backgrounds and interests is the mixing of styles, ranging from the sublime to the profane, and the use of the oratory as spectacle in a calculated barrage of the senses so as to exclude any contradiction. Nazi discourse offered affective and cognitive material for the largest possible number of people to identify with. This "totality" is one of the foremost characteristics of the Nazi propaganda films and mass demonstrations as well; nebulous symbols, sentimental music, and carefully choreographed marches are offered as substitutes for intellectual and political content.

Luther's use of the antonym "Jew" and "German," replacing the traditional "Jew" and "Christian," signals a shift from a religious perspective to national concerns. The new discursive pattern implies that acculturation or absorption, rather than mere conversion (as in the traditional religious paradigm), is required for the integration of the two groups defined as opposites, or rather, for the integration of the Jews into German society. This fact is clearly spelled out in Enlightenment treatises such as Christian von Dohm's *Über die bürgerliche Verbesserung der Juden.*[14] Nineteenth-century anti-Semitism radicalized the binary opposition "Jews and Germans." Its emphasis on race and the superiority of the "races" of Northern Europe ruled out assimilation, absorption, or coexistence which many Jews had come to accept as valid goals. "Semit" and "Germane," "Jew" and "Aryan," were the catch phrases of a segregationist, latently violent discourse. One need only to mention the slogan of the prominent historian, Heinrich von Treitschke, "Die Juden sind unser Unglück."[15]

Prior to the eighteenth century, Jewish authors did not write in German, despite the fact that they had lived for centuries in immediate proximity with the gentile population. In the wake of the emancipation debates, German was adopted by Jewish writers. Many of them attempted to vindicate their culture, for instance Heinrich Heine in *Der Rabbi von Bacharach* (1824–25).[16] However, neither individual efforts to counteract defamation, nor the activities of Jewish and philo-Semitic associations such as the Verein für Kultur und Wissenschaft der Juden, the Verein zur Abwehr des Antisemitismus, B'nai B'rith, and the CV (Central Association of German Citizens of Jewish Faith), succeeded in neutralizing the hostile discourses of the majority.

There was a host of anti-Jewish and anti-Semitic movements and parties for which the Nazi-movement ultimately provided an umbrella. It unified and organized the xenophobes, racial purists, and hooligans. They outnumbered by far their victims, a heterogeneous Jewish population, among them religious Jews, pacifists, and even World War I veterans. Unlike their opponents, the Jews, who had been excluded from military service for centuries, possessed no paramilitary organizations and they were not prepared to fight other than by legal means and public debate.

Throughout the centuries the Jewish minority in Germany had been an easy prey. The European Jewish history of toleration, persecution, and expulsion is evidence that the effects which the easy-to-activate hate rhetoric had at any given historical period depended on the economic conditions and the public atmosphere. Anti-Judaism, derived from numerous different sources, one of the most powerful being the basic texts of Christianity themselves, was firmly embedded in the German language and cultural iconography and could be easily activated at any time.[17] Every improvement of the status of Jews since the anti-Jewish riots of 1819 elicited hostile reactions, particularly among the educated middle class. In times of political and economic instability these conflicts were more severe, often leading to persecutions and the liquidation of entire communities.

The civil rights breakthrough in 1848–49 was preceded and followed by riots.[18] The year 1871, when the Imperial constitution confirmed the citizenship and limited equal rights for Jews, marks the beginning of major anti-Semitic movements. Associations such as Wilhelm Marr's anti-Semitic League (founded in 1879) were considered legitimate and decorous, and the university fraternities adopted anti-Jewish clauses. Anti-Semitism also became a powerful political tool, as is obvious from the success of Otto von Bismarck's anti-Semitic campaign of 1878, the anti-Semitic conventions of the Young-Czech and Hungarian independence movements of 1883, the Dreyfus Scandal in France, the manifesto of the Austrian Christian Social Association (1889) opposing professional freedom for Jews and demanding the restriction of Jewish immigration, as well as the election of the avowed anti-Semite Karl Lueger as mayor of Vienna in 1895. Anti-Semitic rhetoric incited the mob violence in Russia between 1881 and 1891, and, as the increasing number of ritual slaughter trials at roughly the same time suggests, went hand in hand with a renewal of popular superstition, as is obvious from ritual slaughter trials such as the one in Tisla Eszlar, Hungary, in 1882.

Anti-Semitism was supported by popular and academic propaganda, suffice it to mention Richard Wagner's *Das Judenthum in der Musik*, the standard work on race ideology by Wagner's son-in-law, Houston Stewart Chamberlain, *Die Grundlagen des 19. Jahrhunderts;* Sergey Nilus's *Protokolle der Weisen von Zion* which enjoyed great popularity in Germany (1905); and Theodor Fritsch's *Antisemiten-Katechismus.*[19] For Nazi ideologues and pamphleteers such as Julius Streicher, Alfred Rosenberg, Hans F. K. Günther, but also Adolf Hitler, it was only a matter of picking and choosing to concoct their oeuvres.[20] The language for the expression of radical anti-Semitic and racist convictions and doctrines was readily available and, as Klaus Theweleit observed, these writers were so imbued with it that *it* spoke through *them.*[21] Nazi propaganda combined themes from all discourses to turn them into effective tools. Themes such as ritual slaughter, the Jewish world conspiracy, modernity, and decadence as Jewish phenomena resounded in popular pamphlets and films such as *Der ewige Jude* (1939).

As early as 1918, General Erich von Ludendorff, an occultist and anti-Semite, together with Paul von Hindenburg, had convinced large segments of the population that World War I had been lost due to a stab in the back, that the betrayal of Jews had caused the military defeat. The National Socialist Party and *Mein Kampf* built on this theme.[22] Echoing popular sentiments, Hitler made the inequities of the Treaty of Versailles and the supposed treachery his major battle-cries for revenge. In 1919, anti-Semitic fervor sparked a pogrom in the *Scheunenviertel,* the Jewish quarter of Berlin, which was raided again in 1923, the year of the first National Socialist Party rally. In the interwar period, countless politically and racially motivated murders were committed by right-wing extremists and anti-Semites. Among the victims were the left-wing politicians Rosa Luxemburg, Kurt Eisner, and Karl Liebknecht (1919), the foreign minister Walther Rathenau (1922), the novelist and critic Hugo Bettauer, author of *City without Jews* (1926), and the author of the treatise *Jewish Self-Hatred,* Theodor Lessing (1932).[23]

Language conserves ideas. Beyond the official end of Nazi rule, it continues to transmit not only arguments for the persecution of Jews such as the ones Luther had projected into the New Testament, but also popular old wives' tales about the murder of Christ, ritual slaughter, and the poisoning of wells. In the nineteenth and twentieth centuries, the racist and Social Darwinist discourses expanded this heritage, adding to it the concept of the survival of the fittest, and the vision of Superman.

The anti-Semitic and occultist novels of Artur Dinter, for example, give an impression of the hodgepodge of ideas and sentiments crowding the mind of potential Nazi-followers:[24] Christian and heathen concepts, popular superstition, and occult spiritualism, watered-down ideas from classical literature, science, and technology, as well as maudlin perceptions of love, marriage, motherhood, war, and bravery, but most of all, the hatred against an unfathomable entity called Jew. These and similar works are still readily available to readers of all ages in Germany's community libraries, in private reprints, and private book collections.

Neither the discourses nor the ideas of the perpetrators of the Holocaust, but the scope and consequences of their crimes, and the suffering and change they precipitated, are unprecedented. Reading Nazi authors in search of new ideas to explain this worldwide catastrophe yields as few new insights as do the many purposefully vague postwar publications by Nazi veterans. Not the trivial Nazi discourses but the crimes call into question occidental culture, including Christianity, Humanism, the Enlightenment, and German Classicism. The cultural discourses of Germany and Austria and Nazi ideology share the same deep structure. Holocaust authors such as Nelly Sachs, Ilse Aichinger, and Edgar Hilsenrath have suggested that human survival depends on the ability of Western men and women to uncover, scrutinize, and transcend these fundamental conceptual and emotional patterns which structure the languages of the Christian world and have shaped the power relationships in the ghetto and death camp to the same degree as in religious, civilian, military, and corporate life. Paul Celan and Jean Améry, equally convinced that nothing short of a complete revision of linguistic and intellectual paradigms was necessary, did not believe that such a change was possible. The ultimate expression of their skepticism was their suicides in 1970 and 1978 respectively. To this day, many German scholars consider mentioning Goethe and Schiller in the context of the Holocaust anathema, yet the Holocaust is such a significance that it requires the reexamination and reevaluation of all German, and moreover, all Western discourses. Without examining the Holocaust era, a serious analysis of German culture and the Western world is not possible.

Integrating the documents and testimonies of the Holocaust produced by survivors and those directly affected into the dominant discourses is a necessary first step toward revising the perception of reality, historical and present. Even after the demise of the Nazi regime, Holocaust literature written by survivors and intended Nazi victims, particularly Jewish authors, has been deprioritized in one form or another. The German and Austrian media were fast to dismiss them because of their supposed inferior literary quality, declaring a vast body of German-Jewish texts of all genres and caliber substandard. German and Austrian non-Jews, many of them World War II veterans, who wrote about the Nazi era and introduced Holocaust themes, had a much easier time winning critical acclaim.

Despite the fact that the significance of German-Jewish Holocaust literature and the scholarship of survivors has been consistently marginalized, it is precisely these texts as well as the vast memoir literature which could effect major changes in how Germans and Austrians perceive their culture and history, as well as the basic assumptions of their everyday language, because these texts reveal the human dimensions of the Holocaust. Some of them introduce concepts and patterns transcending the binary mode still prevalent in the works of most contemporary gentile writers, even the well-intentioned ones.

The importance of expanding and modifying ingrained discursive patterns cannot be overestimated. Teaching history in the entrenched mode has never effected any fundamental change. According to Walter Benjamin, who distanced himself from the dominant culture, cognizant of its barbarism, historians (and I may add, most other scholars) have sided with the victors, adopted their language, and written their history.[25] Change can only be brought about at the level of the cultural blue-print. Edgar Hilsenrath suggests in his novel about the Armenian genocide and the Holocaust, *Das Märchen vom letzten Gedanken* (1989), that such fundamental change is theoretically possible. He implies that a group's or an individual's identity rests on the discourse they engage in. Their language determines who they are—thus it makes no difference if Hilsenrath's protagonist is an Armenian by ancestry, race, or ethnicity. It is enough that he speaks like an Armenian and tells the story of the Armenian people.

It is necessary to read and understand Holocaust literature and memoirs which traditionally have been perceived as documents of otherness, as an integral part of German or European culture which without the Jewish experience and the perspective of minorities is incomplete. Excluding the Jews or any other participants in the Central European discourse from the privileges engendered by German or Austrian identity prevented those who dominated the German and the Habsburg Empires from recognizing the character and tendencies of their civilization. A realistic assessment by necessity would have to include the awareness of the destructive aspects of the dominant culture, no matter how closely those may be intertwined with sacred traditions. A culture's negative elements, however, are only visible from a marginal point of view.

As is apparent from the current fragmentation and ethnic strife in the countries of the former German and Austro-Hungarian Empires, tolerance or the acceptance of an inclusive cultural and national identity is far from being realized. The enemy images and conflicts which arose after the restructuring of Europe since 1989 indicate quite the opposite, suggesting that no lesson has been learned from recent history. On the contrary, the spreading and rehabilitation of the language of traditionalism, nationalism, and tribalism in a world where nuclear disasters and human cloning are a reality, make for terrifying prospects, indeed.

NOTES

1. Theodor W. Adorno, "Kulturkritik und Gesellschaft," *Soziologische Schriften X,* ed. Tiedemann (Frankfurt am Main: Suhrkamp, 1972), 30.

2. Dagmar C. G. Lorenz, *Verfolgung bis zum Massenmord* (New York: Peter Lang, 1992), 8.

3. Hannah Arendt, *Eichmann in Jerusalem* (München:Piper, 1964).

4. Elias Canetti, *Masse und Macht* (Frankfurt: Fischer, 1980).

5. Lion Feuchtwanger, *Die Geschwister Oppenheim* (Amsterdam: Querido, 1933), 372; Wilhelm Reich, *Massenpsychologie des Faschismus* (Frankfurt: Fischer, 1974, written in 1933), 179. Reich believed that it would take generations to overcome the effects of the brutalization of German society. Karl Kraus, *Die Dritte Walpurgisnacht* (München: Kösel, 1965). Kraus wrote his indictment of the Nazis in 1933, but did not publish it to avoid endangering his German associates. Cf. also Lorenz, *Verfolgung bis zum Massenmord,* 44.

6. One such example is Otto Weininger, the author of *Geschlecht und Charakter: Eine prinzipielle Untersuchung* (Wien: Braumüller, 1906). Sander Gilman, *Jewish Self-Hatred: Anti-Semitism and the Hidden Language of the Jews* (Baltimore: The Johns Hopkins Press, 1986).

7. Martin Luther, "Von den Juden und ihren Lügen." *Luthers Sämmtliche Schriften XX: Reformationsschriften* (St. Louis: Lutherischer Condordia-Verlag, 1890), 1860–2029.

8. Krausnick quotes: "Staatsbürger kann nur sein, wer Volksgenosse ist. Volk-

sgenosse kann nur sein, wer deutschen Blutes ist, ohne Rücksicht auf Konfession. Kein Jude kann daher Volksgenosse sein. . . . Wer nicht Staatsbürger ist, soll nur als Gast in Deutschland leben können und muß unter Fremdengesetzgebung stehen." Helmut Krausnick, "Judenverfolgung," *Anatomie des SS-Staates II* (München: dtv, 1982), 11–13. The "Reich Citizenship Law" of 1935 restates these items almost verbatim. *Nazi Culture: Intellectual, Cultural, and Social in the Third Reich,* ed. George L. Mosse (New York: Grosset and Dunlap, 1968), 336.

9. Luther, "Von den Juden," 1860–2029.

10. Martin Luther, *Weimarer Ausgabe, Tischreden II* (Weimar: H. Böhlau, 1883), No. 2634a.

11. "The Moravian Toleration Edict," in *The Jews of Bohemia and Moravia: A Historical Reader,* ed. Wilma Abeles Iggers (Detroit: Wayne State University Press, 1992), 49.

12. Edgar Hilsenrath's novel *Das Märchen vom letzten Gedanken* (München: Piper, 1989) emphasizes the parallels between both genocides. See Lorenz, *Verfolgung bis zum Massenmord,* 270–75.

13. For example, Joseph Arthur de Gobineau (*Essai sur l'inégalité des races humaines* [Paris: Didot], 1853–55), Houston Stewart Chamberlain (*Die Grundlagen des 19. Jahrhunderts* [1889; reprint, München: Bruckmann, 1944]), and Alfred Rosenberg (*Der Mythus des zwanzigsten Jahrhunderts* [München: Hoheneichen, 1943]).

14. Christian von Dohm, *Über die bürgerliche Verbesserung der Juden* (Hildesheim: Olms, 1973). First published, 1781–83.

15. See Jacob Katz, *From Prejudice to Destruction* (Cambridge, Mass.: Harvard University Press, 1980), 1.

16. Heinrich Heine, *Der Rabbi von Bacharach: Werke I* (Köln: Kiepenheuer und Witsch, 1968), 577–612.

17. Vamberto Morais in *A Short History of Anti-Semitism* (New York: Norton, 1976) emphasizes the common elements of religious, racist, and Nazi anti-Jewish rhetoric and the similarities in their practice of persecution. See Sander L. Gilman, "Chicken Soup, or the Penalties for Sounding Too Jewish," *Insiders and Outsiders: Jewish and Gentile Culture in Germany and Austria,* ed. Dagmar C. G. Lorenz and Gabriele Weinberger (Detroit: Wayne State University Press, 1994), 15–29. Gilman argues: "The stereotype of the Jews' language is rooted in the earliest history of the rise of Christianity (or rather in the separation of the early Church from Judaism) and is mirrored in a static manner in a series of texts—The Gospels, or as the early Christians referred to them, the *New Testament*" (19).

18. Riots took place in Prague in 1844–48, and in 1859–61 following the abolition of the Prague ghetto in 1852; see also literature about the pogroms in

Germany. Else Lasker-Schüler wrote about the mid-nineteenth-century pogrom in Gesecke, Westphalia, in *Arthur Aronymous* (Berlin: Rowohlt, 1932).

19. Dagmar C. G. Lorenz, "Zeittafel," *Verfolgung biszum Massenmord* (New York: Lang, 1992), 362–73.

20. Hans F. K. Günther, *Rassenkunde des deutschen Volkes* (München: Lehmann, 1929); Alfred Rosenberg, *Des Mythus des zwanzigsten Jahrhunderts* (München: Hoheneichen, 1943) was first published 1930.

21. Klaus Theweleit, *Männerphantasien I: Frauen, Fluten, Körper, Geschichte; II Zur Psychoanalyse des weißen Terrors* (Hamburg: Rowohlt, 1980); also, Theweleit, *buch der könige: orpheus und eurydike.* (Basel: Stroemfeld, 1988), 251ff.

22. The National Socialist Party emerged in 1920 from the anti-Semitic National German Worker's Party, which Hitler had joined in 1919. Adolf Hitler, *Mein Kampf,* tr. Ralph Manheim (Boston: Houghton Mifflin, 1971).

23. Hugo Bettauer, *Die Stadt ohne Juden* (Frankfurt: Ullstein, 1988). Tr. Salomea N. Brainin, *The City without Jews* (New York: Block, 1926); Theodor Lessing, *Der jüdische Selbsthaß* (Berlin: Jüdischer Verlag, 1930).

24. Artur Dinter, *Die Sünden der Zeit I: Die Sünde wider das Blut* (Leipzig: Beust, 1928).

25. Walter Benjamin, "Über den Begriff der Geschichte," *Gesammelte Schriften I/II,* ed. Rolf Tiedemann and Hermann Schwepphäuser (Frankfurt: Suhrkamp, 1974), 696.

REFERENCES

Adorno, Theodor W. "Kulturkritik und Gesellschaft." *Soziologische Schriften X,* ed. Tiedemann. Frankfurt am Main: Suhrkamp, 1972.

Arendt, Hannah. *Eichmann in Jerusalem.* München: Piper, 1964.

Benjamin, Walter. "Über den Begriff der Geschichte." *Gesammelte Schriften I/II,* ed. Rolf Tiedemann and Hermann Schwepphäuser. Frankfurt: Suhrkamp, 1974.

Bettauer, Hugo. *Die Stadt ohne Juden* (Frankfurt: Ullstein, 1988).

Canetti, Elias. *Masse und Macht.* Frankfurt: Fischer, 1980.

Chamberlain, Houston Stewart. *Die Grundlagen des 19. Jahrhunderts.* 1889. Reprint, München: Bruckmann, 1944.

Dinter, Artur. *Die Sünden der Zeit I: Die Sünde wider das Blut.* Leipzig: Beust, 1928.

Dohm, Christian von. *Über die bürgerliche Verbesserung der Juden.* Hildesheim: Olms, 1973.

Feuchtwanger, Lion. *Die Geschwister Oppenheim.* Amsterdam: Querido, 1933.

Gilman, Sander L. "Chicken Soup, or the Penalties for Sounding Too Jewish."

In *Insiders and Outsiders: Jewish and Gentile Culture in Germany and Austria,* ed. Dagmar C. G. Lorenz and Gabriele Weinberger. Detroit: Wayne State University Press, 1994.

———. *Jewish Self-Hatred: Anti-Semitism and the Hidden Language of the Jews.* Baltimore: The Johns Hopkins Press, 1986.

Gobineau, Joseph Arthur de. *Essai sur l'inégalité des races humaines.* Paris: Didot, 1853–55.

Günther, Hans F. K. *Rassenkunde des deutschen Volkes.* München: Lehmann, 1929.

Heine, Heinrich. *Werke I.* Köln: Kiepenheuer und Witsch, 1968.

Hilsenrath, Edgar. *Das Märchen vom letzten Gedanken.* München: Piper, 1989.

Hitler, Adolf. *Mein Kampf.* Tr. Ralph Manheim. 1925–27. Reprint, Boston: Houghton Mifflin, 1971.

Iggers, Wilma Abeles, ed. *The Jews of Bohemia and Moravia: A Historical Reader.* Detroit: Wayne State University Press, 1992.

Katz, Jacob. *From Prejudice to Destruction.* Cambridge, Mass.: Harvard University Press, 1980.

Kraus, Karl. *Die Dritte Walpurgisnacht.* München: Kösel, 1965.

Krausnick, Helmut. "Judenverfolgung." *Anatomie des SS-Staates II.* München: dtv, 1982.

Lasker-Schüler, Else. *Arthur Aronymous.* Berlin: Rowohlt, 1932.

Lessing, Theodor. *Der jüdische Selbsthaß.* Berlin: Jüdisches Verlag, 1930.

Lorenz, Dagmar C. G. *Verfolgung bis zum Massenmord.* New York: Peter Lang, 1992.

Luther, Martin. *Luthers Sämmtliche Schriften XX: Reformationsschriften.* St. Louis: Lutherischer Condordia-Verlag, 1890.

———. *Weimarer Ausgabe, Tischreden II.* Weimar: H. Böhlau: 1883.

Morais, Vamberto. *A Short History of Anti-Semitism.* New York: Norton, 1976.

Mosse, George L., ed. *Nazi Culture: Intellectual, Cultural, and Social in the Third Reich.* New York: Grosset and Dunlap, 1968.

Reich, Wilhelm. *Massenpsychologie des Faschismus.* Frankfurt: Fischer, 1974.

Rosenberg, Alfred. *Der Mythus des zwanzigsten Jahrhunderts.* München: Hoheneichen, 1943.

Theweleit, Klaus. *buch der könige: orpheus und eurydike.* Basel: Stroemfeld, 1988.

———. *Männerphantasien.* Hamburg: Rowohlt, 1980.

Weininger, Otto. *Geschlecht und Charakter: Eine prinzipielle Untersuchung.* Wien: Braumüller, 1906.

CHAPTER 5

Secrecy and the Final Solution

RICHARD BREITMAN

On November 30, 1942, Heinrich Himmler, head of the SS, wrote a short letter to Heinrich Müller, head of the Gestapo, that is on the surface one of the stranger documents of the Holocaust.[1] It is nonetheless revealing testimony to a coverup that was part of the killing process almost from the beginning.

Himmler's letter was prompted by a report, passed along to and by Rabbi Stephen Wise, head of American Jewish Congress, that the Nazis were making soap from flesh of Jews who were gassed, as well as fertilizer from bones. It turned out that this report was untrue. But Wise spoke about it at a press conference on November 24 which he had called to publicize the fact that the Nazis had a plan to exterminate the Jewish people as a whole.[2] Wise's statements were reported in some American newspapers, and Himmler may have learned about them through Reich Security Main Office's press monitoring. But it is also possible that Himmler learned of Wise's report earlier, because the Nazi security agencies had broken one of the American diplomatic codes in Switzerland, where this report originated.[3] In any case, in his letter to Müller, Himmler rightly or wrongly referred to Wise's viewpoint of September 1942, a time when Wise had not yet started to speak publicly about the Final Solution. The copy of whatever document Himmler received about Wise does not survive.

A partial text of Himmler's letter read as follows:

In view of the large emigration movement of Jews, I do not wonder that such rumors come to circulate in the world.

We both know that there is present an increased mortality among the Jews put to work. You have to guarantee to me that the corpses of these deceased Jews are either burned or buried at each location, and that absolutely nothing else can happen with the corpses at any location.

Conduct an investigation immediately everywhere whether any kind of misuse [of corpses] has taken place of the sort as listed in point 1, probably strewn about in the world as a lie.

Upon the SS-oath I am to be notified of each misuse of this kind.[4]

This letter did confirm that many Jews were dying, though it denied that they were being killed. The real part of the letter, the business part of the letter, had Himmler reminding a key subordinate that no one was supposed to be misusing the bodies—and he wanted Müller to double-check to make sure. But why did he include the first two sentences about an emigration movement of Jews and an increased mortality? Part of the explanation of such euphemisms was that Himmler and Hitler were addicted to secrecy.

Secrecy was essential for the Final Solution, but it went beyond that; it was Hitler's and Himmler's general style of operation. Call it their conspiratorial style. Keep in mind that the Nazis got started as a conspiratorial movement with a secret plan to overthrow the government, and they never entirely lost this conspiratorial orientation. Hitler, Himmler, and others found advantages in concealing their intentions.

In a meeting with Franz Halder, the new chief of the army general staff in 1938, Hitler boasted that he never revealed his intentions ahead of time, even to key officials. A military man wanted to know what to plan for. Halder said that he and his colleagues didn't like to operate in this way. Hitler answered that it was different in politics.[5]

Hitler once issued something he called his fundamental order. It was not about the war or the structure of the Nazi regime or about propaganda or about ideology. It was about secrecy. The fundamental order, issued September 25, 1941, read:

No one: no office, no employee, and no worker may be informed of a matter which is to be kept secret, if it is not absolutely necessary for him to have cognizance of it for official reasons.

No office, no official, no employee and no worker may have any more information about a matter which is to be kept secret than is absolutely necessary for the execution of his assignment.

No office, no official, no employee, and no worker may be informed of that part of the matter to be kept secret, which pertains to him, any sooner than is absolutely necessary for the execution of his assignment.[6]

With regard to what we would today call criminal activities, secrecy was all important. And so in the Nazi "euthanasia" program, actually a program to murder the handicapped, one of the earliest murder programs, Hitler gave authorization but tried as much as possible to insulate himself, as a careful politician is wont to do, from criminal acts. He was even more careful with the Final Solution of the Jewish question, perhaps having learned from leaks about his written authorization of the euthanasia program. This is a likely explanation why we have no written document by Hitler ordering the mass murder of the Jewish people.[7]

True, Hitler gave speeches threatening or hinting at the destruction of the Jews. But there was a difference between giving a speech that could later be explained away as mere rhetoric and direct personal involvement in mass murder. Indicatively, as far as we know, Hitler never personally visited any concentration or extermination camp. Hitler tried to maintain the image of being selfless, hardworking, above the ordinary world, and we know from scholarly studies of German public opinion that he was generally successful in transmitting this image to the German people.[8] When cases of corruption or abuses of power emerged, people used to say: "If the Führer only knew!" It was possible to give blood-curdling speeches, but through a variety of devices to avoid being incriminated.

Himmler adopted some of the same methods. Since his youth Himmler had followed the imaginary world of espionage, secret plots, and conspiracies. He probably learned a lot from Hitler's style, but he may well have adopted some methods on his own. Some of Himmler's secrecy guidelines in letters and conversations antedate Hitler's fundamental order on secrecy.[9]

With sensitive or criminal instructions, Himmler wherever possible stuck to oral transmission. So much so that ever since historians have had considerable difficulty determining when the orders to kill the Jews was actually given. How much of the process was planned in advance? Let me discuss briefly one relevant document, which had perhaps the greatest impact on me during my research.

I was reading letters from Raymond Geist, the longtime American consul general in Berlin, to his friend and former superior, George S. Messersmith, who had become assistant secretary of State. I had long known that Geist was an astute and well informed observer of Nazi Germany, someone who had met personally with Himmler and Heydrich and appraised them well. In December 1938, Geist warned Messersmith that the Jews in Germany were being condemned to death and urged measures to rescue them. Geist followed in April 1939 with a more specific forecast: Nazi Germany would soon place all able-bodied Jews in work camps, confiscate the wealth of the entire Jewish population, isolate the Jews from the German population, and get rid of as many as possible by force. Geist got at least some of his information, he later testified, directly from Karl Hasselbacher, the *Sicherheitsdienst* (SD) official in charge of the department dealing with Jews and Free Masons.[10] This was not merely a forecast of the general fate of German Jews, but a diagnosis of the forthcoming stages of persecution leading to mass extermination.

Here was good evidence not yet of a continent-wide plan for the extermination of European Jewry, but of a clear phased plan for the murder of German Jews who remained in the country when war broke out—a plan that could and would be expanded to other territories when they were conquered by Germany. Since the plan preceded the war, it could not possibly have resulted from specific wartime pressures and circumstances—the stock line of "functionalist" historians who maintain that the Final Solution was improvised. Mass murder, though not yet on the scale of genocide, was quite premeditated if one believed Geist.

Note that we do not have an SS document spelling out what Geist learned from high SS sources. When criminal, murderous intentions are not recorded plainly on paper by the highest authorities, and they usually are not, we historians have to work harder to pin down the timing of plans and decisions. We know, for example, that Himmler chose to meet privately with Auschwitz commandant Rudolf Höss in the summer of 1941, most likely in mid-July, to tell him about the Final Solution and about the key role he was to play.[11] Höss talked about this meeting in postwar interrogations and wrote about it in memoirs he wrote before he was hanged; otherwise we would not know about it, for there is no documentary record of it.

We do have a contemporary document from Franz Stahlecker, head of *Einsatzgruppe* A, one of four police battalions each carrying out thousands (ultimately hundreds of thousands) of executions of Jews, Communists, and other groups in the conquered territories of the Soviet Union. Stahlecker revealed in early August 1941 that on the Jewish question the Security Police had received fundamental orders that were not to be spelled out in writing. They were connected, however, he said, with the impending complete purge of Jews from Europe.[12]

We have another contemporary document in which Viktor Brack, manager of the "euthanasia" program reminded Himmler that Himmler had told him quite a while earlier that the Final Solution had to proceed as quickly as possible to facilitate camouflage.[13] So there is little doubt that the Final Solution was supposed to be ultra-secret.

At the start of the Final Solution, not even high Nazi government officials knew what Himmler and the SS had organized. That was the way Himmler wanted it: rival Nazi officials might try to block the program or more likely grab off chunks of it for themselves. An additional reason for secrecy was to prevent leaks to the outside world. Though it was hardly possible to prevent the West from learning that Jews were dying, at least the magnitude and nature of the killing process might remain secret.

After a while there were leaks, even about the overall policy. On July 30, 1942, a prominent and well-connected German industrialist named Eduard Schulte met with a Swiss business associate in Zurich. Schulte revealed Hitler's headquarters had a plan to concentrate all Jews from Germany and German-occupied territories in the East and to exterminate them through the use of prussic acid. All together some three-and-a-half to four million Jews would be killed in this operation set for the fall. Certain parts of the anti-Nazi industrialist's information were inaccurate. The plan was not under consideration; it had already begun. The undertaking was so vast that it could not occur suddenly, as Schulte thought, but over many months. Nonetheless, the Breslau businessman, whose company had mines not far from Auschwitz, had uncovered one of the greatest secrets in Nazi Germany. After insisting that his identity be withheld (for he was returning to Germany), Schulte urged his business associate to get this information to Churchill and Roosevelt immediately.[14]

Within days Schulte's warning that the Nazis intended to resolve the

Jewish question "once and for all" reached Gerhart Riegner in Geneva. A German Jew who had left the country after Hitler took power, Riegner, as representative of the World Jewish Congress in neutral, well-located Switzerland, had regularly sent to Washington and London reports of Nazi atrocities and killings of Jews in Eastern Europe and of deportations of Jews from Western Europe to the east. This new information complemented what Riegner had learned from other sources about the brutality of the deportations. He went to the American consulate in Geneva and asked Vice Consul Howard Elting, Jr., to inform the American government and to pass the report on to Rabbi Stephen S. Wise, president of the American Jewish Congress. Riegner also went to the British consulate where he asked officials to transmit the same message to Sidney Silverman, a Labour Party member of the House of Commons who was also the British representative of the World Jewish Congress.

Although he was skeptical of the revelation, Elting dutifully wrote up a memo for his superiors at the American Legation in Bern. Elting assessed Riegner as a serious and balanced individual who would not have come forward if he did not believe the story. Legation officials did send Riegner's message to Washington, but with an accompanying dispatch questioning the accuracy of the information. An intelligence official, summarizing the despatch, called Riegner's message "a wild rumor inspired by Jewish fears." The dominant view in the State Department was to sit on this unconfirmed allegation, not to pass it on to Rabbi Wise. Word went back to Riegner that he would need corroborating information.

Riegner had had better luck with the British. The British Foreign Office was no less skeptical than the State Department, but the officials there had not dared to withhold a message to a member of Parliament. So Silverman received Riegner's telegram, and he passed on the contents to Rabbi Wise in New York.

Wise rushed to see Undersecretary of State Sumner Welles, President Roosevelt's trusted advisor in the State Department. Welles conceded that Riegner's information could be correct, but argued that it would be illogical for the Nazis to kill large numbers of Jews when they needed laborers. Welles urged Wise to refrain from any publicity until further investigation confirmed or refuted the story. Although keeping the story out of the press, Wise did quickly meet with representatives of the major Jewish organizations, such as the orthodox Agudas Israel World Organization, which had received its own reports from Switzerland of horrendous killings of Jews.[15] Wise also contacted some sympathetic government officials. Then he and other Jewish officials and spokesmen carried on their campaign to arouse public attention to Nazi brutalities and mass murder, but without publicly using Riegner's telegram about the Final Solution right away.[16]

Schulte's information was the first report to reach the West of an overall Nazi plan to eliminate the Jewish people entirely—moreover, a report itself emanating from the center of the Third Reich, Hitler's headquarters. It took several months before Undersecretary of State Sumner Welles was willing to concede to Rabbi Stephen Wise that the State Department had gathered enough information from other sources to confirm the original report.[17] Welles's confirmation led to Rabbi Wise's press conference of November 24, to Wise's announcement of the Nazi intention to exterminate all Jews, *and* to Wise's statement about the use of Jewish corpses by the Nazis, which leads us back to Himmler's letter to Müller.

Again, Himmler was hardly trying to fool Müller with his instructions. Müller had been Heydrich's direct subordinate; for the moment, in the period after Heydrich's assassination, he was directly subordinate to Himmler. He was also the superior of Adolf Eichmann. He might not have known the details of deportations of Jews and of the operations of the extermination camps as Eichmann did, but there could not have been more than a few people in Nazi Germany who knew more of what was going on with Jews than Heinrich Müller.

Part of Himmler's message was quite accurate. Bodies of Jews were supposed to be buried or burned. Actually, a large number of bodies had first been buried and then burned. This part of the Final Solution is less known than the gas chambers and crematoria, but directly related to them. The killing process and the results had to be concealed, one way or another. Beginning in June 1942, Heinrich Müller directed the concealment operation carried out by special units known by the numerical designation 1005. Since this was precisely the time when Müller became directly subordinate to Himmler, we may deduce that the inspiration, if not the specific orders, came from Himmler.

Müller called in a man named Paul Blobel, former head of an execution unit known as Sonderkommando 4a. Blobel and his unit had carried out the 33,000 plus executions at Babi Yar in September 1941. In June 1942, Müller instructed Blobel to erase the traces of the shootings of Jews in the East—while preserving absolute secrecy and putting nothing on paper. Blobel actually began, however, with the bodies at the extermination camps Chelmno and Auschwitz-Birkenau, which up until then had been buried. Burning (with or without crematoria) was gradually replacing burial. Then, he proceeded to the extermination camps at Sobibor, Belzec, and Treblinka, where there were a great many buried corpses.

Only then, in the fall of 1942, did Blobel go to the conquered Soviet territories. In the Ukraine, Dr. Max Thomas, commander of the Security Police and SD, resisted what he regarded as an unnecessary operation. Thomas apparently had no fear of leaks of information about the corpses, nor did he think that the Soviets would ever retake the territory. By the spring of 1943, however, such confidence was not so widespread, and Blobel got going in one conquered Soviet region after another. His work extended until the late summer of 1944.[18]

A number of different German units in different regions, all given the designation Sonderkommando 1005, organized the work. Invariably camp prisoners themselves dug for corpses, piled them up, and carried out the burning. Since they thereby became a security risk, they were invariably shot at the end of the operation. A few, however, escaped and lived to tell the tale.

It would be a mistake to read this camouflage operation—and Himmler's letter to Müller—simply as a reflection of Nazi fear of losing the war. Strikingly, Himmler did not think that the German people themselves would understand the necessity of the Final Solution. In his now infamous speech to the SS Gruppenführer at Posen on October 4, 1943, Himmler began by stating that there were certain things that SS did not talk about—a matter of instinctive tact. First, he mentioned the so-called Röhm Putsch, the killings of SA leaders and assorted Nazi enemies on June 30, 1934. Then he turned to what he called the "Jewish evacuation," which he would discuss with this elite group, but never in public. Himmler again used the term Jewish evacuation, then followed it with extermination, making it plain that evacuation was a code word, a cover. He pointed out that many Nazi Party officials and members had long spoken of exterminating Jews, but when it came time for action, each of the eighty million Germans would try to intercede for the one respectable

Jew he or she knew. Such people could never and would never really have carried extermination through, whereas the SS men knew what it was like to have hundreds or thousands of corpses in view. To carry through such work and to have remained respectable made the SS tough. Himmler concluded with reference to the whole operation: "This was an unwritten and never to be written page in our history." [19]

This speech, a direct and lengthy statement of Jewish policy to a select audience, is unique in that we have three forms of evidence of it: a transcript, Himmler's handwritten notes from which he spoke, and a tape recording. Taken together, they form one of the best sets of evidence authenticating the SS policy of extermination of the Jewish people.

So Himmler did not really distinguish between the outside world and the German public. Neither would appreciate what the SS had done and was doing. Martin Bormann apparently agreed. In a bulletin for Nazi Party officials in October 1942, Bormann warned "It is conceivable that not all Volksgenossen are capable of mustering up sufficient understanding of the necessity for such measures (against the Jews)." [20] Bormann did not spell out just what those measures were. It followed naturally that Himmler, Bormann, and others wanted to cloud the historical record of the Final Solution. There was no reason for them to believe that subsequent generations of Germans would appreciate the hard but necessary work performed by the SS in the course of the Final Solution. In this context, Himmler's letter to Heinrich Müller, written well before Himmler had serious fears of military defeat, makes some sense.

The reversal of Germany's military fortune gave Himmler additional and even more essential reasons to continue his camouflage and mendacity. On April 21, 1945, Himmler met with Swedish Count Folke Bernadotte and a Swedish Jew named Norbert Masur, a representative of World Jewish Congress. Himmler's story then was not all that different than what he had written to Müller in November 1942. Yes, he explained, the Jews had been a subversive element in Germany, but he had tried to solve the Jewish problem through emigration. When Germany conquered the East, however, it found masses of poor, diseased Jews, some of whom spread disease to the SS. Himmler did not say that such Jews were killed, but he did concede that he had had to build crematoria to burn bodies of those who had died of epidemics. "And now they want to make a hangman's noose for us," he complained.[21]

A number of postwar Holocaust revisionists subsequently adopted strikingly similar versions of history. As Deborah Lipstadt has described in her book *Denying the Holocaust,* the French fascist Maurice Bardeche, in a work entitled *Nuremberg or the Promised Land* (1948), maintained that the real Nazi policy toward Jews was emigration. The deaths of Jews in concentration camps were primarily the result of starvation and injury. Evidence to the contrary was falsified.

Another revisionist, Paul Rassinier, himself a prisoner at Buchenwald and Dora, wrote in *Crossing the Line* (1948) that there was no official Nazi policy of extermination by gas. Whatever gassings occurred were done by individual perpetrators acting on their own. By 1964, Rassinier concluded that the myth of mass extermination by gas chambers was manufactured by the Zionist establishment.[22]

The basic elements of the "Holocaust deniers creed," according to Lipstadt, were that emigration, not annihilation, was Nazi policy for the Jewish problem, that there was no gassing of Jews in camps, that the crematoria were built for the disposal of corpses of those who died from various means, including Anglo-American bombing and disease, that the majority of Jews who disappeared were in territory under Soviet control, and that the majority of Jews in German hands were subversives, partisans, spies, and saboteurs.[23]

What is more threatening than this implausible rewriting of history is the revisionists' attempts to discredit or cast doubt on the real history of the Holocaust. They use methods such as discovering minor errors or ambiguities in survivor testimony and above all in historical works, trying to explode the credibility of the overall picture given by survivors and historians. Since the real historical events are so shocking that they are indeed hard for many people to believe, it is not so difficult to cast doubts in the minds of the uneducated or the prejudiced.

Some mainstream historians, in search of new findings, have shown the same tendency to raise questions and doubts. In *Why Did the Heavens Not Darken,*[24] Arno J. Mayer suggested that large numbers of victims at Auschwitz died a natural death of typhus and raised doubts that very large numbers of Jews were gassed there. Mayer did not offer any documentary evidence to support his view of the history of the Holocaust, which he termed the Judeocide; he was content to raise questions about what others had found and to provide his own "plausible" reinterpretation.

One of the virtues of the United States Holocaust Memorial Museum is to lay out for the public as well as scholars the visual evidence—artifacts as well as documents—of what happened during the Holocaust. Some items in the Museum in particular, such as the milkcan in which Emmanuel Ringelblum's chronicle of events in Warsaw Ghetto was buried—represent a triumph for Jews and for humanity. Such crucial evidence helped and still helps to overcome the Nazi campaign to destroy the evidence of the Final Solution and to distort its history.

It is still important for historians of the Holocaust to be extremely careful to present accurate information. Mistakes or misinformation may be exploited by those who wish to create new, destructive myths.

In this connection, I have a few misgivings about recent intellectual movements such as deconstructionism which de-emphasize the significance of historical accuracy and substitute the author's imaginative reconstruction of texts and of narrative. It is certainly true that there is no completely objective history, and that an author's selection of information (even if it were accepted by all as factual) always represents a certain subjective orientation toward his or her material. An author's analytical approach or interpretation is even more subjective. So there is no single, universal truth in history. There are truths, and they may be relative in certain ways.

Nonetheless, there are certain questions in the field of history which are not relative. It is not purely a matter of opinion when Himmler gave his speech to the SS-Gruppenführer at Posen in 1943 or what he said to them. We have extraordinarily good evidence about that speech, and valid interpretations must conform to the constraints of this evidence. Anyone who ignores or misconstrues this speech writes bad or mendacious history.

Similarly, an author cannot make an arbitrary judgment when or whether Himmler met with Rudolf Höss to order the use of Auschwitz-Birkenau for the mass extermination of the Jewish people. Here the evidence is far from perfect, which means that different historians may make different judgments. Still, even if we cannot know the past perfectly, we know either that Himmler met with Höss and discussed this subject or he did not; that they met in the summer of 1941 or they did not. Who, what, when, and where questions are factual questions, which the available evidence may or may not allow us to answer with confidence. But we should never pretend that the answer is purely a matter of author's license, or that there is no such thing as an event independent of the author's view. That extreme subjectivity grants equal status as historians to those who would deny the Holocaust.

NOTES

1. Himmler to Müller, 30 Nov. 1942, United States National Archives, Record Group 242 (hereafter NA RG 242), Microfilm Series T-175/Roll 58/Frame 2521486.

2. *New York Herald Tribune,* 25 Nov. 1942, 1.

3. Interrogation of Walter Schellenberg, 13 Feb. 1946, NA RG 319, IRR Walter Schellenberg, Box 195, Folder 3. Confirmation of the leak in Memorandum of Information for the Joint U.S. Chiefs of Staff, 23 June 1945, OSS Operations in Switzerland 1942–1945, William J. Donovan Papers, Box 67B, U.S. Army Military History Institute, Carlisle, Pa.

4. See n. 1 above.

5. Gerald Fleming, *Hitler and the Final Solution* (Berkeley, 1984), 18.

6. Copy of Hitler's Order in NA RG 242, T-175/R 426/2955875.

7. Henry Friedlander, "Euthanasia and the Final Solution," in David Cesarani, ed., *The Final Solution: Origins and Implementation* (London, 1993), 2–4.

8. See Ian Kershaw, *The "Hitler Myth": Image and Reality in the Third Reich* (Oxford, 1987).

9. See Richard Breitman, *The Architect of Genocide: Himmler and the Final Solution* (Hanover, N.H., 1992), 73.

10. Geist to Messersmith, 5 Dec. 1938; Geist to Messersmith, 4 Apr. 1939, George S. Messersmith Papers, Folders 1087 and 1139, University of Delaware. Geist affidavit of 28 Aug. 1945, International Military Tribunal, Trials of the Major War Criminals before the International Military Tribunal (hereafter IMT) (Nuremberg, 1946–49), vol. 28, 242, 1759-PS.

11. Breitman, *Architect of Genocide,* 189.

12. Hermann Graml, "Zur Genesis der Endlösung," in *Der Judenpogrom 1938: Von der "Reichskristallnacht" zum Judenmord,* ed. Walter H. Pehle (Frankfurt am Main, 1988), 170. This document was discovered by Gerald Fleming in the Riga Archive of the former Soviet Union.

13. Brack to Himmler, 23 June 1942, NA RG 238, NO-205.

14. For this and the following section about Schulte and Riegner, see Walter Laqueur and Richard Breitman, *Breaking the Silence: The German Who Exposed the Final Solution* (Hanover, N.H., 1994).

15. The story of the Agudas Israel reporting from Switzerland is sympathetically portrayed by Joseph Friedenson and David Kranzler, *Heroine of Rescue* (Brooklyn, 1984).

16. Friedenson and Kranzler (n. 15 above) charge that Rabbi Wise also withheld the Riegner cable from Orthodox representatives in New York, which is belied by contemporary evidence: Rosenblum to Wertheim, 8 and 9 Sept. 1942, with summaries of two meetings of American Jewish leaders, American Jewish Committee Archives, RG-1, EXO-29, Waldman File, Poland, 1942. Some details of the joint meetings of Jewish organizations were also published several months later. See "Tragedy of European Jewry," *Bulletin of the World Jewish Congress,* Jan. 1943, 1.

17. Richard Breitman and Alan M. Kraut, *American Refugee Policy and European Jewry, 1933–1945* (Bloomington, 1987), 157. Irwin F. Gellman, *Secret Affairs: Franklin D. Roosevelt, Cordell Hull, and Sumner Welles* (Baltimore, 1995), 286–87.

18. Raul Hilberg, *The Destruction of the European Jews* (New York, 1984) III, 976–77; Leni Yahil, *The Holocaust: The Fate of European Jewry* (New York, 1990), 449–50.

19. IMT 29, 115, 1915-PS and Breitman, *Architect of Genocide,* 242–43.

20. Partei-Kanzlei, *Vertrauliche Informationen,* 9 Oct. 1942, NA RG 242, T-81/R 3/64401.

21. Norbert Masur's report of (21 Apr.) conversation with Himmler, 23 Apr. 1945, reprinted in Steven Koblik, *The Stones Cry Out: Sweden's Response to the Persecution of the Jews, 1933–1945* (New York, 1988), 289–92. Masur's report also summarized by Herschel Johnson to Secretary of State, 25 Apr. 1945, War Refugee Board Records, Box 70, German Proposals through Sweden, Franklin D. Roosevelt Library.

22. Deborah Lipstadt, *Denying the Holocaust: The Growing Assault on Truth and Memory* (New York, 1993), 49–56.

23. Lipstadt, *Denying the Holocaust,* 99–100.

24. Arno J. Mayer, *Why Did the Heavens Not Darken: The "Final Solution" in History* (New York, 1988).

A hungry man lying in the street in the Warsaw ghetto.

Jewish child dying on the sidewalk in the Warsaw ghetto.

Hunger and illness in the Warsaw ghetto.

Hunger and illness in the Warsaw ghetto.

Child begging for food in the Warsaw ghetto.

PART II

CONSIDERING

ISSUES OF

TEACHING AND

CURRICULUM

INTRODUCTION

ROBERT P. WELKER

Many cultural myths stand in the way of conjoining the development of intellect with the development of character. The popular depictions of the evil genius, the simple-minded saint, and the morally loathsome artist all indicate that it is possible to be smart but evil and good but intellectually deficient. While most teachers know students whose moral development lags far behind their intellect, we must take care not to separate even further the cognitive and affective domains of education, making it appear that thinking has nothing to do with acting and that skills might be evaluated or developed apart from their appropriate use. It is all too possible to see the world of education as operating in a solar system with two suns. Each may illumine and warm either the heart or the mind, but neither can nourish both at the same time.

The essays included in this section speak forcefully against this disjunction. Whereas the pieces in the first section struggled with the question of universality within the bounds of historical context, the pieces in this section struggle with the demands of moral responsibility as they match with demands for intellectual rigor. They are informed by a definition of intelligence and thinking which has implications for character.[1] All good thinking demands cognitive abilities and particular strategies and skills. Yet, as one of the authors in this section notes, considering the Holocaust is not like thinking about anything else. Teachers engaged in its instruction want to give students intellectual tools, but they would be disappointed if the moral sensibilities of their students weren't also enlarged. Conceived in this way, good thinking has dispositional elements. It requires both sensitivity and inclination—the tendency to be open minded as well as the disposition to evaluate reasons and be intellectually careful. Perhaps most importantly for Holocaust instruction, it requires the need to be reflective and aware, an inclination to monitor the effect of knowledge not only on one's own beliefs but also on the well-being of others.

The chapters in this section can be divided into two groups. In the first, the authors are concerned with curricular development as it relies primarily on the intellectual tools of various disciplinary approaches. These essays generally answer the question: "How do different ways of thinking help students study the Holocaust?" The second group of essays considers special issues that arise as instructors and students encounter the multiple responses the Holocaust evokes. These chapters generally respond to the question: "What instructional approaches will allow students to understand the complexities of Holocaust responsibility?" In all the contributions, the authors have found their own moral identities engaged. Clearly, this is part of the omnipresent urge to place oneself in the time and to wonder what one might have done. Even more fundamentally, these approaches suggest that insofar as thinking and intelligence embody dispositional elements, then teachers also will need to be involved in the learning process. In the study of the Holocaust, knowledge cannot be separated from being; what one knows and learns has implications for who one is as a person.

The chapters by Robert P. Welker and Franklin Bialystok introduce the first group of discussions by reflecting upon the goals of curriculum construction and moral education as they might inform those drafting Holocaust courses. Welker's argument is simple in theory, but perhaps hard to accomplish in practice; it is difficult to design courses which limit their scope and which concentrate objectives and strategies within focused instructional parameters. He argues that this is difficult not simply because so much is known about this complex time, but also because instructors find every aspect so deeply compelling. Weaving intellectual and moral goals establishes the sense of intelligence indicated above, but Welker argues that is not likely to be as powerfully realized if instructors try to achieve too much in a limited time period. His review of several adopted state curriculums illustrates this principle.

Bialystok is even more reserved about using Holocaust education for moral purposes than Welker. While he shares the conviction that Holocaust education has unavoidable moral implications, he argues that too often teachers ill serve their students if they try to make the universal moral point at the expense of a more thorough examination of the Holocaust's situated place in human history. In this respect, Bialystok supports moral aims as they align with the rigors of scholarship. This line of thinking mirrors some of the suggestions of the "Guidelines for Teaching about the Holocaust" as adopted by United States Holocaust Memorial Museum: to avoid the easy generalization, to make intelligent and informed distinctions about sources of information, and to refrain from seizing upon simple answers to a complex history.[2]

The next several chapters give an account of that richness and the ways that creative educators have solved curriculum construction problems. Jacqueline Berke and Ann L. Saltzman describe interdisciplinary approaches using the disciplines of English and psychology. Charles R. Clarke and Sharon L. Dobkin further explore psychological considerations as they uncover motivational constructs. These essays indicate that disciplinary approaches have particular assets and deficiencies. All place their own demands on the intellectual inclinations of students and require that they develop different capacities for judging and weighing evidence and assessing reasons. Berke and Saltzman provide several models for interdisciplinary instruction that not only provide ways to sidestep administrative barriers but also offer separate opportunities to engage the thought of students. Clarke and Dobkin, in focusing on social and psychological research and theory, show how the discipline of the social sciences can add depth and insight to historical and literary narrative.

The pieces by Marsha Carow Markman and Sarah Leuchter Wilkins center on the instructional use of personal narrative. Markman forcefully argues that the diaries and autobiographies of Holocaust participants offer a powerful and authentic means to command student attention and thought. Similarly, Wilkins describes how she has used audio tape narratives of survivors to move students toward human encounter. These authors suggest the documentary power of personal testimony and indicate how such evidence might affect a student's dispositional intelligence both in the opportunity to compare and connect such testimony with other sources and in the opportunity to probe for causes and justifications and to seek clarity and completeness. Teachers will also find the Markman and Wilkins essays valuable for their suggestions about sources and how to incorporate them within the texture of a larger study.

Similarly, the contributions of Rafael Medoff and Andrew Charlesworth offer unique disciplinary perspectives which will challenge the thinking of students to enlarge their imagination as they conceive what it might have been like to live in the Holocaust era. Both pieces rely on primary textual sources, though in very different ways. Medoff describes a research project in which he directs students to examine critically local newspaper reports written during the employment of the Final Solution. In this project, students learn how to use tools of interpretation, comparison and synthesis, and also begin to imagine and judge the appropriateness of the wider public response to accounts of genocide. Andrew Charlesworth, a geographer, describes what it is like to teach a course in which students visit the death camps themselves. This provocative discussion illustrates the use of landscape as text and the challenge such landscapes make upon students who must now regard their current uses and the ways people interact with them. As in Medoff's work, the call to thoughtfulness is immediate. It provokes students not only to place themselves in the time and place, but also to consider what their study means for choices they are currently making.

The second group of pieces in this section turn from investigating different disciplinary approaches to examining the evocative and challenging issues of Holocaust responsibility. Here, students are challenged to think dispositionally as they must search for good reasons and discover underlying grounds, sources, and implications. These papers indicate that a central problem of Holocaust teaching and learning is the rush to judgment and the need to escape the horror of the event by distancing oneself from the complex human dimensions of those who participated in it. Most often this is done by some form of categorization in which perpetrators, victims, rescuers, and bystanders are conceived in simple terms as either wholly evil, good, or helpless. Understanding the different textures of human response to the Holocaust either on the part of those who survived it or those who later entered into its study is one antidote to unqualified misconceptions.

For these reasons, teachers will find the Carlos C. Huerta and Dafna Shiffman-Huerta essay a thought-provoking introduction to the last group in this section. The Huertas' controversial thesis is that the Holocaust denial literature should be a part of legitimate academic study. To be sure, the authors themselves do not argue for the veracity of the denial literature, but they do argue that students need to be exposed to it and need to learn how to think their way through its false claims.

Here, students must be inclined to seek and evaluate reasons and have a hunger for thoroughness, accuracy, and consistency. They must learn to be open minded without relinquishing an alertness to deception and misrepresentation.

Donald G. Schilling, Michael F. Bassman, and Elisabeth I. Kalau approach denial from the far more common if not more damaging domain of the student's own consciousness. Schilling's selection confronts the "dead end" of demonizing the perpetrators. Schilling notes the need to make careful distinctions in this area since the effort to understand evil is at times misconceived as an effort to excuse or justify it. As a history teacher, he is particularly sensitive to matters of veracity, context, and completeness, and he offers a brief critique of several popular accounts of the perpetrators based on those criteria. Demonizing the perpetrators, he argues, "cuts us off from a deeper, more complete understanding of human behavior, of our capacity for evil, and, therefore, of our ability to guard against future atrocities."

Similarly, Bassman and Kalau are concerned with the human capacity for evil, especially as it exposes the student's and the instructor's own biases, misjudgments, and stereotypical thinking. Readers might find it helpful to compare the two very different courses these teachers describe, especially since they originate from such separate disciplinary and instructional points of view. Bassman's essay, which includes a course syllabus, describes how he uses particular literature, video tapes, and student activities to make the event relevant for predominantly white middle-class students. Bassman thus confronts the issue of "we" versus "they," not only as it involves the perceptions of students vastly disconnected by time and circumstance from the event, but also as it concerns the legitimacy of teachers who find themselves in the position of representing it. As a child of a Nazi colonel, Elisabeth I. Kalau must confront the issue of legitimacy and representation from a far different perspective. She offers an inspiring description of how she uses her own battle with the past to inform the struggle that her students and, indeed, all of us must have as we confront intimate and personal capacities for prejudice and cruelty. The fact that her students are preparing to be rehabilitation professionals makes the effort all the more significant. This is dispositional thinking which is metacognitive or self-reflective at the core: our ability to be self-monitoring and to challenge ourselves to consider carefully the images we carry of others.

The final two pieces of this section provide an appropriate response to this struggle by offering us the gift of language. Both Henry Gonshak's essay and the chapter by Milton Teichman and Sharon Leder reflect upon literary responses to the Holocaust on the part of those who have been most wounded by the event. As both essays suggest, a constant struggle for teachers of the Holocaust is to provide an opportunity for meaningful expression, as students confront what Gonshak describes as its "most despairing lessons." His critical review of Cynthia Ozick's "Rosa" provides a model of how a teacher might unpack a piece of literature for this purpose, and indicates how a vivid literary work might provide students both a dramatic representation and a vocabulary of memorable and transforming response.

In a similar fashion, Teichman and Leder describe various pieces of Holocaust literature, classifying them as either a mode of lamentation or truth-telling. In the former category, literature focuses on the way in which "sorrow merges with anger and bitterness toward a seeming uncaring God." In the latter category, literature supports "insights and reflections about the Holocaust as an upheaval in human history." Teichman's and Leder's insightful construction allows students to discriminate between authentic and inauthentic response, between literature meant to shock and literature meant to find words for the unspeakable. Such literature serves as models for the students' own need to express how their own image of humanity or inhumanity has been altered by what they have learned. It provides important lessons about the connection of intellectual clarity with the search for essence and empathetic understanding.

Finally, it might be said of all the pieces in this section that this enlargement of perception and imagination remains the central goal. Through such teaching, student character as well as cognitive ability is developed, though certainly these teachers would want to avoid all instruction which is morally self-serving. As a transforming event in human history, the Holocaust itself speaks to the malicious outcome of separating learning and skill from the service of tolerance, compassion, and good will. In connecting thinking to behavior and in developing ways that intelligence can be considered dispositionally, Holocaust education provides a telling response to an education that dares to be silent about larger social responsibilities.

NOTES

1. I owe this analysis of dispositional thinking to the work of Shari Tishman, David Perkins, and other fellows involved with Project Zero at Harvard University. For a fuller analysis of the concept of dispositional thinking see Shari Tishman, "The Concept of Intellectual Character and Its Connection to Moral Character" (Paper delivered at the Annual Meeting of the American Education Research Association, San Francisco, 1995), and D. N. Perkins, Eileen Jay, and Shari Tishman, "Beyond Abilities: A Dispositional Theory of Thinking," *Merill-Palmer Quarterly* 39, no. 1 (1993): 1–21.

2. William S. Parsons and Samuel Totten, "Guidelines for Teaching about the Holocaust" (Washington, D.C.: United States Holocaust Memorial Museum, 1994), 2–8.

CHAPTER 6

Searching for the Educational Imperative

in Holocaust Curricula

ROBERT P. WELKER

Eleven states now recommend the teaching of the Holocaust and have developed a curriculum or teacher's guide for that purpose. Four more states recommend Holocaust education and/or are presently exploring avenues of resource development and teacher training.[1] This trend toward state mandates of Holocaust or genocide studies comes at a time of great ferment in American education. Curriculum revision in nearly every subject area has followed numerous studies which document inadequacies in student achievement and school delivery systems. At the same time, student misconduct as evidenced by indicators of rising school violence, substance abuse, and teenage pregnancy has prompted a revival of moral education. Holocaust education lies within the conflicting web of these different concerns. Its inclusion in the present educational reform movement will depend upon the viability of connecting its moral and intellectual aims.

This chapter explores that possibility in three ways. The first section offers an overview of the social context in which Holocaust education must vie for consideration. This section will outline directions in curricular and instructional reform as well as some current research in moral education. Such investigations suggest criteria by which present Holocaust curricula may be judged. The second section uses those criteria to examine three state-adopted curricula. That review yields areas for improvement in the specific curriculum under review, but more importantly suggests general principles that any Holocaust curriculum might consider. The last section consolidates those points and suggests how stories might provide a particularly powerful instructional vehicle for achieving Holocaust education's academic and moral purposes.

THE CONTESTED SPACE OF EDUCATIONAL REFORM

One might begin to uncover principles for developing Holocaust curriculum by first noting how many curricular disputes arise quite simply out of the truism that "you can't teach it all." The need to prioritize and order content obliges any curriculum to provide a clear rationale for what is taught and what is excluded. Much of the modern impetus for curriculum reform arises out of the dual concern that many students leave school without basic factual knowledge of their past and current world and without the intellectual tools to participate in its reconstruction and renewal. Despite the perennial struggles between the back-to-basics and thinking skill movements, recent research indicates that the two are connected.[2] John Goodlad's study of schools mirrors many others in noting that while students are required to study massive amounts of material (almost always delivered by direct instruction and teacher talk), they are provided very little opportunity to extend such information, to apply it, analyze it, and make it their own.[3] The inability of students to reconstruct basic timelines that might allow them to place the Civil War within fifty years of its occurrence or to connect the rise of Nazism with World War II comes not from the fact that they were never taught such information. It more likely arises out of the fact that such information never became part of their cohered vision of a world which concerns them and requires their learned and extended participation. Holocaust curricula can answer a dual challenge when they allow for extended practice and analysis, and when they provide opportunities for discovering information and organizing it. The gap between content and thinking skills is bridged when students encounter a subject matter by understanding how they can create and represent knowledge within it.

Instructional practice cannot be divorced from curriculum in this respect. One of the strongest movements in curriculum currently is for teacher collaboration and interdisciplinary instruction,[4] a movement which arises out of the "more is less" principle and the historical lesson that curricula are neither teacher proof nor by themselves likely to have lasting effect on student achievement.[5] Unless instructional practice is itself implicated in curriculum design, then students are likely to encounter the subject matter in the same fragmented and nonengaging ways that hobbled student learning in the first instance. Holocaust curricula can draw upon a rich treasury of music, art, literature, and history. The claim to universality, in this instance, has disciplinary content, for it impacts upon the different ways we come to understand and allows for teachers from different disciplines to take part in the same instruction. It appeals to students because, like the rest of us, they retain better what they are allowed to practice, and because they can encounter material in the specialized ways they best learn.

Unfortunately, interdisciplinary learning frequently works better in design than practice. Both teachers and students have long been trained to work alone. The bureaucratic structure of the school itself creates barriers to integration. Any curriculum that employs interdisciplinary instruction, therefore, must give students and teachers explicit directions about how to make connections and must point out those materials or activities that provide solid instructional bridges. In this regard, little research has been done on the actual employment of Holocaust curricula or on their effect on student learning. One study of three different curriculums used in different schools indicated that teaching methods changed very little.[6] In every case, students clearly found the subject matter engrossing and left their study more factually informed, less likely to blame the Shoah on a single factor, though more likely to emphasize racism and prejudice as a cause.[7] Teacher training was not emphasized or carried out in any school; and, while teachers reported more student interaction and a heavy reliance on media, it was not clear that students were provided the type of instruction that might allow them to engage the material in transformative ways. Current learning theory emphasizes the creation of intellectual scaffolds to support long term memory and lasting student achievement.[8] There was little evidence provided in the study to suggest that students were given opportunities to participate in interdisciplinary work, to develop analytical skills, or to encounter documents, fiction, music, or art in ways that might engage multiple ways of knowing and provide the web upon which cohered understanding depends.

Beyond providing these intellectual opportunities, any Holocaust curriculum must also be forthright about its moral aims. Admittedly, this is a significant risk. One does not have to turn too many pages of the daily paper to learn of a community group protesting some element of curriculum on the basis of its moral implications. In Pennsylvania, the entire state directive toward outcome-based education was scrapped when the public discovered that moral outcomes were identified as well as cognitive ones.[9] Within the field of Holocaust education, the National Endowment for the Humanities denied funding for two years to "Facing History and Ourselves" on the basis of disagreements over its explicit moral intent.[10] Ironies abound. Each year the Gallup Poll on education reveals that the public places its highest priority on matters directly connected with moral education—youth violence, discipline, student attendance, and drug abuse.[11] Clearly, moral choices in education are unavoidable as we select curricular priorities, determine instructional approach, demand of teachers high standards of conduct, or provide for local and national youth service initiatives. Just as clearly, decades of moral education research reveal how difficult it is to make a lasting moral imprint on the character of a youth.[12] All moral education efforts, whether directed at youth violence, teenage pregnancies, or substance abuse, struggle against the powerful cultural messages of instant gratification, self promotion, and materialism. As John Dewey noted long ago, even instructional exhortations toward more democratic social relations have little impact when the very life and organization of the schools teach a contradictory version of social reality.[13]

The Holocaust, of course, provides stark and chilling evidence of the fragility of character and the susceptibility of ordinary people to acts of unspeakable cruelty. This conveys a moral message itself as students come face to face with violence made legitimate and race hatred made normal. The professional and ethical obligations of teachers to provide developmentally appropriate material for their students is sharpened in Holocaust curricula by the need, at the very least, to avoid characterizations that might demonize the perpetrators, sanctify the victims, or deify the rescuers. This again speaks to the "more is less principle" because only by attending in an extended fashion to the complexities of the history can one avoid one-dimensional description and easy stereotype. The moral messages need not be Herculean to be both significant and warranted. Following the "Guidelines for Teaching about the Holocaust," published by the United States Holocaust Memorial Museum, these are the commandments of careful scholarship: to avoid the easy generalization; to make careful distinctions about sources of information; to avoid comparisons of pain; and to avoid simple answers to a complex history.[14]

Beyond these academic virtues, all Holocaust curricula must provide as coherent an account of their affective objectives as they do of their cognitive aims. Given the difficulties of providing effective moral education, one principle should be to keep the instructional aims simple and consistent. The tendency may be to cast the net too broadly and too confidently. Moral claims regarding duty, courage, rectitude, sympathy, loyalty, citizenship, and obedience abound. One unavoidable aim focuses on the dangers of prejudice and racism, but even here curricula must describe exactly what such a goal means in the positive sense of encouraging the capacity for sympathy and human filiality. Such positive direction and precision may be guided by the research which suggests that one grows in moral sensibility by participating in acts of kindness rather than by denigrating the callousness of others.[15] Children who are more likely to aid, comfort, and help others are sociable, competent, and assertive.[16] Such children are like adults in that sympathy is most likely to be extended to those most like themselves,[17] a finding which suggests that teachers need to avoid the easy, simple characterization and offer opportunities for students to discover connections within the complexities of lived lives. Just as clearly fragile capacities for sympathy must be protected against numbing collisions with the vast dimensions of the Holocaust horror. Compassion fatigue may be one result of subjection to graphic accounts of mass destruction, and the danger also looms of suggesting helplessness or fatalism. These suggestions can themselves undermine the social confidence felt and exhibited by those most likely to interfere when faced with the distress of others.[18]

Clarity of moral intent by itself does not yield efficacy. In the research noted above, students showed no increase in their levels of moral reasoning skills after extended instruction about the Holocaust.[19] Teachers gave anecdotal accounts of student interest, and students themselves reported the dramatic effect of the curriculum, accounts which have been repeated in other contexts.[20] But moral competence is composed of so many variables experienced over the course of a person's life, that connecting a sustained ethical sensibility to a particular instruction would be difficult to claim or assess. The profile of Holocaust rescuers are themselves instructive. Their moral identities depended upon the supportive foundation of cultivated, close friendships and a legacy of parental modeling that revealed a long history of tolerant acts that served to extend justice and universal rights to others.[21] One can not help but be impressed by how such profiles clash with the fragmented and fragile social lives of so many students. Many are victims themselves of violence and neglect. If independence, dependability, trust, and good will are the attributes of the altruistic personality, many students now find refuge in social isolation, mistrust of adult authority, and a terminal sense of the future.[22] Such are the stark reminders that safety itself remains an immensely strong and determinate factor in moral behavior.

Such a reminder is the final lesson the research provides with regard to the proper moral direction of Holocaust curricula. As James Q. Wilson has noted, we should foster sympathy as a moral virtue not merely to increase helping behaviors, but to increase the possibility that people are less likely to harm others.[23] Again, the history of the Holocaust is itself instructive, for in many cases the perpetrators were, in the words of Christopher R. Browning, "ordinary men."[24] Sociability, the human need to seek the company and approval of others, lies at the basis of our capacity for sympathetic behavior, but it can also be seen as the agent of cruelty when people fall into the safe confines of the crowd, obey the immediate authority, and seek their primary worth and validation outside themselves.[25] Much of the research on the likelihood of people coming to a stranger's aid indicates that personal intervention increases as people determine the situation depends on them rather than the crowd.[26] Rescuers frequently felt a personal positive connection to the people they helped.[27] In contrast, perpetrators denigrated the victim and attached to people much like themselves qualities that made victims appear to deserve their own fate.[28]

This argues for the need when teaching the Holocaust to present a richly textured account. I will argue in more depth below that we must provide personal stories behind the overwhelming statistics, stories which in their very narrative sweep can help students make personal connections and discover life courses that indicate how human decisions impact upon the present and the future. Such stories provide moral spaces that allow for a recognition of personal circumstance and the opportunity for student description, reflection, and explanation. Again, it must be said that the collision with horror itself yields neither understanding nor kindness nor even the capacity for outrage.

State-Adopted Curricula and the Holocaust

At its best, Holocaust education involves a training of the imagination and a training in the vocabulary of sensibility. This can be recommended as an increasingly important goal when information surplus, sensory overload, and the impenetrability of bureaucratic function threaten to deaden our capacity to distinguish and describe the human voices that claim us. Still, moral aims cannot be purchased at the price of intellectual rigor and a review of state curricula of New York, Pennsylvania, and Ohio reveal the difficulty of balancing both demands.

The Human Rights Series: Teaching about the Holocaust and Genocide, 3 volumes (New York, 1985 and 1986)

In the words of one scholar, this curriculum presents "the most extensive state-developed teacher/student guide on genocide."[29] The assessment seems apt given the sheer size of the document. Three volumes totaling 553 pages cover a subject matter that includes the Holocaust as well as the Armenian and Cambodian genocide and the Ukrainian famine. This breadth indicates the intent of the designers to locate the Holocaust within the larger scope of genocide studies and the study of human prejudice and cruelty generally as they are aided by institutions of the modern state. The foreword, along with a brief description on "how to use this guide," serves as the only rationale for the document. It notes the deeper questions which students should begin to answer as they study the Holocaust:

> What does the Holocaust tell us about our conceptions of what constitutes civilized or rational human beings?
> What does the Holocaust suggest about the notion of progress as it applies to medicine, law, and technology?
> What can we do to prevent violations of human rights in the future?[30]

The first two volumes of the curriculum concern us the most and comprise our review since they are most directly connected with the Holocaust. Volume three focuses primarily on the Ukrainian famine and the Cambodian genocide and appears to have been added later. The volumes are divided into four units which include a statement of purpose, a list of objectives, a group of learning activities, and student materials. The authors caution teachers to use their own professional judgment in choosing among each unit's many readings and activities, though they do present a model two-week unit outline with selected objectives and goals. This strategy indicates the intent of the guide to be flexible enough to ensure coordination with local programs. It also suggests, as do the other two state curricula, that two weeks is a minimal amount of time for the study. The model itself offers no rationale that might direct teachers to consider conceptions of student learning, vehicles of instruction, or even prerequisite knowledge and skills. As indicated previously, rationales give reasons for the order and content of instruction since "you can't teach it all" and good practice matches subject matter to appropriate instructional strategies. Teachers would profit by the addition of best practice recommendations and by a model program that provides direction in sequential skill development. Suggestions of instructional strategies might increase the likelihood of personal engagement and reflection as it meets with local time commitments and the maturity of students.

The New York curriculum shines in its extensive collection of historical readings and primary source documents. It also provides supporting material in art, literature, music, and film. While this by itself is a marvelous contribution, the issue of textual coherence plagues any topic as complex and sensitive as the Holocaust. The matter extends beyond subject content to include the cultivation of specific academic skills and moral dispositions. The "more is less" principle would move curriculum designers to keep objectives simple and consistent while at the same time allowing students to engage different disciplines and ways of knowing. The challenge is both to encounter information and to extend it through analysis and creative activities. In these respects, the impressive wealth of material referenced in the New York curriculum can have a downside if vehicles for instruction do not have a coherent, developmental approach. The architecture of the design must provide the recurring themes and intellectual structures upon which a deeper, more enduring knowledge depends.

Such concerns arise immediately in volume one of the New York curriculum which introduces the field of genocide studies. In the first of the two units which comprise the volume, students study the importance of Holocaust education and the roots of intolerance and persecution. Readings highlight the human capacity to forget, deny reality, hide behind indifference, or actually participate in acts of prejudice and discrimination. The strength of this section, like the curriculum as a whole, is that students are provided a wide variety of readings, short stories, accounts, and poems. All point to circumstances which resemble the everyday life choices of students themselves. Yet the approach seems fragmented. No coherent narrative thread connects the material. Similarly, while group activities and role plays lead students to consider personal susceptibility, such considerations easily can seem hypothetical if they are not reinforced by actual historical connection. This perception seems to be reinforced as students move quickly to an analysis of the Armenian persecutions. While this serves as an important case study of genocide, relationships to the first unit are not adequately drawn. Similarly, later instruction about actual Holocaust participants makes only scant reference to these earlier discussions.

Volume two carries the bulk of the instruction on the Holocaust. It is divided into two units that have a sequential structure which resembles that given in the curricula of Ohio and Pennsylvania. Beginning with sections on anti-Semitism and Nazi thought, the curriculum then traces the Nazi rise to power through the "final solution" and its effects. Sections on perpetrators and victims and then "responses by individuals, institutions, and nations" lead to the final unit that discusses "implications for our future." This is a reasonable and coherent structure, and again the supporting material is impressive and engaging. Included are biographical selections on perpetrators and fictional accounts of life in the Weimar Republic and under Nazi rule. Selections from larger historical works document the Nazi organizational structures and life in the ghettos and concentration camps. For each reading, teachers are provided with possible activities which include research, discussion, and various activities such as the development of timelines. To their credit, curriculum designers also include opportunities for students to imagine themselves in various settings using different forms of writing prompts.

The issue for this curriculum is neither the richness of the material nor even the opportunities for students to engage the material in thoughtful and creative ways. Clearly, the developers of the curriculum have taken great care to provide a variety of learning activities and supportive resources. What is lacking are those explicit conceptual scaffolds that might provide students the recurring foundation to support their understanding. Various instructional vehicles might have been employed to help here. For example, each of the units in volume two might have highlighted the themes of human frailty which were discussed in volume one. Revisiting those themes (denial, forgetfulness, indifference, unrestrained intolerance) would not only have reinforced previous learning, but also would have provided valuable tools of academic and moral analysis and understanding. Using such a conceptual lens could help teachers select the most useful activities and resources from those provided.

Conceptual focus is perhaps most noticeable and most needed in regard to moral or affective objectives. Again, the "more is less principle" applies, since so much stands in the way of moral efficacy, and since the promise of moral lessons relies on their recurring connection to the circumstances of lived lives. The designers were appropriately explicit about their moral intent only at selected points in the curriculum. Various objectives direct students to empathize with the victims, recognize the implications of one person's suffering on the human community, and "appreciate the specialness of each living person on earth."[31] The latter goal occurs as one of the last objectives of volume two, supported only by short readings on the homeless, Mother Teresa, and rescuers. Little is done throughout the volume to provide explicitly the type of ongoing personal connection that might make such an objective feasible or to suggest on a more modest level how the moral principle of opposing cruelty can be manifested not simply in heroic interventions but in the growing moral sensibility of the effect of personal action. To do the latter, the volume would have had to concentrate more fundamentally on the effect of the Holocaust on ordinary people. Here perhaps only extensive work with narrative as represented in literature or other works of the creative imagination would do. In the New York curriculum, glimpses of such work are lost in an analysis that focuses primarily on the machinations of the state and the evil of selected figures within it.

The Holocaust: A Guide for Pennsylvania Teachers (Pennsylvania, 1990)

Developed seven years after the New York curriculum, the Pennsylvania guide was able to make use of its materials as well as materials from other Holocaust curricula. The writers were explicit about their aim not to duplicate other curricula and to provide a tool for teachers to find their way through the complexities of Holocaust and genocide studies. Like the New York curriculum, this guide lacks a well-developed rationale that might take into account present social needs as well as concepts of student learning as they apply to specific material. The introductory material, however, does indicate the intent of the authors to "permit students to understand types of thinking and behavior which led to genocide" and to "develop the necessary tools to not only avoid this themselves, but also to condemn such thinking and behavior of others." [32] Introductory notes indicate the responsibility to "teach the event first" and then to inquire into questions of human nature. Suggestions are made to make use of literature, art, and music as well as to explore questions of scientific responsibility. [33]

The guide is divided into thirteen chapters which follow the conceptual outlines also employed in the New York and Ohio curricula. Each chapter includes a synopsis, a list of instructional objectives, an overview of topics and issues, a list of vocabulary words, activities, discussion questions, assessment tools, and suggested teacher strategies. The vocabulary and assessment sections are valuable additions though the assessment is built primarily around memory work and revisiting the chapter material rather than around performance assessments that would require students to extend the material and create their own work. Many of the activities and strategies suggested in the design would require students and teachers to access material not provided in the curriculum. Reading, film, and video suggestions are made in the text and in an appendix. One strength of the appendix is the inclusion of references to music. This reference stands in contrast to the lack of other specific interdisciplinary activities and teacher strategies throughout the design.

This design has several strengths in relation to the New York curriculum. It includes a set of more general instructional objectives for the entire guide as they impact on student knowledge, values, and skills. The guide lacks, however, any coherent plan for sequential knowledge and skill development, and therefore, it would be difficult for teachers to see how such general objectives are carried through the specific chapters. Still, this might allow for teachers to select their own objectives out of the inclusive list provided. Like the New York curriculum, this design spends time not only on the origins of stereotypes and prejudices in relation to history and the study of human nature, but also on Jewish life, which has been the object of so much ill will and misunderstanding. The description given in the Pennsylvania guide lacks the historical precision of the New York curriculum as it relates to European Jewry. It does provide, however, an account of Jewish culture and beliefs which is more positive and descriptive and seems more likely to escape the victimization characterization. This can provide students some opportunity to prize uniqueness and seek personal connections, two elements directly associated with the research on the development of capacities for sympathy.

Unlike the content-rich New York curriculum, the Pennsylvania curriculum does not include any primary source material in terms of documents, photographs, or eyewitness accounts. Each chapter, instead, has a narrative section which identifies and gives some definition to specific topics. At times such narratives are fairly long and descriptive, as in the case of the section on classical and Christian anti-Semitism, but at times the material is distressingly cursory as in cataloguing the Nazi murder of non-Jews. Teachers coming to the topic without much background can profit from the overview provided in the guide, though they will not find much guidance about how to select, prioritize, and enlarge specific sections. Even more distressing would be the inclination to use the material in the guide as the primary reading for the study. Not only would such misuse lead to a highly fragmented and incoherent curriculum, but it would also act against the development of academic skills and moral sensibilities dependent on richer, more contextualized sources. It would be difficult to see how some of the guide's better objectives, activities, and strategies could be accomplished given the material the guide provides.

Like the New York curriculum, moral values and dispositions are explicitly identified at selective points throughout the guide. The general objectives for the curriculum itself are appropriately modest, indicating the intent for students to "recognize value problems and opposing viewpoints," "describe their own reactions to traumatic events," and "wonder if the Holocaust could happen today."[34] Such objectives indicate that students must first develop a capacity for recognition of moral issues before they can begin to develop strategies for resolving them. Similarly, the vocabulary of moral sensibility must be developed as it relates to identifying and validating one's own deeper emotional responses before one can extend and recognize those values in others. This seems reasonable. The telling wisdom of many nonviolent curricula today depends on students first determining sources of anger, mistrust, and pain in themselves. Only then do students discuss appropriate ways to deal with such emotions and then practice strategies to avoid foisting personal pain or anger upon others. While this seems some distance from "prizing the uniqueness and worth of all people," such a course is much more in keeping with the lessons of moral development especially as they apply to young people seeking safety from violence themselves. It speaks clearly to the reverse side of the sympathetic response: the need to do no harm to oneself or others, and to recognize the full impact of one's actions as they extend beyond the daily quest for personal survival.

Any curriculum design which wants to enlarge capacities for reflective care must provide opportunities for students to describe, imagine, and name the effect of personal response. Here, the lesson of moral obligation that was assumed by those who actively resisted the Nazi evil might be modestly mirrored in instructional activities that allow for students to listen to the voices of participants in the Holocaust and reconstruct in their own language what they hear people say about beliefs, feelings, and needs. This is the primary gift of story as created in personal narrative, literature, and art. In the Pennsylvania curriculum, little opportunity is provided to engage in the transporting medium of stories, primarily because the guide does not include content in which personal voices can be heard. Even when provided such accounts, students must develop capacities for description and a vocabulary which allows for deeper, more profoundly differentiated images. Much of the Pennsylvania curriculum provides students vocabulary relating to human pain and the institutional machinery of destruction. As unavoidable and important as such vocabulary is, kindness like cruelty depends upon articulation and expression. The moral imagination becomes malnourished without it.

The Holocaust: Prejudice Unleashed (Ohio, 1994)

The lesson plans, content materials, and classroom strategies in the Ohio Holocaust curriculum were developed by teachers reflecting upon their most successful teaching strategies in Holocaust education. Unlike the Pennsylvania Guide and the New York curriculum, this plan was developed as a complete ten day unit. Each daily lesson includes instructional objectives and materials, procedures, and supplementary materials. The introductory program instruction includes program goals and objectives that correspond with the lessons themselves. In this respect, the Ohio program promises a coherence which the New York and Pennsylvania curricula cannot deliver. The procedures governing instruction are so tightly bound to resource material in each unit that teachers are provided daily timelines. As with the other two curricula, the architecture of the curriculum is roughly chronological, first examining foundations of the Holocaust before moving on to the "final solution" and its aftermath. Later chapters provide additional learning activities and resources as well as a selection of poetry written by students who have completed the unit.

While the Ohio Holocaust curriculum fails to include a rationale which clearly outlines considerations of student learning and social context, best practice concepts were operating in its construction. Students are given reasons for attending to readings, filmstrips, or films in the form of pre-reading reaction guides, questions, or vocabulary. Follow-up activities are provided which allow students to organize and extend material. In many ways, the mark of practicing teachers prevails in this unit. Every lesson includes a variety of activities and homework assignments; lectures extend no more than fifteen minutes; and even supplementary materials are matched with teacher guides. Far more than the other two units, the narrative/personal dimension of Holocaust study is accentuated. Excerpts from *Night* by Elie Wiesel, for example, are at the core of the lesson on concentration camps. Maps and primary source material from the Nuremberg Trials buttress the lesson. This variety of material is typical of the curriculum. Poetry, eyewitness accounts, and films are provided along with primary source material.

In a unit as tightly bound as the Ohio study, it would be difficult though not impossible to articulate a developmental account of cognitive and affective skills. While the activities in the unit allow students to analyze, interpret, and evaluate the material, there is no obvious attempt to have students develop any of those skills as they work through the resource material. Matches have been made between curriculum and different instructional vehicles. For example, lecture is matched with understanding Eastern and Western European models of Jewish community; group work is used to help distinguish between the many ways civil law deprived the Jewish people of rights and personhood. Point of view seems to be a generative academic consideration that winds its way throughout this document. The design could be much more intentional about building student awareness of point of view as it relates to the different skills of description, identifying sources, detecting bias, and evaluating or suggesting implication.

Similarly, the unit lacks any explicitly formulated moral premise on which to build and attach its affective aims. Within the objectives identified by the unit designers, students are variously directed to evaluate the effects of "world apathy," "examine the issue of following a nation's law in lieu of a higher standard," and "appreciate the situation of non-Jews who risked their lives to save Jews." [35] Time constraints act against any deep consideration of such objectives, and it is difficult to attach specific activities or strategies to their fulfillment. Yet, the design provides many opportunities in its activities and instruction for students to identify and describe the perceptions of others, to evaluate the effects on others of state and individual actions, and to imagine one's own reactions if confronted with similar circumstances. In conjunction with the point of view as an academic consideration, these types of opportunities can be much more deliberative and can be sequenced in a more coherent and developmental fashion.

As with the Pennsylvania curriculum, story, art, and literature are key instructional vehicles here. To its credit, the design provides additional avenues for teachers to reference such material including in addition to Elie Wiesel's *Night,* material on *Town beyond the Wall,* Gerda Klein's *All but My Life,* and *The Diary of Anne Frank.* In each case, such reference includes corresponding teaching guides. Of the three curricula reviewed, the Ohio study is the most coherent and structured, providing the practicing teacher with a valuable ease of use tool. Yet even here one encounters at every step the restrained and unspoken wish to include additional room for discussion and material. For example, the design barely mentions the effect of the Nazi destruction on non-Jewish populations. Similarly, one may wish more room for students to locate, describe, and develop beliefs, feelings, and human need within themselves even as they develop the capacity to describe such sensations in others. Here, the less is more principle can operate only as the Holocaust becomes an event described by more than one class using the tools of more than one discipline. This touches upon the organization of a school as it corresponds to its own instructional mission. While this seems to go beyond the parameters of curricular review, it is for this reason that curriculum reform in the 1990s has become so intimately tied to the structural reform of education institutions themselves.

Principles of Holocaust Instruction: The Narrative Dimension

Time—around this element all Holocaust curricula must gather their deliberative intent. In some ways the differences in the Holocaust programs we have reviewed originate in how the developers deal with time constraints. The New York genocide curriculum has enough material for an entire college course and for a year of high school study. Still, one reviewer faulted it for cursory treatment of the Cambodian genocide,[36] and we have criticized its lack of attention to moral instruction. The Pennsylvania curriculum dealt with time constraints by providing a guide that catalogued major elements of the Holocaust. We noted that this was an unfocused approach and raised the possibility that students might never investigate the period in sophisticated and integrated ways. Finally, the Ohio curriculum most forthrightly faced the time element by explicitly noting that two weeks (scarcely ten hours of class) is the minimal period for Holocaust instruction. Accordingly, their curriculum is a tightly structured ten-lesson study which merely touches upon the riches of the subject. One wonders about the opportunities for students to process what they see and hear, and how they might develop academic and moral skills in reference to the subject matter.

Time becomes a crucial element in Holocaust education in part because so much scholarly attention has been focused upon the Shoah, and so much historical, literary, and artistic material can be used to support its study. Yet teachers with little background in Holocaust education will have a difficult time sorting through sources themselves, much less coordinating such material with specific objectives. In addition, the social situation in which teachers practice may act against any focused, integrated approach. Not only do state testing mandates direct teaching away from such learning, but also students themselves can pose barriers to instruction. Many enter the classroom burdened by their own moral and social issues which must be acknowledged and dealt with before instruction can begin. Much of the material about the Holocaust can exceed their academic skills. Integrative learning and performance-based assessments require tolerance for instructional ambiguity. While current learning theory would encourage teachers to provide opportunities for students to analyze, evaluate, and extend information, only practicing teachers can contextually determine what strategies are appropriate.

The New York and Pennsylvania efforts at Holocaust education prefer the word "guide" over "curriculum." Teacher choice becomes the unavoidable corollary to constraints of time and place, yet reasons must be given for professional judgment. Like any other justifiable study, Holocaust curricula require well-developed rationales which reflect social needs and conceptions of student learning as they relate to content and instructional strategy. Instructional approaches will always vary, but we have argued they still need to take into account solid principles of curricular design.

1. To keep the knowledge, skill, and value objectives simple and related, in this way covering less but integrating more.
2. To provide avenues for students to work with material in creative ways allowing them to extend content and make it their own.
3. To develop intellectual scaffolds upon which students might come to understand material in ways that develop categories of understanding and tools of reflection.
4. To make value objectives explicit but modest and allow students to describe, imagine, and name the effects of personal ethical response.

This review has repeatedly recommended the use of story as an instructional vehicle. Stories help students attend to the personal voices behind the Holocaust horror and help them avoid simplistic generalizations. Educators are just now rediscovering the full moral import of stories.[37] While some educators see stories as providing exemplary models in the sense of parable or allegory, the power of stories extends much deeper. In the sense of memory as understood by tradition and legend, stories tell who we are as a people and what kind of life we are supposed to lead. As a type of autobiography, stories provide the bridge between the private and public space and allow us to construct personal meaning out of the caldron of experience. Finally, as literature, stories require that we attend to the tales of others. They become islands of narrative safety where we are permitted to feel and imagine, embraced in audience by the confidence of the writer.

To a certain extent, all of the curricula reviewed here employ story and provide ways to use it to develop moral imaginations. In particular, the New York curriculum employs story as a creative device where students must attend to setting, adopt the pose of a Holocaust participant, and establish a contextual and reflective response. A danger lies in such creative presumption since one's efforts to see from "over there" may not be accurate or genuine. Yet when properly guided, students can come to honor perspective and begin to feel and imagine difficulties, dilemmas, and choices with increased complexity. One may overuse stories, given the construction of experience. Yet story is easily balanced, as it was in the Ohio curriculum when Wiesel's account in *Night* is connected with other historical descriptions and documents. One way to use story is to move from fiction to non-fiction and back again, as students are required to translate a historical description into a dialogue or retell what they have seen and heard in first person narrative. The latter can be an important academic and moral obligation not only because one is called to get it right, but also because inevitably one is forced to use and develop a personal moral vocabulary to describe the circumstances of others. In all events, it is important to extend beyond what is told and heard. All stories raise the questions of what has not been told and what could not be imagined.

Storytelling by itself represents an instructional event. Most Holocaust curricula recommend, if possible, having survivors visit to tell their own stories. This is story in its most generous dimension, the inspirational presence of the speaker. Yet if this is not possible, one cannot forget the presence of storytellers as they are represented by the students and teachers themselves. In telling our own stories as they relate and interrelate with the experience of Holocaust study, we cannot help but order experience, select compelling and significant events, and make judgments of how one's account might gain an audience. In this respect, the inclusion of student poetry is not simply an attractive gesture on the part of the designers of the Ohio curriculum. Rather, it allows for the opportunity for testimony, as students reflected on how they themselves have been affected and are being formed by their study.

In conclusion, this type of reflection might be said to be the strongest recommendation for the inclusion of Holocaust education as a vital part of a school's curriculum. Especially in the current social climate, any education which promotes tolerance, sympathy, and moral imagination makes a valuable contribution. To use story in this teaching can locate the student in a moral space that has both direction and place, where the course of events is filled with the portent of both choice and possibility. Only here do we find that actions do have determinate consequences for our own lives and for others. Here, the story which makes the most difference is the student's own.

STATE-DEVELOPED TEACHERS' GUIDES AND CURRICULA ON THE HOLOCAUST AND GENOCIDE

Human Rights: The Struggle for Freedom, Dignity, and Equality. State of Connecticut Department of Education, 1987.

Model Curriculum for Human Rights and Genocide. California State Board of Education, 1988.

South Carolina Voices: Lessons from the Holocaust. South Carolina Humanities Council, 1992.

Teaching the Past Describes Today . . . Tomorrow . . . Human Rights Education. Virginia Department of Education, 1987.

The Holocaust: A Guide for Pennsylvania Teachers. Pennsylvania Department of Education, 1990.

The Holocaust and Genocide—A Search for Conscience: A Curriculum Guide and a Student Anthology. Anti-Defamation League of B'nai B'rith, 1983.

The Holocaust: A North Carolina Teacher's Resource. North Carolina Council on the Holocaust, 1989.

The Holocaust: Can It Happen to Me? State of Florida Department of Education, 1990.

The Holocaust: Prejudice Unleashed. Ohio Department of Education, 1994.

The Human Rights Series: Teaching about the Holocaust and Genocide. 3 Volumes. The University of the State of New York, 1985 and 1986.

NOTES

1. United States Holocaust Memorial Museum, "State Requirements and Holocaust Studies" (United States Holocaust Memorial Council, Washington, D.C., photocopy), 1, 2.

2. John Goodlad, *A Place Called School* (New York: MacGraw Hill, 1984), 229–32. For a discussion of this tendency as it relates to environmental factors, see Zaine Ridling, "The Effect of Three Seating Arrangements on Teachers' Use of Selective Interactive Verbal Behaviors" (Paper delivered at the Annual Meeting of the American Education Research Association, New Orleans, La., 1994). ERIC Document Reproduction Service No. ED 369757.

3. See also Jere Brophy, "Probing the Subtleties of Subject Matter Teaching," *Educational Leadership* 49, no. 7 (April 1992): 4–8; and Robert D. Tennyson,

"An Educational Learning Theory for Instructional Design," *Educational Technology* 32, no. 1 (January 1992): 36–41.

4. This is particularly the case in the "essential schools" movement as conceived by Theodore Sizer, but it has also been a part of school intervention efforts using other models. See Heather McCollum, "School Reform for Youth at Risk: Analysis of Six Change Models," (Washington, D.C.: Policy Studies, 1994). ERIC Document Reproduction Service No. ED 370201.

5. Seymour B. Sarason, *The Predictable Failure of Educational Reform* (San Francisco: Jossey Bass, 1991), 9–31.

6. Mary T. Glynn, *American Youth and the Holocaust: A Study of Four Major Holocaust Curricula* (New York: National Jewish Resource Center, 1987), 58.

7. Ibid., 100.

8. Brophy, "Probing the Subtleties of Subject Matter Teaching." Also see Barak Rosenshine and Carla Meister, "The Use of Scaffolds for Teaching Higher-Level Cognitive Strategies," *Educational Leadership* 49, no. 7 (April 1992): 23–33.

9. Judith McQuaide and Ann-Maureen Pliska, "The Challenge to Pennsylvania's Education Reform," *Educational Leadership* 51, no. 4 (Dec.-Jan. 1993–94): 16–21.

10. U.S. Congress, House Subcommittee of the Committee on Government Operations, *Department of Education's Refusal to Fund Holocaust Curricula,* 100th Cong., 2nd Sess., 19 October 1988. ERIC Document Reproduction Service No. ED 320787.

11. Stanley M. Elam, Lowell C. Rose, and Alec M. Gallup, "The 26th Annual Phi Delta Kappan/Gallup Poll of Public Attitudes toward the Public School," *Phi Delta Kappan* 76, no. 1 (September 1994): 41–56.

12. Edward B. McCellan, "Schools and the Shaping of Character: Moral Education in America, 1607 to the Present," (Bloomington, Ind.: ERIC Clearinghouse for Social Studies/Social Science Education, 1992). ERIC Document Reproduction Service No. ED 352310.

13. John Dewey, *Moral Principles in Education* (Carbondale: Southern Illinois University Press, 1975), 7–17.

14. William S. Parsons and Samuel Totten, "Guidelines for Teaching about the Holocaust" (Washington, D.C.: United States Holocaust Memorial Museum, 1994), 2–8.

15. Bela Kozeki and Rita Berghammer, "The Role of Empathy in the Motivational Structure of Children," *Personality and Individual Differences* 13, no. 2 (February 1992): 191–203; and Nancy Eisenberg, Paul A. Miller, Rita Shell, Sandra McNalley, et al., "Prosocial Development in Adolescence," *Developmental Psychology* 27, no. 5 (September 1991): 849–57.

16. Nancy Eisenberg and Paul A. Mussen, *The Roots of Prosocial Behavior*

in Children (Cambridge: Cambridge University Press, 1989); and Jane A. Pilavin and Hong-Wen Charng, "Altruism: A Review of Recent Theory and Research," *Annual Review of Sociology* 16 (1990): 27–65.

17. Harvey A. Hornstein, *Cruelty and Kindness: A New Look at Aggression and Altruism* (Englewood Cliffs, N.J.: Prentice-Hall, 1976), 102–14.

18. Samuel P. Oliner and Pearl M. Oliner, *The Altruistic Personality: Rescuers of Jews in Nazi Europe* (New York: Free Press, 1988). Researchers using the Oliners' data also report that self-conceptualization may also have a gender bias. See Vicky Anderson, "Gender Differences in Altruism among Holocaust Rescuers," *Journal of Social Behavior and Personality* 8, no. 1 (1993): 43–58.

19. Glynn, *American Youth and the Holocaust.*

20. Kim Kunczt, "Beyond Anne Frank," *Educational Leadership* 51, no. 3 (November 1993): 35; Thomas Gerrity and Robert Clark, "Holocaust Studies: An Approach to Peace," *Momentum* 14, no. 4 (December 1983): 36–37; and Margot-Stern Strom, "The Holocaust and Human Behavior," *Curriculum Review* 22, no. 3 (August 1983): 83–6.

21. Oliner and Oliner, *The Altruistic Personality,* 155–70.

22. James Garbarino et al., *Children in Danger: Coping with the Consequences of Community Violence* (San Francisco: Jossey Bass, 1992), 1–15.

23. James Q. Wilson, *The Moral Sense* (New York: The Free Press, 1993), 39.

24. Christopher R. Browning, *Ordinary Men* (New York: Harper Collins, 1992).

25. Wilson, *The Moral Sense,* 50–4.

26. Bibb Latane and John M. Darley, *The Unresponsive Bystander: Why Doesn't He Help?* (New York: Appleton Century Crofts, 1970).

27. Oliner and Oliner, *The Altruistic Personality,* 149–50.

28. Browning, *Ordinary Men,* 159–89. Browning suggests that the cruelty of the soldiers in Police Battalion 101 had causes which eclipse simple explanations of race hatred. However, controlled studies have revealed denigration to be an all-too-human rationalization for cruelty. See Melvin J. Lerner, *The Belief in a Just World* (New York: Plenum, 1980), 39–53.

29. Samuel Totten and William S. Parsons, "State Developed Teacher Guides and Curricula on Genocide and/or the Holocaust: A Succinct Review and Critique," *Curriculum Research and Instruction* 28, no 1 (Spring 1992), 30.

30. Adam Clayton et al., *Teaching about the Holocaust and Genocide, The Human Rights Series* (Albany: New York State Education Department, 1985), I, iii.

31. Clayton et al., *Teaching about the Holocaust and Genocide,* II, 312.

32. Gary Grobman, *The Holocaust: A Guide for Pennsylvania Teachers* (Harrisburg: The Pennsylvania Jewish Coalition, 1990), i.

33. Ibid., iii.

34. Ibid., 2–3.

35. Leatrice B. Rabinsky and Carol Danks, eds., *The Holocaust: Prejudice Unleashed* (Columbus: Ohio Department of Education, 1994), chapters 1 and 3.

36. Totten and Parsons, "State Developed Teacher Guides and Curricula on Genocide and/or the Holocaust," 32.

37. For a good review of research around narrative see Paul C. Vitz, "The Use of Stories in Moral Development: New Psychological Reasons for an Old Educational Method," *American Psychologist* 45, no. 6 (June 1990): 709–20. For a guide to using literature to teach about the Holocaust see Judith R. Klau, "Literature of the Holocaust: The Imagination after Auschwitz," (Washington, D.C.: Council for Religion in Independent Schools, 1986). ERIC Document Reproduction No. ED 345257.

REFERENCES

Anderson, Vicky. "Gender Differences in Altruism among Holocaust Rescuers." *Journal of Social Behavior and Personality* 8, no. 1 (1993): 43–58.

Arendt, Hannah. *Between Past and Future*. New York: Viking Press, 1961.

Brophy, Jere. "Probing the Subtleties of Subject Matter Teaching." *Educational Leadership* 49, no. 7 (April 1992): 4–8.

Browning, Christopher R. *Ordinary Men*. New York: Harper Collins, 1992.

Clayton, Adam, et al. *Teaching about the Holocaust and Genocide*. The Human Rights Series. Vols. I and II. Albany: New York State Education Department, 1985.

Dewey, John. *Moral Principles in Education*. Carbondale: Southern Illinois University Press, 1975.

Eisenberg, Nancy, Paul A. Miller, Rita Shell, Sandra McNalley, et al. "Prosocial Development in Adolescence." *Developmental Sociology* 27, no. 5 (September 1991): 849–57.

Eisenberg, Nancy, and Paul A. Mussen. *The Roots of Prosocial Behavior in Children*. Cambridge: Cambridge University Press, 1989.

Elam, Stanley M., Lowell C. Rose, and Alec M. Gallup. "The 26th Annual Phi Delta Kappan/Gallup Poll of Public Attitudes toward the Public School." *Phi Delta Kappan* 76, no. 1 (September 1994): 41–56.

Garbarino, James, et al. *Children in Danger: Coping with the Consequences of Community Violence*. San Francisco: Jossey Bass, 1992.

Gerrity, Thomas, and Robert Clark. "Holocaust Studies: An Approach to Peace." *Momentum* 14, no. 4 (December 1983): 36–37.

Glynn, Mary T. *American Youth and the Holocaust: A Study of Four Major Holocaust Curricula*. New York: National Jewish Resource Center, 1987.

Goodlad, John. *A Place Called School*. New York: MacGraw Hill, 1984.

Grobman, Gary. *The Holocaust: A Guide for Pennsylvania Teachers.* Harrisburg: The Pennsylvania Jewish Coalition, 1990.

Hornstein, Harvey A. *Cruelty and Kindness: A New Look at Aggression and Altruism.* Englewood Cliffs, N.J.: Prentice-Hall, 1976.

Kozeki, Bela, and Rita Berghammer. "The Role of Empathy in the Motivational Structure of Children." *Personality and Individual Differences* 13, no. 2 (February 1992): 191–203.

Kunczt, Kim. "Beyond Anne Frank." *Educational Leadership* 51, no. 3 (November 1993): 35.

Latane, Bibb, and John M. Darley. *The Unresponsive Bystander: Why Doesn't He Help?* New York: Appleton Century Crofts, 1970.

Lerner, Melvin J. *The Belief in a Just World.* New York: Plenum, 1980.

Litynsky, Walter, et al. *Case Studies: Persecution and Genocide. The Human Rights Series.* Vol. III. Albany: New York State Education Department, 1986.

McCellan, Edward B. "Schools and the Shaping of Character: Moral Education in America, 1607 to the Present." Bloomington, Ind.: ERIC Clearinghouse for Social Studies/Social Science Education, 1992. ERIC Document Reproduction Service No. ED 352310.

Oliner, Samuel P., and Pearl M. Oliner. *The Altruistic Personality: Rescuers of Jews in Nazi Europe.* New York: Free Press, 1988.

Parsons, William S., and Samuel Totten. "Guidelines for Teaching about the Holocaust." Washington, D.C.: United States Holocaust Memorial Museum, 1994.

Pilavin, Jane A., and Hong-Wen Charng. "Altruism: A Review of Recent Theory and Research." *Annual Review of Sociology* 16 (1990): 27–65.

Rabinsky, Leatrice B., and Carol Danks, eds. *The Holocaust: Prejudice Unleashed.* Columbus: Ohio Department of Education, 1994.

Sarason, Seymour B. *The Predictable Failure of Educational Reform.* San Francisco: Jossey Bass, 1991.

Totten, Samuel, and William S. Parsons. "State Developed Teacher Guides and Curricula on Genocide and/or the Holocaust: A Succinct Review and Critique." *Curriculum Research and Instruction* 28, no. 1 (Spring 1992): 27–47.

Vitz, Paul C. "The Use of Stories in Moral Development: New Psychological Reasons for an Old Educational Method." *American Psychologist* 45, no. 6 (June 1990): 709–20.

Wilson, James Q. *The Moral Sense.* New York: The Free Press, 1993.

CHAPTER 7

Americanizing the Holocaust:

Beyond the Limit of the Universal

FRANKLIN BIALYSTOK

Two recent events have unveiled the American agenda in the teaching of the Holocaust. The first was the release of *The Liberators,* a film that depicts the supposed liberation of German concentration camps by African-American soldiers. According to a memorandum on the documentary, the film will be used to "examine the effects of racism on African-American soldiers and on Jews who were in concentration camps . . . to explain the role of African-American soldiers in liberating Jews from Nazi concentration camps and to reveal the involvement of Jews as 'soldiers' in the civil-rights movement." Following the film's release it was discovered that all-Black battalions were not the first units of Allied soldiers to enter the camps at Buchenwald and Dachau. This challenge to historical accuracy has not deterred the film's promoters from proceeding with the distribution of *The Liberators* to public television and school boards. After a gala presentation at the Apollo Theatre in Harlem, where Jesse Jackson embraced a Hasidic rabbi, an organizer of the event claimed that the film was "good for the Holocaust . . . what we're trying to do is make New York a better place for you and me to live" since it creates a "dialogue" between Jews and Blacks. She concluded that "there are a lot of truths that are very necessary. This is not a truth that's necessary." [1]

The second event was the opening in February of the Museum of Tolerance in Los Angeles under the sponsorship of the Simon Wiesenthal Center for Holocaust Studies. The promotional pamphlet describes the Museum as "an exciting experiential museum that promotes understanding among all people. Two themes are explored through unique interactive exhibits—the dynamics of racism and prejudice in American life, and the history of the Holocaust—the most monumental example of man's inhumanity to man."[2] The museum creates an experiential environment by utilizing multimedia technology to depict the Los Angeles riots where "*all* aspects of the . . . Riots are explained from various viewpoints"[3] (author's emphasis) and creating replicas of the Wannsee Conference and the gas chamber at Auschwitz. For one observer, the museum's purpose is "bold and blatant: To assault people's sensibilities and shock them into realizing that bigotry, hate and prejudice can only be defeated by tolerance."[4]

Michael Berenbaum, the project director of the United States Holocaust Museum in Washington, D.C., states that the museum's mission is twofold: (1) to memorialize the victims of the Holocaust; (2) to "Americanize the Holocaust" by trumpeting the ethical ideals of the Republic in contrast to the ideals of National Socialism.[5]

In the last fifteen years, the Americanization of the Holocaust has been widely adopted as the paradigm for learning about this event. This decision is ill-founded and unworkable. There are three central problems with this paradigm.

1. The Holocaust is shoe-horned into the context of the American experience, thus both denying the uniqueness of time, place, and motivation, and expanding the boundaries of universality.
2. The Holocaust is taught so that Americans will become more tolerant and understanding and less disposed to racism and prejudice, thus hoping that students will create a more just society.
3. The Holocaust is reduced to a mono-causal phenomenon which can be understood, perhaps even "experienced," thus both simplifying a complex historical process and ascribing comprehension to a situation which even the participants are at pains to describe.

Each of these problems requires further exploration. The first problem is the presumption that the universal implications of the Holocaust can be applied willy-nilly to American history, popular culture, and social discord. Documentaries such as *The Liberators* and institutions such as the Museum of Tolerance are symptomatic of the misplaced agenda of American educators and cultural promoters regarding the teaching of the Holocaust. They contend that to study the Holocaust, one must learn about racism in general, whether it be as the causal factor for the beating of Rodney King and the initial acquittal of his attackers, or as state sponsored mass murder, that is, "other genocides" in human history. In this ideological construct, the study of the Holocaust is meant to awaken society to what Franklin Littell calls the warning signs of genocide. This wake-up call for American society necessitates the preservation of liberal democratic principles, the building of bridges of understanding among ethnic communities in the United States, even to the point of conflating the beating of Rodney King with Auschwitz and falsifying the genuinely heroic actions of African-American soldiers to promote racial harmony in New York City.

This problem is not confined to a small number of programs. It is endemic in American public education. The widespread, thoughtful, and influential curriculum, *Facing History and Ourselves* in Brookline, Massachusetts, presents the universal implications for the American setting as the center piece of its study. It posits that "any discussion of racism in the context of this study almost invariably draws parallels to racism within our own society and particularly within our own schools and neighborhoods." Drawing on student journals, the Americanization is explicitly stated in the methodology section. One student wrote, " 'I don't think there will be another Holocaust if we keep on teaching about the Holocaust and the Constitution; all men are created equal.' "

In the last few years, the *Facing History* curriculum has been revised.[6] Nevertheless, the universalization of the Holocaust on the theme of Americanization remains in the forefront of the Institute's work. *Facing History* marked its fifteenth anniversary with a conference in May 1992. A panel discussed the intellectual and cultural roots of racism and anti-Semitism. One speaker presented a document and poem from the nineteenth century on anti-Chinese discrimination; another on the depiction of African Americans in the literature and popular culture in the last century. One workshop dealt with the depiction of African Americans on television. What was not discussed is how the Holocaust, the murder of European Jews during World War II, should be taught, especially in light of the most recent research on rescuers, the functionalist-intentionalist debate, the role of Churches, collaborators, resisters, and so on.[7] *Facing History* has moved the boundaries from a discussion of the universal implications of the Holocaust to an analysis of the crisis in American society. One can understand the anxiety felt by educators in May 1992 in the immediate aftermath of the acquittal of Rodney King's attackers in Simi Valley and the subsequent riots in Los Angeles; one cannot support, however, the conflation of the Holocaust with the roots of those events.

The central premise of the Americanization of the Holocaust is that by learning about this event students will create a less racist, more caring, and increasingly tolerant society. This raises the second problem with this paradigm—to what extent should the study of history be an object lesson in moral education? This question has been and continues to be at the root of the debate about public education in the United States. Teaching about the Holocaust, therefore, is subsumed within an exploration of American-style democracy and safeguarding its principles in order to prevent a recurrence of the events that led to Auschwitz. Concern about the preservation and efficacy of democracy is a constant in this paradigm, as Lucy Dawidowicz pointed out in her critique of this agenda.[8] This concern is undeniably a laudable goal. One fervently hopes that a study of the Holocaust will enable the student to see the patterns and currents that allowed democracy to fail in Germany leading to state-sponsored racism and descending to state-sponsored murder. One trusts that this study will persuade students to condemn the forces and opinions that articulate the canards that enable racism and discrimination to flourish in our society.

Without denying the inherent nobility of this motivation, it contains a major flaw. How is one to determine whether fifteen-year-olds who learn about the Holocaust change their attitudes about race and tolerance? Will this determination be made a generation from now, when one examines the attitudes and more important the statutes of that time? If society in the year 2020 is willing to admit refugees and immigrants from all lands and disavow discrimination and harassment on the grounds of race, ethnicity, or religion, will this provide some validation for the teaching of the Holocaust today? In fact, there is no vehicle which can measure the longterm outcome of such a study. While no analysis of history can prepare the student to foresee the warning signs of genocide, it can be argued that the Holocaust does provide a model of inhumanity. This factor, however, should not be the central premise of Holocaust education. Rather, the rationale for teaching the Holocaust is for students to know about a central event, what some observers call a *caesura*, of our time, that is circumscribed by place, time, and context.

The third problem of this educational agenda is that the Holocaust is explicable. In this paradigm anti-Semitism is the European version of racism; racism is the reason for the Holocaust. According to this mono-causal construct, when racism is unchecked it leads to the crematoria. Moreover, the Holocaust can be "experienced" in the United States by entering models of camps, ghettoes, gas chambers, and genuine transport wagons. By learning about why the Holocaust occurred, by "entering the gates" so to speak, students, of all ages will recognize the evil of racism in their own society and its current manifestations, and will acquire the tolerance to prevent a repeat of the Holocaust in the United States. At its essence, this approach leads the student along a straight path, from racism to the gas chambers, implying that this is why the Holocaust occurred.

Anti-Semitism as a European variant of racism and as the reason for the Holocaust is a simplification and a distortion of a complex historical process. Anti-Semitism was not racism. It was a phenomenon *sui generis*. As Emil Fackenheim has written,

> The Holocaust was not a case of racism although, of course, the Nazis were racists. But they were racist because they were anti-Semites, not anti-Semites because they were racists. Racism asserts that some human groups are inferior to others, destined to slavery. The Holocaust enacted the principle that Jews are not of the human race at all but "vermin" to be "exterminated." [9]

A brief overview of the confluence of anti-Semitism and National Socialism between 1920 and 1945 reveals the inappropriateness of a mono-causal explanation. Anti-Semitism was central to the ideology, policies, and actions of National Socialism which resulted in the planned extermination of European Jewry by 1941.[10] Anti-Semitism, however, was not central in the Nazi takeover. In fact, anti-Semitism may have been a deterrent in gaining popular support.[11] Anti-Semitism was not a consistent policy in prewar Germany and the so-called decision to enact the "final solution" was a subject of debate in the party, armed forces, and bureaucracy.[12] Anti-Semitism ultimately was of marginal importance in the act of mass murder, as depicted so chillingly by Christopher R. Browning.[13] In the final analysis, Michael Marrus states, "antisemitism in Germany may have been a necessary condition for the Holocaust, but it was not a sufficient one." [14]

Anti-Semitism as a mono-causal explanation of the Holocaust does not reveal the complexities of historical process to the student. It leads to the assumption that there was a straight path from racist ideology to the extinction of a people. It overlooks the possibility that there was a "twisted road to Auschwitz." This simplistic view is further diluted by attempting to "import" the Holocaust to the United States. Replicas of places and reenactments of conferences, rallies, ghettoes, camps and crematoria, and the reduction of the experience of the victims and victimizers to computerized games of choice and chance are banal. As an educational tool, the logic of this approach is faulty; the presumption of experience is absurd. Anyone who has visited the museums at Auschwitz or Maidanek realizes, upon reflection, that they have not "experienced" the camps; they have visited the museums there, they have been brought to the gates of hell, but they have not entered hell, even when entering into the bowels of the gas chambers and barracks, because they were free to leave. If anything, visitors understand that they cannot understand—they can only learn.

Important curricula, such as *Facing History and Ourselves,* and the U.S. Holocaust Museum, recognize this problem of mono-causality and comprehension and deal with it by examining the long and varied legacy of anti-Semitism and the factors that accounted for the success of National Socialism. The weakest curricula and the "experiential" museums resist the mandate to teach. Their approach is grounded in asking the student "How do you feel?" rather than demanding "What do you know?" The key to learning about the Holocaust is knowledge, as it is about any other topic. Educators and cultural promoters in the Americanization paradigm are stressing the affective domain and relegating the cognitive domain to a secondary status. This is unnecessary and unfortunate. It is unnecessary because the resources, while presenting the required content, elicit an emotional response without it needing to be embellished by games and artificial presentations. It is unfortunate because it masks the complexity of the historical process. One may feel drawn into the historical event but the student remains removed by sheer ignorance of the phenomenon.

Americanization of the Holocaust exceeds the boundaries of the debate on the unique/universal qualities of the Holocaust. That debate focuses on why the Holocaust was unique, to what extent there is comparability with other acts of genocide in history, to what degree current events, such as "ethnic cleansing" are symptomatic of the Holocaust, and the question of so-called other victims of Nazi policies.[15] Within the parameters of this debate most scholars agree that there are universal implications and most educators support the necessity of drawing on some of these implications in teaching about the Holocaust. There are limits to this debate, however, that are broached by the Americanization paradigm.

Several intertwined factors are responsible for exceeding the limits of universalization in the United States. The foremost factor is the necessity by Americans to view history and culture through their own prism. Perhaps this is indicative of ethno-centric preoccupation or so it appears to this Canadian observer. Thus, the Holocaust, while an event that occurred in Europe and ended almost fifty years ago, is automatically submerged into the context of the American experience of racism, democracy, and civil liberties. A second factor is the difficulty that educators have in teaching a multicultural audience that views the war in Vietnam as ancient history. The all-pervasive dictum of *relevance* prescribes that learning about the past, whether that past is two thousand years ago, or fifty years ago, must be placed into the context of here and now. A third factor is that complicated information is a disincentive in the classroom and in the museum. This postulates that a simplistic view of events that elicits an emotive response is preeminent. As a result, the study of history becomes homogenized and even distorted, as in the case of *The Liberators,* for the sake of the Americanized agenda.

Two of the most scathing critiques of the Americanization of the Holocaust have been Lucy Dawidowicz's attack on secondary school curricula in the December 1990 issue of *Commentary* and Philip Gourevitch's condemnation of the United States Holocaust Memorial Museum as theme park in the July 1993 issue of *Harper's.*[16] Both articles and the resultant letters to the editor, however, have missed the most salient problem of the Americanization paradigm. If the Holocaust is to be taught in the public arena, it is because it was an event of major importance in the history of modern Europe, with significant lessons and connections to other developments in our time, and not primarily because it is a vehicle for introspection about racism and democracy in the United States. The criteria which determine how and why the Holocaust is to be taught should be the same criteria for all other events in history—as unique occurrences circumscribed by time, place, and perspective.

NOTES

1. Jeffrey Goldberg, "Film Fraud—The Liberation that Wasn't," *The New Republic*, reprinted in *Globe and Mail*, February 6, 1993, D2.

2. Simon Wiesenthal Center, *Beit Hashoah Museum of Tolerance*.

3. Ibid.

4. Michael Miller, "An Assault on Bias at 'Museum of Tolerance,' " *Globe and Mail*, February 13, 1993.

5. Philip Gourevitch, "Behold Now Behemoth—The Holocaust Memorial Museum: One More American Theme Park," *Harper's* 287:1718 (July 1993): 55–6.

6. *Facing History and Ourselves—Holocaust and Human Behavior* (Brookline, Mass.: Facing History and Ourselves National Foundation, 1994).

7. "Legacies of Inequality: Exploring the Intellectual and Cultural Roots of Racism and Antisemitism," *Facing History and Ourselves*, Conference Agenda—May 7, 1992. Workshops, May 8, 1992. Author's notes on the conference.

8. Lucy Dawidowicz, "How They Teach the Holocaust," *Commentary*, December 1990, 25–32.

9. Emil L. Fackenheim, "What the Holocaust Was Not," foreword to Yehuda Bauer, *The Jewish Emergence from Powerlessness* (Toronto: University of Toronto Press, 1979), i-xiv.

10. This is not a point of controversy among historians of the Holocaust. For a sampling see Yehuda Bauer, *A History of the Holocaust* (New York: Franklin Watts, 1982); Lucy Dawidowicz, *The War against the Jews 1933–1945* (New York: Bantam, 1975); Martin Gilbert, *The Holocaust—The Jewish Tragedy* (London: Collins, 1986); Raul Hilberg, *The Destruction of the European Jews* (New York: Holmes and Meier, 1985).

11. See Sarah Gordon, *Hitler, Germans, and the Jewish Question* (Princeton: Princeton University Press, 1984); Ian Kershaw, *The "Hitler Myth"—Image and Reality in the Third Reich* (Oxford: Oxford University Press, 1987); Detlev J. K. Peukert, *Inside Nazi Germany—Conformity, Opposition and Racism in Everyday Life*, trans. R. Deveson (Toronto: Penguin, 1987).

12. See David Bankier, "Hitler and the Policy-Making Process on the Jewish Question" in *Holocaust and Genocide Studies* 3:1 (1988): 1–20; Yehuda Bauer, "Who Was Responsible and When? Some Well-Known Documents Revisited" in *Holocaust and Genocide Studies* 6:2 (1991): 129–49; Christopher Browning, *The Path to Genocide—Essays on Launching the Final Solution* (New York: Cambridge University Press, 1992); Gerald Fleming, *Hitler and the Final Solution*, English edition (Los Angeles: University of California Press, 1984); Ian Kershaw, "Hitler and the Holocaust" in *The Nazi Dictatorship—Problems and*

Perspectives of Interpretation, 2d ed. (London: Edward Arnold, 1989); Berel Lang, "The Concept of Intention and the Final Solution" in *Remembering for the Future* (Oxford: Pergamon, 1988). Supplementary Volume. A paper presented at the International Conference, Oxford, July 1988; Michael Marrus, *Entering History: Scholarly Study of the Holocaust,* paper presented to a joint session of the Canadian Historical Association and the Canadian Jewish Historical Society, Kingston, June 5, 1991. Draft Copy, May 1991; Karl A. Schleunes, *The Twisted Road to Auschwitz—Nazi Policy toward German Jews 1933–1939* (Chicago: University of Illinois Press, 1990).

13. Christopher R. Browning, *Ordinary Men—Reserve Police Battalion 101 and the Final Solution in Poland* (New York: Harper Collins, 1992), 160–84.

14. Michael Marrus, *The Holocaust in History* (Toronto: Lester and Orpen Dennys, 1987), 18.

15. For a sampling of the debate, see Yehuda Bauer, *The Holocaust in Historical Perspective* (Seattle: University of Seattle Press, 1973), 30–49; Yehuda Bauer, "Whose Holocaust?" *Midstream,* November 1980, 42–46; Peter Hayes, ed., *Lessons and Legacies: The Meaning of the Holocaust in a Changing World* (Evanston, Ill: Northwestern University Press, 1991); Papers by Emil Fackenheim, John Fox, Zev Garber and Bruce Zuckerman, Yehuda Bauer, Vahakn Dadiran, Henry Huttenbach, and Steven Katz presented at *Remembering for the Future—The Impact of the Holocaust on the Contemporary World,* International Scholars Conference, Oxford, July 10–13, 1988.

16. See notes 5 and 8.

CHAPTER 8

Teaching the Holocaust:

The Case for an Interdisciplinary Approach

JACQUELINE BERKE AND ANN L. SALTZMAN

By definition, the study of the Holocaust is—and must be—interdisciplinary, for each discipline in and of itself allows us to understand only one aspect of the Holocaust: history tells us what happened; psychology probes the psyches of those involved: perpetrators, victims, survivors, rescuers, bystanders (what made them behave as they did?); literature and the arts shape what happened in the Holocaust into an aesthetic form which enables us to enter events imaginatively and vicariously, to feel them "on the pulse" as Coleridge put it; philosophy and theology raise questions about morality and ethics, the nature of good and evil, and the possibilities of leading a meaningful life in the post-Holocaust world.

Only in combination do the disciplines provide the many perspectives required for understanding at any depth or breadth. Although the advantages of an interdisciplinary approach seem self-evident, there appear to be relatively few courses built around multiple perspectives. Indeed, as James Waller of Whitworth College has aptly observed, "We tend to under-utilize insights from other disciplines."[1]

This paper describes three models for teaching the Holocaust, each designed to incorporate interdisciplinary objectives and to demonstrate the value of the interdisciplinary approach. Each model evolved from the previous one during a five-year period of experimentation with various formats. Throughout this process of refining and revising, we have been responsive to the needs of both students and instructors as well as the special demands of working with Holocaust materials.

MODEL I: "SHARED CLASSES"

The authors, a professor of English and a professor of Psychology, began their collaborative work during the fall 1990 semester when both were teaching First-Year Seminars focusing on the Holocaust. Jacqueline Berke's course was entitled "*SHOAH:* The Film, the Text, the Art and Ethic of the Interview"; Ann Saltzman's was called "Obedience to Authority: The Holocaust and Beyond." During that semester, we scheduled six "shared classes" at which our students met together at six appointed sessions in a common classroom and for which we assigned a given number of common texts.

During the first shared meeting, students from one seminar were paired with students from the other and asked to take turns "teaching" one another something they had learned about the Holocaust in their respective seminars. From literature, for example, a student might cite the images of death in Elie Wiesel's classic memoir *Night*, a "bullet of a book," as one student described it. Similarly, from psychology, a student might describe to his or her literary partner the profile of the "altruistic personality," as defined by psychologists Samuel and Pearl Oliner, and as embodied in the character of Lorenzo in Primo Levi's *Survival in Auschwitz*.

Other shared classes alternated between literary, cinematic, and psychological perspectives. For example, during one session we watched a videotaped interview with Claude Lanzmann, director-producer of the film *SHOAH*,[2] then discussed a particular segment of the film, the famed interview with Abraham Bomba. In this segment, the former Polish barber, succumbing to the relentless pressure of the interviewer erupts, as it were, into a truth he has long repressed, the emotional truth of his horrific experience cutting the hair of women about to enter the gas chamber. We watch him return to a time too horrific to recall. We watch his face, contorted with grief, shame, humiliation, despair, a stark contrast to the mask he had been wearing earlier as he dutifully recited the bare facts, detached from all feeling.

This film excerpt exemplifies a "text" which was illuminated by both disciplines. Psychological and literary perspectives conjoin as Bomba begins to thaw emotionally, to face the horror and to try to express it in words. Further, this most controversial segment of Lanzmann's documentary masterpiece parallels, in many interesting respects, the controversial procedures practiced by Stanley Milgram—as described in his landmark text, *Obedience to Authority*—whereby Milgram gained information and insight into some of the "awful truths" about human nature—procedures that some investigators regarded as "off limits."[3]

At the end of our First-Year Seminars, we were so pleased with our collaboration and eager to repeat and expand it that, in Fall 1992, we composed a second model of interdisciplinary course work that offered more than selected shared classes; we offered in their place upper-level "paired seminars."

MODEL II: "PAIRED SEMINARS"

The upper-level seminars entitled "Literature of the Holocaust" and "Psychology of the Holocaust," as offered in Fall 1992, were each complete and self-contained courses within the separate disciplines and available to students as separate offerings. Our goal in "pairing" these courses was to give our students as broad an interdisciplinary experience as possible. Ideally, we would have preferred to offer one six-credit course entitled "Literature and Psychology of the Holocaust." However, due to departmental constraints we were unable to do this. Instead, we encouraged students to take both courses simultaneously. First, we sent a note to our colleagues asking them to alert their students to the "paired seminars"; then, we described them in meticulous detail in the pre-registration listing. Finally as students signed up for one of the courses, we advised them to think about the advantages of signing up for the other course as well, pointing out that they would get a much fuller understanding of the Holocaust if they participated with us in this first-time experiment in Holocaust education at Drew.

Fourteen students enrolled in the Literature seminar; thirteen in the Psychology seminar; five enrolled in both. However, again, because we believed that a multidisciplinary understanding of the Holocaust was crucial, we chose to provide *every* student with an interdisciplinary experience by attending each and every session of the other's classes where we served as co-instructors.

Clearly, as the literature professor, Berke retained authority in her class, with Saltzman—at moments—helping the literature students understand the psychological motivations and responses of the characters in the memoirs, short stories, novels, and so forth. Likewise, Berke brought to Saltzman's students literary examples which made the psychological processes under investigation more personal, more vivid, more concrete—capable of carrying the materials "alive to the heart."

Further, by collaborating in this way, we were able to demonstrate to students that different disciplines ask different questions. The literary questions involve style, structure, point of view, tone of voice, and the like, whereas the psychological questions involve causation, motivation, methodology, intrapsychic processes, and so on. Certain literary works such as Cynthia Ozick's *The Shawl* and its companion story *Rosa,* for example, require and permit questions drawn from both disciplines; similarly, psychological texts such as Samuel and Pearl Oliner's *The Altruistic Personality* are illuminated by a literary explication of formal interviews in which rescuers tell their stories to a researcher.

We felt most confirmed in our collaboration when our shared students spontaneously drew from both disciplines, transcending classroom boundaries. Thus, in the middle of a discussion of Jerzy Kosinski's *The Painted Bird,* students not only noted that the young protagonist had himself become a perpetrator but were able to draw on psychological theory as put forth in Ervin Staub's *The Roots of Evil,* for example, to explain why.

Evaluation of the Paired Seminar Approach

Based on responses to the post-course interviews and questionnaires, all five students who took both courses were more than satisfied. As they testified (and as reported below—in their own words), they felt that they had "learned about several aspects of the Holocaust which complemented each other"; that "the knowledge from one course facilitated learning in the other"; and that they had gained "a fuller picture of the Holocaust." One student also noted that the "presence of two professors who were not afraid to disagree with each other facilitated the desired environment of a community of scholars" (a goal we set at the outset of the seminars). This student noted that the presence of two professors, only one of whom was the "expert" in the specific discipline, legitimized the observation that we all (including the "non-expert" faculty member) can learn from one another.

Ten of the seventeen students (59 percent) who took only one of the two courses returned their questionnaires. Although we recognize that this is a small sample, we feel that these responses are compelling and relevant. For example, when asked how they thought the experience of students who had taken both seminars differed from their own, responses of the one-course students paralleled those of the both-course students. Those taking both courses were perceived to have gained a more complete picture of the Holocaust, to have gained ideas from multiple perspectives, and to be more involved in the study because they were reading twice as much material and meeting twice as often.

However, when asked "If the semester were starting now and you could sign up for both courses, do you think you might consider doing that?", five of the ten students said "no," one said "maybe," and only four said "yes." Two major reasons were offered for this hesitancy to take both Holocaust seminars: First, the reading for one course was perceived to be demanding enough; reading for two seemed prohibitive. Second, studying both perspectives on the Holocaust was perceived to be far too emotionally draining.

Interestingly, our data suggested that students who chose to take both courses were—indeed—differently oriented from those who took only one. Even though both groups of students had been drawn to Holocaust study out of interest, only students who had elected to take both courses described themselves as wanting to understand the larger picture and as willing to enter the "total experience." They too indicated that the material was often "hard to get through"; at times, they felt that they were "under assault." Nonetheless, if again faced with the choice of taking only one or both courses, *all would choose to take both*. In comparison to those who were taking one course and who were fearful that taking both courses would overwhelm them, those taking both courses seemed to welcome the intense experience, acknowledging at the same time that for those taking only one course "the intensity was probably dulled."

This finding becomes even more meaningful when placed into the context of how those taking both courses defined themselves. During the post-course interview, four of these students spontaneously self-described themselves as "survivors" of some traumatic experience such as rape, child abuse, or the tragic and unexpected death of a loved one. Indeed, they *identified* with the traumas of Holocaust victims and found the material on coping strategies for survival personally relevant. In contrast, only two students who were taking only one course and who returned the post-course questionnaire self-described themselves as "survivors" in the same way (although three saw themselves as survivors by virtue of taking a Holocaust course).

While it was the exceptional student who was attracted to taking multiple Holocaust seminars simultaneously, our data also revealed that even those taking one course had connected with and appreciated the rounded, multidisciplinary approach. Nine of the ten reported that the presence of a co-instructor from another discipline added to the course. One student even commented on the one class session where guest lecturer and historian Yaacov Lozowick of Yad Vashem, Israel, and the two instructors "came together to present different viewpoints" that were controversial in some respects but deeply affirming in others.

If a single course entitled "Literature and Psychology of the Holocaust" were to be offered, seven of the ten students said that they would take it. The other three cited reasons for *not* taking it: they felt that the impact of each of the original courses might be diluted; they feared that the amount of reading would be prohibitive and that the emotional strain of such an intensive six-credit course would be "more than they could take."

In sum, our data suggest that although students are decidedly interested in a rounded, multiperspective approach to studying the Holocaust, they want to make certain that the course will not "undo" them. (Our response to this finding is to sound an alert to ourselves and to any instructor planning an interdisciplinary course on the Holocaust: Be sure to provide safeguards against overwhelming or overpowering students, mentally or emotionally; indeed, assure students that a concerted effort is being made to avoid this possible "downside" to an otherwise positive approach.)

It is important to add here that as instructors, we too felt certain reservations about the format of our "paired seminars" model. It was extremely time intensive. In sitting in on each other's classes and in reading assigned texts for each other's courses, our workload was virtually doubled; we taught one class and "took" the other.

Further, while we attended and contributed to each other's classes, our initial unfamiliarity with the texts in the other's discipline often prevented us from anticipating where common themes would emerge. In fact, during post-class discussions and evaluation, we began to see the many missed opportunities which had simply "passed us by." We concluded that in order to harness the true potential of this interdisciplinary approach, we needed to do more extensive planning and preparing. To provide us with a more compressed and more sharply focused experience, we created a third interdisciplinary format, "planned visitations."

MODEL III: "PLANNED VISITATIONS"

In this model, we will not "sit in" on all sessions of each other's classes. Rather, we will make four planned visitations and assign a given number of common texts. Further, we hope to use our shared students as "coteachers." Table 1 summarizes these planned visits and the new role of shared students.

During the introductory sessions, we will introduce each other and review the interdisciplinary components of our respective courses. We will then outline how the disciplines differ, both in the types of questions each asks about the Holocaust and in the nature of the "data" each compiles and presents. Thus, in the literature class, the psychological approach will be introduced by citing specific studies and established theories that help to explain why perpetrators, victims, survivors, bystanders, and rescuers behaved as they did, exploring behaviors which seem to range from "monsters" to "saints." (Or, we might ask, were they just ordinary people, induced by circumstances, into behaving in extraordinary ways?) The literary approach will be introduced to the psychology students through selected literary works such as the sonnet "If We Must Die" (written by Claude McKay of the Harlem Renaissance); Yevgeny Yevtuchenko's "Babi Yar" (wherein a non-Jew speaks out as a Jew); and the haunting lamentations of Nelly Sachs's *O the Chimneys!*

The second class session in both seminars will be devoted to history, where the common text, *Never to Forget: The Jews of the Holocaust,* will be studied.

During the third and fourth planned visitations, we will trade places: Berke will teach psychology students; Saltzman will teach literature students. Here, our choice of texts was guided by feedback from students in our previous model, "paired seminars." When asked to recommend which texts from their course they felt students in the other discipline should read, the top three choices by the literature students were Elie Wiesel's *Night,* Cynthia Ozick's *The Shawl/Rosa,* and Tadeus Borowski's

TABLE I AN OVERVIEW OF THE
"PLANNED VISITATIONS" APPROACH

Literature	*Psychology*
I. Introductory class	Introductory class
The psychological approach is introduced through a review of studies and theories.	The literary approach is introduced through selected poems, including "If We Must Die."

II. History of the Holocaust. We use a shared text: Milton Meltzer's *Never to Forget: The Jews of the Holocaust* (1976).

III. Obedience to authority and other social psychological processes.	Literary illustrations of coping via numbing and eruptions of feeling during the rehumanization process.
Assigned reading, Milgram's *Obedience to Authority*, and viewing the film "Obedience."	Assigned readings: *Night* and *This Way to the Gas, Ladies and Gentlemen*.
Shared students lead discussion about other social psychological processes: numbing, development of the "Auschwitz self," use of language, and dehumanization.	Shared students talk about literary devices: lyric quality in Elie Wiesel, ironic tone in Borowski.
(Week 5 of Literature class)	(Week 7 of Psychology class)

IV. The Psychology of Rescuers	The Literature of Coping after Liberation
A review of the major findings from Samuel and Pearl Oliner's book *The Altruistic Personality*	Ida Fink's short story *Crazy* and viewing of the Abraham Bomba episode in the film *SHOAH*.
Shared students discuss the more subtle findings of the text.	Shared students discuss Cynthia Ozick's *Rosa*.
(Week 12 of Literature class)	(Week 11 of Psychology class)

V. Concluding class: final report from the other discipline. Discussion is led by visiting professor and shared students.

This Way for the Gas, Ladies and Gentlemen. Similarly, top choices by the psychology students were Stanley Milgram's studies on *Obedience to Authority* and related social psychological theories and *The Altruistic Personality* by Samuel and Pearl Oliner. As indicated in Table 1, our shared students will augment our comments with presentations on pre-assigned topics.

Finally, we will allot time in our final class sessions for a report from the other discipline: what have we learned? what questions have we asked? what answers have we gleaned? what remains for further study? what are the limitations of our separate disciplines?

We believe that the five "planned visitations" reviewed above (five points of interdisciplinary articulation) satisfactorily address the concerns of students fearful of being overwhelmed. At the same time, we believe that our present approach will enable us to weave an interdisciplinary perspective into our courses with subtlety and strength so that the data of each discipline illuminates the data of the other. How successful we are in creating a course that is powerful yet not overpowering remains to be seen—and will be the subject of a future (and hopefully positive) report.

Notes

1. Professor Waller made this observation at a conference, held at Wittenberg University in October 1993, entitled "Teaching the Holocaust: Issues and Dilemmas." The title of his talk was "Social Psychological Analyses of the Holocaust: The Next Chapter."

2. Claude Lanzmann's epic nine-and-a-half hour documentary (1985) chronicles the events of the Holocaust through a series of provocative interviews with survivors, bystanders, historians, former Nazi guards, bureaucrats, and SS officers.

3. Stanley Milgram's text *Obedience to Authority* (New York: Harper Colophon Books, 1974) describes a series of eighteen experiments in which naive subjects were induced into administering electric shocks to "subjects" who were really confederates of the experimenter. Although no shocks were actually administered, the confederates acted as if they were and the subjects believed that, in fact, they had been punishing people who made errors during a learning task. These experiments were highly criticized for the deception employed to induce subjects into delivering these "shocks" and for the high levels of stress which the subjects experienced.

REFERENCES

Borowski, Tadeus. *This Way for the Gas, Ladies and Gentlemen.* New York: Penguin, 1976 (1959).

Fink, Ida. "Crazy" in *A Scrap of Time and Other Stories.* New York: Pantheon Books, 1987. 20–22.

Kosinski, Jerzy. *The Painted Bird.* New York: Bantam Books, 1981.

Levi, Primo. *Survival in Auschwitz: The Nazi Assault on Humanity.* 1958; Rpt. New York: Collier Books/Macmillan, 1987.

McKay, Claude. "If We Must Die" in *The Holocaust Years: Society on Trial.* Edited by Roselle Chartock and Jack Spencer in cooperation with the Anti-Defamation League. New York: Bantam Books, 1981. 245.

Meltzer, Milton. *Never to Forget: The Jews of the Holocaust.* New York: Harper Row, 1976.

Milgram, Stanley. *Obedience to Authority.* New York: Harper Colophon Books, 1974.

Oliner, Samuel, and Pearl Oliner. *The Altruistic Personality: Rescuers of Jews in Nazi Europe.* New York: The Free Press, 1988.

Ozick, Cynthia. *The Shawl.* New York: Vintage International, 1990.

Sachs, Nelly. *O the Chimneys!* New York: Farrar, Straus and Giroux, 1967.

SHOAH. France, 1985. Directed by Claude Lanzmann (documentary).

Staub, Ervin. *The Roots of Evil: The Origins of Genocide and Other Group Violence.* New York: Cambridge University Press, 1989.

Waller, James. "Social Psychological Analyses of the Holocaust: The Next Chapter." Paper presented at the conference on "Teaching the Holocaust: Issues and Dilemmas." Wittenberg University, Wittenberg, Ohio, October 1993.

Wiesel, Elie. *Night.* New York: Hill and Wang, 1960.

Yevtuchenko, Yevgeny. "Babi Yar" in *The Holocaust Years: Society on Trial.* Edited by Roselle Chartock and Jack Spencer in cooperation with the Anti-Defamation League. New York: Bantam Books, 1981. 242–44.

CHAPTER 9

Holocaust: Transcendent Case Study

for the Social Sciences

CHARLES R. CLARKE AND SHARON L. DOBKIN

This chapter explains the rationale for locating a course on the Holocaust within the framework of the social sciences, and within a format for guiding students on a journey that explores the social and psychological processes that can help us better understand human behavior in extremity and in our daily lives. Typically, courses on the Holocaust are likely to be located within departments of history, religion, or Judaic studies. Such courses reflect a perspective that locates the phenomenon that has come to be known as the Holocaust as either a historical event or one which has unique and transcending meaning to the Jewish experience. While we acknowledge that historical framework is essential for understanding events that culminated in the Final Solution, and that the Holocaust has special qualities that inform the Jewish experience, we suggest that these two paths have serious limitations. It is our contention that, unless the Holocaust assumes an interdisciplinary direction by interweaving fields that do not normally intersect (Brown 1991), we are unlikely to be able to view this "event" through the multiple lenses of varied disciplines necessary to go beyond the description bias of history or the transcendent analyses of theism.

In our opinion, history or religion, taught without the interdisciplinary vantage point that includes the social sciences, constrains the audience and misses an opportunity to provide parallels and connections to contemporary social science models and metaphors. By limiting one's focus to either "the historical event" or its secular and religious impact on the Jews, the student runs the risk of having the Holocaust not inform the present social psychological context. In our opinion, this is a significant loss, since one goal should be to have the student move beyond information to knowledge and ultimately to integration in a balance of compassion and wisdom. Understanding the Holocaust necessitates deconstructing the historical event through many prisms including contemporary social science models and metaphors. However, this process runs the risk of trivializing the fact and meaning of this historical event and relativizing it to the point of rendering it distant, irrelevant, or excusable.

Lest we be accused of negating the unique meaning of the Holocaust to the Jewish experience by universalizing its "lessons," or denigrating the significance of history, what we hope to accomplish is to go beyond the unique/universal dialogue by presenting the Holocaust as both a prototypical and an archetypical case to explore the simplicity of good, the banality and seductiveness of evil, and the danger of indifference.

The social and psychological research and theory of the past forty-five years provides the necessary framework to analyze the narrative of both history and literature. The work from such seminal social scientists as G. W. Allport on the nature of prejudice, Solomon Asch on conformity, Leon Festinger on cognitive dissonance, Stanley Milgram on obedience, Herbert C. Kelman on compliance, identification, and internalization, and J. M. Darley and C. D. Batson on bystander intervention, helps to build the bridge from the descriptive pattern of historical presentation and the idiosyncratic of the literary form, to the dilemmas of the students' present lives and circumstances. Both good and evil are shown to be banal and mundane to all, in both the laboratory and in real life.

Let us briefly elaborate on how each one of these areas of research and theory respectfully can be applied to the analyses of the historical and literary sources on the Holocaust. It is a blend of information that makes this archetypical-prototypical event more understandable without excusing it. At the same time, we can draw upon those social science principles in extracting parallels to our everyday life. It allows for interpretation that permits a more personal relationship with the event. The outcome is to place this historical event as part of a historical process that is neither singular nor yet complete. In contrast to Bertrand Russell's dictum on philosophy, social science takes that which is paradoxical and almost unbelievable and makes it into something intuitively obvious.

The work of Allport on the nature of prejudice (Allport 1954) has helped us in our understandings of ethnocentricity, ethnic conflict, and the escalation of hostilities whether at the macro level of nations or the micro level of the dyad. Our studies of ethnocentrism push us to understand more clearly the underlying individual processes and the prompt-ing and supporting social context in the development of stereotypes. The consequence of stereotypes is to isolate and diminish while helping to develop and sustain irrational prejudice and discrimination. These are principles that can assist students to quickly identify with the dilemmas of their contemporary lives. In turn, the research of Solomon Asch (1952) helps us focus on the subtle ways in which both the individual and its manifestation in the aggregate come to form impressions of personality so critical to our understanding of the stigmatizing of Jews, gypsies, homosexuals, feminists and Communists during the 1933–1945 Nazi era.

Next, we can look at the complex relationship between actions and attitudes so powerfully introduced and derived from the work of Leon Festinger (1980). The student sees the parallels of how subtle, small personal commitments of behavior in support of the ideology of Na-tional Socialism impacted upon individual attitudes and subsequently informed and guided their behavior. We ask students to understand that so much of who they are is contained in what they do, and how so much of what they do is imbedded in the social context in which they operate. They quickly achieve the uncomfortable realization that indifference to continuing human suffering and injustice was commonplace then and remains so today.

The power of social circumstance, particularly as it relates to institu-tional authority, is profoundly highlighted in the work of Stanley Mil-gram on obedience (1977). Milgram reminds us that the majority of normal, healthy individuals faced with the order to obey, even without explicit or implicit threat of sanction by institutional authorities, will usually obey even if action is dissonant with their existing values. The power of social circumstance as it relates to institutional authority has been more completely and subtly elaborated on in the work of Kelman (Kelman and Hamilton 1989). Here, we understand that the social power of controlling means, attractiveness, and credibility impacts on the individual by generating progressively higher levels of personal com-mitment sometimes reflected in orderly acts of evil and human destruc-tion. In applying this to the Holocaust, we assist students in understand-ing that the social and psychological processes that make the Holocaust understandable also continue to inform our daily lives.

Finally, with some hopefulness, we look at the complexity of how individuals intervene to affirm and support those in need (Darley and Batson 1973). Such work has helped us understand that bystander intervention is, in fact, both complicated and subtle. Although the decision to help appears to be instantaneous, the process itself can be broken down into successive stages. We now know that before intervention occurs the event must be noticed; bystanders must see it as an emergency; potential rescuers must perceive themselves as responsible; and they must know and be skilled at the appropriate forms of assistance. Finally, they go through an often unconscious, cost-benefit analysis in coming to the decision to help. It is in this context that we can both dissect the conditions where rescue did or did not occur, while crafting a better understanding of how these processes impact upon our own lives today.

The interweaving of social science theory and research brings us to the most difficult challenge. At this junction, students are asked to define and explain indifference to human suffering. When introducing the concept of indifference, one must differentiate between the committed collaborator, uncaring bystander, and the uninformed, confused, and/or fearful but caring bystander. Once students begin to understand the extremes of good and evil, they are challenged to explain how these groups of bystanders either intentionally or incidentally facilitated behavior at either end of the continuum. Furthermore, this collage of factors diminishes the notion that the Holocaust was orchestrated by one deranged but charismatic leader or a small group of psychopaths.

Several suggested works for confronting indifference and bystander behavior include *The Good Old Days* by Klee et al., *Ordinary Men* by Christopher R. Browning, and the poem by Maurice Ogden entitled "The Hangman." The first presents a collection of diary entries, letters home, confidential reports, and photographs from sympathetic observers. In vivid detail, *The Good Old Days* (Klee 1988) describes what the ordinary person witnessed, often as sport or spectacle, as the process of killing moved across Eastern Europe. It employs context analysis to look more closely at all three groups of bystanders. It artfully dispels the concept that bystanders were people who "did not know" what was happening to the Jews, and suggests that many "partisans" were quite willing to take part in the killings where execution was "popular entertainment." It challenges the student to deal with the notion that indifference is every bit as difficult to confront as evil or good. In fact, it shakes them to their very core because of its paradoxical simplicity and complexity.

In *Ordinary Men* (1992), Christopher R. Browning introduces the student to Police Battalion 101. Meeting the cast of characters, the reader is faced with troubling questions regarding acts that either facilitated or circumvented evil. Browning skillfully invites one to integrate the narrative with the more "scientific" data, viewing the work of Milgram and others through the experiences of ordinary policemen. Browning cites Milgram's findings as useful in shedding light on police behavior during the Holocaust, but suggests that conformity rather than obedience to authority may have played a more crucial role.

Further, Browning explores Milgram's notion of ideological indoctrination, and concludes that in the case of Reserve Police Battalion 101, it falls short of explaining how ordinary men became killers. Finally, through Browning's vivid portrayal of the ordinary group of men as they became active participants in genocide, students face the most difficult challenge yet—given the state of modern society with its emphasis on bureaucracy and diffusion of personal responsibility—how can we depend on the strength of individuals to choose connectedness, personal commitment, and responsibility?

"The Hangman," a poem by Maurice Ogden, lures the student into the town where indifference in its multiple forms empowers evil. "He who serves me best," says the Hangman, "shall earn the rope on the gallows tree." The student is invited to watch from afar as the tale unfolds and is at the end transformed into the henchman himself as the Hangman cries, "First the alien, then the Jew . . . I did no more than you let me do." When the Hangman straps the last person to the gallows, the student, no longer afar, no longer indifferent, faces evil alone.

We press our students to go beyond the metaphysical question of guilt and responsibility of all humans, as was suggested in Karl Jaspers (1947): "A solidarity among men, as human beings, that makes each co-responsible for every wrong and every injustice in the world" (32). Rather, we ask them to consider their connectedness to all life forms. If they are willing to acknowledge and affirm this connectedness, can they continue to be bystanders? Paraphrasing what Karl Jaspers wrote (Kohler and Saner 1993) of Heidegger, are we going to be someone with impure soul; that is, soul that is unaware of its own impurity, and is constantly trying to expel it, but continues to live thoughtlessly in filth? Can someone living in that kind of dishonesty perceive and ultimately actualize in their ordinary lives, a community of justice, gently interweaving compassion and wisdom in the creation of an inclusive, life-affirming community? In the end, the Shoah is the prototypical and archetypal vehicle that propels us from the safety of complacent spectator and engages participation.

REFERENCES

Allport, G. W. *The Nature of Prejudice*. Cambridge, Mass.: Addison-Wesley, 1954.

Asch, Solomon. *Social Psychology*. New York: Prentice Hall, 1952.

Brown, Michael. "The Holocaust as an Appropriate Topic for Interdisciplinary Study." In Gideon Shimoni, ed., *The Holocaust in University Teaching*. New York: Pergamon Press, 1991.

Browning, Christopher R. *Ordinary Men*. New York: Harper Perennial, 1993.

Darley, J. M., and C. D. Batson. "From Jerusalem to Jericho: A Study of Situational and Dispositional Variables in Helping Behavior." *Journal of Personality and Social Psychology* 27, (1973): 100–108.

Festinger, Leon. *Retrospections on Social Psychology*. New York: Oxford University Press, 1980.

Jaspers, Karl. *The Question of German Guilt*. New York: Dial Press, 1947.

Kelman, Herbert C., and V. Lee Hamilton. *Crimes of Obedience: Towards a Social Psychology of Authority and Responsibility*. New Haven: Yale University Press, 1989.

Klee, Ernst, et al. *The Good Old Days*. New York: Free Press, 1988.

Kohler, Lotte, and Hans Saner, *Hannah Arendt and Karl Jaspers: Correspondence, 1926–1969*. Translated by Robert and Rita Kimber. New York: Harcourt Brace Jovanovich, 1993.

Milgram, Stanley. *The Individual in a Social World*. Reading, Mass.: Addison-Wesley, 1977.

Ogden, Maurice. *Hangman*. Tustin, Calif.: Media Masters, Inc., for Regina Publications, 3d ed., 1968.

Rosch, E. *Principles of Categorization*. In E. Rosch and B. L. Lloyd, eds., *Cognition and Categorization*. Hillsdale, N.J.: Erlbaum, 1978

CHAPTER 10

Teaching the Holocaust through Literature

MARSHA CAROW MARKMAN

Why teach the Holocaust through literature? It is clear to all of us who teach about the Holocaust that it is so singular, so catastrophic, so unimaginable an event, that the process of annihilating six million Jews cannot be visualized unless it is somehow personalized. Poetry, drama, fiction, biography, the unlikely comic strip, and especially the literature of individual experience (diaries, letters, memoirs) can help students to visualize the ghettos and concentration camps, the hiding places and hidden identities, the bystanders and perpetrators, the rescuers and those who resisted—and can do so in courses across the curriculum.

For students of history, English, psychology, sociology, philosophy, religion, and the sciences, Holocaust literature not only paints vivid pictures of countless personal experiences, but provides a plethora of perspectives from which to view this event: the firsthand, eyewitness testimonies of diaries and letters that transport readers to an historical moment as it occurs; the retrospective view of the memoirist, no longer insulated as diarists and letter writers often are; and the poetry, drama, fiction (and faction) that recreate the Holocaust experience. Holocaust literature, in addition, invites discussion and reflection about the historical moment and countless personal and social issues and dilemmas, including those of responsibility, guilt, and innocence and the extremes of human behavior—all of which can lead to understanding and, ultimately, peace.

From a wealth of Holocaust literature, come works written by survivors and victims from countries throughout Nazi-occupied Europe. Out of the broad landscape of Holocaust experience, their personal narratives focus on, and magnify, the personal experience, a factor which was reflected in the dialogue journal entry of one of my students: "It's not easy to think in terms of six million Jews suffering or dying," she wrote. "The number is so large, so distant. But in the books that we are reading I feel along with each one of them . . . it is personal."

IN THE BEGINNING

A study of the extermination of six million of Europe's Jewish community should begin with an autobiographical work which is both personal and from which the seeds of the Holocaust were planted. Hitler's *Mein Kampf,* published worldwide in 1924, is a frank espousal of views reflecting subsequent policies and actions in regard to Europe's Jewish community. Those views are important for students to recognize at the outset of a study of the Holocaust through its literature. For example, referring to Germany following World War I, Hitler made the following declaration:

> If we pass all the causes of the German collapse in review, the ultimate and most decisive remains the failure to recognize the racial problem and especially the Jewish menace.[1]

His solution to this "menace," he writes, is to *"set race at the center of all life . . . and take care to keep it pure."*[2] *"By mating again and again with other races,"* he adds, *"we may raise these races from their previous cultural level to a higher stage, but we will descend forever from our own high level."*[3]

Hitler states, furthermore, that he will accomplish his goals through Germany's youth: *"No boy and no girl,"* he writes, *"must leave school without having been led to an ultimate realization of the necessity and essence of blood purity."*[4] Children, he declares, must be educated to believe that they are "absolutely superior to others."[5] And to his theory, he boldly adds:

> I believe that I am acting in accordance with the will of the Almighty Creator: *by defending myself against the Jew, I am fighting for the work of the Lord.*[6] (Italics are Hitler's)

Students should be aware that Hitler's words, which became a template for his actions and for the philosophy and legislation adopted by the Third Reich, were widely read.

On January 30, 1933, fewer than ten years after *Mein Kampf* was published, the Jewish journalist and then member of Germany's wealthy diplomatic and aristocratic society Bella Fromm recorded in her diary:

> At 11:00 this morning, Hitler was appointed Chancellor of the Reich. It took him another ten minutes to form his cabinet. . . . It seems an ironic foreboding that the new Hitler cabinet should start off without a Minister of Justice.[7]

Fromm's diary is a record of government functions she attended early in Hitler's regime and a vivid picture of the rise of Nazism with its party rallies, the 1936 Olympic games, state dinners (including conversations with Hitler and members of the party elite) . . . and the mounting, legislated attacks on Germany's Jews. On February 14, 1938, just seven months before she fled Germany, she writes,

> Mounted S.S. and S.A. trot along the sidewalks, clattering their collection boxes. An S.S. man knocked down two children and did not even bother to dismount! There is no one in this country to call them to account.[8]

Indeed, the unbridled actions of the Nazis were repeated and redoubled in every country they conquered. And in those countries, men, women, and even children recorded their observations and reflections in diaries. Writing at great personal risk, their acts of resistance are the raw materials from which much of Holocaust history is constructed. This witness literature provides us with an immediate and intimate record of those personal observations, experiences, and thoughts that reflect the broad landscape of the Holocaust.

Several of those works are appropriate for students in high school and college. If I emphasize *diary* literature, it is because it takes students, however vicariously, on a journey with the writer that has no rival in literary genres or in the proximity to the Holocaust experience. That journey can begin with Nazi occupation.

In the Early Days of Nazi Occupation

The Diary of David Rubinowicz reveals much about the early days of Nazi-occupied Poland and reflects the plight of Jews throughout Europe. Dawid began his diary less than seven months after Germany invaded

Poland. He was twelve years old. His entries over the next two years record steady and increasingly severe sanctions against the Jews: forced labor, indiscriminate public beatings and murders, deportations, the wearing of the Star of David on clothing, ejection from schools, prohibition from theaters and parks, and finally evacuation to ghettos—a plight that would be shared by Jews throughout the occupied territories. On February 12, 1942, Dawid recorded an incident involving the hateful propaganda that was a daily assault:

> the village constable came up and began putting up a notice . . . a caricature of the Jews. On it a Jew is shown, mincing meat and putting a rat into the mincer. Another is pouring water from a bucket into milk. In the third picture a Jew is shown stamping dough with his feet, and worms are crawling over him and the dough. The heading of the notice reads: "The Jew is a Cheat, Your only Enemy," And the inscription ran as follows:
>
> Dear reader, before your very eyes,
> Are Jews deceiving you with lies.
> If you buy your milk from them, beware,
> Dirty water they've poured in there.
> Into the mincer dead rats they throw,
> Then as mincemeat it's put on show.
> Worms infest their home-made bread,
> Because the dough with feet they tread.
>
> When the village constable had put it up, some people came along, and their laughter gave me a headache from the shame that the Jews suffer nowadays. God give that this shame may soon cease.[9]

Dawid's diary ends on June 1, 1942, fewer than four months after this entry. It is believed that he and his family were deported to Treblinka death camp where they were murdered. But his diary, like so many others written in secret, is both a testimony and a legacy. Its immediacy makes it invaluable for students both as an historical document and one which illustrates and typifies this event.

Like Dawid, thirteen-year-old Eva Heyman, a Hungarian Jew, kept a diary in which she describes the unrelenting confiscation of Jewish property: "One day it's typewriters," she writes, "the next day carpets, and today . . . bed linens."[10] On April 7, 1944, she writes of another appropriation:

Today they came for my bicycle. I almost caused a big drama. . . . Now that it's all over, I'm so ashamed about how I behaved in front of the policemen. . . . I threw myself on the ground, held on to the back wheel of my bicycle, and shouted all sorts of things at the policemen: "Shame on you for taking away a bicycle from a girl! That's robbery! . . . One of the policemen was very annoyed and said: "All we need is for a Jewgirl to put on such a comedy when her bicycle is being taken away. No Jewkid is entitled to keep a bicycle anymore." . . . But you know, dear diary, I think the other policeman felt sorry for me. "You should be ashamed of yourself, colleague," he said. "Is your heart made of stone? How can you speak that way to such a beautiful girl?" Then he stroked my hair and promised to take good care of my bicycle. He gave me a receipt and told me not to cry, because when the war was over I would get my bicycle back.[11]

Eva Heyman did not survive the war. She was deported on June 2, 1944, three days after her final diary entry—first to the city's "ghetto-camp" and then to Auschwitz where she died in the gas chambers. Her story is yet another window into the lives of children affected by the Holocaust and the edicts and actions taken by the Nazis and their collaborators.

THE GHETTOS OF EUROPE

The ghettos of Europe are reflected in much of Holocaust literature, significant contributions to our knowledge coming from diaries of ghetto life. In the Warsaw ghetto, for example, both individual diarists and those working with the Oneg Shabbat, a group of scholars led by historian Emmanuel Ringelblum, joined in the pursuit to collect testimony in spite of the personal risk.

Ringelblum's diary, more a social history than a personal account as are so many Holocaust diaries, has a sense of urgency about it. The diary abounds with fragmented sentences and changing topics. Observations, reports, rumors, all with minimal commentary, combine to give the impression that time and paper are running out.

On November 19, 1940, three days after the Warsaw ghetto was established, Ringelblum recorded several incidents in which Jews were penalized for disobeying one of countless Nazi regulations:

those who are slow to take their hats off to Germans are forced to do calisthenics using paving stones or tiles as weights. Elderly Jews, too, are ordered to do push-ups. They [the Nazis] tear paper up small, scatter the pieces in the mud, and order people to pick them up, beating them as they stoop over.[12]

Scroll of Agony: The Warsaw Diary of Chaim A. Kaplan is another detailed account of ghetto life spanning the period from September 1, 1939 (when the Nazis conquered Poland), until August 4, 1942, shortly before Kaplan and his wife were transported to Treblinka. A teacher in a private Jewish school, Kaplan wrote in Hebrew in his diary, with allusions and references that give his writing a biblical flavor. His diary is for him a mission, an intellectual pursuit . . . and an "obligation" that he says he is "not free to relinquish."[13] He reports and reflects upon the propaganda films the Nazis make in the ghetto, the unrelenting typhus epidemic, the roundups and deportations, and the random murders in the ghetto streets. Every aspect of the endless and sadistic treatment of Warsaw's Jews are revealed in these and other ghetto diaries.

LIFE IN HIDING

Jews who saw the dangers of waiting out the war and were able to "go under" required a benefactor who would provide a hiding place and sustenance. For these Jews, life in confinement was filled with fear. Anne Frank's diary describes life in her hiding place in Amsterdam: "how oppressive it is never to be able to go outdoors," she writes, and tells her diary of her fear "that we shall be discovered and be shot."[14] But her diary is also filled with hope and with her faith in the goodness of people.

As we know, the Frank family was discovered and deported, and Anne died in Bergen Belsen concentration camp. Her diary, however, is a vivid record of a girl coming of age in the Holocaust. The dilemmas she faced in hiding are important for our students to examine.

The plight of Jews who fled the Nazis and roamed from town to town seeking shelter is reflected in Jerzy Kosinski's powerful novel *The Painted Bird*. The six-year-old protagonist, whose life closely parallels the author's, is sent to live in safety with foster parents and tells of the death of the foster mother and his subsequent odyssey through rural Poland.

The relentless parade of humiliation and maltreatment that he relates are as surreal and unimaginable as the Holocaust itself. Nameless and ultimately voiceless, with a heritage that is either Jewish or Gypsy, the child is a painted bird, different from the rest of the flock, a victim who becomes a victimizer. Students soon discover that the boy's repetitive and inconceivable suffering is a metaphor for brutality and a symbol of the Holocaust itself.

"Passing" as a Christian

The dilemma of passing as a Christian is revealed in Renee Roth-Hano's book *Touch Wood*. This memoir by a French Jew is the story of an eleven-year-old girl who was sent with her two younger sisters to live in a Normandy convent. In order for her to survive, she—and all Jews who passed as Christians—had to maintain the pretext of a Christian identity. It required that she learn the Catholic prayers and rituals and, in essence, lead a double life. She is "torn," she writes in the voice of the child she was, and doesn't know "which way to go." [15]

The fear of exposure and, at the same time, the guilt of survival while fellow Jews faced deportation and death, is evident in Roth-Hano's book and in works about Jews who "passed" as Christians.

Deportation and the Concentration Camp Universe

Deportation to the concentration camps of Europe is reflected in much of Holocaust literature. Etty Hillesum's diaries and her letters from Westerbork in Holland describe those deportations East. In a letter written to friends outside the camp, she writes:

> One night last week a transport of prisoners passed through here. Thin, waxen faces. I have never seen so much exhaustion and fatigue as I did that night. They were being "processed": registration, more registration, frisking by half-grown NSB men, quarantine, a foretaste of martyrdom lasting hours and hours. Early in the morning they were crammed into empty freight cars. Then another long wait while the train was boarded up. And then three days' travel eastwards. . . . How many, I wondered, would reach their destination alive? And my parents are preparing themselves for just such a journey. [16]

Etty Hillesum took that journey and lost her life. Her letters and diaries, however, are testimony to her struggle for life and the plight of so many other Dutch Jews.

In *Survival in Auschwitz,* Primo Levi describes his journey to Auschwitz and the interminable sentence meted out to prisoners who, like himself, were convicted of nothing more than being Jewish. He describes the ceaseless roll calls, the beatings and shootings, the sickness and starvation, the slave work force, and the smoke that rose endlessly from the crematoria. Students will see that, retrospectively, Levi has the benefit of time, hindsight, and knowledge from which to reflect and draw conclusions—perspectives limited in diaries and letters. Along with his other Holocaust books are his volumes of poems, which contribute to the wide range of Holocaust poetry.

Probably the most widely read Holocaust memoir is Elie Wiesel's *Night,* which describes his deportation, the upside-down, nightmare world of the concentration camps, and the long, lingering night of the Holocaust that has followed him, as it has other survivors, through his life. On the final page of his book, he describes his looking into the mirror for the first time shortly after liberation. "a corpse gazed back at me," he writes. "The look in his eyes, as they stared into mine, has never left me." [17]

The endless night that Wiesel describes is evident too in Isabella Leitner's slim volume, *Fragments of Isabella.* Like Wiesel, Leitner, a Hungarian Jew, struggles to survive alongside a close family member. And through her memoir, we see the concentration camp as producing a new culture, with its own organization and rituals. Like Wiesel, Leitner survives the Holocaust only to discover that her life is in fragments. "I am condemned to walk the earth for all my days," she writes, "with the stench of burning flesh in my nostrils," [18] a feeling shared by other camp survivors, and in many ways passed on to their children.

THE GENERATION AFTER

Works that reflect the children of survivors abound and should be read by our students, for they portray the effects of this event over the generations. Art Spiegelman's nontraditional books, *Maus* and *Maus II* are as much Holocaust biographies as they are memoirs. Written and illustrated in comic-book form, with Jews depicted as mice and Nazis as cats, *Maus* is anything but comic. Its black and white illustrations do much to tell the story that words alone do not convey. Nontraditional as its format is, it contains a powerful example of the Holocaust's effect on the generation after.

BYSTANDERS AND PERPETRATORS

Rolf Hochhuth's drama, *The Deputy,* is a searing attack on Pope Pius XII whom Hochhuth accuses of dereliction of duty. Through his characters, the author asks provocative questions about the church's responsibility, providing an important work by which students can explore the issues of action and inaction.

A work by an infamous perpetrator is the diary of Joseph Goebbels, whose entries testify to his virulent anti-Semitism and the role he played in the persecution and annihilation of millions of Europe's Jews with what he describes as "cold ruthlessness" and a lack of "squeamish sentimentalism."[19] His comments on March 7, 1942, are reiterated throughout the diary: "There can be no peace in Europe until the last Jews are eliminated from the continent."[20]

THE RESCUERS

A vast number of books reveal the heroic deeds of people who rescued Jews—hiding them and helping them escape to safety. These works reflect the generosity of people throughout Nazi-occupied Europe. A few examples are *The Hiding Place,* a memoir by Corrie ten Boom, a Dutch Christian who hid Jews in her home and helped them to find hiding places throughout Holland; *Schindler's List,* a biography by Thomas Keneally about Oscar Schindler, a German industrialist in whose factory-camp he rescued hundreds of Jews; and the several biographies such as those by Linnea and Werbell about Raoul Wallenberg, the Swedish diplomat who saved the lives of 30,000 Jews by issuing them Swedish passports.

These and many other accounts of heroism enable students to consider the valiant efforts of humanitarians and the dilemmas faced by those who, at great personal risk, resisted Nazi rule.

Holocaust literature is replete with works that represent every phase in the process of exterminating Europe's Jews. Each story reflects the many untold stories that this event has produced; each is an image of that which cannot be fully imagined; and each is a memorial to those who perished and a tribute both to those who survived and those who jeopardized their lives for that survival. But most importantly, each of these literary works can bring students closer to knowledge, compassion, and ultimately a world of peace. For it is peace which is our ultimate goal in teaching about the Holocaust. The poet Aaron Schmuller speaks to that peace in his poem, "Peace Now," in which he writes that "The standard-bearer of all life on earth/The breathless harbinger of tidings brought/To generations yet unborn—the true/Redeemer of all races and all creeds" is peace. Schmuller reminds us in the last lines of his poem: *"The word is peace,/the word is peace,/the Word."* [21]

Through its myriad genres and the events and experiences it vivdly portrays, Holocaust literature can recreate for our students one of the most calamitous events in history. It can also provide the kinds of insight which can lead to a world of understanding and peace.

NOTES

1. Adolf Hitler, *Mein Kampf,* translated by Ralph Manheim (Boston: Houghton Mifflin, 1971), 327. Italics throughout are Hitler's.

2. Hitler, 403.

3. Hitler, 428.

4. Hitler, 427.

5. Hitler, 411.

6. Hitler, 65.

7. Bella Fromm, *Blood and Banquets: A Berlin Social Diary* (New York: Carol Publishing Group, 1990), 75–76. Originally published by Harper and Brothers, 1942.

8. Fromm, 266.

9. Dawid Rubinowicz. *The Diary of David Rubinowicz,* translated by Derek Bowman (Edmonds, Wash.: Creative Options, 1982), 43. This book is currently out of print.

10. Eva Heyman, *The Diary of Eva Heyman* (New York: Shapolsky, 1988), 65. This book is currently out of print, although manuscript copies may be purchased from the publisher.

11. Heyman, 72–73.

12. Emmanuel Ringelblum, *Notes from the Warsaw Ghetto: The Journal of Emmanuel Ringelblum,* edited and translated by Jacob Sloan (New York:

Schocken, 1974), 86. See the current reprint, translated by Danuta Dabrowski and edited by Shmuel Krakowski with an introduction by Yehuda Bauer (Northwestern University Press, 1992).

13. Chaim A. Kaplan, *Scroll of Agony: The Warsaw Diary of Chaim A. Kaplan,* translated and edited by Abraham I. Katsh (New York: Collier, 1973), 104.

14. Anne Frank, *The Diary of a Young Girl* (New York: Pocket, 1953), 19. See also Anne Frank's *Tales from the Secret Annex,* stories she wrote while in hiding (New York: Doubleday, 1983). Also of interest are *Anne Frank: Beyond the Diary, a Photographic Remembrance* (New York: Viking, 1993) by Ruud van der Rol and Rian Verhoeven; and *Anne Frank Remembered: The Story of the Woman Who Helped to Hide the Frank Family* (New York: Simon and Schuster, 1987) by Miep Gies.

15. Renee Roth-Hano, *Touch Wood: A Girlhood in Occupied France* (New York: Puffin, 1989), 161. Another book that reflects a girl in hiding and "passing" is Nechama Tec's autobiography, *Dry Tears: The Story of a Lost Childhood* (New York: Oxford University Press, 1984).

16. Etty Hillesum, *Etty Hillesum: Letters from Westerbork,* translated by Arnold J. Pomerans (New York: Pantheon, 1986), 76–77. Hillesum's diary, *Interrupted Life* (New York: Pocket Books, 1991), is another good source for her experiences.

17. Elie Wiesel, *Night* (New York: Bantam, 1982), 109.

18. Isabella Leitner, *Fragments of Isabella: A Memoir of Auschwitz* (New York: Dell, 1978), 102. A more recent edition of this book, which includes her later experiences, is *Isabella: From Auschwitz to Freedom* (New York: Doubleday and Company, 1994). For younger readers (grades 4–7) is Leitner's *The Big Lie: A True Story* (New York: Scholastic, 1994).

19. Joseph Goebbels, *The Goebbels Diaries, 1942–1943,* translated and edited by Louis P. Lochner (New York: Doubleday, 1948), 86; reprinted by Greenwood Press, 1970. See also *Final Entries, 1945: The Diaries of Joseph Goebbels* (New York: G. P. Putnam's Sons, 1978).

20. Goebbels (1948), 116.

21. Aaron Schmuller, *While Man Exists: A Collection of Poems and Translations from the Yiddish by Aaron Schmuller* (New York: Parthenon, 1970), 10.

REFERENCES

Frank, Anne. *The Diary of a Young Girl.* New York: Pocket, 1953.
Fromm, Bella. *Blood and Banquets: A Berlin Social Diary.* 1942; rpt. New York: Carol Publishing Group, 1990.

Goebbels, Joseph. *The Goebbels Diaries, 1942–1943*. Translated and Edited by Louis P. Lochner. New York: Doubleday, 1948.

Heyman, Eva. *The Diary of Eva Heyman*. Introduction and Notes by Judah Marton. New York: Shapolsky, 1988.

Hillesum, Etty. *Etty Hillesum: Letters from Westerbork*. Introduction and Notes by Jan G. Gaarlandt. Translated by Arnold J. Pomerans. New York: Pantheon, 1986.

Hitler, Adolf. *Mein Kampf*. Translated by Ralph Manheim. Boston: Houghton Mifflin, 1971.

Hochhuth, Rolf. *The Deputy*. New York: Grove Press, 1978.

Kaplan, Chaim A. *Scroll of Agony: The Warsaw Diary of Chaim A. Kaplan*. Translated and edited by Abraham I. Katsh. New York: Collier, 1973.

Keneally, Thomas. *Schindler's List*. New York: Simon and Schuster, 1993.

Kosinski, Jerzy. *The Painted Bird*. New York: Bantam Books, 1981.

Leitner, Isabella. *Fragments of Isabella: A Memoir of Auschwitz*. New York: Dell, 1978.

Levi, Primo. *Survival in Auschwitz: The Nazi Assault on Humanity*. New York: Collier, 1959.

Linnea, Sharon. *Raoul Wallenberg: The Man Who Stopped Death*. Philadelphia: Jewish Publication Society, 1993.

Ringelblum, Emmanuel. *Notes from the Warsaw Ghetto: The Journal of Emmanuel Ringelblum*. Edited and Translated by Jacob Sloan. New York: Schocken, 1974.

Roth-Hano, Renee. *Touch Wood: A Girlhood in Occupied France*. New York: Puffin, 1989.

Rubinowicz, Dawid. *The Diary of David Rubinowicz*. Translated by Derek Bowman. Edmonds, Wash.: *Creative Options*, 1982.

Schmuller, Aaron. *While Man Exists: A Collection of Poems and Translations from the Yiddish by Aaron Schmuller*. New York: Parthenon, 1970.

Spiegelman, Art. *Maus: A Survivor's Tale*. New York: Pantheon, 1986.

———. *Maus II: A Survivor's Tale: And Here My Troubles Began*. New York: Pantheon Books, 1991.

ten Boom, Corrie. *The Hiding Place*. New York: Bantam, 1971.

Werbell, Frederick E. *Lost Hero*. New York: McGraw Hill, 1982.

Wiesel, Elie. *Night*. New York: Bantam, 1982.

CHAPTER 11

Witness to the Holocaust:

History from a First-Hand Perspective

SARA LEUCHTER WILKINS

The magnitude of the Holocaust—the annihilation of some six million Jews and four million others—is beyond the comprehension of most of us. It is difficult indeed to grasp the meaning of such enormous numbers. One tends to become detached, void of any kind of personal connection with six million, or ten million, of anything. In the case of the Holocaust, especially, identification with the victims as individuals becomes a virtual impossibility. For students, this is certainly the case. And it is compounded by textbooks and photographs about the Holocaust, which often fail to convey the individual, personalized experiences of the victims—presenting the event instead in the aggregate.

I have learned that helping my audience identify with the victims on a personal level is key to ensuring interest, empathy, and enthusiasm for learning. My classes at Marshall University, therefore, are structured not only to introduce the students to the Jewish victims as a whole, but also to introduce them to certain Jews in particular with whom they can make a personal connection.

In my classes, which I call "Witness to the Holocaust: History from a First-Hand Perspective," I supplement lectures with first-hand tape-recorded interviews I have conducted with survivors, and by showing documentary films.[1] The poignancy and vivid details of these tapes and films have more impact than anything the students could read or I could teach them. The tapes, especially, provide an immediate, indelible, and unique link with my students and history as it really happened—to people with names, voices, families, and emotions.

My class is presented in a mostly chronological manner, tracing the historical roots of anti-Semitism from Biblical times through the early Christian theologians, the Middle Ages, the Reformation, the Enlightenment, nineteenth-century European nationalism, and early Nazi doctrine. I then discuss Germany during the 1920s, the rise of Hitler and his ascendence to power, the Nuremberg Laws, and the worsening situation for Jews in Germany in the late 1930s. I move to the invasion of Poland, the creation of the ghettoes, life in the ghettoes, the invasion of France and the Low Countries, the invasion of Russia, the fate of the Jews in the eastern province, the Jews of Italy and Greece, and the Final Solution. I conclude with the last years of the Holocaust, the fate of the Jews of Hungary, life in the concentration camps, and resistance and rescue.

One of the first tasks I assign my students is to learn the prewar map of Europe (including national capitals), and I quiz them on this each week until I am satisfied they have mastered the geography of the region. I find that this helps the students to make a greater connection with the victims and to better understand the enormity of the Nazi undertaking in a geographical sense.

During the semester, the class meets once a week for two and one-half hours each. The first two weeks are entirely lecture, but during the third week, when I discuss the Jews of Germany from 1933–1939, I play my first tape. Before I begin each tape, I introduce the class to the survivor they will be hearing by giving them a brief biography of his or her life: where they were born, where they grew up, what happened to them during the war, what happened to them immediately after the war, and where they were and what they were doing at the time the interview was conducted. In addition, I pass around the class a copy of *Guide to Wisconsin Survivors of the Holocaust,* which includes a photograph of each of the survivors who were interviewed. In this manner, the students can see that these are indeed real people, whose experiences are etched indelibly on their faces.

On this first tape, for the better part of a half-hour, the German survivor, Fred Platner, speaks eloquently about his childhood years in prewar Germany, about his growing isolation, and the loss of friends who must chose between him and their allegiance to the Nazi Party.[2] Even after all these years, Platner's voice chokes with grief as he recalls the pain he felt upon separation from his friends, and his inability to grasp what was happening to him. "I could not understand why the children who had been my friends now would not talk to me," Platner remembers. "My best friends suddenly joined the Hitler Youth and tried to physically attack me," he continues. While Platner's accent is somewhat difficult to master, his message is riveting, and this provides a good introduction to the students about what will follow.

The next week, I lecture on the prelude to war and the siege of Poland, and I play a half-hour tape of Rosa Katz, a survivor of the Lodz ghetto, who discusses her childhood and teenage years as a "second-class citizen" in Christian Poland.[3] She talks about her extended family, her father's business, the richness of their religious and cultural life in Lodz, and the growing anti-Semitism she encountered in the mid- to late-1930s. One of Mrs. Katz's greatest strengths is the softness of her voice, her unquestionable enthusiasm for life, and her ability to "tell it like it is." I always see a strong connection with my students and Mrs. Katz as the interview progresses—how they nod in agreement and laugh at her jokes.

The next week is devoted entirely to life in the ghetto. Mrs. Katz's tapes are used again in this class, because she remained in the Lodz Ghetto until its final liquidation in August of 1944. This interview takes a much more serious bent, and provides the students with their first descriptions of the horror that was life in the ghetto. Mrs. Katz keeps the students mesmerized as she describes the "walking dead," the constant fear of being deported, and the agony of starvation and disease.

"One day, somebody spilled some soup on the street," Mrs. Katz remembers. "Everybody who walked by it said, 'Oh, look at that soup on the street.' They all made a big fuss about it. But nearby a person could be lying dead, covered with flies, and no one would pay attention," she says.[4]

The following week, I show the documentary film *Lodz Ghetto,* which introduces the students to actual photographs and unpublished manuscripts of life in the ghetto. It leaves them shaken, as one can well imagine, and I am already able to discern a difference about them—a disbelief and a revulsion that this event happened to people with whom they are now identifying.

The next week, I discuss the invasion of France and the Low Countries. I supplement my lecture with a riveting forty-five minutes of interview with a Dutch survivor, Herb DeLevie, who as a boy spent four and one-half years hiding in a single room of a Dutch farmhouse on the German border with twelve other people.[5] He describes the continual overwhelming fear of discovery, the excruciating boredom of being trapped "in a cage like a wild animal," the lack of privacy, and the mental and physical deterioration of everyone around him. Since most of the class is familiar with the story of Anne Frank, the DeLevie interview provides reinforcement of this particular type of Holocaust experience.

Following a mid-term exam and a brief lecture on the invasion of Russia, I then move on to the Jews in the eastern province and introduce the notion of the Final Solution. I am fortunate at this juncture to share an interview with Lucy Baras.[6] Mrs. Baras lived in eastern Poland, under Russian control, until the German invasion in June 1941. At that time, her little village was ghettoized and reduced by numerous *aktions,* and Mrs. Baras fled into the forest and survived with the help of the partisans. Mrs. Baras is a bright and articulate woman; she vividly describes hiding in the family's underground bunker during the *aktions* and listening to the screams and wails of her neighbors as they are dragged off by the Nazis. She takes particular delight in describing how her family was able to fool the Nazis by disguising the route to their underground bunker as an outdoor privy.

The next week, I present the last years of the Holocaust and the fate of the Jews of Hungary. For this lecture I use an extraordinary tape with a Hungarian survivor of Auschwitz, Magda Herzberger, who was separated from her family upon her arrival at the concentration camp at the age of seventeen. Mrs. Herzberger, in chilling detail, recounts her first hours at Auschwitz as she wanders around in a dream, naked and confused. We learn of her horror as her long braid is chopped off; we share her humiliation as the SS guards watch her try to cover her naked body; we agonize with her as she debates whether or not to touch the electrified barbed wire fence:

> When we finally got to Auschwitz and they threw open the doors of those cattle wagons, we could see great flames belching from the chimneys. People were running around screaming, families were being separated. The Nazis were beating us with little rubber sticks and yelling at us to get out from the wagons. . . . All of a sudden, I was separated from my mother and I was marched into the undressing room. There, they forced us to undress, still hitting us with those little rubber sticks. I was 17 years old; no one, except my

mother, had ever seen me naked before. But now I had to get totally undressed in front of an SS guard, who was laughing and joking with his girlfriend, an SS woman. Can you imagine my humiliation? I was totally naked, and they were laughing and making jokes. . . . I heard a cutting sound and I looked behind me and there was my beautiful braid, just lying there in one piece on the floor.[7]

The next week, I spend a full class session on life in the concentration camp. Having previously assigned Terence Des Pres's *The Survivor,* we discuss a number of the issues raised in the book. In addition, I play an interview with Walter Peltz, a native of Warsaw who survived for almost five years in a number of concentration camps including Majdanek and Auschwitz.[8] Peltz, another survivor who spares no details when describing his experiences, shares the futility of his years in slave labor, the resourcefulness of the "professional survivor" who learns how to play the system, and the pain and discouragement of believing that God has abandoned the Jews to this most catastrophic of fates.

The following week, I discuss resistance and rescue, and I ask the students what they think they would have done if they had been given the chance to save Jewish lives. It's remarkable how strongly they are now connected with the victims. I also show the film *Avenue of the Just,* which recounts the rescue of Jews by a number of different righteous Gentiles.

If I have the time, I also show the documentary film *Witness to the Holocaust,* an excellent six-part encapsulation of the Holocaust produced by the CLAL, the National Jewish Learning and Resource Center. The semester concludes with at least two full weeks of segments from Claude Lanzmann's landmark documentary film, *SHOAH.* Here, the students are introduced to the perpetrators as well, and are afforded a glimpse into the psyches of these evil men who were "just doing their jobs."

I also assign a final project. On the first day of class, I ask the students to count from one to four, then assign a country to each student—either Germany, Poland, Holland, or Hungary—depending on the number each student was assigned. This particular country becomes the student's "country of origin," because for the final project, each student must write a first-hand account of what happened to him or her during the Holocaust, as if he or she had experienced it personally as a Jewish native of that assigned country. These first-hand accounts can be in the form of a fragmented diary, letters, memoirs, or even poems. The historical details must be accurate, but otherwise the students can write about any experience they wish. The writer need not have survived the war, but could have written the account sometime during the Holocaust period, only to have it discovered after his or her death.

This exercise has a profound impact on my students, forcing them, in effect, to exchange their safe and comfortable lives of today with the horrors of the past. These first-hand accounts are filled with warmth, depth, emotion, and pain, and I know my students will now be able to find the strength to stand up to what they know to be wrong, to challenge hatred and bigotry.

I am convinced that my overall approach to teaching about the Holocaust, through the use of first-hand documentation in the form of interviews, photographs, and films, allows students to develop a personal and intense connection to this tragic event. They cannot help but wonder what would have happened to them, to their families, to their friends. They recognize the need to speak out against evil and oppression, and they find the strength within themselves to champion the cause of justice.

Notes

1. While employed as an archivist with the State Historical Society of Wisconsin during the 1980s, I co-conducted a two-year oral history and photographic documentation project with survivors of the Holocaust who had resettled in Wisconsin after the war. More than one hundred sixty hours of interview and greater than sixteen hundred photographs of the survivors in their prewar, immediate postwar, and contemporary environs were collected during this project—all of which became a part of the permanent collection at the State Historical Society and therefore available to the public. I also wrote and edited a guide to the collection for the Historical Society, entitled *Guide to Wisconsin Survivors of the Holocaust,* which helps ensure that the tapes and photographs are more accessible to researchers and the general public alike. It is these tapes which I use as first-hand documentation in my classes. At the State Historical Society of Wisconsin, our philosophy about oral history was that the tapes themselves were the historical documents. We wanted people to listen to the actual tape-recorded interviews. So, instead of creating word-for-word typed transcriptions of each interview (which leads one to read the transcript rather than to listen to the tape), we created abstracts—brief paragraphs synopsizing the interview—which

encouraged researchers to listen to the tapes themselves to achieve the fullest impact of the testimony. We believed that a person's voice and emotions are an important part of the story, and that the interviews should be listened to and savored—not merely read as a written piece. *The Guide,* the one hundred sixty hours of tape, and the photographs are available by writing to: Wisconsin Survivors of the Holocaust Oral History Project, State Historical Society of Wisconsin, 816 State Street, Madison, WI 53706, or by calling (608) 264–6400.

While I personally collected the films from a number of sources, university and/or local libraries should have access to them through interlibrary loan programs. The library's reference desk can also help you find sources from which you can rent the films. Ergo Media, P.O. Box 2937, Teaneck, NJ 07666 (201) 692–0404, is an excellent source of Holocaust films, but does not carry the ones I used.

2. The interview with Fred Platner was conducted in Wausau, Wisconsin, by Jean Loeb Lettofsky on October 1, 2, and 22, 1980. In class, I play tape 3, side 1.

3. My interview with Rosa Katz was conducted in Oshkosh, Wisconsin, on October 28–29, 1980. In class, I play tape 2, sides 1 and 2.

4. This section is from Rosa Katz, tape 2, side 2.

5. My interview with Herb DeLevie was conducted in Madison, Wisconsin, on March 11, 13, and 20, 1980. In class, I play tape 3, sides 1 and 2.

6. My interview with Lucy Baras was conducted in Sheboygan, Wisconsin, on November 12–13, 1980. In class, I play tape 3, side 2.

7. My interview with Magda Herzberger was conducted in Dubuque, Iowa, on July 21–22 and August 27, 1980. This section is from tape 3, side 2.

8. My interview with Walter Peltz was conducted in Milwaukee, Wisconsin, on February 26–27 and March 1, 1980. In class, I play tape 4, side 1.

CHAPTER 12

Teaching about International Responses to News of the Holocaust: The *Columbus Dispatch* Project at Ohio State University

RAFAEL MEDOFF

Recent scholarship has unearthed a wealth of new information concerning how the international community responded to news of the Holocaust. In addition to studies of the responses of the Allied governments and Jewish communities in the Free World, important work has been done on American media coverage of the Holocaust. The role of the media is a topic that can provide an important avenue for teachers to help their students comprehend the variety of complex moral questions surrounding international reaction to Nazi atrocities.

Through the lens of the major American newspapers, one may begin to grasp the broader context in which international responses to the Holocaust must be viewed. Examining press coverage offers a glimpse at the crucial question of how much was really known about what was happening to Europe's Jews. In addition to confronting the obvious question of whether or not the U.S. press responded appropriately to the news of Nazi genocide, students may also grapple with the equally important issue of whether America's response to Holocaust news was commensurate with the amount and quality of the information available about the annihilation of the Jews.

Incorporating these issues into Holocaust curricula has become especially important in light of recent studies which have found that many high school and college-level history textbooks leave the impression that Americans had no idea what was happening to the Jews during the Holocaust years. A comprehensive analysis by Glenn S. Pate, which was published in 1987, found that of sixty-five leading high school-level

American history textbooks, only two acknowledge that news of the Holocaust did reach the United States. Pate's study of twenty-eight high school-level world history textbooks revealed that all but two "give the impression that no one knew of the extermination camps until the Allied armies found them."

Pate's findings at the university level were similar. He examined twenty-eight textbooks that are routinely assigned in college-level history, political science, and sociology courses covering the years that the Holocaust took place. He concluded that with only a few exceptions, the books are "woefully inadequate" in their treatment of the entire range of Holocaust issues, including the issue of American awareness of the events in Europe.[1] There is, therefore, reason for concern that many college students, having learned about the Holocaust largely through such textbooks, may share in the popular misconception that Americans were unaware of the Holocaust and therefore unable to alter the course of events.

This was one of the reasons I deemed it appropriate to assign the students in my Holocaust course at the Ohio State University, in 1991–1992, to undertake a team research project concerning how their local daily newspaper, the *Columbus Dispatch,* covered a number of major events related to the Holocaust. The project was intended to provide a framework for teacher-student discussions about issues such as: the ethical obligations of the press; the interaction between public opinion, media coverage, and governmental policy; and the array of American societal factors that helped shape America's response to the Holocaust.

A project of this nature is most likely to be successful with a relatively small group of students, preferably those who have had at least limited experience in the use of microfilms and possess other basic research skills. The small size of the class involved in the project at the Ohio State University facilitated interaction between myself and the students as they did their research.

For background information, context, and general guidance on the issues raised by the research, my students consulted selections from *Beyond Belief: The American Press and the Coming of the Holocaust,* by Deborah E. Lipstadt (1986).[2] Lipstadt documented the manner in which the American press covered the Nazi persecution of the Jews. She showed how major newspapers and wire services downplayed news about the Holocaust, universalized the identity of the victims by blurring the fact that they were Jews, and in some cases even displayed a certain amount of understanding for the behavior of the Nazis. The Ohio State University students read selections from *Beyond Belief* prior to looking at the microfilm copies of the *Columbus Dispatch,* to give them an idea of what to expect, and to help alert them to ways in which the *Dispatch* might have differed from other major newspapers in Holocaust coverage.

In order to keep the subject matter to a manageable size, nine major events of the Nazi period were singled out for study. Each of the students was assigned to analyze specific aspects of the *Dispatch*'s coverage of those events, including news coverage, editorials, political cartoons, and letters to the editor. What they discovered was that many of the same tendencies which Lipstadt found elsewhere in the U.S. press were echoed in the pages of the *Columbus Dispatch*.

For example, the *Dispatch* responded to Hitler's rise to power in 1933 with the same sort of naive optimism that was characteristic of much of the American press. A *Dispatch* editorial defended the selection of Hitler as chancellor on the grounds that Hitlerism was already "ebbing" and would "recede more rapidly" now that the Fuehrer would have the opportunity to fall from the highest office.[3] The notion that Hitler was not necessarily a serious danger was echoed in an editorial cartoon which depicted Hitler as an enigma who was equally likely to opt for democracy, communism, or totalitarianism.[4] Even many years later, the editors of the *Dispatch* still seemed to approach Hitler in a rather flippant manner: indulging in a bit of amateur psychology, one *Dispatch* editorial in 1943 theorized that Hitler was able to devise his racial theories only because his years as a painter had provided him with too much time to think while he was working.[5]

The *Dispatch* did provide adequate news coverage of some of the subsequent events related to the Nazis' persecution of the Jews, the students found. For example, the Kristallnacht pogrom and its aftermath made the front page of the *Dispatch* on seven separate days in early November 1938,[6] and the tragic journey of the *S.S. St. Louis* (the boatload of Jewish refugees that Roosevelt refused to let land in Miami) was front page news three times in June 1939.[7] Yet at the same time, other news stories related to the plight of Europe's Jews were ignored by the *Dispatch*. For example, the Evian refugee conference in 1938, and the Congressional hearings in 1939 over the Wagner-Rogers bill (legislation that would have allowed 20,000 refugee children to enter the United States), both of which were covered by other leading newspapers, were not covered at all by the *Dispatch*.

The most troubling aspects of the *Dispatch*'s coverage during the 1930s were its repeated attempts to "explain" Hitler's persecution of the Jews as being somehow less grave than it appeared to be. In the summer of 1938, and again that autumn, editorials in the *Dispatch* claimed that Hitler's persecution of the Jews was "not so much ideological in motive as it is a 'purge' dictated by sheer economic and political necessity." According to the editors of the *Dispatch,* the Nazis were not so much haters of Jews as they were merely desirous of "their property and their money." [8] The editors of the *Dispatch* apparently had not considered that if their theory were correct, the Nazis would have limited their attacks to wealthy Jews, instead of attacking all Jews, rich or poor.

One wonders if the editors' attitude may be explained in part by their erroneous assumption that virtually all German Jews were wealthy. A 1933 *Dispatch* editorial rationalized German anti-Semitism as simply targeting "the large Jewish element in the financial, commercial, professional and official life of present-day Germany." [9]

In *Beyond Belief,* Lipstadt cited numerous examples of how newspapers confined Jewish suffering to the back pages while highlighting the suffering of non-Jewish Europeans. My students found a graphic example of this in the *Dispatch* as well. On November 24, 1942, the *Dispatch* reported that the Nazis had murdered 250,000 Polish Jews in September of that year, and were planning to murder many times that number in the months to come. The story was allotted just six paragraphs and relegated to page 13 of the *Dispatch,* alongside the City News Briefs. Yet the news that the Nazis were charging Dutch citizens high prices for exit permits was given fifteen paragraphs on page 6 of that same day's *Dispatch.*[10]

One of the purposes of this research project was to provide the students with a framework for understanding the broader context in which America's response to the Holocaust took place. In our classroom discussions, I tried to help the students understand that the *Dispatch*'s coverage did not take place in a vacuum. Both the *Dispatch*'s response to the Holocaust, and the American public's response to the Holocaust— which the *Dispatch* helped shape—were influenced by what was happening in the United States during the 1930s and 1940s. Skepticism about the reliability of atrocity reports, isolationist attitudes regarding the conflict in Europe, the public's preoccupation with local issues, and the competition for news space during wartime, all affected America's response, and the American media's response, to news of the Holocaust.

BELIEVABILITY

The skepticism with which both the American media and the American public greeted some of the earliest reports of Nazi persecution was rooted in their experience during the World War I. Many newspaper reports about German atrocities in Belgium during World War I later turned out to be false. As a result, both newspaper editors and newspaper readers were not always ready to believe the reports about what the Germans were doing to the Jews. Not surprisingly, more than a few Americans suspected that stories about Germans using gas chambers to kill millions of people were no more reliable than stories about German cannibalism in Belgium twenty-five years earlier. I also discussed with the students how the reports about the Nazi mass murders differed in quantity and quality from the atrocity stories of World War I; how the Nazi atrocities were verified by the Allied leaders as early as 1942; and why the initial skepticism of many Americans became an increasingly unreasonable approach as the Holocaust continued.

ISOLATIONISM

The editorial stance of the *Dispatch* was strongly isolationist prior to the war, a position which the editors described, correctly, as a view shared by "the masses of the plain people, particularly in the Middle West."[11] Isolationism played an important role in shaping the attitude of both the *Dispatch* and its readers toward Hitler and the plight of Europe's Jews. Strongly committed to the idea that events in Europe were none of America's business, the *Dispatch* repeatedly chided the Roosevelt administration for getting the United States involved in Europe's problems. Roosevelt was denounced for "speaking too harshly" about Hitler and for unfairly attributing "villainous motives" to the Fuehrer.[12] The *Dispatch* sometimes carried its isolationism to such an extreme that it almost seemed to be defending the Nazi regime. In one editorial in 1939, it argued that the Soviet Union was "a bloodier dictatorship" than Hitler's Germany.[13] On another occasion, a *Dispatch* editorial contended that Germany's characterization of the post-World War I Versailles treaty as an act of aggression against it, was just as valid as the claim by Britain and France that the German dismemberment of Czechoslovakia was an act of aggression.[14] Not all Americans embraced such an extreme view, but public opinion surveys during the 1930s did find that the overwhelming majority of Americans were staunchly opposed to any kind of U.S. intervention in Europe's affairs. Whatever humanitarian sympathy for European Jewry many Americans felt, it was not sufficient to persuade them to risk a conflict between their country and Germany.

APATHY

Typical residents of Columbus, Ohio, like most Americans, were primarily interested in local issues, or in the nationwide Depression (during the 1930s), or in the war effort (during the 1940s). The news and editorials of the *Dispatch* catered to the views of its readers, featuring the issues which interested them most. The letters-to-the-editor column of the *Dispatch* vividly illustrated the public disinterest in the fate of the Jews. The students who searched through the *Dispatch*'s letters columns for letters related to the plight of the Jews found themselves searching for a needle in a haystack. After combing through more than four hundred letters that were published in the weeks immediately following instances of Nazi brutality, they found just two letters about the plight of European refugees—and neither of those two mentioned Jewish refugees.[15] The subjects that letter-writers typically addressed provided a good indication of the public mood. They wrote about the lack of parking spaces in downtown Columbus, the success of the Ohio State University football team, and the dilemma of disposing of empty cough syrup bottles, among other issues.[16] Surveying the *Dispatch*'s letters column is not a scientific method of measuring public opinion, but it certainly sheds some light on the public mood in central Ohio during the period under discussion.

PREOCCUPATION WITH THE WAR EFFORT

I urged the students to keep in mind that once America entered the war, both the public and the *Dispatch* editors understandably focused the bulk of their attention and concern on the war effort. There was fierce competition for news space following Pearl Harbor. Reports from the battlefront naturally dominated the limited space that the *Dispatch* allotted for international news—just as they occupied the hearts and minds of average Americans. There was little space left for the plight of Jews in Poland.

At the same time, however, competition for news space does not adequately explain why the editors of the *Dispatch* chose to confine the news about the annihilation of Polish Jewry to just six paragraphs on page 13 of its November 24, 1942, edition, while awarding a much larger amount of news space, on page 6, to the Nazis' price-gouging in Holland. Once the editorial decision had been made to devote enough space for two stories about Nazi misdeeds on November 24, why spotlight high prices in Holland and downplay the high death toll in Poland?

This is just one of the many Holocaust-related questions that cannot be answered easily. We cannot easily understand what could impel an ordinary person to take part in the most heinous of atrocities. Nor, conversely, can we comprehend how other, equally ordinary, people, mustered the superhuman courage to resist their oppressors. We are likewise puzzled at the fact that so many of the victims apparently did not resist. For my students, one troubling mystery was why the *Dispatch* downplayed news about the mass murder of Jews, in comparison to its coverage of the difficulties experienced by Dutch refugees. The students likewise had difficulty understanding how it was that not a single letter-writer in the *Dispatch* expressed concern about the Nazi genocide during the periods they examined.

Were these phenomena evidence of a fundamental indifference to Jewish suffering, in the media and among the public at large? Is such indifference rooted in centuries of ingrained prejudice against Jews, that is, anti-Semitism? Questions such as these offer additional opportunities for discussion and debate, as we explore how to most effectively teach about international responses to the Holocaust.

NOTES

1. Glenn S. Pate, "Part III: The United States of America," in Randolph L. Braham, ed., *The Treatment of the Holocaust in Textbooks: The Federal Republic of Germany, Israel, the United States of America* (Boulder, Colo.: Social Science Monographs and Institute for Holocaust Studies of the City University of New York, 1987).

2. Deborah E. Lipstadt, *Beyond Belief: The American Press and the Coming of the Holocaust, 1933–1945* (New York: The Free Press, 1986).

3. *Columbus Dispatch* [hereafter CD], "Giving Hitler Plenty of Rope," February 2, 1933. Regarding how other newspapers reported Hitler's rise to power, see Margaret K. Norden, "American Editorial Response to the Rise of Adolf Hitler: A Preliminary Consideration," *American Jewish Historical Quarterly* (October 1968): 290–301.

4. CD, February 4, 1933.

5. CD, April 28, 1943.

6. CD, November 12, 13, 15, 16, 18, and 20, 1938.

7. CD, June 3, 4, and 6, 1939.

8. CD, June 24 and November 23, 1938.

9. CD, April 16, 1933.

10. "Himmler Reportedly Orders Half of Polish Jews Murdered," CD, November 24, 1942; "Dutch Charge Nazis with Extorting Large Sums from Refugees," CD, November 24, 1942.

11. CD, September 11, 1941.

12. CD, April 27 and April 17, 1939.

13. CD, April 27, 1939.

14. CD, April 19, 1939.

15. CD, November 11, 1938; June 2, 1942.

16. CD, November 22 and 15, 1938, and December 14, 1943.

REFERENCES

Laqueur, Walter. *The Terrible Secret: Suppression of the Truth About Hitler's "Final Solution."* Boston: Little, Brown and Company, 1980.

Lipstadt, Deborah E. *Beyond Belief: The American Press and the Coming of the Holocaust, 1933–1945.* New York: The Free Press, 1986.

Norden, Margaret K. "American Editorial Response to the Rise of Adolf Hitler: A Preliminary Consideration." *American Jewish Historical Quarterly* (October 1968): 290–301.

Pate, Glenn S. "Part III: The United States of America." In Randolph L. Braham, ed., *The Treatment of the Holocaust in Textbooks: The Federal Republic of Germany, Israel, the United States of America.* Boulder, Colo.: Social Science Monographs and Institute for Holocaust Studies of the City University of New York, 1987.

Wyman, David S. *The Abandonment of the Jews: America and the Holocaust 1941–1945.* New York: Pantheon, 1984.

CHAPTER 13

Teaching the Holocaust through

Landscape Study

ANDREW CHARLESWORTH

Since 1990 I have taught a course on "The Geography of the Holocaust." As far as I know this is the first time in the world that a university degree level course has been offered on this topic in a geography syllabus and also the first time a degree level course on the Holocaust has had as its central component an extended period of field study in Eastern Europe and the former Soviet Union. The course has been offered as a final year option on four occasions. Eighty-eight students in total have taken the course to date. All of them have been non-Jewish, though two on the first course would have been adjudged "Jews" by Nazi racial classification. On all four courses we were accompanied, emotionally supported, and taught for some part of the time in Poland by Ben Helfgott, a Holocaust survivor, retired businessman, and chairperson of the British Yad Vashem Committee. The places visited have included prewar Jewish districts, settlements, and cemeteries and the sites of the wartime ghettoes in Warsaw, Krakow, Lodz, Lublin, Lvov, and Piotrkow, slave labor camps at Piotrkow, Janowska, and Plasow, and the death camps of Majdanek, Treblinka, Sobibor, Belzec, and Auschwitz-Birkenau. The period of field study averaged ten days. The field class was preceded by twelve hours of lectures and workshops and on our return there was an opportunity for students to present their work.

As soon as the idea of teaching a course on the geography of the Holocaust came to me, I knew that I wanted to teach the course with a field element. I was reminded of this when I read David Cesarani's account of his visit to the former Soviet Union with Tony Kushner and Carrie Supple to advise Russian Jews on the teaching of the Holocaust.

He commented that after visiting a site of Nazi atrocity and an exhibition on the Minsk ghetto, their lectures acquired an immediacy impossible to acquire in a classroom in the United Kingdom.[1] Immediacy of place, site, and landscape are ingrained in a geographer and provided one of my starting points.

If I had a geographer's intuition that one could add a new dimension to teaching the Holocaust through a field course, it was an essay by George Steiner and Claude Lanzmann's *SHOAH* that pointed the way forward. Writing about the Holocaust, George Steiner has underlined the importance of questions of "relations." He discusses the time relation in these words:

> Precisely at the same hour in which . . . Langner [was] . . . flayed alive, "blood splashing slowly from his hair," . . . the overwhelming plurality of human beings, two miles away on the Polish farms, 5,000 miles away in New York, were sleeping or eating or going to a film or making love or worrying about the dentist. This is where my imagination balks. The two orders of simultaneous experiences are so different, so irreconcilable to any common norm of human values, their coexistence is so hideous a paradox—Treblinka is both because some men have built it and almost all men have let it be— that I puzzle over time. Are there, as science fiction and Gnostic speculations imply, different species of time in the same world . . . ? If we reject some such module, it becomes exceedingly difficult to group the continuity between normal existence and the hour at which hell starts. . . . On the fake station platform at Treblinka, cheerfully painted and provided with window-boxes so as not to alert the new arrivals to the gas-ovens half a mile further, the painted clock pointed to three. Always. There is an acute perception in this on the part of Kurt Franz, the commander of the extermination camp.

Steiner writes that this hideous paradox should force us

> to discover the relations between those done to death and those alive then, and the relations of both to us; to locate, as exactly as record and imagination are able, the measure of unknowing, indifference, complicity, commission which relates the contemporary or survivor to the slain . . . [to] make oneself concretely aware

that the "solution" was not "final," that it spills over into our present lives is the only but compelling reason for forcing oneself to continue reading these literally unbearable records, for going back or, perhaps forward into the non-world of the sealed ghetto and extermination camp.[2]

In writing about the time relation, Steiner cannot avoid making statements and provoking questions about the space relation. These events seem to be on another planet or to be in hell but they are not—they are on earth. They occurred cheek by jowl with working farms, were set in landscapes alive with men and women. On one side of the fence Polish farmers work their fields, on the other side Jews await death. On one side are living children, on the other a twelve foot deep pit full of dead children.

Lanzmann's *SHOAH* takes exactly the same stance on the question of spatial relations. Lanzmann constantly relocates the camps of Chelmno and Treblinka by his shots of the movement of the gas vans and the death trains through the surrounding landscapes and their eventual arrival at the sites of the camp. The repetition allows the viewer no escape from the conclusion that the camps were set in living landscapes, not in remote Siberian wastes. He makes the point more discursively for the ghettoes but it is made all the same. The ghettoes were in the centers of Polish cities, not distant suburbs. The geography of the bystander is brought into sharp focus by Lanzmann. Thus study at the sites of the death and slave labor camps and the ghettoes could become a way of raising questions of "relation." For example, how was knowledge of hell not passed on farm to farm, village to village, village to town, town to city? How was that spatial chain of knowledge broken or not acted upon? Questions of "relation" raise questions, as Steiner says, relating to the present. How do the present surrounding populations relate to these sites of terror and horror? How do we relate to them? Do we fail to relate to those events because of what Steiner calls "the sheer incapacity of the 'normal' mind to imagine and hence give active belief to the enormity of the circumstance and the need"?[3]

The "sheer incapacity" to believe is at the very heart of Lanzmann's *SHOAH* and is articulated in his interview with Raul Hilberg concerning a German document recording the transport of Jews to Treblinka—an interview that is tellingly placed near the center of the film's nine-hour span. Lanzmann questions Hilberg concerning what is special about this document. But the question is an attempt by Lanzmann in his own mind to reconcile tensions of evidence. Lanzmann says, "Because I was in Treblinka, and to have the two things together, Treblinka and the document." [4] In other words, I have been to the place of extermination. I have stood there, stamped on the ground. And here is this document which I can touch. Lanzmann even strikes it as he says the word "document." Yet there is still disbelief about connecting the table of transports even when correctly interpreted by a historian — the thousands of deaths it records — and the site of the place where they were put to death. With Hilberg's authentication and interpretation the document becomes a record of historical event and by so doing becomes a metaphor of written history, the history of the Holocaust we can all read. But then juxtapose that history with the landscape of Treblinka, the mute stones, where what F. Edholm has described as "the imperviousness of place" dominates. [5] The wish to disbelieve becomes greater because of the enigmatic nature of landscape and place. That tension between documentary evidence, oral testimony, and Lanzmann's shots of the sometimes idyllic, bucolic landscape as at Chelmno and of the almost surreal landscapes of Treblinka and Birkenau is one of the great hallmarks of *SHOAH*.

From *SHOAH* I thus drew out two further reasons for the need to go to Poland. First, once there, students themselves would be confronted with the same tension of belief that exists between the historical record and the places and the landscapes themselves. Second, vital necessity behooves us to read and interpret these landscapes, however intractable that task may appear. [6]

THE FIELDWORK

The fieldwork is structured around group and individual experiences, the latter associated with project work the students undertake. The approach to fieldwork is one of nonparticipant observation for the most part. This is partly pragmatic: only one student so far has had a working knowledge of Polish. It is also born of a conviction that participant observation can at times muddy the waters. In survey-type analysis, people can give you the answers they think you want to hear or refuse to answer one's questions. This is particularly so given the level of suspicion of the outsider amongst many older Poles and the sensitivity over the relations between Poles and Jews during the Shoah.

The interpretation of landscape, particularly through the sharing of each individual's reading of the landscape with the group, provides a focus for discussion not possible in the classroom, where the student expects the landscape to be "read" to them by the teacher.

For example, being in a Jewish cemetery like the one in central Warsaw can be the opportunity to discuss the imagery of the neglect and dereliction of sites of importance in Jewish-Polish history. Here, nature is reclaiming the graveyard as she is at some of the death camps. But what images do the presence of trees, ivy, bush undergrowth, and partly ruined graves evoke? For some, the deserted nature of place, the silence, leads to a view of a peaceful scene. Here is high nineteenth-century romanticism; cultivated neglect, nature embracing civilization, which can mask the scandal of the neglect. To others, the image is almost one of discovering a long lost civilization in the jungle—how Hitler would have been pleased by that image. The questioning of the neglect has to break through these images. Closed off behind their high walls, the vast majority of Poles appear to be little disturbed by what is happening to these national treasures. The cemeteries at Warsaw and Lodz are keys to the richness of the Polish-Jewish heritage. There can be no sharper contrast for students but for them to compare Jewish and Catholic cemeteries, or to look at how the Poles tend their war graves, their sites of atrocities such as Palmyry.

Students need to be alerted to keep their eyes and ears open at all times. The scene before them is ever-changing, and fresh images have the ability to force the student to deconstruct what is happening around them at first hand. Two vignettes from Treblinka spoke volumes to the students: the Polish family picnicking by the side of their van but one hundred yards from the memorial within the inner perimeter of the death camps and the four Polish boys chasing each other on bikes across the camp memorial. Such incidents I have to say did strain our nonparticipant observer role.

Going as a group has its advantages. We take the opportunity to have the landscapes of former Jewish areas and the slave labor and death camps explained to us by official guides. All that the students need to be alerted to are the intonation of the guide's voice, what they do tell us and what they do not, what they show us and what they do not. Most times the guides assume we know nothing and hence provide the students with an account that is revelatory to the whole problem of Polish national memory and its self-selecting propensities. For example, a guide, a Polish academic moreover, begins an account of the Holocaust by the balancing of six million Poles killed under Nazi terror against the six million Jews killed in the Holocaust. He offers no qualification that of the six million Poles, three million were Polish Jews.

Even tourist trips can yield unexpected benefits—for example, in the Wieliczka salt mine, used as a slave labor camp for Jews during the war, a Star of David carved in one wall, visible for all to see, was ignored by our guide. All he related was the fact that during the war, prisoners here were involved in the construction of aircraft. To hear an official guide, a former academic, state that it was well known that Jews kept gold under their floorboards, without clarification, explanation, contextualization, has an impact that is only heightened by being related whilst we stand in a courtyard in Kazimierz, the former Jewish quarter of Krakow. Or a guide may completely drop their guard and say that "the Jews were not good as resistance fighters—see how quietly they went to the gas chambers. It was the Poles who had to do the fighting." On no occasion should students challenge these statements, however offensive. The guide would then censor his or her comments for the rest of the tour. The guide certainly would not have said these remarks to a group of Jewish students.

With the rapidity of change in Eastern Europe there is constant change and flux in the landscape. The increasing appearance of anti-Semitic and Nazi graffiti (words often written in English), at memorial sites and other places are again something students stumble on—not just at the big public memorials but in the huts and the "sauna," that is the showerhouse, at Birkenau and in a side street in Lodz. These highlight graphically the rise of neo-Nazism in Eastern Europe since the weakening and subsequent ending of communist rule. When guides and others dismiss these as the actions of a very small minority of hooligans, the students have further cause to think deeply about the nature of anti-Semitism and neo-Nazism.

But this sense of change is also occurring within the former Jewish landscapes. To come across the restoration work at the Lublin New Jewish cemetery can jolt one out of complacency. The strident nature of the new outer wall standing opposite as it does a Catholic cemetery is sure to be interpreted by many Poles as a sign of returning Jewish wealth and influence; particularly as this and other sites of restoration work at cemeteries and synagogues are usually accompanied by a large sign in a foreign language. How long before anti-Semitic graffiti are daubed on these, one wonders.

I have also learned to leave some sites to the students, with only prior reading and a map of the site. They are free to wander over the site where their curiosity takes them. This works particularly well at sites where there is apparently nothing there. Guides are at a loss without the "authentic" artifacts of Nazi terror. They can talk their heads off in Auschwitz I and Majdanek but in Birkenau and even more so in Monowitz (Auschwitz III), Belzec, and Plasow they are struck dumb. This is surprising in the case of Monowitz and Plasow, the site of two of the most famous writings on the Shoah, respectively Primo Levi's "If This Is a Man" and Thomas Keneally's "Schindler's Ark/List." The reading of text and the reading of landscape, when there is superficially nothing there, can be a revelatory experience. With Keneally's text and his accompanying map of Plasow, the landscape of the camp can be read: the pre-camp landscape with the remains of the Jewish cemetery and mortuary; the camp landscape with key features such as the hill fort where prisoners were shot and later bodies were burnt, the quarries, Amon Goeth's house with its "shooting gallery" balcony, the outlines of the foundations of the barracks, the Apellplatz, the road through the camp; the post-camp landscape of memorials, mountain bike and scrambling bike tracks, dog walks, picnic sites, parkland aspect, and of course in the adjacent quarry, the remains of Spielberg's film set of Plasow. Questions of authenticity, memorialization, and remembrance of past things crowd in upon the student where the guide's soothing factual account might displace such a problematic.

The sense of discovery is present all the time. The landscapes of horror change with and are even challenged by the weather. To see Treblinka or Birkenau on a hot sunny day really stretches the imagination to believe these events happened here; as Srebnik tells Lanzmann in *SHOAH* standing on the site of Chelmno death camp on a beautiful day.

> "I can't believe I'm here. No, I just can't believe it. It was always this peaceful here. Always. When they burned two thousand people— Jews—every day, it was just as peaceful. No one shouted. Everyone went about his work. It was silent, peaceful. Just as it is now."[7]

To see the landscape of chimney stacks, the only remains of many of the prisoners' huts at Birkenau, emerge from an April mist can be both terrifying and surreal. To allow students to roam at will and not in a group can heighten their awareness of certain issues. To see a man reconstructing a brick wall in Crematoria III and to come across a prisoner's hut and a watchtower being reconstructed, the former, moreover, by a German company, can be the most shocking discoveries of all. It leaves students wondering whether the museum authorities are trying to give succor to Holocaust deniers, many of whom claimed that Auschwitz was constructed after the war by the Poles as a tourist attraction.

We are, however, participants in the sense that our presence draws out reactions from those who encounter us and those reactions can be revelatory. Two instances must suffice. First, there is the reaction of passersby. In Piotrkow a man has shouted out "Juda" on two different occasions when the group has crossed the same square. That meant, I am sure, "outsider." By using the German for "Jew"—for surely he didn't think we were German Jews—he saw us as "the other," "the foreigner," "the exploiter" be it German, Jewish, American, anyone who is not Polish. Poland as both geopolitical and geo-economic victim has so shaped the Polish consciousness that the non-Pole is generally viewed with great suspicion. That incident became a vivid insight for students into how Poles view themselves and the outside world and how in that cosmology Jews have figured.

Secondly, there is the reaction of those who act as our academic hosts or guides. For example, in Lodz a Polish academic with whom I had been in correspondence made the assumption that I and my students were Jewish. Why else would we have an interest in the Holocaust, was the implication. Later the same day, our Jewish guide to the Jewish cemetery and the recently restored synagogue in Lodz also assumed we were Jews. To Poles, non-Jewish and Jewish alike, an interest in the Holocaust and perhaps, particularly a study course on the Holocaust must be by and for Jews. Once again questions are raised in the students' minds about how Poles have come to construct the Holocaust within their worldview.

If the immediacy of place is the central reason for taking students to Holocaust sites, certain responsibilities are required of the teachers. Those who take the course are asked to undergo emotional strain of a character they have not been exposed to before. All I have said about reading landscapes, observing site and situation, go for nothing if the student is numbed by the emotional immediacy of a place like Treblinka, Auschwitz I, or Birkenau.

The encounter with the site of a death camp has to be dealt with sensitively if the intellectual endeavor is to be achieved. The students are not undertaking visits to the camps as occasions to be alone with their thoughts. The nature of the intellectual quest is that students have to open their minds, to observe, to reflect. They do not have the option to run away. That is hard and it needs a lot of sensitive handling. It is why I have kept the groups under twenty-five in number. It has also to be said that I was blind to certain of these aspects, because my own way of coping with the emotional pain has been through intellectualizing, through observing, reading, asking questions of the landscapes. Thus, on a number of occasions I misread the coping strategies necessary for the emotional pain. Without the presence of a survivor of the emotional sensitivity and intellectual capacity of Ben Helfgott, these situations would have become irretrievable.

If such sensitivity is not shown, then the encounter with such horror can prove too much and students are unable to intellectualize what they have experienced. It can thereby undermine their ability to complete projects and to prepare for the examination in the course. But more fundamentally it blocks the learning experience of such a study of the Holocaust. A number of coping strategies appear to work. Besides the group discussions that go on until well into the night, two A.M. is not unusual, getting students to keep a daily journal of their thoughts is such an aid. One of the students found writing a fictional account, a short story, helped in coping with the horror and hence moving on to the intellectual plane. If this had not been done, this student would have been trapped within the emotional plane and would without a doubt have failed the course. For at that emotional level there is a distaste with intellectualizing the horror, dehumanizing of the victims yet again this time in neat explanatory constructs, of seeing the human victims as "Figuren."

The evidence of the course is that those who are able to pass through the barrier of trauma and pain and then ask critical questions about the landscapes of horror, death, and fear that they have encountered come away with a greater and deeper commitment to an understanding of the Holocaust. On their return from Poland, it leads to an engagement with texts and historiographical debate that is the true mark of a university graduate.[8]

The Encounter Itself

All education is about change—making us more human and more open to the needs of others, the views of others, and more ready to defend the rights and values of others. In an educational system from primary to higher that is being valued in terms of skill acquisition, in terms of parts of the person, rather than the whole, the making of whole personalities is taking a lower priority. Therefore, as a teacher to feel you are part of a course that has as its impact on the individual that process of remaking is a very humbling experience. To hear students talk about themselves before and after the field course, being clearly able to mark out in their lives a watershed, is something I never expected when I embarked on this endeavor. Students who have been on the field course talk of the time before they went, when they were apathetic to social, political, and moral issues, when they bought a tabloid newspaper daily and the time after, when they will not allow a racist stereotype or sexist joke to pass by without telling the perpetrator of such views their disapproval, when they will write to their M.P. on some issue, when they take a quality newspaper on a regular basis and follow closely world events.

Students will speak of their disbelief that other graduates still carry the attitudes of the British middle-class that Kitty Hart and survivors encountered in the early postwar days. "Don't tell us about that, it is too shocking." "That's past now—forget it and get on with life."

Engaging so deeply with the Shoah through an experience of place and landscape and the experiential encounter of the sense of death at places like Birkenau, Treblinka, Majdanek, or at small town selection sites marks many into being witnesses, bearers of testimony, just as the survivors were. And for such people rebuffs hurt and astound. Like survivors they find they can at times only talk to those who have shared the same experience. It must be very rare for members of any field class wanting to hold reunions well after graduation but the groups I have taken have wanted that opportunity.[9]

For many, there is the experience of trauma itself. The nature of this particular encounter with the Shoah can release within the person a level of shock, horror, and even something that teaches grieving that they have not experienced before. It can thereby better prepare one for other traumas. One student found that coping with their parents' divorce, announced on their return from Poland, proved much easier than they could have expected. The pit of the Shoah puts other aspects of one's life into perspective.

For some students the trauma works in a different way. They come back, as did many survivors, unable to talk about the emotional, the painful, and the moral aspects of the experience, even though they can handle the material from an intellectual perspective. But gradually there develops a desire, a wish to talk about the experience, to tell others of it. This is again something that needs to be taken into account by teachers. As this is a final year course done in the Easter vacation before finals, then the ability for these persons to have the support of the field course leader or the group itself is limited. Graduation occurs with two months of the field class. Arrangements should be made for students to contact others and the field course leaders. Yet even here I feel we may underestimate how long it will take individual students to come through this type of trauma. More importantly, we need to be very sensitive to students in that period following the Polish experience. Reactions that show a lack of engagement with the course should not be automatically read as the sign of a person who only came "along for the ride" or because "their mates were going." No student will have enrolled lightly for the course. That seriousness of purpose needs to be clear to us as the teachers at all times, even when evidence points to the contrary. Perhaps that sensitivity to students' motivation and needs should be borne in mind on other occasions during their university careers.

I can only end with the reaction of a fellow geographer who showed visible revulsion at the idea of taking students to the death camps, to Auschwitz. To be repulsed by the death camps to the point of ignoring them is the collective amnesia that is allowing ethnic cleansing in what was Yugoslavia. Moreover, it indicates a distorted view of European, Christian civilization. Geographers have long been happy to take students to the imperial cities of Europe and to read the monumental landscapes of empire and nation state, perhaps often uncritically. Yet those cities, but particularly Berlin at the heart of one of the Great Powers of the nineteenth and twentieth centuries, are inextricably linked to Auschwitz, the *anus mundi*. As my former colleague John Dickenson has pointed out to me, we select particular landscapes to conserve and to take pride over, others we attempt to eradicate or change. A study of the geography of the Holocaust particularly through the landscape approach allows us to give students the keys to the part of our collective biography which an older generation would perhaps rather forget but which daily events in Central and Eastern Europe are forcing us to remember.

NOTES

This course originated in the Department of Geography at the University of Liverpool in England. I have now taken an appointment in the Department of Geography and Geology at Cheltenham and Gloucester College of Higher Education in England and the course has moved with me. It is no longer offered at Liverpool. I am grateful to the comments on my paper especially from Pamela Hope-Levin, Sister Mary Noel Kernan, and William Seidelman. Comments on an earlier version of the paper were made by Colin Richmond, Martin Gilbert, Ben Helfgott, and John Dickenson. This is a revised version of an essay that appeared in *Immigrants and Minorities*, vol. 15 (1995): 33–45.

1. "Don's diary," *The Higher,* May 15, 1992.
2. G. Steiner, "Postscript" in *Language and Silence: Essays 1958–1966* (New York, 1967), 156, 157.
3. Ibid, 183.
4. The dialogue is not reproduced word for word in the published text of the film. C. Lanzmann, *SHOAH: An Oral History of the Holocaust* (New York, 1985), 141.
5. F. Edholm, "*SHOAH:* A Film by Claude Lanzmann," *History Workshop* (1988), 204.
6. Lanzmann himself has said *SHOAH* is a "topographic film." C. Lanzmann, Seminar, Yad Vashem, Jerusalem, July 24, 1991.
7. C. Lanzmann, *SHOAH,* 6.
8. I am grateful to Rabbi Sidney Brichto for access to notes he made at a reunion in May 1992 of students who had been on the first two field courses. I would also like to thank the students who have come on the field courses, especially those who came back for the reunion and those who have sent me written comments on the course.
9. An even rarer event surely must be students wanting to help to finance future field courses in however small a way they can, given the level of student indebtedness at graduation. I obviously have been concerned that students have taken out loans just to take the course. Fortunately, outside funding is now helping to ease some of this financial burden. Students have contributed on average £220 from their own pockets.

CHAPTER 14

Holocaust Denial Literature:

Its Place in Teaching the Holocaust

CARLOS C. HUERTA AND
DAFNA SHIFFMAN-HUERTA

If one said, ten years ago, that Holocaust denial literature should be taught when one teaches Holocaust literature, a flurry of criticism would have descended upon the person who had said it. Even five years ago, to suggest to a Holocaust studies teacher that some time should be spent in introducing the student to the claims that the denialists were making would have drawn heated debate. Now the story is very different. In the last decade, Holocaust denial has made such in-roads into the fibre of American and world thinking that it has become self-evident to those that study the phenomenon that it must be addressed. This paper will look at the need to introduce the study of Holocaust denial literature during the study of the Holocaust and will then offer a quick survey of the more readily available literature Holocaust denial produces, analyzing some of the works and their authors. Finally, it will address the issue of how one can, most effectively, incorporate denial literature into the teaching the Holocaust.

Why teach it?[1] It is difficult to frame an answer to someone not knowledgeable in the scope, volume, and effect of Holocaust denial today. This is similar to explaining to a high school student why he or she needs to learn algebra, or a foreign language. What is self-evident to someone studying the Holocaust denial phenomenon can be quite obscure to one not acquainted with it. The fact of the matter is that one out of five Americans believing it is possible that the Holocaust may not have happened is indicative of something more than just a lack of knowledge of the Holocaust.[2] Not knowing about the Holocaust is very different from believing that it may not have happened. Rather, the belief that an event such as the Holocaust may not have happened is indicative of some *inadequate* knowledge, and a rejection of that knowledge. This rejection is not created in a vacuum, but rather through contact with those arguments that attempt to show that the Holocaust either did not occur, or did not occur in the way depicted by Holocaust historians. This contact with Holocaust denial arguments and views is primarily through the printed word. Not exposing students to Holocaust denial literature leaves them open to denialist arguments when they eventually and inevitably encounter them. Assuming that students will not come across the works or arguments of Butz, Faurisson, Leuchter, Smith, and the like exhibits a dangerous naivete on the part of the Holocaust educator. One would like to live in a world with no crime, but only a suicidal nation would not create a police force. One would like to think that Holocaust denialism is insignificant or does not exist, but only a naive and uninformed educational system would not create a curriculum to meet the challenges created by Holocaust denial.

The first problem encountered in introducing Holocaust denial in Holocaust education is resistance. In some cases this resistance will be quite vocal and unrelenting. A story best serves to exemplify this. The author, wanting to analyze the statements of *The Leuchter Report,* a report that says that the presently existing gas chambers at Auschwitz were not used to gas human beings, went to the chemistry department of a large world-known university. An appointment was made with the chairperson of the department to discuss the report and see where the errors were. The author explained to the chairperson, at the start of the meeting, that he was seeking to combat Holocaust denialism and wanted to prove *The Leuchter Report* wrong. The chairperson, after being handed the report and scanning it for a few minutes, suddenly went into an uncontrollable tirade and proceeded to verbally abuse the author and almost physically throw him out of the office.

What should be clear from this is that even when one's motives for discussing Holocaust denial are explained, one will encounter many highly educated people who will resist its introduction as a *concept,* into Holocaust studies. These people have little patience in talking about something a main purpose of which is to tell them that their loved ones did not suffer, were not murdered, or maybe did not even die. This resistance can come not only from one's audience, but also from one's colleagues (other Holocaust educators), one's supervisors, and even from one's family.

What is interesting is that one will often find support in addressing

Holocaust denial from the survivors themselves. Survivors seem to understand instinctively that people should be more aware about Holocaust denial so that its challenges will be effectively met. One of the best ways to introduce denialism to an audience is to have a survivor precede the discussion or presentation by explaining to the audience, in his or her own words, why he or she feels there is a need to study and understand what the denialists are saying. One should not underestimate this resistance, because unless it is properly dealt with and fears assuaged, it will be counter-productive to introduce Holocaust denial literature into the Holocaust curriculum.

After this resistance is overcome, then the next hurdle that must be dealt with is what to introduce. This can be most easily answered when one considers the question: What denial literature will the student most likely first encounter? Experience has taught both the Holocaust denialist and the Holocaust educator that the first literary contact the student will probably make with denialism is through a denialist leaflet or pamphlet. The success of a leaflet/pamphlet blitz was quickly recognized by Holocaust denialists. Mark Weber, author of three leaflets and editor of the *Journal of Historical Review,* a denialist journal, readily admits that much of the success Holocaust denial presently enjoys is due to the grass-roots work of the leaflet pushers.

> Much of the credit for our steady progress is due to the quiet work of activists across the United States. A good example . . . is Jack Riner, a long-time IHR supporter who recently passed out 2,400 IHR leaflets to students on two university campuses. . . . We applaud and strongly encourage such grass-roots efforts. Experience has shown that, even when they might not seem to have any noticeable effect, the real long-term impact of such efforts is very difficult to measure. Don't forget the example of Bradley Smith—now one the most active of activists—who was introduced to all this quite a few years ago when someone handed him a denial leaflet. Reading that short item jolted Bradley and transformed his life.[3]

There are several reasons for the success that these leaflets/pamphlets have. The most obvious are their portability and brevity. One will not bother to read, let alone buy, the major denial works by Butz, Faurisson, or Staeglich until one is motivated by the seeming reasonableness of their positions. Their works cover many hundreds of pages, are rather technical and, no doubt, boring to a high school or college student whose reading load is already more than he or she thinks can be handled. The leaflets/pamphlets motivate the need for these full-length works by giving the reader a concise overall view of what Holocaust denial is, demonstrating the reasonableness of its position, depicting the problems and lies of the official Holocaust story, and showing the great cost and burden the Holocaust myth is creating in American society in particular and the world as a whole.

The IHR, Institute for Historical Review, publishes these denial pamphlets. There are seven that deal directly with the Holocaust, one on the Dead Sea Scrolls,[4] and one on historical revisionism.[5] Of the seven that deal with the Holocaust, three are written by Mark Weber, editor of *The Journal of Historical Review*, two by Robert Faurisson, the leading French Holocaust denialist, one by Theodore J. O'Keefe, an editor for the Institute for Historical Review, and one by Fred A. Leuchter, a gas chamber consultant in the United States and author of *The Leuchter Report*.[6]

The three tracts Mark Weber has written are entitled *Auschwitz: Myths and Facts, The Holocaust: Let's Hear Both Sides*, and *Simon Wiesenthal: Bogus "Nazi Hunter."*[7] In these pamphlets, Weber exhibits, with fine precision, the use of argument by extrapolation. One can see a good example of this in *Auschwitz: Myths and Facts*. Here he starts his argument by quoting from the transcripts of the Nuremberg trials, correctly one should add, that the official death toll at Auschwitz was four million human lives. He then shows, through various news clippings, that the Soviets and other historians supported this number until 1986. He then quotes Holocaust historians to show that this number has been constantly decreased. First, he quotes Yehuda Bauer saying that the four million is too high, then he moves on to Raul Hilberg's one million, then to Gerald Reitlinger's seven hundred thousand minimum. The reader is given the impression that given enough time the Holocaust historians will get the numbers correct and will hit the rock bottom number of the denialists of a couple of hundred thousand, maximum. He quotes some of the testimony cited at Nuremberg, but now universally discredited, to show, again by extrapolation, that perhaps all of the mass killing stories coming out of Auschwitz could be a lie.

To understand the effectiveness of these and similar arguments, one must read these leaflets, not as a Holocaust educator, but rather as an open-minded college student or other adult, detached from the subject matter and perhaps not so well educated in the Holocaust. When one learns that there was testimony at the Nuremberg trials of mass electrocution, soap making from human fat, use of devices that could instantaneously vaporize twenty thousand people, and that all of these have since been discredited, it is not hard to make the jump to challenge all other aspects of the data and evidence presented at the trial. This is what the pamphlets are designed to do. They are not written to turn one into a Holocaust denialist on the spot, but rather written to have their readers question various aspects of the Holocaust, then hopefully move on to question the entire thing.

The pamphlet *The Holocaust: Let's Hear Both Sides* addresses an entirely different aspect of the issue of denialism. One of the more sacred things to the American citizen is the right to free speech. In general, Americans abhor anything that limits or appears to limit this right. In this pamphlet Mark Weber has drawn on this concept of free speech and the American instinct for fair play to try to paint the picture that important work of Holocaust denial is being systematically suppressed by various "hate" groups (which invariably turn out to be Jewish) in America. Again he uses argument by extrapolation, showing how the "official" Holocaust story has changed over the years, clearly implying that there exists another, suppressed, side to which the "official" position must ultimately come. He would have us believe that in other countries around the world this "other side" is freely discussed, but in America it is not.

> For several years now, the Holocaust story has been the subject of legitimate controversy in Europe. It was debated for several hours on Swiss television and over French radio. The leading French daily, *Le Monde,* and the respected Italian historical journal, *Storia Illustrata,* have given extensive coverage to both sides of this issue. Here in America, though, powerful organizations have so far prevented any real public exchange of views on this issue. Many thoughtful Americans are having growing doubts about at least some of the more sensational Holocaust claims, but all the public ever sees and hears is the orthodox view of the extermination story. That's not right. Americans have the right to judge this important issue for themselves.[8]

This purported open debate in Europe stands in direct contradiction to articles and speeches by European denialists on the state of Holocaust denial in Europe.[9] This other side that he would like to have one believe exists, and is debated openly in Europe, simply does not enjoy the open publicity and acceptance he describes.

The set of pamphlets written by Robert Faurisson entitled *A Prominent False Witness: Elie Wiesel*[10] and *The "Problem of the Gas Chambers"* follow the general pattern described above. What makes *The "Problem of the Gas Chambers"* unique is that a version of it enjoyed publication in the French newspaper *Le Monde*.[11] Robert Faurisson is arguably the leading French Holocaust denialist. Looking at his constant stream of articles to *The Journal of Historical Review,* his many speeches at the conferences for historical denial sponsored by the IHR, and to denialist groups around the world, he is easily the world's leading Holocaust denialist. This alone warrants the need to address his works, first through his pamphlets then through his many articles published in denialist journals.[12]

The pamphlet by Theodore J. O'Keefe entitled *The "Liberation of the Camps": Facts vs. Lies* uses various documents and eyewitness testimony of American military officers to try to induce the reader to believe that it was the Allied destruction of Germany's infrastructure that inevitably led to massive deaths in the concentration camps by first impeding, then destroying, Germany's ability to properly care for the camp's inmates as it had done before 1942. He rehashes many of the points of the previously discussed pamphlets to try to have the reader believe that there was no systematic murder in the camps condoned by the German authorities in Berlin, and where corruption and cruelty did occur it was addressed, with the instigator or perpetrator quickly punished.

This pamphlet would be a good way to introduce the student to the misuse of historical documents. Here the student would see the use of some of the classic tricks of the trade, like taking a document out of its historical context, extrapolating the data and meaning of a document to have it apply to another unrelated situation, use of a document designed for propaganda purposes as one that factually describes the situation, or taking the one document that supports one's position and ignoring the hundreds that do not. In analyzing any of these pamphlets one should be sure that one's audience is aware of good historical methodology. The flaw in many of the pamphlets is not necessarily one of fact but rather in use of fact. The student must be exposed to good historical technique to fully appreciate how it is misused by many Holocaust denialists. In using the pamphlets as a means to discuss Holocaust denial, the educator should not bite off more than he or she can chew; there is too much material in the collected pamphlets to be effectively addressed. Rather, the Holocaust educator should choose to address one or two pamphlets he or she feels most comfortable with and limit his or her discussion to those, the remainder being available for independent student analysis.

After the pamphlets,[13] the next classics of Holocaust denialism that students are most likely to encounter are the works of Fred A. Leuchter, *The Leuchter Report*,[14] Arthur R. Butz, *The Hoax of the Twentieth Century*, Wilhelm Staeglich, *Auschwitz: A Judge Looks at the Evidence*, Thies Christophersen, *Auschwitz: Truth or Lie*, or by an anonymous author, *The Myth of the Six Million*. One should not consider this list all-inclusive. Instead of an above-mentioned book or booklet, the next contact could be with a past issue of *The Journal of Historical Review*, or one of the denial newsletters or articles put out by Bradley Smith.[15]

The point to be made here is that the Holocaust educator cannot and should not try to address the entire gamut of denial literature. He or she should be familiar with it, but must pick and choose which of the denial material to address. The decision should be based on the educator's personal expertise in an area and on the audience's ability to deal with the subject matter. *The Dissolution of Eastern European Jewry* by Walter N. Sanning,[16] whose thesis is that most European Jewry disappeared through emigration, is a highly technical book filled with demographic tables and charts. This book would be totally unsuitable to bring to the attention of high school or most college audiences.

If at all feasible, the Holocaust educator should poll the audience and encourage them in the beginning of the course to inform him or her of what denial material they have come into contact with and would want to discuss. In doing this the educator must have complete command and control of the class or audience to permit an open discussion of any denialist leanings a participant may have. No one should feel ashamed to admit to his or her views, and the educator should not let any participants condemn or verbally abuse anyone who wishes to discuss denialist views. Only in an open and free discussion of the facts can Holocaust denial be effectively dealt with. If the Holocaust educator opens up the environment to free discussion of denialism, he or she will be quite surprised to find out just how many of his or her students or audience members have come into contact with denial literature or share some sort of denialist view.

By tailoring the discussion of Holocaust denial literature to the needs and exposure of the class, the Holocaust educator will best meet the challenge that such literature poses in the minds of many Americans today. The Holocaust educator must always maintain an honest environment in discussing denial literature. If there are points that the educator is not properly prepared to address, he or she should admit it to the students. If there are legitimate points that Holocaust denialists make—and there are some—the Holocaust educator must openly acknowledge them.[17] The Holocaust educator should always realize that the truth is on his or her side, and should not fear, after proper preparation, to deal with denialism and teach students how to deal with it. In so doing, the educator will help insure that the lessons of the Holocaust will be learned.

Notes

A version of this chapter appeared in *Conservative Judaism,* vol. 47, no. 1 (Fall 1994), under the title "Revisionist Literature: Its Place in Holocaust Literature and Its Role in Teaching the Holocaust."

1. For a fuller treatment of this subject, see Carlos C. Huerta, "Holocaust Revisionism in the Classroom," *Ten Da'at: A Publication of the Torah Education Network,* vol. 5, no. 2 (Spring 1991): 5–6.

2. A survey conducted by the American Jewish Committee in 1993 showed that at least one in five Americans think it is possible to believe that the Holocaust never took place.

3. Mark Weber, "From the Editor," *Journal of Historical Review,* vol. 13, no. 4, (July/August, 1993): 3. Jack Riner passed out 1,200 pamphlets at Indiana State University, Terre Haute, on January 20, 1993, in front of the student union building. Earlier he had passed out a similar number of revisionist pamphlets at Bowling Green State University in Ohio. The majority of these pamphlets challenge the Holocaust or some aspect of it.

4. This pamphlet, *Whatever Happened to the Dead Sea Scrolls,* by Martin A. Larson, Ph.D., deals with the lack of publication on the contents of the scrolls after over forty years since their discovery. This very problem has been addressed by various writers, among them Hershel Shanks, editor of the *Biblical Archaeology Review.* This is a situation where many scholars are in agreement with this

denialist position. Here is an example that shows the danger of sweeping all denialist positions with the same brush.

5. This pamphlet is entitled *The Tradition of Historical Revisionism* and is written by Tom Marcellus, the Director of the Institute for Historical Review. This pamphlet makes the very reasonable argument for the need of historical revisionism. Most people, in principle, would agree with the comments that Tom Marcellus makes here concerning damaging effect that war has on the truth. After the experience in Vietnam, most Americans would agree with him concerning "the existence of the underlying causes of war and what our own leaders have done to encourage war, and prolong it." One should differentiate between the need for good historical revisionism versus the rewriting of history to promote a pet political theory. One needs to point out to one's students that historical revisionism and Holocaust denialism are two separate camps that many Holocaust deniers would like to combine: they would legitimize Holocaust denialism by riding on the coattails of legitimate historical revisionism.

6. *The Leuchter Report* is a report compiled by Fred Leuchter for use at the Zündel trial in Canada. Ernst Zündel was on trial for "dissemination of false news," in particular for distributing books like *The Auschwitz Lie,* which is a Nazi officer's eyewitness account of the non-existence of gas chambers at Auschwitz. Fred A. Leuchter, a prominent U.S. execution gas chamber consultant, was sent by the Zündel defense team to visit Auschwitz and give his professional opinion about the existence of gas chambers there. He ends his report with the conclusion that the facilities at Auschwitz, Birkenau, and Majdanek "could not have been, or now be utilized or seriously considered to function as execution gas chambers."

7. This pamphlet is a personal attack on Simon Wiesenthal. Since it does not directly attack the Holocaust it will not be addressed here. It, however, should be included in the Holocaust curriculum on revisionism as it attacks a well-known person, who to many represents the Holocaust. This also applies to the pamphlet written by Robert Faurisson entitled *A Prominent False Witness: Elie Wiesel.* Again, this is an attack on an important person who has done much to bring the Holocaust into proper focus in history. Though space does not allow it to be addressed here, it would be proper to look at this pamphlet in a discussion of Holocaust denialism.

8. Mark Weber, *The Holocaust: Let's Hear Both Sides,* Institute for Historical Review Pamphlet, 7.

9. In the March/April 1993 issue of *The Journal of Historical Review,* 26–28, one sees an article describing the tremendous legal entanglements that the French denialists, among them Robert Faurisson, are involved in for their publication and distribution of Holocaust denialist material. On pages 29–30 one can read about the Nazi general Otto-Ernst Remer sentenced to twenty-two months of

imprisonment for publishing articles disputing the gas chambers and mass killings at Auschwitz. The apparent acceptance of Holocaust denialism, that Mark Weber would have us believe is a legitimate point for debating in Europe, flies in the face of data supplied by the denialists themselves.

10. See note 7.

11. Many Holocaust deniers constantly use this fact to demonstrate the legitimacy and acceptance of their position. This was the pamphlet that converted Bradley Smith to become a Holocaust denialist activist.

12. The Institute for Historical Review is publishing a compilation of his articles entitled *Faurisson on the Holocaust*. This book was scheduled to appear late in 1993 but as of September 1995, has not yet appeared. It is to contain all of the articles published by Robert Faurisson in the journal published by the IHR, and also include previously unpublished articles in English.

13. A page handout, flyer type, entitled 66 *Questions and Answers on the Holocaust*, published by the IHR, also has a wide distribution. This flyer is published in Spanish, French, English, Portuguese, and soon Arabic.

14. Fred A. Leuchter's pamphlet entitled *Inside the Auschwitz "Gas Chambers"* serves as an introduction to *The Leuchter Report*. This pamphlet describes the background to the report, his description of his trip to the camp, and his conclusions.

15. For a more complete description of Bradley Smith and his work on the college campus, see Carlos C. Huerta, "Revisionism, Free Speech, and the Campus," *Midstream,* vol. 38, no. 3 (April 1992): 10–11.

16. This book was published by the Institute for Historical Review in 1983 and has a foreword by Arthur R. Butz.

17. For example, one of the legitimate points they have made in the past concerned the proof of soap made from human fat. They claimed that the evidence during the Nuremberg trials was not convincing, and it was not. Holocaust scholars have also made the same point, but not as loudly as the denialists would have liked.

CHAPTER 15

The Dead End of Demonizing: Dealing with the Perpetrators in Teaching the Holocaust

DONALD G. SCHILLING

In the autumn of 1992, I taught my first course on the Holocaust. The preparation for and teaching of this course proved to be one of the most demanding, challenging, draining, and rewarding experiences in my two decades of teaching. I suspect that most who have offered courses on the Holocaust could make the same affirmation and would agree with Michael Marrus that "Researching and teaching the Holocaust . . . is not quite like researching and teaching everything else."[1] Among the many issues confronting me as I designed and taught the course was how to treat those three groups so central to any analysis of the Holocaust: the perpetrators, victims, and bystanders. Each of these groups presents unique challenges, but given space limitations in this chapter I will focus on the perpetrators, the "people," according to Raul Hilberg, "who played a specific role in the formation or implementation of anti-Jewish measures."[2] I began my consideration of this group with the very general question, "What did I expect my students to learn about the perpetrators of the Holocaust?" The following subquestions seemed especially relevant to elucidating this general query. Who were the perpetrators? As a group were they identifiably different from others in the general population? Were there significant differences among perpetrators? What functions did perpetrators perform? Why did they perform those functions and become active agents in the process of genocide? How did perpetrators justify their actions and live with themselves? What can we learn about ourselves and human behavior from the study of the perpetrators?

I hoped to assist students in addressing these questions through various means, but given the nature of the course as an honor's seminar, its small size, and my reliance on discussion as the primary instructional method in the classroom, the course reading would have to play a central role in facilitating the exploration of these questions. My strategy for this chapter, therefore, is to evaluate potential texts, considering their ability to engage students, and to frame the issues raised by the above questions. I will consider the following: Raul Hilberg, *Perpetrators, Victims, Bystanders: The Jewish Catastrophe;* Robert Jay Lifton, *The Nazi Doctors: Medical Killing and the Psychology of Genocide;* Christopher R. Browning, *Ordinary Men: Reserve Police Battalion 101 and the Final Solution in Poland;* Richard Breitman, *The Architect of Genocide: Himmler and the Final Solution;* Hannah Arendt, *Eichmann in Jerusalem: A Report on the Banality of Evil;* Rudolf Höss, *Commandant of Auschwitz;* and Gitta Sereny, *Into That Darkness: An Examination of Conscience.*[3]

Before I turn to individual analysis of these works, one overarching issue requires attention. In perusing the relevant literature treating the perpetrators, I was struck by the frequency of authors' comments about the difficulties of dealing with this group. Joel Dimsdale, for example, writes,

> As controversial as the study of the victim may be, the controversy pales in comparison with the tempest engendered by the study of the perpetrator. Efforts to understand the behavior of the Nazis are frequently mistaken as efforts to forgive or justify their actions. One finds strong convictions about the Nazis that on the one hand they are uniquely evil or uniquely abnormal psychologically . . . (or else that they are not fundamentally different from other people.)[4]

Given the evil perpetrated by the Nazis, especially by the SS, it is not surprising that they, and particularly figures such as Adolf Hitler, Heinrich Himmler, Reinhard Heydrich, Adolf Eichmann, Ernst Kaltenbrunner, and Dr. Josef Mengele have been depicted as demonic.[5] This depiction serves a number of useful functions. First, it provides a straightforward explanation of many aspects of the Final Solution. Simply put, the Final Solution in all its corrosive horror was the work of evil, psychologically deformed men. Second, this explanation lifts much of the burden of guilt from "normal, average" citizens in Germany and other countries. Third, it frees all of us from troubling questions about the capacity of normal human beings to participate in an evil project and commit acts of brutality and murder. We are obviously fundamentally different from the perpetrators and thus can preserve our sense of humanity and morality.

There are, however, two immediately evident problems with this approach to the perpetrators. First, studies of the perpetrators and the mechanisms and processes of the Final Solution have revealed its grave limitations. In this respect, the early 1960s was a particularly crucial period, with the publication of Raul Hilberg's monumental *Destruction of the European Jews* (1961), which highlights the bureaucratic, technocratic machinery of destruction staffed by thousands of ordinary persons, and of Hannah Arendt's penetrating, if controversial, *Eichmann in Jerusalem* (1963). If Arendt's depiction of Eichmann's normality and banality can be challenged in certain specifics, her general point that one can not dismiss Eichmann as an insane or demonic figure has been reinforced by important studies of other perpetrators.[6] In short, while there were perpetrators who fit the demonic, psychologically disturbed image—one thinks, for example, of Kurt Franz, Treblinka's deputy commander—the empirical evidence does not support this characterization of most perpetrators.

Second, demonizing the perpetrators cuts us off from a deeper, more complete understanding of human behavior, of our capacity for evil, and, therefore, of our ability to guard against future atrocities. Robert Jay Lifton addresses this issue in the forward to his powerful study, *The Nazi Doctors*. He encountered critics of his investigation who asserted, "rather than make it [Nazi evil] an object of study; one should simply condemn it."[7] In response, Lifton writes,

> I had no doubt about the reality of Nazi evil. . . . To avoid probing the sources of that evil seemed to me, in the end, a refusal to call forth our capacity to engage and combat it. Such avoidance contains not only fear of contagion but an assumption that Nazi or any other evil has no relationship whatsoever to the rest of us—to more general human capacities. While Nazi mass murder and brutality tempt one toward such an assumption, it is nonetheless false and even dangerous.[8]

Christopher R. Browning, in his stunning *Ordinary Men,* explores this issue in even more personal language:

Another possible objection to this kind of study concerns the degree of empathy for the perpetrators that is inherent in trying to understand them. Clearly the writing of such a history requires the rejection of demonization. The policemen in the battalion who carried out the massacres and deportations, like the much smaller number who refused or evaded, were human beings. I must recognize that in the same situation, I could have been either a killer or an evader—both were human—if I want to understand and explain the behavior of both as best I can. This recognition does indeed mean an attempt to empathize. . . . Not trying to understand the perpetrators in human terms would make impossible not only this study but any history of Holocaust perpetrators that sought to go beyond one-dimensional caricature.[9]

My point, based on Browning, Lifton, and many others, is simple: any book that I select on the perpetrators must reject demonization as its primary characterization or explanation. The kind of understanding I want my students to achieve is only possible if we avoid the dead end of demonizing.

As is obvious in the comments above, some persons fear that seeking to understand and to empathize with the perpetrators will result in an inability to condemn evil, in a loss of moral judgment, or in the moral confusion Reagan exhibited in going to Bitburg. They feel the power of the old French adage. *"Tout comprendre c'est tout pardonner."* This is a concern, yet where the moral compass remains steady, understanding does not necessarily lead to forgiveness. Browning is very emphatic on this point, "What I do not accept . . . are the old clichés that to explain is to excuse, to understand is to forgive. Explaining is not excusing; understanding is not forgiving." [10] In my students and myself, the capacity for empathy must be linked with the capacity for discerning moral judgment.

The rejection of demonizing and stereotyping opens the door for a serious confrontation with the questions I originally raised about the perpetrators. Of the works under consideration, part 1 of Raul Hilberg's recent book *Perpetrators, Victims, Bystanders,* provides the most broad ranging answers to the questions, "Who were the perpetrators?" "What functions did they perform?" It also indicates important differences among perpetrators. In eight chapters beginning with one on Hitler, "the supreme architect of the Third Reich" and "the first and foremost perpetrator," Hilberg describes the "vast establishment of familiar functionaries and ascending newcomers," [11] who transformed Hitler's intentions into reality. The strength of Hilberg's work lies in classification— categorizing the wide array of perpetrators—description, and documentation. His vast knowledge and total immersion in the archival material are noticeable as he delineates the actions of perpetrators all over the continent in a flat, dry prose style, but he "seems more convinced than ever that the terrible events he describes speak, in a sense, for themselves." [12] Hilberg's work is surprisingly short on analysis. The section on perpetrators has the briefest of introductions (less than a page in the preface) and no concluding discussion or judgments. He eschews exploration of motivation and psychological makeup. He does note, "The personality characteristics of the perpetrators did not fall into a single mold. The men who performed the destructive work varied not only in their backgrounds but also in their psychological attributes." [13] The point, however, is not developed. Hilberg sees the perpetrators as vital, self-aware cogs in the machinery of destruction. As cogs they are able to diffuse responsibility for their actions. This explanation has merit but is too limited; hence, I did not and would not choose Hilberg's book, despite its strengths, as the assigned reading on perpetrators. I would recommend it to students as supplementary reading or as essential reading if they were doing a paper on perpetrators. I would also want to convey some of the information to students through handouts or minilectures. I fear, however, that Hilberg would not stimulate engaged class discussion, especially on the critical questions of motivation and justification. [14]

In many instances the willingness to sacrifice breadth for depth can result in more acute examination of essential issues. Two studies of groups of perpetrators offer this possibility, those by Lifton and Browning. Extremely ambitious, Lifton's *The Nazi Doctors* confronts the terrible paradox that healers became killers. Lifton dissects the medical profession's role in developing, legitimizing, and actualizing the Nazi "biomedical vision." After discussing the euthanasia program, he turns to the heart of his book, Auschwitz, where doctors supervised "mass murder from beginning to end." [15] Lifton argues that the systematic genocide represented by Auschwitz was enabled by the "medicalization of killing—the imagery of killing in the name of healing" which destroyed "the boundary between healing and killing." [16] Accepting the argument that Jews and others with racial or genetic defects threatened the health of German society, Nazi doctors sought a cure in the surgical removal of the offending agents. Mass murder became a form of therapy. The murderers themselves were disturbingly ordinary, "neither brilliant nor stupid, neither inherently evil nor particularly ethically sensitive." In short, "Nazi doctors were banal," but "in performing demonic acts . . . the men themselves changed, . . . they themselves were no longer banal." [17] According to Lifton, a variety of factors including ideological conviction, socialization to the SS and the routines of "planet Auschwitz," and the psychological mechanisms of "distancing" and "doubling," allowed doctors to accept their roles as killers.

Much commends *The Nazi Doctors* for classroom use. Although dealing with only one type of perpetrator (treating in five hundred pages a group that Hilberg discusses in seven), Lifton provides incredibly rich material and analysis relevant to all the questions raised at the beginning of this paper, but his work is especially strong on the issues of motivation, psychological defense mechanisms, and justification. The ambiguities, the complexities, the problematics of human behavior in the infernal world of Auschwitz are strikingly presented. Lifton describes the investigator who never loses sight of the humanity of the perpetrators and yet retains his morally grounded critique of their actions.[18] It is impossible to do justice to Lifton's multilayered analysis in this brief commentary, but I have little doubt that students would find this book both engaging and provocative. The one major drawback for classroom use is its length. Even highly motivated students will find daunting its 503 pages of small type. Excerpting and assigning several chapters might be a happy compromise, allowing students exposure to significant dimensions of Lifton's presentation without requiring an inordinate time commitment. I would recommend using the introduction, one or more of his case studies of individual Nazi doctors (chapters 16, 17, and 18 dealing with Ernst B., Josef Mengele, and Eduard Wirths respectively), and chapter 19 on psychological doubling. Whatever one chooses to use, the whole or some of its parts, students will only benefit from exposure to this remarkable book.

Few recent books have had the impact of Christopher R. Browning's *Ordinary Men*. Based on court records unusual in their scope and candor which "starkly juxtaposed the monstrous deeds of the Holocaust . . .

with the human faces of the killers," [19] this study presents in disturbing detail the actions of Reserve Police Battalion 101 in liquidating Jewish communities and ghettos in Poland from July 1942 to November 1943. Of the five hundred men of this unit, "most came from Hamburg, by reputation one of the least nazified cities in Germany, and the majority came from a social class [the working class] that had been anti-Nazi in its political culture"; yet, when given the choice, 80 percent to 90 percent of these middle aged men killed Jews in large numbers.[20] Why? Browning addresses this difficult question in his concluding chapter after he has described the role of the Order Police in the Final Solution and presented the history of this unit. The rich descriptive material in the body of the book, enveloping the reader in the gruesome processes of killing and the behaviors of the killers, creates an essential context for the concluding analysis.

This final discussion has the virtues of modesty—Browning reminds us that "the behavior of any human being is . . . a very complex phenomenon, and the historian who attempts to 'explain' it is indulging in a certain arrogance" [21]—of offering a multifaceted explanation for that behavior, of assessing the findings of this case study in the light of other research—most importantly that of Dower, Hilberg, Steiner, Zimbardo, and Milgram—and of preserving the capacity for both empathy and judgment. In the end, for Browning, the men of Reserve Police Battalion 101 murdered 38,000 Jews not because they were preselected for the task due to prior brutality or because they had been brainwashed to kill, but because of the brutalizing consequences of war and racism, the segmentation and routinization of the task, careerism, deference to authority, obedience to orders, and, perhaps most importantly, conformity to the group. From the chilling cover photograph to the haunting concluding question, "If the men of Reserve Police Battalion 101 could become killers under such circumstances, what group of men cannot?," *Ordinary Men* commends itself for classroom use. If not as weighty or subtle as Lifton's work, this book benefits from relative brevity, lucidity, compelling material, careful analysis, and judicious judgments.

A final category of books requiring evaluation is that treating individual perpetrators. While biography or autobiography may not be the most fashionable of historical genres, it can be of particular value in dealing with complex questions and fragmentary evidence.[22] Studies of key perpetrators potentially allow the reader the benefits of a depth of insight into an individual's background, psychological makeup, motivation, behavior, and role in the Holocaust. Although the case could certainly be made for using one of the many fine biographies of Hitler, "the first and foremost perpetrator," I would caution against this choice, since Hitler was too removed from the implementation of the Final Solution to illumine critical aspects of the perpetrators' roles; however, that of Richard Breitman dealing with Himmler deserves consideration.[23]

Breitman's *The Architect of Genocide* gives us a much needed examination of the individual who was arguably the critical figure in the execution of the Final Solution. Breitman focuses "on Himmler's role in the decisionmaking of what the Nazis formally called the 'Final Solution of the Jewish Question.' "[24] Having combed a vast array of archival sources and made imaginative use of Himmler's log books, Breitman is able to reconstruct in considerable detail the steps leading to mass murder, thrusting Himmler into the center of debate about when the decision for genocide was actual made. By the late summer of 1941, ideological commitment, external circumstances, and the removal of practical obstacles made it possible for Himmler to move forward with plans to exterminate the Jews in Europe.[25] This is important work and Breitman deserves praise for his careful, if at times speculative, analysis of decisionmaking and his contribution to the intentionalist-functionalist discussion. Given this emphasis, however, the book is less helpful in addressing the questions about the perpetrators posed at the beginning of this paper. At points, even Himmler disappears in the detailed recording of meetings, memos, trips, and orders. Although Breitman does seek reasons for Himmler's behavior, he reminds us, "There is no simple environmental or psychological explanation as to why Himmler became a mass murderer on an unprecedented scale."[26] In the end, Breitman presents Himmler as the bureaucrat, skilled in intrigue and political infighting, and as the idealistic, ideological fanatic willing to use any means to destroy the enemies of Germandom while maintaining a rigid bourgeois morality in his personal life. This interpretation is sound, but *The Architect of Genocide,* lacking the rich personal material of Browning and Lifton, or a prose style that is particularly accessible to undergraduates, has limitations as the primary work on perpetrators in a course on the Holocaust.

A more promising alternative is Hannah Arendt's classic study of one of Kaltenbrunner's subordinates, Adolf Eichmann, who worked in the Reich Security Main Office (*Reichsicherheitshauptamt,* RSHA) as the Gestapo expert on Jewish affairs. *Eichmann in Jerusalem* interweaves three narrative strands: (1) a study of Eichmann; (2) an examination of the stages and processes of the Holocaust, based largely on Hilberg's *Destruction of the European Jews,* to assess the extent of Eichmann's responsibility; and (3) an evaluation of Eichmann's trial before the District Court of Jerusalem. The result is a compelling, insightful, passionate, and controversial book. Given the purposes of this chapter, I will comment on Arendt's treatment of Eichmann and the light it sheds on perpetrators. According to Arendt, Eichmann lacked both a demonic nature ("half a dozen psychiatrists have certified him as 'normal' ") and a commitment to virulent anti-Semitism ("his was . . . no case of insane hatred of Jews, of fanatical anti-Semitism or indoctrination").[27] What disturbs was his very ordinariness, his "banality." Unable to think independently, Eichmann "was genuinely incapable of uttering a single sentence that was not a cliché."[28] Language was one protection against the reality of his deeds. There were others. Eichmann saw himself as a man who in good conscience responded to the imperatives of duty and the law, who worked with Zionists toward a common end (emigration) until the Führer's decision for extermination cost him "all joy in my work, all initiative, all interest,"[29] and who never personally inflicted pain on others. Arendt notes, "He showed unmistakable signs of sincere outrage when witnesses told of cruelties and atrocities committed by SS men."[30] Eichmann emerges from Arendt's pages as the zealous, middle-level bureaucrat, representative of one crucial category of perpetrator. If Arendt's work does not provide systematic analysis of all types of perpetrators, it does give students enough material to construct partial answers to virtually all the questions I posed at the beginning of the paper and is especially rich on the nature of perpetrators, their motivations, and self-justifications. A variety of courses have successfully used this book, and I would not hesitate to use it in part, or in its entirety, for a segment on perpetrators.[31]

If Eichmann represents the perpetrator as bureaucrat who engineered the movement of Jews to the death camps in Poland but was removed from the actual processes of killing, Rudolf Höss and Franz Stangl, as death camp commandants, were centrally involved in the murder of several million Jews and other victims of the Holocaust. As such, they constitute horrifying but fascinating subjects of study. Both Höss's auto-biography, *Commandant of Auschwitz,* and Gitta Sereny's impressive reconstruction of the life and thought of Stangl, *Into That Darkness,* plunge the reader into the world of the perpetrator and facilitate the exploration of key issues of role, motivation, and self-justification.

Written in January and February of 1947 in a Polish prison as he was about to stand trial for his crimes, Höss's work must be used with caution for it is not always accurate and is rife with self-justification. But even when Höss pursues obfuscation, there is much this book reveals to the reasonably discerning student. Despite that fact that Höss loved his wife and family and noted that "I was no longer happy at Auschwitz once the mass extermination had begun,"[32] it is not difficult to under-stand why he ended up as the commander of the major death-labor camp. Taught by parents whom he respected but did not love that "the state had to be obeyed unconditionally"[33] and that duty was everything, Höss lied about his age—he was fifteen—and joined the army in 1916, seeing extensive action in the Middle East. Following the war he entered a *Freikorps* unit and fought in the Baltic, became a member of the National Socialist party in 1922, and was soon thereafter convicted of the murder of a political opponent. After six years in prison he was released in an amnesty and threw himself into the anti-urban, neo-romantic, farming movement, the Artaman League. This put him in contact with Himmler, who invited him to join the SS and appointed him to the guard unit at Dachau. He rose through the ranks at Dachau and Sachsenhausen, becoming in May 1940 Commandant of Auschwitz, a position very different from the priesthood that his parents had desig-nated for him in his youth or the farmer that he claimed was his desired goal in life. If Höss's career path is unsurprising, so too are the self-justifications of this man who finally in 1947 recognized "that the extermination of the Jews was fundamentally wrong," not because it was morally reprehensible, but "because . . . these mass exterminations [have] drawn upon Germany the hatred of the entire world" and "in no way served the cause of anti-Semitism."[34] Scattered throughout *Com-mandant of Auschwitz* are numerous "explanations" for Auschwitz and his role there. To summarize: (1) his primary role at Auschwitz was as builder, that is to make Auschwitz into a giant center of munitions production (104); (2) his good intentions were often undermined by his subordinates, trained under the brutal regime of Theodore Eicke, who paid little attention to his orders which he could not enforce since he was far too busy with other functions (97–101, 105); (3) he personally did not hate Jews or mistreat prisoners and always sought the most humane methods of killing (123, 137, 170); (4) prisoners themselves often exhibited the greatest brutality toward other prisoners (106–7) and Jews suffered higher levels of mortality primarily because of their psychological fatalism (123); (5) as a National Socialist and SS man he had no choice but to follow orders and do his duty to the best of his ability, especially since he lacked the broader view to determine whether extermination was justified (135); (6) he had to adopt a hard exterior to hide his own softness (his tendency to identify with the prisoners) and because the goal of winning the war was more important than his own feelings (70, 134). Pathetic attempts at self-exoneration no doubt, but encountering them in print gives students insights into how perpetrators could do what they did. At another level, the Höss autobiography allows students to construct an answer to the question "Why?" One could reasonably hypothesize that Höss, coarsened by the brutalizing experiences of war and prison, acted out of ideological commitment, a strong sense of duty and loyalty to his superiors and the SS, and a passion to excel in completing the tasks assigned, regardless of their nature.

The parallels between Höss and Franz Stangl, commandant at Sobibor and Treblinka, are striking. But if Höss had only to face his conscience, such as it was, and the judgment of history as he wrote, Stangl confronted the searing examination of Gitta Sereny, who had covered his 1970 trial in Düsseldorf for the *Daily Telegraph,* then engaged him in seventy hours of interviews in his prison cell between April and June 1971. While she sought "to assess the circumstances which led up to his involvement, for once, not from our point of view, but from *his,*" she was also unfailing in her commitment to probing, however painfully, beneath his clichés and self-justifications. Her examination of Franz Stangl is woven into a masterful reconstruction of his life based on interviews with other key figures and significant historical research. The result is a work of impressive breadth, yet with the searing power that comes from the sharply focused study of an individual perpetrator. *Commandant of Auschwitz* cannot compete on these dimensions. *Into That Darkness* also offers the reader important insights into the roles and attitudes of other perpetrators—for example, of Dieter Allers, the chief administrator of the T4 office that controlled the euthanasia program, who responded to Sereny's question, "Do you regret what was done [in the Holocaust]?" with,

> Well yes, that goes without saying. But, on the other hand, if one realizes what the situation was in Germany in the early 1930s: I remember when I said I wanted to study law, somebody in my family took me to the Ministry of Justice in Berlin. We walked along a corridor and he told me to read the names on the office doors we passed. Almost all of them were Jews. And it was the same for the press, the banks, business; in Berlin all of it was in the hands of Jews. That wasn't right. There should have been *some* Germans.[35] (italics in the original)

In addition, her interviews (five in number) with survivors from Sobibor and Treblinka and her examination of the actions of the Roman Catholic Church and the Vatican in response to the Final Solution and in assisting perpetrators, including Stangl, to escape from Europe offer valuable insights about both victims and bystanders.

The examination of Stangl remains at the heart of the book, whose merit rides on the quality of that investigation. Like that of Höss, Stangl's road to Treblinka has an internal logic. Trained as a weaver in the small Austrian town of Altmünster, Stangl abandoned his trade at twenty-three and joined the police in 1931, earning a posting to the political (security) division in 1934. That, according to Stangl, "was the first step on the road to catastrophe,"[36] for after the Anschluss this section of the police was incorporated into the Gestapo, which in turn led to his assignment to the euthanasia program, a training ground for almost four hundred individuals subsequently involved in the Final Solution.[37] In the spring of 1942, Stangl was ordered to report to SS Headquarters in Lublin where Odilo Globocnik, coordinator of the Final Solution in Poland, assigned him to the building of the death camp at Sobibor. Transferred to Treblinka in September 1942, he supervised the murder of 900,000 people over the course of the next eleven months.

How does one reconcile this fact with the descriptions of Stangl as "an incredibly good and kind father . . . the best father, the best friend anyone could ever have had"?[38] There is no pat answer to this question, but it is apparent that Stangl rigidly compartmentalized his life, separating family from his professional work. Sereny writes "of extraordinary manifestations of a dual personality" and of the physical transformation that affected Stangl "when he had to speak about a new and terrible phase in his life." [39] Stangl also resorted to other common stratagems to diffuse any sense of guilt or personal responsibility. He argued that at the time of his appointments he was in the dark about the realities of the euthanasia program and Sobibor; that he never personally harmed anyone, and that he had no choice but to follow the orders of his superiors. As he put it, "It was a matter of survival—always of survival. What I had to do, while I continued my efforts to get out, was to limit my own actions to what I—in my own conscience—could answer for." [40] No matter that he commanded two death camps with energy and dedication; as long as he personally did not pull the trigger or start the engines for the gas chambers, he was not guilty. This separation of his function as death camp commandant from his personal actions was delusional, and only at the end of his long journey with Sereny did Stangl finally speak haltingly of " 'my guilt': but more than the words the finality of it was in the sagging of his body, and on his face." [41] Nineteen hours later he was dead of heart failure.

I used *Into That Darkness* in my course on the Holocaust and it fostered informed, engaged student discussion about the roles and functions of perpetrators, their motives, and their self-justifications. My students were both appalled and fascinated by Stangl; they acknowledged his humanity while condemning the choices he made in his life. In the end, they gave the book high marks for the contribution it made to the course. On a scale of 1 (excellent) to 5 (wretched), *Into That Darkness* earned a 1.25. Although I have indicated other works that deserve strong consideration when I next teach the course, I would be loath to discard this outstanding book.

I have argued that an effective unit on perpetrators in a course on the Holocaust depends on moving beyond the dead end of demonizing while sustaining a creative tension between understanding and moral judgment. The ability to engage significant questions about perpetrators is greatly enhanced by the quality of the reading selected for the unit. While no single text can address all issues equally well, we are fortunate to have a number of books that powerfully delineate the backgrounds, behaviors, motivations, and justifications of perpetrators. The best of them confront the difficult task of explaining how and why perpetrators became part of the system of mass murder, while recognizing that no explanation can ever fully illuminate these painful issues. They also remind us of our own vulnerability, that "everywhere the human soul stands between a hemisphere of light and another of darkness."[42]

NOTES

1. " 'Good History' and Teaching the Holocaust," *Perspectives* 31, no. 5 (May/June 1993): 6.

2. *Perpetrators, Victims, Bystanders: The Jewish Catastrophe, 1933–1945* (New York: HarperCollins, 1992), ix.

3. I am obviously omitting discussion of the rich periodical literature and visual material on perpetrators. For readers interested in the possible use of these sources in the classroom the following information should be helpful. Hilberg is available as a HarperPerennial paperback from HarperCollins (1993), as is the Browning (1993). A paperback edition of Lifton is published by Basic Books (1988), while paperback editions are also available for Breitman from University Press of New England (1992), for Arendt from Penguin (1977), and for Sereny from Random House (Vintage, 1983). The Höss is only available in hardback at the present time as *Death Dealer: The Memoirs of the SS Kommandant of Auschwitz*, ed. Steven Paskuly (Buffalo: Prometheus Books, 1992).

4. Dimsdale, ed., *Survivors, Victims, and Perpetrators: Essays on the Nazi Holocaust* (Washington, D.C.: Hemisphere Publishing, 1980), 284.

5. For example, Robert Jay Lifton discusses "the cult of demonic personality" surrounding Mengele in *The Nazi Doctors* (New York: Basic Books, 1986), 337–38. Eichmann, who in the minds of many was chiefly responsible for the implementation of the Final Solution, was according to Gideon Hausner, the prosecutor at his trial, "a man obsessed with a dangerous and insatiable urge to kill" and "a perverted, sadistic personality." Quoted in Hannah Arendt, *Eichmann in Jerusalem* (New York: Viking Press, 1964), 26. John Steiner notes, "the SS are viewed as utterly evil and sadistic, and criminal motives are attributed to all of them," in "The SS Yesterday and Today: A Sociopsychological View," in *Survivors,* ed. Dimsdale, 406. Peter Black, *Ernst Kaltenbrunner* (Princeton: Princeton University Press, 1984), 3, writes that the portrait of Kaltenbrunner which emerged at the Nuremberg War Crimes Trial was that of "an insensitive murderer, a callous super-criminal whose actions placed him beyond the human pale."

6. For example, Breitman (1991), Browning, Hilberg (1992).

7. xi–xii. This point was also made by Bruno Bettelheim, who writes, "Having devoted much of my life to this problem, I restricted myself to trying to understand the psychology of prisoners and I shied away from trying to understand the psychology of the SS — because of the ever-present danger that under-

standing fully may come close to forgiving. I believe there are acts so vile that our task is to reject and prevent them, not to try to understand them empathetically." "Their Specialty Was Murder," review of *The Nazi Doctors* by Robert Jay Lifton, *New York Times Book Review*, October 5, 1986, 62.

8. Ibid. Lifton also wisely reminds us that there are limitations to our understanding of the Holocaust when he quotes a survivor, "The professor would like to understand what is not understandable. We ourselves who were there, and who have always asked ourselves the question and will ask it until the end of our lives, we will never understand it, because it can never be understood" (13).

9. (New York: HarperCollins, 1992), xix-xx.

10. Ibid.

11. Hilberg, *Perpetrators*, 10, ix.

12. Michael R. Marrus, "Acts that Speak for Themselves," review of *Perpetrators* by Raul Hilberg, *New York Times Book Review*, September 20, 1992, 14.

13. Hilberg, *Perpetrators*, 51.

14. Hilberg includes some fascinating biographical sketches of perpetrators, but he does not use this material to examine the issues of motivation or justification. In addition, I am concerned about his dry prose style and the lack of analysis and explicit argument. The very breadth of Hilberg's discussion makes it more difficult to zero in on some of the key issues. I also would agree with Marrus's judgment that Hilberg "remains aloof from much of this new work [of younger scholars] and material." Review of *Perpetrators* by Marrus, *New York Times Book Review*, September 20, 1992, 15.

15. Lifton, *The Nazi Doctors*, 4.

16. Ibid., 14.

17. Ibid., 4, 14. In these comments Lifton is responding directly to Arendt's "banality of evil" thesis. While much of his evidence appears to confirm her thesis, Lifton makes the argument stated here, that their involvement in such evil actually changed *The Nazi Doctors*.

18. The dynamics of his interaction with Ernst B., "a unique Nazi doctor in Auschwitz: a man who treated inmates (especially prisoner doctors) as human beings, who saved many of their lives; who had refused to do selections in Auschwitz; who had been so appreciated by prisoner doctors that, when tried after the war, their testimony on his behalf brought about his acquittal," (303) as described on pages 328–32, reflect in dramatic fashion the duality of Lifton's relationship to these individuals.

19. Browning, *Ordinary Men*, xvi.

20. Ibid., 48, 159.

21. Ibid., 188.

22. The point is made by Breitman, *The Architect of Genocide* (New York: Alfred A. Knopf, 1991), 17.

23. Given the absence of a written order authorizing the Final Solution, the degree to which Hitler bears primary responsibility for it has been the subject of some controversy. Gerald Fleming, *Hitler and the Final Solution* (Berkeley: University of California Press, 1984), confronts this issue and should be consulted.

24. Breitman, *Architect,* 18.

25. Ibid., 206.

26. Ibid., 9.

27. *Eichmann in Jerusalem,* 25–26.

28. Ibid., 48.

29. Ibid., 84.

30. Ibid., 109.

31. I would, of course, have to provide students with a broader view of the Judenräte and Jewish resistance than she offers in the book.

32. *Commandant of Auschwitz* (New York: Popular Library, 1959), 146. This raises the question whether Höss's happiness had been the product of "normal" numbers of dead as the result of hard labor and brutal conditions.

33. Ibid., 23.

34. Ibid., 168.

35. Gitta Sereny, *Into That Darkness* (New York: Random House, Vintage Books, 1983), 90.

36. Ibid., 29.

37. Ibid., 84.

38. Ibid., 348–49.

39. Ibid., 14, 50.

40. Ibid., 164.

41. Ibid., 364.

42. To introduce her book, Sereny quotes these words of Thomas Carlyle along with those of Origen, "The power of choosing between good and evil is within the reach of us all."

CHAPTER 16

Teaching the Holocaust and Making It

Relevant for Non-Jewish Students

MICHAEL F. BASSMAN

As faculty members in present-day American universities, we are often, out of a need for professional "survival," forced to undertake an added task to the traditional ones of teaching, research, and service; namely, that of trying to "sell" our courses to students. With fewer requirements, young people may now pick and choose more often. As a result, their priority for the most part is not learning for its own reward but learning so that down the road they will have an edge on landing a better job with a higher salary. On the one hand, we can understand this way of thinking; on the other, especially for those of us who are products of the late 1960s, the obsession with money perplexes us. And for those of us in the humanities, we are painfully aware of the increasingly more prevalent occurrence of having a class cancelled because of insufficient enrollment. It seems that the powers-to-be are obsessed with numbers. In addition, we must continue to push for a multicultural vision which is not, as skeptics claim, simply a "fad." In the early 1980s, with cognizance of the above, I developed a course on the Holocaust. A description of my university is appropriate here before describing the course.

East Carolina College (ECU) was founded in 1907 as a teacher-training institution serving the rural eastern portion of North Carolina. In 1960, the college became a university and then, eight years later, one of the sixteen constituent institutions of the University of North Carolina system. In fact, ECU today, with a student population of 18,000, has become the third largest school in the system. A clear majority of students are still from eastern North Carolina—a region that has remained predominantly rural. Greenville, the home of the university, is situated between Raleigh and the coast. The population has recently reached 50,000, with the growth spurt linked primarily to the opening of the ECU School of Medicine in the late 1970s.

As a faculty member in foreign languages and literatures, I have traditionally taught French and Latin. I did, however, harbor an undisclosed passion for Yiddish studies, but there was not much if any demand for this field here. Fortunately, there was a growing Honors Program for which an instructor could submit a course proposal and, if approved by the appropriate committees, offer the course during one semester. I had already had a positive experience of team-teaching a course on "The World as Seen by Nobel Prize Winners in Literature." As my interest in Yiddish studies blossomed and I actively pursued it as an area of research, I was soon exposed to Holocaust literature. In time, I drew up a course proposal which was then approved and publicized as "Literature of the Holocaust." In 1982, when first offered, eight students enrolled. Naturally, as with any new course, an instructor needs time to feel that he or she is on terra firma. A year later, I requested permission to teach the course again and twelve students enrolled this time. As I began to gain confidence and feel comfortable with the material, I decided to propose "Literature of the Holocaust" as a permanent component of the university's curriculum. I did specify, however, that the course be open to all students, as only those in the Honors Program could enroll previously. The "new" course was in place by the mid-1980s and was listed as a free elective counting towards the General Education requirement in the Humanities. Today, the course has also become required for the minor in Ethnic Studies.

"Literature of the Holocaust" has in the last four years become one of the most popular courses on campus. In fact, forty-five to fifty students regularly enroll every spring semester when the course is given. My intent was to offer a seminar class, an impossibility with so many students. I suggested that the course be taught every semester; my department, however, would release me only one time per year. Therefore, I do not turn away a student who genuinely expresses interest in the class but cannot take it the following year. It should be noted that I make every effort to conduct the class in the style of a seminar. Discussions are, therefore, intense and emotional; it is rare that the students do not leave the class troubled but also reflective. I have chosen to teach the class during a three-hour block in the evening. Admittedly, it is an exhausting experience for all involved; however, I believe it is preferable to continue a passionate discussion rather than to cut it off and try to recapture it the next time. By selecting evening hours for the class, I try to make it available to our nontraditional students, who are usually older and working full-time.

Interestingly, the number of minority students in the class has been low, although last spring's enrollment included three African Americans. I hope to attract more minority students in the future and this can be done by clearly demonstrating that the course material is relevant to their lives (to be discussed later). Concerning the number of Jewish students, there are usually two or three, not surprising given the low enrollment of this religious-ethnic group at the university. So the class has almost entirely consisted of white, Protestant students from the central and eastern regions of North Carolina.

In addition to all of the above, I was keenly aware of a problematic situation that had arisen in 1990 while attending a seminar on the Holocaust in Jerusalem. The participants, all college professors, had gathered at Yad Vashem for intensive work on teaching the Holocaust. Our daily discussions were always animated and, at times, heated. One of the recurring moot issues involved the resentment, frequently expressed by several of the participants, towards the few non-Jews in attendance; in other words, how could "they" (the "outsiders") truly understand the Shoah, which was for the most part a Jewish experience (in terms of the victims). I, for one, was appalled by this view and considered it to be entirely insensitive. Granted that a chasm exists between an "insider" (or "victim," in this case) and an "outsider." The latter can, of course, never truly put him/herself "into" the experiences of the former; nevertheless, there is certainly a need for empathy, sensitivity, and awareness on both sides. Further, I believe that the adamant refusal to bridge the gap and remain insular in the end will be detrimental, perhaps, even leading to "Holocaust-type" events. In my opinion, what must become a pivotal statement for all of us is George Santayana's "those who ignore the past, are condemned to repeat it." For me, "those" connotes each and every person.

Now, to look at the actual course by using the syllabus (minus the "Selected Bibliography") prepared for the spring semester of 1993.

Spring 1993 Dr. Michael Bassman
"Literature of the Holocaust"

SYLLABUS

January 12 Introduction
Lecture and Discussion: Definition of "Holocaust" and
the unique/universal aspects of the Holocaust
Video: "Night and Fog"

19 Quiz
Lecture and Discussion: Anti-Semitism
Discussion: *The Painted Bird*
Video: "Triumph of the Will"

26 Quiz
Discussion: *The Diary of a Young Girl* Lecture and Dis-
cussion: The Weimar Republic and the Rise of Nazism
Video: "Last Seven Months of Anne Frank"

February 2 Quiz
Discussion: *This Way for the Gas . . .*
Lecture and Discussion: Hitler's Henchmen
Video: "Jews of Poland"

9 Quiz
Discussion: *Night*
Lecture and Discussion: Polish Jewry between the Wars
Speaker: Dr. Linda Allred, Psychologist
Slides: Warsaw Ghetto

16 Quiz
Project Approval
Discussion: *A Scrap of Time*
Lecture and Discussion: Stages of the Final Solution
Video: "Shoah"

23 Quiz
Discussion: *Anton the Dove Fancier*
Lecture and Discussion: Jewish Responses to the Holo-
caust
Video: "Shoah" (continued)

March 2 Quiz
Project dates assigned
Discussion: *Man's Search for Meaning*
Lecture and Discussion: Transports and the Death
Camps

Video: "Memory of the Camps"

9 Spring Break

16 Quiz
Discussion: *An Interrupted Life*
Lecture and Discussion: Literature of the Holocaust
Speaker: Dr. John Moskop, Professor of Medical Humanities Slides and recordings: "I Never Saw Another Butterfly"

23 Quiz
Discussion: *Maus*
Lecture and Discussion: World Response
Speaker: Holocaust Survivor
Video: "Interviews with children . . ."

30 Quiz
Discussion: *Maus II*
Lecture and Discussion: Impact
Speaker: Dr. Susan McCammon, Psychologist
Video: "Safe Haven"

April 6 Quiz
Discussion: *Children of the Holocaust*
Lecture and Discussion: Anti-Semitism Today
Speaker: Dr. Irena Klepfisz, Poet and child of a survivor
Video: "A Generation Apart"

13 No Class

20 Scrapbooks due
Student Presentations

27 Student Presentations/Exams due
Video: "They Risked their Lives"

May 4 Student Presentations
Video: "California Reich"

REQUIREMENTS

1. As the seminar meets only one time/week, class attendance is essential. You will be allowed one absence; however, I urge you not to miss any classes. More than one absence will result in the lowering of the final grade. In addition, you are expected to remain for the entire class.

2. In determining the final grade, the following will be taken into
   account:
Class discussion	10%
Quizzes (11) to be added	25%
"Creative" Project	20%
"Scrapbook": (minimum of 3 articles/week)	20%
Final Exam	25%
	100%
3. Required readings (there may be additions and/or deletions):
   Borowski, Tadeusz. *This Way for the Gas, Ladies and Gen-
   tlemen.* (Penguin)
   Epstein, Helen. *Children of the Holocaust.* (Penguin)
   Fink, Ida. *A Scrap of Time.* (Pantheon)
   Frank, Anne. *The Diary of A Young Girl.* (Simon and
   Schuster)
   Frankl, Viktor. *Man's Search for Meaning.* (Pocket Books)
   Gotfryd, Bernard. *Anton the Dove Fancier.* (Pocket Books)
   Hillesum, Etty. *An Interrupted Life.* (Washington Square)
   Kosinski, Jerzy. *The Painted Bird.* (Bantam)
   Spiegelman, Art. *Maus,* and *Maus II.* (Pantheon)
   Wiesel, Elie. *Night.* (Avon)

Basically, the class is divided into two one-hour twenty-five minute
sessions with a ten-minute break in the middle. The first part includes
the quiz, lecture, and discussion. The second is devoted to a video and/
or slides or a speaker. As noted on the syllabus, the class usually begins
with a ten-minute quiz on the assigned book for that day. I would prefer
to assign journal writing instead of a quiz; this, however, becomes
impossible with 40-plus students. At the first meeting, the hand-outs
include a detailed chronological listing of the events occurring during
the Holocaust. I also recommend but do not require Lucy Dawidowicz's
The War against the Jews 1933–1945.

CONCERNING THE BOOKS

We begin with Kosinski's *The Painted Bird,* a shockingly graphic novel.
My reason for doing this is to immediately immerse the students in the
horrific so that they will always be aware of it, but not become obsessed

with it to the exclusion of everything else. This usually happens; in a way, however, it is frightening to realize how quickly a person can become immune to the violence.

The selection of the other required readings is difficult as many poignant books go out-of-print so quickly (such as Kuznetsov's *Babi Yar,* Leitner's *Fragments of Isabella,* Hochhuth's *The Deputy,* and Sherman's *Bent*). Among the criteria used in selecting a book, I always consider the length (no more than 200–250 pages), as a book is read for each class. With this in mind, some superlative books (David Wyman's *The Abandonment of the Jews,* for example) must be excluded from consideration. Additional criteria for selection include the book's "readability" for the students (most of whom are sophomores) and its relevance not only to the course but also to their lives. As the members of the class have frequent opportunities to critique the readings, it becomes apparent to me which books have truly had an impact on them. In some cases, and with reluctance, I discontinue a book that I have considered meaningful and appropriate if many students have complained about it. Such was the case with Hannah Arendt's *Eichmann in Jerusalem,* a powerful book in my opinion but one that students repeatedly disliked. One book, however, that I have continued to require in spite of student laments is Etty Hillesum's *An Interrupted Life.* This book always polarizes the students and, as a result, the discussions tend to be heated but interesting, with older students generally on one side and younger ones on the other.

The readings to which the students best relate have usually been *The Diary of a Young Girl* by Anne Frank and *Night* by Elie Wiesel. In addition, *Maus* and *Maus II,* which are in comic-strip form with animals representing people, are popular and stimulate absorbing discussions. Videos/slides/films are all vital to the course but, again, selectivity is crucial. "Night and Fog," "Memory of the Camps," and excerpts from the nine-and-a-half hour "Shoah" have all been effective. A video that quickly showed me the need to be extremely careful in my choices was "Jud Süss." Although I thought I had adequately prepared the class before showing this Nazi-propaganda film, I came to realize how unsophisticated and young the students truly were. We did not have the time to discuss the film as it was longer than expected. I told the class that we would discuss it at the beginning of class the following week. In the interim, I ran into several students from the class who expressed their outrage at what the "deceitful Jews" had done to the "innocent Germans." I therefore began the next class with the comment that the propaganda was so clever that even the students had fallen for it.

Equally important is the selection of guest speakers. I have found that it is important to invite diverse guests, ranging from Holocaust survivors and their children to psychiatrists/psychologists to people who deny the Holocaust. A priority in selecting a speaker is to find someone who will generate class discussion while furthering the students' understanding of the goals of the course.

Perhaps one of the most useful learning experiences for the students is the "scrapbook." The assignment involves the collection of three newspaper/magazine articles weekly. The students must use three different sources and the articles must relate to a "Holocaust-type" event, such as the "ethnic cleansing" in Bosnia. The students summarize the articles and then comment on them while relating them to the course. By the end of the semester, they express in amazement the number of "Holocaust-type" events still going on; in other words, it is not past history for them but something that continues on in their lifetime.

Lastly, each student is required to present a "creative" project before the class at the end of the semester. They are free to choose what they would like to do, but it must first be approved by me. Members of the class grade each other based on "originality," "learning experience," "relevance to the course," and "preparation time." The projects vary from original short stories, poems, paintings, to creative dances and shooting a video about racism on campus.

An interesting example of how the students relate the concerns of the class to their own lives occurred when a student recounted a story in class about her minister's "joke" concerning a Jew and his money. She was offended at the idea that her religious leader would use this tasteless stereotype. She expressed her outrage to the class and was encouraged by the other students to address the issue with the minister.

The students, from their angle, have also mentioned such things as:

1. The realization that horrific, Holocaust-type events continue.
2. The Nazi perpetrators were, for the most part, "normal" human beings and, under certain conditions, many of us are capable of acting in a similar way. In other words, the students no longer continue to say "I never could have committed such an atrocity

towards someone else." They become more and more cognizant of the complexities of human nature and, in fact, by the end of the semester, they realize that brutal acts of violence are "easier" to perpetrate than they had originally thought.

3. The importance of studying the Holocaust at the high-school level or even earlier. A number of students have mentioned the fact that they have returned to their high schools to share the syllabus with a teacher and/or librarian; and, at times, they have even volunteered to speak to a class about the Holocaust.

4. The students have also mentioned the need to "require" a course on the Holocaust or a class dealing with diversity.

In conclusion, I would like to say that the experience of teaching the class has been monumental for me as I feel, in a small way, that I am helping to prevent the realization of George Santayana's statement while increasing student awareness and sensitivity. Throughout the semester, as student empathy and understanding increase, my level of satisfaction, as an effective teacher, also increases. I feel that I am influencing these young people, not only making them more informed but also more alert to what is happening around them.

References

I. Books—all of the following are readily available except for those preceded by an asterisk (*), indicating that the book is out-of-print.

Arendt, Hannah. *Eichmann in Jerusalem*. New York: Penguin, 1965.

Borowski, Tadeusz. *This Way for the Gas, Ladies and Gentlemen*. Trans. Barbara Vedder. New York: Penguin, 1980.

Dawidowicz, Lucy. *The War against the Jews 1933–1945*. New York: Bantam, 1975.

Epstein, Helen. *Children of the Holocaust*. New York: Penguin, 1979.

Fink, Ida. *A Scrap of Time*. Trans. Madeline Levine and Francine Prose. New York: Pantheon, 1987.

Frank, Anne. *The Diary of a Young Girl*. New York: Simon and Schuster, 1972. See also *The Diary of a Young Girl: The Definitive Edition*. Ed. Otto H. Frank and Mirjam Pressler. New York: Doubleday, 1995.

Frankl, Viktor. *Man's Search for Meaning*. New York: Pocket, 1984.

Gotfryd, Bernard. *Anton the Dove Fancier.* New York: Pocket, 1990.

Hillesum, Etty. *An Interrupted Life.* Trans. J. G. Gaarlandt. New York: Washington Square, 1985.

*Hochhuth, Rolf. *The Deputy.* Trans. Richard and Clara Winston. New York: Grove, 1964.

Kosinski, Jerzy. *The Painted Bird.* New York: Bantam, 1972.

*Kuznetsov, A. Anatoli. *Babi Yar.* Trans. David Floyd. New York: Pocket, 1971.

*Leitner, Isabella. *Fragments of Isabella.* New York: Laurel, 1988.

*Sherman, Martin. *Bent.* New York: Avon, 1979.

Spiegelman, Art. *Maus.* New York: Pantheon, 1986.

———. *Maus II.* New York: Pantheon, 1991.

Wiesel, Elie. *Night.* Trans. Stella Rodway. New York: Avon, 1969.

Wyman, David. *The Abandonment of the Jews.* New York: Pantheon, 1985.

II. Video cassettes—all are readily available.

"California Reich." A film by Walter Parkes and Keith Critchlow, 1986.

"A Generation Apart." A film by Danny and Jack Fisher, 1993.

"Interviews with Children of the Architects of the Holocaust." Segment done on "60 Minutes" in 1991.

"Jews of Poland." A film by Yitzhak and Shaul Goskind, 1988.

"Jud Süss." Nazi-propaganda film directed by Veit Harlan, 1941.

"Last Seven Months of Anne Frank." A 1988 Dutch documentary directed by Willy Lindwer.

"Memory of the Camps." British documentary from 1945 focusing on Bergen-Belsen and other death camps.

"Night and Fog." French documentary directed by Alain Resnais, 1955.

"Safe Haven." American documentary directed and written by Paul Lewis, 1991.

"Shoah." Claude Lanzmann's nine-and-a-half hour oral history of the Holocaust, 1985.

"They Risked their Lives." A film by Gay Block, 1991.

"Triumph of the Will." Nazi-propaganda film directed by Leni Riefenstahl, 1935.

CHAPTER 17

Teaching the Holocaust: Helping

Students Confront Their Own Biases

ELISABETH I. KALAU

At a recent meeting of children of Holocaust survivors and children of Nazis, one woman was asked which side she was on. "On the human side," was my immediate response which I voiced when introducing myself that day. Notwithstanding the uncomfortable fact that I am a child of the Third Reich and the daughter of a Nazi army colonel, I am on the human side. My roots bring neither pride nor joy. Quite to the contrary, they have engendered the opposite. Recognition of my father's contribution to Nazi murders brought me to an abyss of shame—shame for me, for him, for all of Germany and those who share my conviction that all human beings are connected. Living in the United States most of my adult years, I tried not to draw attention to my Germanness and considered speech therapy to rid myself of my accent.

My last ditch effort to get my Nazi heritage out of my system failed in 1988 when I researched my father's assignments at the German Military Archives. At that point, I realized that knowing some of the men whose names I found in the Nazi documents made me a living link to those dreadful times. I despaired about the brutalities against defenseless people in which my father had participated. His support of Nazi crimes and his silence enrage me still—as does the fact that in 1945 he slipped off his Nazi army uniform and in fastidious Prussian manner wrapped those years in silence until he died in 1983. Religious teachings to honor him, my elder, do not ease my rage, which I am likely to take to my grave.

Before discussing three of my courses which focus on the Holocaust, I want briefly to describe the setting. Unlike a great number of Maine's residents, people living or summering on Maine's long and rocky coast are relatively wealthy. Several large paper mills operating in the state are located not at the coast but in mountainous and rural areas, as is our campus. The one million people who call Maine home are predominantly (98.4 percent) white; nearly four thousand of these are Jewish. The majority of our students at the University of Maine at Farmington (UMF) call Maine home and have rarely met someone not Caucasian and not Christian. Some with Franco-American backgrounds may be bilingual, speaking French at home and English in school; therefore, hearing English spoken with such an ethnic accent is not new to them. Few students have heard people like me, however, who "talk funny," that is, someone who speaks English with a German accent. Some have difficulty in understanding me and say so.

Approximately one hundred fifty of UMF's two thousand students are rehabilitation services majors whom, and I quote here from UMF's catalogue, we prepare "to assist disabled and at risk persons to function effectively in their living, learning, and working environment." Compared to other students, we find that those majoring in rehabilitation services are outstanding in their compassion and kindness; they are committed to making ours a better world.

Imparting basic knowledge about psychosocial rehabilitation can be done readily by lecturing. The more challenging aspect of teaching is to get students to examine their own attitudes toward people whom they wish to help, including those who have different ethnic traditions, religious beliefs, and life styles. The repository of good will notwithstanding, many embrace attitudes that put barriers between themselves and other people, including future clients. For that reason, I ask my students to confront these attitudinal barriers which I call prejudices. The courses I teach are generally required for graduation and their enrollment is small. A class of fifteen to twenty-five students allows for a good deal of interaction. I make a point of creating as accepting an atmosphere as possible so that students will feel free to express their opinions. Those who do so without being asked need little or no encouragement. But the reticent ones who do not speak up on their own accord, I call on, acknowledging their inner discomfort. However, my more immediate objective is for them to have an opportunity to speak up in front of a small group of people whom they hardly know and to be more comfortable while doing so. My long term goal is for them to learn to speak up against injustice in any setting.

In a course designed for second year students entitled "Basic Counseling and Interviewing," I go beyond mere discussion of attitudinal barriers. I focus specifically on how these obstruct the client/helper relationship and assign a paper, worth one-quarter of the course grade, which students are to call *My Biases*. For this paper, students examine their prejudices. They scrutinize their attitudes towards persons who have different religious practices, cultural traditions, sexual orientation, and/or disabilities. They are to search their souls and ask themselves: Do I prejudge? Do I see an individual as a person or a stereotypic member of his or her group? Am I biased? What are my prejudices? Why do I have these? Where did I learn them? Who taught them to me? Do I diminish the worth of the person in that way? Since I deem a mere identification of their biases insufficient, I ask them to seek ways to reduce these biases; better yet, to abandon them.

Needless to say, a good many questions are generated by so personal an assignment. Anxiety about exposure runs high, as does worry about getting a failing grade. In an effort to restore some degree of equanimity, I make the following two points:

1. Biased behavior is learned. Until scientists find the genes for racist attitudes, or sexist ones for that matter, we can assume that infants are born without prejudice. Parents, relatives, and others in the social and educational environment impart biases to children who are keen observers as well as imitators. Children absorb these prejudicial attitudes long before they are able to examine whether or not they want to live by them. If identified, examined, vigilantly watched for during interactions with people, confronted, and talked about with others who are supportive of such self-examinations, these stereotypic attitudes and behaviors growing out of them can be unlearned, a process that is not easy, sometimes even painful, but certainly possible.

2. I talk about my childhood in the most biased nation in modern history when Hitler's henchmen, among them my own father, justified their prejudices on the basis of biology and then lethally acted upon them.

I tell my students that I was taught Nazi ideology that claimed Aryans, or Germans, to be a superior "race." It also claimed that by nature men were superior to women. My purpose as a female was to grow up to have many, many children, preferably boys, because Hitler needed men for his army. The life purpose of males, on the other hand, was to fight for the fatherland and Lebensraum (space to live) which served as justification for Nazi attacks on any country Hitler desired. That was why the Hitler Youth boys sang "Germany is ours today and tomorrow the whole world." I learned that certain groups of people were considered "useless eaters"; for example, children with mental retardation had no right to go to school, because when they became adults they would be unable to work and adults who do not work had no right to eat. The same held for people with mental illness and the Gypsies, who, I was told, were thieves, dirty, dishonest, did not hold down a steady job, and were continually on the go.

I tell my students that when I was seven and my sister eleven years old, she told me about the burning of the synagogue in town. At the time, I did not know that the fire was set by government decree and fire fighters were instructed not to put out the flames; nor did I know that police officers received orders to arrest Jewish store owners instead of those who destroyed their properties. When one neighboring family who was Jewish moved away, no one seemed to have noticed their empty house; not one word was said about their furniture factory standing idle. No one in school, none of the neighborhood children nor their parents spoke about it. And my parents? Well—they were silent, too.

In elementary school, each class began and ended with the Hitler salute and every textbook I opened showed a full-page picture of him. At age ten in 1941, I became a Hitler Youth and during the next four years was instructed that Hitler was the savior of Germany and that our victorious soldiers were helping him shape the thousand-year-Nazi Reich. He himself had been a fighter, my Hitler Youth leaders stated, as had been his comrades, who, in all their brutality, were held up to us as role models. We girls were taught that murdering, killing, causing death was the "good" Nazi German way. And, I was to hate our enemies: the English, the French, the Americans, particularly the Poles and Russians who, like blacks, were considered subhumans. As a matter of fact, I was to hate anyone not thought of as German.

But my Nazi teachers did not succeed. As an adult, I began to reflect on my encounters with people and to examine my own reactions by asking myself: why did I feel uncomfortable with that person? How did I get so negative an impression? What assumptions am I making? Do I know enough about the individual? By confronting myself with these as well as those questions my students are to ask themselves for their biases papers, I have removed one layer of prejudice after another—a process that continues to this day.

My personal example opens the door for students to ask questions. Those who from high school classes know something about the Holocaust never fail to ask about our neighbors who were Jewish: "Was I not taught to hate them?" More so than any other, this question sends me on a renewed search through my childhood memories. In class, I say that I remember no adult in my presence making an anti-Semitic remark: not my mother, none of my teachers, not even a Hitler Youth leader. I can't remember hearing one on the radio. Perhaps they were made and I did not understand them; perhaps they were made and I have repressed them. On the other hand, information learned by indoctrination seeps into a person's psyche so that the source cannot be readily identified. That may be the reason why I am unable to recall. But it is more likely, I say in class, that having retained a minimum of what I would call conscience, my mother shielded me from such hateful propaganda. So when it was expressed outside the home, which is very likely, I was unable to grasp its implications. Extended discussions follow, during which the informed students have an opportunity to teach others what they know about the Holocaust. I fill in the gaps. Though shameful to me, I want students to know some basic facts about Hitler's regime, while I express at the same time my adult horror about Nazi acts against humanity, my sorrow about the tremendous suffering, as well as my regret.

Students frequently interject their own religious beliefs, citing God's word as justification for their prejudices. Dismayed at the Christian clergy and German parishioners, so few in number, who helped their Jewish neighbors during Nazi persecution, I feel compelled to query the class: "Were you not taught in Sunday school 'to love your neighbors as yourself?'" Most say "yes," so I pursue the point: "Was the neighbor whom you are to love described in any special way, for example, as being Greek, Catholic, African, and heterosexual?" Students' eyes open wide with astonishment at such an unexpected line of thought and admit that they had not viewed it quite that way. Since I am neither qualified nor willing to lead a denominationally biased Bible study, the discussion continues around the idea and the subsequent difficulty of accepting people of religious faith not like their own, differences in appearance and dress, ethnic traditions and customs, and sexual orientation. The students conclude themselves that "the neighbor" has no description and that they need further to reflect on what they had been taught, how *they* really feel about it, and above all, how they wish to act. I encourage them to be honest with themselves.

Many a student has begun the paper by writing: "I thought myself an open minded and unbiased person but writing this paper I am no longer sure." To me, this uncertainty is an indication that they were open to self-examination. The 270 papers I have read thus far have been refreshing in the honesty expressed, but very troubling in regards to the biases students have revealed; two wrote about their anti-Semitic sentiments. I was shocked even at that small number.

My knowing that unchecked prejudice in Nazi Germany led to evil makes grading these papers an exacting task. I cannot, in all conscience, give a passing grade for a paper, however well written, that is filled with blatant, unexamined biases. If student writers provide no evidence that they searched for the source of their prejudices, that they have either considered the effect their biased acts might have on others or shown me that they explored avenues for changing them but unquestioningly accepted what they had been taught, those students have not met the criteria for a passing grade. If on the other hand, they show a glimmer of earnest soul searching and of having attempted to explore ways of overcoming the barriers of biases, but got stuck in their own prejudicial mire, I might consider a satisfactory grade. But I do so only after deliberation with the student in my office and by submission of a rewritten version of the paper together with the first version. I have to be able to compare and see how and whether they are different. Of the 270 students, only one young woman was unwilling to confront her biases which she had simply listed. She refused both to look at herself and to rewrite her paper. She earned a failing grade.

I turn now to "The Holocaust Process," an interdisciplinary course which after two years of planning was approved by the UMF Honors Council and offered for the first time during the spring semester 1994. We started with the premise that there is one race, the *human* race, and that real or perceived physical differences among individuals or ethnic groups are indicators of neither inferiority nor superiority. Dr. Mary Schwanke, a biologist, therefore began the course by debunking Nazi mythology regarding race and so-called racial traits. She lectured on what was known in the 1930s and updated students' scientific understanding about the human race. Dr. Jon Oplinger, a sociologist, laid the sociological basis for the events leading to the Holocaust by first describing the political and cultural milieu in central Europe, the alliances of World War I, and the events leading up to Hitler's becoming chancellor. He detailed the Nuremberg laws and Nazi activities which resulted in Kristallnacht, and discussed the accelerating persecution of Jewish people during the Nazi attack on Poland. Oplinger also spoke about the establishment of ghettos, the early successes of the Nazi army, and the occupation of nearly all of Europe. A film reenacting the Wannsee Conference helped focus on the "final solution." Then, Oplinger discussed the work of the SS mobile units, the establishment of the death camps, and the murder industry they housed. My contribution as a member of the rehabilitation services faculty consisted of depicting the slow moral devolution of the German people. Based on my research in primary documents, I presented the army's collusion with Hitler's most monumental crime.

Guest speakers brought reality to the classroom experience. Lore Segal,[1] author and visiting scholar to my university's creative writing program, graciously agreed to talk to our students about her frightening experiences as a child when the Nazis incorporated Austria into the Third Reich. She described leaving her family on a children's transport to England, living in the Dominican Republic, and arriving at long last in New York City. Judith Isaacson,[2] a survivor of Auschwitz, now a Maine resident and author, was also on campus, as was a hidden child, Charles Rotmil, now in his early sixties. He was UMF's main speaker for its annual Holocaust Memorial events. All eighteen students themselves had contributed to the remembrance events by presenting to the campus community synopses of their term papers. A liberator, living not far from Farmington, told of his shock and horror as a young, American GI when entering a concentration camp. He reflected on seeing the human misery and encouraged students not to let it happen again.

A colleague, inquiring how our course was going, remarked in jest that one should never teach a new course for the first time! Student evaluation during the last class which we had prudently allotted for "decompression" made us realize the accuracy of her statement. The students' principle criticism of the course was lack of class discussions. My two colleagues and I were too intent on getting every bit of information and human experience into one short semester. Each lecture was crammed full with events, injustices, cruelties, murders, inhumanities, and human suffering. At the beginning of each class session, we assured ourselves and the students that the lecture would be brief and there would be time to talk. Each class we lost track of time. In the end, we realized that too much class time was taken up with our compulsion to impart in detail what actually had taken place. At the first class meeting we had said, "Don't endure this alone; if you need to, find someone to talk to." But the students, none of whom were Jewish incidentally, wanted and needed time to process in class. They found reading, hearing, and viewing information on the Holocaust frightening and horrifying—some had bad dreams the night after class or when reading about it prior to retiring for the night. We, the instructors, also needed time to talk. It is clear: ongoing class discussions are a must.

At the last session, members of the class expressed forcefully that they had become more aware of their own prejudices and saw themselves as more accepting of other people's beliefs and customs.

Lastly, I want to talk about my Elderhostel course which I entitle "A Family Portrait—World War II Researched and Remembered—the autobiographical/historical journey taken by the daughter of a Nazi army officer." Discussion focuses on my personal odyssey as it relates to the larger historical/societal picture both then and now.

In this forum, I described my father as the prototype of a Nazi army officer. His military career began in 1914 and continued in the armed forces of the Weimar Republic. His and my mother's typical East Elbian families allow me to illustrate the social climate in which the Nazis so successfully operated. Using Nazi military documents, some written by my father, I juxtaposed his route and that of SS Mobile Unit C in the Ukraine,[3] his duties in Warsaw, Poland, and Minsk, Russia, with the transports to the death camps, and show how these intersected. I also spoke of my sense of betrayal by my mother and my father as well as my rage focused on him for his work as a handmaiden to the Nazis' evil deeds. I admit my anger with myself that only after his death did I question his role, participation, and after-the-war silence.[4]

Unlike the undergraduates, those attending my Elderhostel course were informed about World War II and about Hitler's "Final Solution." All were eager to hear my perspective, while a few expressed preferring straight lecturing to the vigorous discussions that actually ensued.

In each of the Elderhostel groups, there was at least one person who suspected Nazi intent in me and feared my whitewashing Nazi murders. At the end of the last course, one participant admitted that he had in his suitcase a striped outfit that slave laborers were forced to wear in Nazi camps. Had I denied the Holocaust, he would have worn it to class. Since I had not, he judged such protest unnecessary and concluded: "Jews will love you and Germans hate you for it."

His remark points to the chasm between those who were persecuted and their German persecutors to whom I am inextricably linked. This link, instead of blinding me, augments my understanding that Nazi agents tore asunder our human connections and also ripped apart my community when they forced the Jewish neighbors of my childhood out of their homes, out of our town, our province, our Germany, and nearly all of Europe. More to the point, this link informs me that biases lead to hatred, hatred to brutality, and brutality to murder. This compels me to expose the varied faces of prejudice. By teaching about the Holocaust, I do my part in reweaving Jewish-German connections that are safe and without fear, reciprocal and respected, trustworthy and trusted. But I am prompted to remember that prior to the Nazis, such connections existed when many perceived themselves as much German as Jewish and accepted their relationships with non-Jewish neighbors as amiable and trustworthy. Tragically, most of these relationships turned vacuous and then lethal because few non-Jewish Germans publicly opposed prejudice.

These then are my reasons for helping students to confront and to abandon their biases; for teaching them to speak out when individuals are humiliated and assaulted simply because of who they are. In fact, I think we all must make public our belief that we accept the commonalities *and* the differences among us and that relationships between us are embedded in tolerance and understanding. If, as some suppose, evil is the absence of good, then such good and public acts in support of this belief will keep evil at bay.

NOTES

Throughout this chapter the words bias(es) and prejudice(s) are used interchangeably, as are their other grammatical forms, such as biased or prejudiced. I am thankful for the helpful comments by the Reverend Marriotte Churchill, Dr. Jon Oplinger, and Dr. Margaret Stubbs.

1. Her book *Other People's Houses* (New York: Harcourt, Brace and World, 1964) is a gripping story.

2. In her Memoirs *The Seed of Sarah* (Urbana: University of Illinois, 1991), Judith Isaacson gives a vivid picture of her family and the changes they endured as Hungary fell under Nazi influence. Her dream to study at the Sorbonne in Paris, France, was brutally halted by deportation to Auschwitz and the slave labor camp in Hessisch Lichtenau. The second edition includes her return visit to Hungary as well as the camps. She leaves the reader with her thoughts on forgiveness.

3. At the start of my research, I was influenced by Jon Oplinger's book *The Politics of Demonology: The European Witchcraze and the Mass Production of Deviance* (Selingrove, Pa.: Susquehanna University Press, 1990). I am very grateful to Raul Hilberg for helping me identify my father's military unit and telling me where I would find that unit's documents. My efforts to put the army and SS mobile unit routes side by side were guided by Dr. Hilberg's definitive work *The Destruction of the European Jews* (New York/London: Holmes and Meier, 1985). German works in which I found additional, critical information were by Helmut Krausnick and Hans-Heinrich Wilhelm, *Die Truppe des Weltanschauungskrieges,* and Christian Streit, *Keine Kameraden: Die Wehrmacht und die sowjetischen Kriegsgefangenen 1941–1945* (both Stuttgart: Deutsche Verlags-Anstalt, 1984 and 1978 respectively).

4. At this writing, I am looking for a publisher for my manuscript, *Poison in My Roots: Nazi Germany Remembered and Confronted.*

CHAPTER 18

"A Madwoman and a Scavenger":

The Toll of Holocaust Survival

in Cynthia Ozick's "Rosa"

HENRY GONSHAK

Critiquing Holocaust literature presents uniquely vexing dilemmas. The most obvious is the issue of whether there isn't something trivializing, if not sacrilegious, in the very notion of turning the Holocaust into art. However, to discredit the very existence of Holocaust literature is to misunderstand some of the chief aspects and functions of art. Since all Holocaust texts, regardless of genre, are aesthetically shaped by their authors, it seems unfair to devalue Holocaust literature because of its aesthetic concerns. Moreover, one crucial function of art has always been to encapsulate tragedy and social injustice in vivid and memorable form. Surely, literature provides a means of "testifying" to the Holocaust which cannot be expressed through more scholarly disciplines.

If a critic of Holocaust literature must avoid automatic suspicion of the genre itself, he or she must also avoid the opposite: the celebration of all Holocaust literature, regardless of artistic merit, simply because it seeks to call public attention to the worst act of genocide in human history. Such a stance, however well intentioned, forgets that in literature the moral and the aesthetic are complexly but inextricably intertwined. In the case of Holocaust literature, if the writer succumbs to the temptation to sentimentalize the tragedy by depicting the Holocaust through the simplistic moral categories purveyed by popular culture, he or she will inevitably profoundly distort the awful reality, since what is most important about the Holocaust is precisely the fact that it shatters our culture's most self-serving moralistic notions.[1] The Israeli journalist Amos Elon makes this same point more succinctly when he cautions against indulging in "Holocaust kitsch."[2]

No such criticism can be leveled against "Rosa," a brilliant novella by the contemporary Jewish-American fiction writer and essayist, Cynthia Ozick.[3] The title character is a Holocaust survivor, now middle-aged and living in Miami. From the story's opening sentence, in which Ozick bluntly characterizes her as a "madwoman and a scavenger," we know Rosa has descended into lunacy: driven mad, it appears, by the traumatization of her experience in general, and specifically by her repressed grief over the murder at the hands of the Nazis of her beloved daughter Magda. Consumed by paranoid delusions, Rosa lives hermetically in a fetid, cramped hotel room. She had once resided in New York City with her niece Stella, where she had owned and managed a dusty antique store. However, several years back, she had destroyed her business—for reasons which are never made entirely clear, though it seems to have been simply a deranged, unpremeditated rampage—whereupon she had been swiftly shipped off to Miami by her disgruntled niece. Over the years of her isolation, Rosa has grown convinced that her daughter Magda is still alive. In her native Polish, she writes long, lovely letters to Magda (whom she believes has grown up to be a distinguished professor of classics at Columbia), epistles which Ozick intersperses throughout the narrative, and which are filled with sharp philosophical reflections, vivid recollections of Rosa's pre-Holocaust girlhood, sudden flashes of insight into her present decrepitude, and, most of all, soaring expressions of a mother's endless love for her child.

Little happens in "Rosa," at least in terms of overtly consequential action. (In fact, the apparent slightness and randomness of its plot might lead one to call the novella "minimalist," if its exuberant prose-style wasn't so fervently "maximalist.") At the story's start, Rosa is eagerly awaiting a package from Stella containing Magda's shawl, the only possession of her daughter's which her mother was able to salvage from the concentration camp. Instead, a letter arrives from a psychology professor, who explains that he is conducting a study into the lives of trauma survivors, whose sufferings he has labeled with the nebulous neologism, "Repressed Animation," and which he has somehow connected to, among other things, Buddhism and experiments with baboons. Intending to visit Miami for a conference, he requests an interview with Rosa.

Scornfully discarding the letter, Rosa hauls her clothes off to the local laundromat, where she meets an elderly but still sprightly Jew named

Persky, a shameless flirt, who, indifferent to Rosa's unkempt appearance, flatters and cajoles her until she grudgingly agrees to lunch with him at a nearby kosher restaurant. Over lunch, Rosa bluntly informs Persky that she is crazy, but he counters by informing her that his wife is, too (in fact, she's currently institutionalized); thus, Rosa's insanity is no obstacle to romance.[4]

The following day, sorting her laundry, Rosa discovers, in horror, that she's missing a pair of underpants. She grows increasingly convinced that her undergarments are in the possession of Persky, who, in the most damning scenario she concocts, has stolen them in a deliberate act of perversion. On the off chance that she might simply have dropped them instead, Rosa embarks on a late-night search, in the course of which she ends up at, of all places, a private gay beach adjoining a posh hotel. Seeking escape from the swarm of naked, entwined male bodies, Rosa charges into the swank hotel lobby, where she's soon plunged into a heated debate with the peeved manager, an officious employee, and fellow Jew, named Finkelstein. Abruptly, Rosa becomes convinced that the hotel is the very site of the academic conference attended by the pompous psychology professor. By the time she is forcibly evicted, Rosa is accusing Finkelstein of membership in the Gestapo.

Back at her own hotel, Rosa discovers the dogged Persky, who beats a hasty retreat after she accuses him of stealing her underpants. The anticlimactic finale of the underwear escapade occurs the next day, when Rosa finds the garment buried among her laundry. She also finally receives Magda's shawl, but possessing the article of clothing fails to rapturously transport her. On an apparent whim, she decides to have her long disconnected phone repaired, and immediately places a long-distance call to Stella. Her chagrined niece chides her aunt for her extravagance, responds negatively to Rosa's suggestion that she might move back in with Stella and reopen her antique store, offers her usual trite advice that her aunt should try and "get interested in something . . . for a change," and eventually loses all patience as Rosa's side of the conversation turns increasingly maniacal.[5] But Rosa is no longer listening. Some stimulus has mysteriously incarnated Magda's presence in the room. Swaddling the phone receiver in her dead daughter's shawl, Rosa delivers a climactic soliloquy to Magda. The phone rings; it's the desk clerk, saying that Persky is in the lobby. "He's used to crazy women, so let him come up," she laconically replies. The story's final words soon follow: "Magda was not there. Shy, [Magda] ran from Persky. Magda was away."⁶

Clearly, Ozick has not provided us with a predictable portrayal of a Holocaust survivor. The most obvious feature of Rosa's personality is that, to put it bluntly, she isn't all that nice. While not entirely unkind, she does not fit any picture of heroic martyrdom, which is how Holocaust survivors are often commonly portrayed, at least in popular culture.⁷ On the contrary, she is a "madwoman and a scavenger," and her madness often takes a frighteningly aggressive form. Surely, she should be at least a bit more civil to the innocuous Finkelstein and especially to the remarkably tolerant Persky, who seems to be offering a genuine friendship that might assuage her intense isolation. Even Stella, for all her fatuousness, seems more shallow and insensitive than deliberately cruel.

Rosa also isn't much of a Jew. Her family, whom she describes in her letters to Magda, were cultured Jews who felt a disdainful superiority to what they saw as the vulgar, cloistered world of Eastern European Jewry. Rosa has also inherited her parents' fervent anti-Zionism. Boasting to Magda of having "saved" Stella, after the liberation of the camps, from the "kidnappers" who wanted to drag her off to a kibbutz in Palestine, she seems not to realize, even after the Holocaust, that her parents' Polish patriotism proved tragically misguided. Most importantly, the experience of living through the Holocaust, of seeing her brethren herded off to the gas chambers, of witnessing her own daughter's murder by the Nazis, somehow has not enabled Rosa to transcend her parents' provincialism and to recognize her profound connectedness with her fellow Jews. If the term had not been so debased through overuse, one might almost call her a "self-hating Jew."

Why does Ozick appear to take such pains to make her protagonist so unsympathetic? Why create a character who seems, in her addled solipsism, blind to the deepest meanings of her tragic past? If a crucial function of Holocaust literature is to educate, would a teacher be better off avoiding such a problematic story, and instead teaching Holocaust fiction that set forth less ambiguously the lessons we fervently wish our students to learn?

By way of answering these questions, let me refer to a deliberately shocking essay by the psychologist and Holocaust survivor Bruno Bettelheim, called "The Informed Heart," about the best known victim of the Holocaust, Anne Frank.[8] Bettelheim criticizes the Frank family (in particular the family patriarch, Otto Frank) for hiding together, rather than splitting up, which Bettelheim argues would have greatly increased their individual chances for survival. He also attacks Otto Frank for clinging to his nonviolent principles, instead of arming his family against the Nazis. Such steps were not taken, Bettelheim contends, because the Franks were attempting to retain the illusion of normalcy in a situation whose utter abnormality they refused to confront. When Anne, in her famous diary, maintains her belief in the essential goodness of humanity, for all the poignancy of her remark, in Bettelheim's view she has failed to comprehend the great, terrible lesson of the Holocaust, which is that, under the right circumstances, humanity is capable of almost limitless evil.

Bettelheim is most concerned, however, with the uses to which the story of Anne Frank has been put since her death. Noting that Anne's words about essential human goodness are placed at the climax of a popular play based on her experiences, he insists that, paradoxically, we read Anne Frank's diary not to learn about the Holocaust, but to *not* learn about it, to insulate ourselves from its unmitigated horror in somewhat the same way the Frank family did. "Her story found wide acclaim," he writes, "because for us, too, it denies implicitly that Auschwitz ever existed. If all man are good, there was never an Auschwitz."[9]

Surely Bettelheim is rather glibly callous in his attacks on the Frank family; even if Anne had kept a pistol atop her diary, would she really have been able to ward off the Gestapo? Nonetheless, Bettelheim's essay is valuable in revealing the countless "distancing strategies" we devise, consciously or not, to avoid facing the black truths of the Holocaust. However, if Anne Frank's diary permits us this sort of escape, "Rosa" assuredly does not. Holocaust survivors, the story tells us in no uncertain terms, are not necessarily ennobled by their experiences. On the contrary, they may, like Rosa, go mad, live in a fantasy world, shun all ties to fellow survivors, cling to petty snobberies and resentments, lapse into senseless violence and paranoid accusations, and repel anyone who tries to offer friendship and assistance.

Indeed, to insist too strongly on Holocaust survivors being ennobled by their suffering may itself be a subtle distancing strategy. Of course, some survivors were ennobled, but framing their experience this way allows us to find at least something redeeming in the genocide, a response which lets us evade, or at least blur, the truth about the Holo-caust—that it is a catastrophe devoid of anything even faintly re-deeming.[10] Moreover, if we insist on perceiving Holocaust survivors as saints, we automatically withhold sympathy from all those survivors who fail to meet such exacting criteria. The truth about the Holocaust is that the Germans' systematic slaughter massacred sinners and saints alike. The vices and virtues of the victims before they were caught in the Nazis' web become utterly irrelevant.[11] Reading "Rosa," as our empathy grows for the flawed protagonist's plight, we slowly come to grasp, in the depths of our consciousness, the Holocaust's despairing lesson.

The story's disturbing comedy can be defended along somewhat simi-lar lines. Without question, many scenes in "Rosa" are darkly funny. The character's mock-odyssey in search of her missing underpants, her firm conviction that the geriatric Persky is a cunning pervert, her crazed confrontation with naked love-makers on a homosexual beach, the inter-twined subplot concerning that pretentious pedant: these and many other examples display Ozick's fondness for shocking burlesque. Of course, some would argue that it is inappropriate, if not offensive, to depict any aspect of the Holocaust in a tone of such madcap farce. While surely not automatically dismissible, such claims tend to reflect a blinkered understanding of the nature of comedy. At least at its best, comedy does not merely dramatize the "lighter" side of existence. Rather, great comedy is usually just another kind of response, different from but not inferior to tragedy, to the catastrophes large and small which checker the human condition. Surely it is no accident that the Jewish literary tradition (a tradition in which Ozick is steeped as a fiction writer and has often analyzed as a critic) is largely comic. Sholom Aleichem, I. B. Singer, Saul Bellow, Bernard Malamud, Philip Roth, Art Spiegelman: the list of Jewish comic literary geniuses, all of whose work has explored anti-Semitic persecution, is virtually endless. A professor of mine once called this kind of comedy "laughing at the devil," an attempt through humor to strike back at satanic evil.[12] Indeed, one might argue that when trying to render fictionally a catastrophe such as the Holo-caust, whose proportions are so overwhelming as to border on the surreal, perhaps harrowingly absurdist "tragicomedy" is the most "real-istic" approach.

These complex and disturbing issues are precisely the ones which an instructor teaching "Rosa" in a Holocaust course should try to get students to grapple with directly. Why does Ozick create such an unsympathetic protagonist? For all Rosa's flaws, do students still find her a deeply moving, even oddly appealing character? What underlies our culture's strong disposition to perceive Holocaust survivors as saints who have been ennobled by their suffering? Can the black comedy in "Rosa" be defended? The story's strangeness, its firm refusal to allow the reader any glib, self-indulgently maudlin response, should push students to formulate original answers to these provocative literary and ethical questions, which touch on some of the deepest dilemmas posed by the Holocaust. Put another way, if analyzed fully and fearlessly, "Rosa" will force students to transcend their conventional ways of thinking, to move beyond stock moral and philosophical categories—in short, to take that intellectual leap which is a prerequisite for anyone hoping to grasp the grim mysteries of the Holocaust.

While no teacher or critic should ignore this tone of pathos and horror pervading the novella, "Rosa" does end with a hint of subtle, ambiguous, but nonetheless unmistakable affirmation. After all, at the story's conclusion Rosa makes several genuine attempts to reestablish contact with the "real world." Her superficially trivial decision to have her telephone repaired implies a desire, both literal and figurative, to "reconnect" to humanity. When she then calls Stella and suggests returning to her niece's home, Rosa is making a real effort to repair their estranged relationship, even though the conversation eventually devolves into futile bickering. Most importantly, when Rosa readmits the indefatigable Persky to her room, the implication is that Rosa and the old man—who, in less obvious ways, is every bit as alone as she is—will develop some oddball but still meaningful, reciprocal friendship.

However, the price of Rosa's reconnection to reality is suggested in the story's terse but haunting last sentence: "Magda was away." If Rosa becomes sane, she must inevitably discard her treasured fantasy that Magda is still alive. In other words, Rosa's decision to rejoin humanity requires that she release her repressed and bottomless grief over the death of her daughter. By confronting her creation with such a bleak and inescapable choice, Ozick once again refuses to succumb to even a trace of sentimentality.

The novella's conclusion introduces a second rich complication. Although Rosa refuses to the last to recognize her blood-ties with her fellow Jews, by the story's end it is no longer clear that she has learned nothing from the Holocaust. In her last letter to Magda, she refers to her life not in the camps, but earlier, in the Warsaw ghetto. Rosa muses over the incongruous fact that a streetcar ran through the center of the ghetto, daily carrying ordinary Poles on various humdrum errands past scenes of incredible suffering. "Every day they saw us," she recalls, "women with shopping sacks; and once I noticed a head of lettuce sticking up out of the top of a sack—green lettuce!" She concludes, her final words to Magda: "And in this place now I am like the woman who held the lettuce in the tramcar . . . I [have become] like the woman with the lettuce." [13]

In the conclusion of the second volume of Primo Levi's memoirs, *The Reawakening,* which describes Levi's difficult, protracted journey home after being freed from Auschwitz, the author, one of the greatest chroniclers of the Holocaust, describes a recurrent nightmare he suffered from even years after his liberation:

> I am sitting at a table with my family, or with friends, or at work; in short, a peaceful, relaxed environment . . . yet I feel a deep and subtle anguish. . . . And in fact, as the dream proceeds . . . each time in a different way, everything . . . disintegrates around me, the scenery, the walls, the people, while the anguish becomes more intense and more precise. Now . . . I am alone in the center of a grey and turbid nothing, and now, I *know* what this thing means, and I also know that I have always known . . . I am in the Lager once more, and nothing is true outside the Lager. All the rest was a brief pause, a deception of the senses, a dream; my family, nature in flower, my home. Now . . . this dream of peace is over, [while] a well-known voice resounds: a single word, not imperious, but brief and subdued. It is the dawn command of Auschwitz, a foreign word, feared and expected: get up, "*Wstawach.*" [14]

For Levi, after Auschwitz, the ordinary world has assumed forever the illusory nature of a dream. Having glimpsed, in the ashes of the crematorium, the evil lurking below the surface of everyday existence, he can never again take that existence at face value, never again mistake that dream for reality. A comparably horrific awareness seems to lie behind Rosa's transformation of herself into that Polish woman with her lettuce. The Holocaust has taught Rosa that, even in Miami Beach, below its sunny surface the world *is* the Warsaw ghetto, and Rosa, by dint of her tragedy, is forced to face this malevolent inner reality every day of her life, just like the Polish peasant staring at the ghetto's emaciated inhabitants. It is the sort of knowledge that can drive one mad. After reading "Rosa," we all become, in a sense, that Polish woman on the tram, clutching our lettuce while gazing out at the Warsaw ghetto—that is, if we have the courage not to turn away.

NOTES

1. For a provocative, if debatable, argument that Steven Spielberg's film *Schindler's List*, its strengths notwithstanding, is guilty of sentimentally distorting the Holocaust, see critic Philip Gourevitch, "A Dissent on *Schindler's List*," *Commentary* 97:2 (February 1994): 59–76.

2. Amos Elon, "Politics of Memory: Reflections on the Israeli Holocaust," *The New York Review of Books* 40 (October 7, 1993): 3. As the essay's title implies, Elon's specific concern is with Israel, specifically with how he thinks some Israeli politicians have employed "Holocaust kitsch"—the sentimentalizing of the Shoah—as a means of manipulating the Israeli public into supporting militaristic policies toward Israel's Arab neighbors, in particular the Palestinians.

3. Ozick has also written a short story, "The Shawl," which portrays Rosa's experience decades earlier in a concentration camp, and concludes with Magda's murder. The two stories, both originally published in *The New Yorker*, have been brought together in a single volume, *The Shawl* (New York: Vintage Books, 1990). However, in its cursory characterizations, sketchily detailed setting, and melodramatic ending, "The Shawl" is much inferior to "Rosa."

4. The relationship between Rosa and Persky may suggest, on one level, the inherent estrangement between American Jews who safely viewed the Holocaust from afar, and Jewish Holocaust survivors who emigrated to the United States after the war. One particular exchange between the two supports such an interpretation. Shortly after they meet in the laundromat, Rosa and Persky discover that they were both born in Warsaw, although Persky, unlike Rosa, emigrated in 1920, before the Nazi takeover. "Imagine this," Persky says, "Two people from Warsaw meet in Miami, Florida." Rosa replies, "My Warsaw isn't your Warsaw." Cynthia Ozick, *The Shawl* (New York: Vintage Books, 1990), 19.

5. Ibid., 64.

6. Ibid., 70.

7. See Judith Miller, *One by One by One: Facing the Holocaust* (New York: Simon and Schuster, 1990). Miller perceptively analyzes how the cultures of countries implicated, to varying degrees, in the Holocaust—Germany, Austria, the Netherlands, France, the former Soviet Union, the United States—have often mythified the Shoah in general, and Holocaust survivors in particular, usually in

self-serving ways. For example, Miller argues that the Dutch have raised Anne Frank to the level of national saint in large part to conceal, or at least obscure, Holland's record of extensive collaboration with the Nazis.

8. Bruno Bettelheim, "The Informed Heart," in *Out of the Whirlwind: A Reader of Holocaust Literature,* ed. Albert H. Friedlander (New York: Schocken Books, 1976), 35. Recently, a team of scholars commissioned by the Dutch government—bent on disproving once and for all charges leveled by Holocaust deniers that Anne Frank's diary is really a clever forgery—have published, after years of work, a definitive edition of the diary, complete with extensive annotations and editorial comments.

9. Ibid., 40.

10. Surely Elie Wiesel is an example of a Holocaust survivor who was ennobled by his youthful imprisonment in Auschwitz and Buchenwald. Wiesel's fine memoir, *Night* (New York: Avon Books, 1960), documents how this harrowing experience, in particular his witnessing of the deaths of his parents and younger sister, forced him to confront for the first time basic questions of good and evil. Since his liberation, Wiesel has become the preeminent spokesman for Holocaust survivors. Comparably, Austrian Holocaust survivor Simon Wiesenthal probably would not have become the heroic figure he turned into—hunting down escaped Nazis and bringing them to justice—had it not been for his own experience in a concentration camp.

11. See Lawrence L. Langer, *Holocaust Testimonies: The Ruins of Memory* (New Haven: Yale University Press, 1991). Langer offers an important, if controversial, analysis of three hundred of the over fourteen hundred interviews with Holocaust survivors kept at the Fortunoff Video Archive at Yale. Langer finds little in the survivors' testimony that evinces "spiritual uplift" or the "nobility" and "indomitability of the human spirit," and he strongly opposes such mythologizing of the Holocaust. See also Primo Levi, *Survival in Auschwitz,* trans. Stuart Woolf (New York: Collier Books, 1961). Particularly in the chapter titled "The Drowned and the Saved," Levi argues brilliantly that the traditional moral categories of civilized societies are utterly inapplicable to the experiences of the inmates in the camps.

12. The professor who made this remark was Gerald Chapman, with whom I studied during my graduate school days at the University of Denver. Although Professor Chapman was discussing Augustan satire, his memorable phrase seems equally applicable to Jewish humorists—not only writers but also actors and stand-up comedians.

13. Cynthia Ozick, "Rosa," in *The Shawl* (New York: Vintage Books, 1990), 69.

14. Primo Levi, *The Reawakening,* trans. Stuart Woolf (New York: Collier Books, 1965), 207–8.

CHAPTER 19

Truth and Lamentation:

Two Modes of Literary Response

to the Holocaust

MILTON TEICHMAN AND SHARON LEDER

Yitzhak Katzenelson, Warsaw poet who wrote *The Song of the Murdered Jewish People* in Vittel, the German concentration camp for foreigners in France, buried his poem in three glass bottles so that it could live and speak the truth after his own destruction. Even writers who did not experience the Holocaust directly have felt compelled to transmit the truth of evil and suffering so that some form of justice be done. As Cynthia Ozick writes, "I am not in favor of making fiction of the data, or of mythologizing or poeticizing it. . . . [yet] I constantly violate this tenet; my brother's blood cries out from the ground, and I am drawn and driven." [1]

Our recent work compiling an anthology of poetry and short fiction on the Holocaust has helped us to see more clearly how central truth-telling has been as a motive for writing. Authors have felt obligated to let the world know what indeed took place in our civilized time—not only in terms of crimes and extraordinary suffering, but also in terms of resistance, rescue, the experiences of women and children, the sometimes agonizing moral conflicts of victims and survivors. But truth-telling, we have learned, can be psychological or philosophical as well as historical in character. Psychological truth-telling, for example, may attempt to render the twisted mind of the perpetrator or the injured mind of the survivor. Philosophic truth-telling may offer observations on the nature of Holocaust and post-Holocaust reality or reflections on the human capacity for evil and for good.

A second dominant literary response to unspeakable atrocity—a response coming mainly but not exclusively from Jewish authors—is elegiac in character: it is the expression of sorrow and loss. As Israeli fiction writer Aharon Appelfeld puts it, "A religious person will certainly argue in favor of silence, but what can we do? By his very nature . . . man has a kind of inner need for ritualization, not only of his joy, but also and perhaps essentially, of his pain and grief." [2] In his poem "Lament for the European Exile," Israeli poet A. L. Strauss asks,

> *Can I mourn?*
> *I am an elegy.*
> *Lament?*
> *My mind is lamentation.* [3]

Lamentation, like truth-telling, can be a complex and many-sided response. It may include a passionate remembering of victims, along with tribute and homage to them. It may include the remembering of the rich East European culture that has vanished. It may include criticism of Western cultural values which proved to be a veneer hiding extraordinary cruelty and inhumanity. It may attempt to answer the question: How does one live in the aftermath of the Holocaust? It may express anger at and disillusionment in an uncaring God.

Viewing Holocaust literature through the perspectives of truth-telling and lamentation alerts the student, we have found, to significant and recurring themes in Holocaust literature; it also helps the student to perceive some order amidst diversity. The authentic literature on the Holocaust, we believe, is likely to reflect these two dominant modes of response. It will be a literature faithful to the historical reality, avoiding distortions of history in order to entertain, romanticize, or realize some ideological end.

Because truth-telling and lamentation are multi-leveled responses, we wish to focus here on a single aspect of truth-telling we call "philosophic" and on that facet of lamentation that reflects the criticism of God. We select these two aspects because our classroom discussion of them has engaged students deeply, intellectually, and emotionally.

In what we call "philosophic" truth-telling, details of atrocity are presented less to underscore the historic truth than to support insights and reflections about the Holocaust as an upheaval in human history. Some writers in the philosophic mode tend to compare pre-Holocaust reality, when civilization and humanism seemed to have some meaning and value, to the reality of the Holocaust itself. As a consequence, these writers are likely to focus upon the new meaning of death under the Nazis—that is, the hideous process of dying, the unheroic aspects, the lack of ritual—and, directly or indirectly, compare such gruesome death to the way individuals died in previous historical periods.

American poet Anthony Hecht in "More Light! More Light!" presents a sixteenth-century Christian martyr who is burnt at the stake to suggest that brutal death is not a new invention; but Hecht's contrast between that death and the deaths of two Jews and a Pole under the Nazis implies a dimension not seen before—the destruction of the spirit as well as the body of the victim. A rupture has thus taken place between past and present.

This same attention to the Nazi transformation of death appears in two poems by American poet Randall Jarrell who served in World War II at the time the camps were liberated. His poem "Protocols" implies a new tragic world we inhabit after the Holocaust by presenting children who, in contrapuntal voices, remember how they died in Birkenau.

> *There was a smoke-stack, then they made me wash. It was a factory, I think.* My mother held me up and I could see the ship that made the smoke. . . . *And I said to my mother, "Now I'm washed and dried."* My mother hugged me, and it smelled like hay. And that is how you die. And that is how you die.

Jarrell's second poem, "A Camp in the Prussian Forest," juxtaposes the barbaric nature of death under the Nazis with more civilized ways of dying. In this poem, the speaker fashions a wreath for a grave, the wreath implying age-old rituals for remembering and honoring the dead. But this very wreath is "chalked with ash" from the crematoria.

In "Season of the Dead," by French writer Pierre Gascar, a work which Irving Howe has called "one of the very few masterpieces of Holocaust fiction,"[4] death in the inherited, civilized conception appears in the burial ground which the narrator, Peter, helps to create, adorn, and tend for fellow French prisoners who die in the German camp. Death as atrocity—anonymous, markerless—is emblemed in the hastily covered mass grave which the narrator and his fellow gravediggers discover at the edge of their own beautifully cared for cemetery. Death as atrocity is emblemed, furthermore, in the endless trains of Jewish deportees "full of stifled cries and shouts" which the narrator sees on their way to gas chambers and incineration. As in the poetry of Hecht and Jarrell, two distinct eras in human history are represented in Gascar's story—an earlier one in which there was still adherence to civilized values and the present era in which those values are overturned and abandoned. This new era, suggests Gascar, is the "season of the dead," a season in which death has taken on a meaning hitherto unknown to humankind. Students have speculated on the various implications of Gascar's title. Since seasons change, is Gascar also suggesting some hope that the "season of the dead" may be followed by a season more respectful of human life?

Other writers in the philosophic mode of truth-telling use the Holocaust as a heightened example of the way reality always has been and will continue to be, though disguised by a veneer of civilization. This view is reflected, for example, in Jacov Lind's surrealistic and grotesquely humorous story "Journey through the Night." An Austrian Jew who survived the war, Lind presents our post-Holocaust world as rational and civilized on the surface only but cannibalistic at its core. Deliberately alluding to the outward sophistication of many a Nazi, Lind fashions a cannibal in his story who could be taken for a doctor with his black bag, except that the cannibal's bag contains instruments for neatly severing the body parts of his victims. Amusing and shocking is the cannibal's perversion of reason as he justifies eating a fellow-passenger. The urbane cannibal is not simply a reference to Nazis but is Lind's symbol for what humanity essentially has been, is, and will be.

Finally, there are those writers in what we have termed the philosophic mode of truth-telling who resemble Lind in viewing the Holocaust as a magnified version of the past but who, unlike Lind, are hopeful that individuals yet have the power to improve the world. Included in this group are a number of poets who see in the Holocaust a reminder of the capacity for good as well as for violence in each one of us. American poets Denise Levertov in "When We Look Up" and W. D. Snodgrass in "A Visitation," for example, both use the figure of Adolf Eichmann to symbolize the tendency in each one of us for the fierce and the savage. But they imply our capacity, nevertheless, to see in another face "a person . . . an I," to quote Levertov, to see ourselves related to one another—"member/one of another."

Snodgrass's stylized dialogue "A Visitation" creates the fiction of

Eichmann's ghost still roaming the world attempting to absolve itself of guilt by pointing to the hypocrisy of others. The ghost of Eichmann says to the poem's speaker, who may represent all of us:

> *Once your own hand*
> *Held a nightstick, .45 and sheath knife;*
> *You've chained men to a steel beam on command.*

Reluctantly, the poem's speaker faces the truth in Eichmann's words— that even decent people can slip into the very evil that initially repels them: "How subtle all that chokes us with disgust/Moves in implacably to rule us unaware." But the speaker ultimately can not regard Eichmann as guiltless, implying that we do have the power to reject the impulse toward the violent and the savage.

Poems like these can lead students to ponder important questions: Does our acknowledgment of our own potential for cruelty and inhumanity clear Nazi leaders of their crimes? Are we helpless in the face of our own propensity for evil?

The literary response of lamentation has its own complexity. We focus here on the way in which sorrow merges with anger and bitterness toward a seemingly uncaring God. Jewish writers who lament the devastation stand in a literary tradition that goes back to the biblical Book of Lamentations, a work of elegiac poetry occasioned by the destruction of the first Temple in Jerusalem in 586 B.C.E. Later persecutions produced additional elegiac works, *kinoth,* whose authors (Solomon ibn Gabirol, Yehudah Halevi, Moses ibn Ezra, Abraham ibn Ezra, to name a few) expressed deep sorrow over the sufferings of their people. Only a selection from the vast number of these dirges is now recited in the synagogue, along with the Book of Lamentations, on the holy day of *Tish'ah b'Av,* the day commemorating the destruction of the Temple. The underlying beliefs of traditional lamentation literature are that Israel's suffering was caused by her sins and that repentance and submission to God's just punishment could bring an end to suffering.[5]

Jewish writers lamenting the Holocaust do not share the theological assumptions of earlier writers in this genre who view both the destruction of the Temple and succeeding catastrophes as caused by Israel's sins. Rather, most writers responding to the cataclysm of the Holocaust perceive the suffering as grossly unmerited, as a violation of God's

Covenant with the people of Israel. They see the destruction of their people as a sign of God's impotence rather than God's control of events. If the traditional lamentation literature presents God as showing wrath against Israel, Jewish Holocaust writers often direct their anger at an uncaring God. If humility is the characteristic tone in traditional lamentation literature, a certain spiritual audacity characterizes the response of modern Jewish authors.

Hebrew poet Hayyim Nahman Bialik (1873–1934), who in his poem "In the City of Slaughter" responded with shock and rage to the 1903 Kishinev pogrom against Jews in Czarist Russia, was the first major Jewish writer to express anger at the absent God. In the poem "Spring 1942," Lodz Ghetto poet Simcha Bunim Shayevitsh responds in grief and indignation to the mass deportations of Jews from the ghetto and calls upon the revered Bialik to wake from their sleep mother Rachel and the Saint of Berdichev.[6] Shayevitsh implores all three — Bialik, the Biblical Rachel, and the Hassidic Saint — to go before God to thunder, demand, plead that God be "the Savior/Of Living Jews" and not "the Savior of Corpses." The questioning of God's justice is implicit throughout the poem as Shayevitsh asks again and again how a beautiful spring can coexist with deportations. Shayevitsh is well aware of Bialik's famous and bitter lines: "The sun shines, the acacia blossoms/and the slaughterer slaughters."

More explicit in his criticism of God is Warsaw Ghetto poet Yitzhak Katzenelson, whose epic poem "The Song of the Murdered Jewish People" is sometimes regarded as a latter-day Book of Lamentations. Also with Bialik in mind, Katzenelson asks angrily,

> *O why are you so beautiful, you skies, while we are*
> *being murdered, why are you so blue? . . .*
> *Millions . . . raised high their hands to you before*
> *they died. . . .*
> *You have no God above you. Naught and*
> *void—you skies! (Canto IX, stanzas 9–12)*

The criticism of God, appearing in various degrees of audacity and springing from sorrow and anguish, is expressed in such postwar poems as Kadya Molodovsky's "God of Mercy," Jacob Glatstein's "Without Jews," and Paul Celan's "Psalm." To denote God's absence, Celan refers to God in the repeated words "No one," as if God no longer deserves a name after the destruction.[7] The conventional language of piety in the second stanza and indeed the title of the poem—"Psalm"—suggest a mocking of the absent God.

Sometimes the criticism of God for abandoning the people of Israel is expressed indirectly in the form of an inversion of Biblical themes or archetypes. The poem "Lekh-lekho" by Simcha Bunim Shayevitsh, written in response to the first deportations of Jews from the Lodz Ghetto in January 1942, concludes with a traditional affirmation of faith, but the poem's very title suggests the author's equivocal attitude toward God. The Hebrew words of the title, which mean "Go forth," allude to God's words in Genesis 12:1 and constitute a mocking of God's promise to Abraham; for now it is the Nazis and not God who are giving the command, and the promise of greatness is now the reality of destruction. Similarly, Israeli poet Dan Pagis subverts Ezekiel 37:1–10 with its consoling vision, at the time of the Babylonian exile, of the dry bones of the Israelites coming back to life. In his poem "Draft of a Reparations Agreement," Pagis implies that there is no return to life for the millions slain in our terrible time. This same archetype is even more explicitly employed for critical purposes in Katzenelson's "The Song of the Murdered Jewish People":

> *Woe and grief!*
> *Not even a bone remains from my murdered people.*
> *No bone is left for new flesh, new skin,*
> *For a new spirit of life—(Canto II, stanzas 5–6)*

The *akeda,* or the binding of Isaac, is the Biblical episode dramatizing Abraham's unquestioning submission to the divine will and God's intervention to spare the life of Isaac. But Israeli poet Amir Gilboa rewrites the episode in his poem "Isaac" to emphasize the absence of divine intervention during the Holocaust. In Gilboa's poem, it is the child who witnesses the slaughter of his father just as countless child survivors witnessed the extermination of their parents' generation. It is the child— that is, the survivor—who will be haunted and scarred by what he has seen.[8]

The inversion of Biblical passages is not new in the history of Jewish literature, but modern Jewish writers frequently employ this technique as a way of questioning God's justice and mercy during the great tragedy. By noting in the classroom inversions such as those described above, we help students to appreciate the richness of many contemporary poems on the Holocaust and the ways in which the Biblical text continues to engage the imagination of modern writers in surprising and daring ways.

There are, of course, exceptions to this pattern of criticism and accusation which is part of the lamentation response. For example, Canadian-Jewish poet A. M. Klein in "Elegy" turns to God asking that God avenge the murdered, heal the survivors, and "renew our days . . . as they were of old." [9] In a like manner, the character Hersh in Chaim Grade's story "My Quarrel with Hersh Rasseyner" holds fast to his faith in God in spite of the catastrophe. But such uncritical attitudes toward God are hardly representative in modern lamentation literature. More prevalent are the questioning and confrontation we find in writers mentioned earlier.

In spite of complaint, accusation, and defiance, however, Jewish writers cannot altogether reject the God of their ancestors. The narrator in Chaim Grade's story affirms: "However loudly we call out to heaven and demand an accounting, our outcry conceals a quiet prayer for the Divine Presence." Similarly, beneath the reproach of God in Jacob Glatstein's "Without Jews" is a longing for a God to whom the poet can feel bound. If your people vanish, says Glatstein addressing God,

> *Who will dream you? . . .*
> *Who yearn for you?*
> *Who, on a lonely bridge,*
> *Will leave you — in order to return?*

In spite of Auschwitz then, Jewish writers cannot separate themselves altogether from their God.

The categories of truth-telling and lamentation can help students understand more fully what compelled writers to express themselves on so painful a subject. Attention to these categories can also help students to discriminate between the more authentic and the less authentic literary treatments of the Holocaust—the latter being those which use atrocity for purposes of shock, sensation, or conventional entertainment. These categories can assist students to relate one piece of Holocaust literature to another and to see how, at times, truth and lamentation may interweave to form the texture of a single work. Finally, because truth-telling and lamentation are grounded in historical reality, students have an additional basis for countering claims that the Holocaust never happened.

NOTES

1. Cynthia Ozick, "Roundtable Discussion," *Writing and the Holocaust,* ed. Berel Lang (New York: Holmes and Meier, 1988), 284.

2. Aharon Appelfeld, "After the Holocaust," *Writing and the Holocaust,* ed. Berel Lang (New York: Holmes and Meier, 1988), 83.

3. Quotations from poetry and fiction in this essay are taken from the anthology *Truth and Lamentation: Stories and Poems on the Holocaust,* ed. Milton Teichman and Sharon Leder (Urbana: University of Illinois Press, 1994). One exception is the quotation from Canto II of Yitzhak Katzenelson's "The Song of the Murdered Jewish People" which appears in *The Literature of Destruction: Jewish Responses to Catastrophe,* ed. David G. Roskies (Philadelphia: The Jewish Publication Society, 1989), 533.

4. Irving Howe, "Writing and the Holocaust," *New Republic,* 27 October 1986, 36.

5. The following passage from the Book of Lamentations, the prototype of all later *kinoth,* illustrates the idea of Israel's sufferings as caused by her sins:

> *Alas!*
> *Lonely sits the city*
> *Once great with people! . . .*
> *Her enemies are now the masters,*
> *Her foes are at ease,*
> *Because the Lord has afflicted her*
> *For her many transgressions. . . .*
> *Jerusalem has greatly sinned,*
> *Therefore she is become a mockery. (1:1–8)*

See also Lamentations 4:6 and 4:11–13. The idea of repentance and submission to God's punishment is reflected in the following lines:

> *Let us search and examine our ways,*
> *And turn back to the Lord;*
> *Let us lift up our hearts with our hands*
> *To God in heaven:*
> *We have transgressed and rebelled. (3:40–42)*

See also Lamentations 3:25–32 and 5:21. Passages cited are from *The Writings, Kethubim: A New Translation of the Holy Scriptures According to the Masoretic Text,* Third Section (Philadelphia: The Jewish Publication Society of America, 1982).

6. In the Jewish tradition, Rachel, wife of Jacob, is identified as a mother who cares for the afflicted among the children of Israel. According to the prophet

Jeremiah (31:14), the matriarch Rachel weeps for the children of Israel who are slain or driven into Babylonian captivity. Jewish legend tells that Jacob buried Rachel near Ramah because he foresaw that his descendants would pass Ramah on the way to exile in Babylonia and that she would weep and intercede for them.

The "Saint of Berdichev" is the renowned Hassidic rabbi Levi Yitzchak of Berdichev (d. 1802), known for his great love of his people Israel and his confrontation of God in their behalf.

7. Celan's words may be an ironic play on Maimonides' doctrine of God's negative attributes as conveyed in part I, chapters 57–58 of *The Guide of the Perplexed,* trans. M. Friedlander (New York: Hebrew Publishing, 1881).

8. It is interesting that the medieval Biblical commentator Rashi also imagined Isaac as scarred by what he had seen and experienced. In his comment on Genesis 27:1, Rashi notes that the trauma of the *akeda* caused Isaac's later blindness. *The Soncino Chumash: The Five Books of Moses with Haphtaroth,* ed. A. Cohen (London: The Soncino Press, 1983), 149.

9. These words echo Lamentations 5:21–22. They also appear in the Jewish liturgy at the close of the Sabbath Torah service.

REFERENCES

Appelfeld, Aharon. "After the Holocaust," *Writing and the Holocaust,* ed. Berel Lang. New York: Holmes and Meier, 1988, 83–92.

Cohen, A., ed. *The Soncino Chumash: The Five Books of Moses with Haphtaroth.* London: The Soncino Press, 1983.

Howe, Irving. "Writing and the Holocaust," *New Republic* (27 October 1986), 27–39.

Maimonides. *The Guide of the Perplexed,* trans. M. Friedlander. New York: Hebrew Publishing, 1881.

Ozick, Cynthia. "Roundtable Discussion," *Writing and the Holocaust,* ed. Berel Lang. New York: Holmes and Meier, 1988, 277–84.

Roskies, David G., ed. *The Literature of Destruction: Jewish Responses to Catastrophe.* Philadelphia: The Jewish Publication Society, 1989.

Teichman, Milton, and Sharon Leder, eds. *Truth and Lamentation: Stories and Poems on the Holocaust.* Urbana: University of Illinois Press, 1994.

Writings, The, Kethubim: A New Translation of the Holy Scriptures According to the Masoretic Text. Third Section. Philadelphia: The Jewish Publication Society of America, 1982.

Gitta Bauer

Gitta Bauer was an award winning journalist who after the war covered the Nuremberg trials and the Harlem race riots. Her lifelong concern with racism was manifested during the war as she housed and protected a Jewish friend in Berlin. Honored by Yad Vashem for her effort, she was given a medal inscribed with the saying, "Who saves one life, it is as if they saved the whole world." Yet she was ashamed by what her generation had done. "But that (the inscription) doesn't help." she said. "I am still deeply ashamed for my people, my country, still ashamed, deeply ashamed. And it doesn't help me that I was able to save one life. It doesn't help me. We did it."

Amfian Gerasimov

Amfian Gerasimov lived in his native Riga with his wife and six children when the town was overrun and occupied by German forces. Jewish people were forced to move into a ghetto of six or seven small streets. Gerasimov, a mailman, aided them by delivering packages and relaying messages. Later, he housed a Jewish man in his home for several days until the man could join the advancing Russian forces. When asked why he helped when the risk was so great, he answered by quoting the Bible, the New Testament, John, Chapter 15: "There is no greater love than sacrificing your own soul for another's soul." This passage, he noted, comes directly from the Old Testament, Proverbs, Chapter 24.

Gertrude Babilinska

When his mother became ill and died, young Mickey Stolowitzky went to the woman who had worked for his family for over fifteen years. "I have no mother. Will you be my mother?" he asked. Gertrude Babilinska wondered how she, a forty-year old Catholic woman living in occupied Poland, could take on such a responsibility. Yet three days later she began a life-long commitment to Mickey raising him as her son. Not long after the war she realized that for her son's sake she would need to go to Israel. Soon they were on the ship "The Exodus" headed for Palestine. "As soon as the war ended I knew I had to get Mickey to Israel," she said. "There was no other way that I could raise a boy to be a Jew."

Jan Karski

Jan Karski was a Polish spy for the underground who was asked to take information about the systematic killing of the Jews to the leaders of the Allied governments. As part of his preparation he visited the Warsaw Ghetto and the Belzec death camp. "I vomited blood that night," he reported. "I saw horrible, horrible things I will never forget." Karski completed his mission carrying reports to high level leaders in England and later having a personal audience with President Roosevelt in the United States. "Helping Jews was no advantage to the Allied war strategy," he recounted. . . . "Only individuals might help and were helping. The help had to come from the powerful Allied leaders, and this help did not come."

Zofia Baniecka

Zofia Baniecka's work with the Polish underground in Warsaw began when she acted as a liaison relaying orders from one group to another and delivering underground newspapers. Later she and her mother used their apartment to hide guns and ammunition as well as people. Their apartment was divided by curtains and behind everyone was a different Jewish family. This work had a lasting personal effect. "There are many people who saved my belief in humanity," she reflected. "And that is why it is important for people to know about this time . . . that there were those of us who did try to save Jews. It is necessary for the children to know that there were such people."

Aart and Johtje Vos

Aart and Johtje Vos housed and hid many Jews in their Amsterdam home and in the adjacent tunnel they had dug for that purpose. Despite the risks they took, they were quick neither to portray their acts as extraordinary nor to deride those taking no role since "some people who said no often had very good reasons." Johtje was quick to disclaim any special status, "I want to say right away that the words 'hero' and 'righteous Gentile' are terribly misplaced because, first of all, I don't feel righteous and, secondly, I certainly don't feel Gentile. . . . And we certainly are not heroes, because we didn't sit at the table when the misery started and say, ''Okay, now we are going to risk our lives to save some people.''

All of the photographs in this section are courtesy of Gay Block and Malka Drucker from *Rescuers: Portraits of Moral Courage in the Holocaust* by Gay Block and Malka Drucker. New York: Holmes and Meier, 1992. Originals in color.

PART III

TEACHING TOWARD DIALOGUE: SPIRITUAL AND MORAL ISSUES

INTRODUCTION

TIMOTHY A. BENNETT

According to Sander L. Gilman, we do not live in the post-Modern era as contemporary thinkers would have us believe; we live in the post-Holocaust era.[1] Therefore, as Matthias Heyl suggests in his chapter, we must confront what Auschwitz and the Holocaust mean for us as educators. Although Heyl writes of education in Germany, his point nevertheless applies to the North American context as well: occidental traditions of education did not prepare the West to prevent the inhumanity and cruelty for which the name Auschwitz itself has become a symbol. The studies presented thus far in this volume help educators develop historical, literary, psychological, and documentary approaches to the teaching of the Holocaust. Typically, however, teachers find that the study of the Holocaust leads students (as well as educators) to fundamental questions about the very possibility of meaning and human dignity in a world where the Holocaust occurred. Having examined the systematic massacre of six million Jews as historical fact, teachers and students will inevitably confront questions that are spiritual in nature. Do religious traditions still have meaning? Can Germans and Jews, or can Christians and Jews, be reconciled despite the legacy of German and Christian anti-Semitism? Can we create new forms of education and symbols that transcend the limitations of intellectualism?

Teachers must be prepared to engage students' questions about spiritual and moral issues. Unfortunately, educators may often feel that religious and spiritual issues are beyond their competence. Ironically, despite the historical role that religious intolerance played in the Holocaust, religious and spiritual traditions may well provide the best hope for arriving at a deeper understanding of what the Holocaust means for our future as a pluralistic society. Richard L. Rubenstein describes a need that secular knowledge cannot meet and that religious insight alone can answer:

> If we concentrate less on what our religious inheritances promise and threaten and more on the human existence that we share through these traditions, we will achieve the superlative yet simple knowledge of who we truly are. Through our religious traditions we come to a knowledge deeper than words of our guilt, our alienation, and our pathetic finitude. Nothing so humbles and teaches us our true station as do our traditions.[2]

Religion, Rubenstein's statement suggests, can perhaps best equip us to deal with the kinds of issues of guilt, alienation, and failure raised by the Shoah. Furthermore, these qualities are, he argues, intrinsic to human identity. If we are to acquaint students with the horror of the Holocaust, we must also be prepared to help them work through its consequences for them as spiritual, moral beings.

The essays in this section correspond to two salient factors identified by Rubenstein in *After Auschwitz* as related to genocidal anti-Semitism: "the religiocultural conflict between Judaism and Christianity," and "the triumph of value-neutral, functional rationality as the predominant mode of problem solving in advanced technological societies such as Germany."[3] These factors point to a crisis of spirituality. In the first, religious traditions prove incapable of treating each other with respect. As a result, they foster conflict. In the latter factor, spiritual and moral issues have become at best irrelevant. The Holocaust demonstrates that a rationality deprived of its moral and spiritual anchor can be manipulated to murderous ends. The first four studies address how religiocultural factors influence an individual's understanding of identity and history as Christian or Jew and of the other whose history or culture intersects in modern, pluralist societies. The final two chapters address the failure of "value-neutral, functional rationality" and point to the danger of failing to see the spiritual dimension as an essential part of the educational enterprise.

The studies presented in this section suggest that education must lead to genuine, open dialogue. Only by engaging in frank discussion with persons of different beliefs, different traditions and histories can we hope to seek answers to the troubling questions raised by the Shoah. In the end, the Holocaust does more than invite our academic attention: it demands a commitment to dialogue between Germans and Israelis, between grandparents and grandchildren, between Christians and Jews, and among the practitioners of the professions that helped pave the way for the crimes against humanity committed by the National Socialists. In an age when cultural relativism seems to have undermined our faith in a common humanity, these writers suggest that by preparing honestly for a radical dialogue we may yet be able to forge a greater community that respects difference and thus create a common vision of humanity.

The first two chapters deal with issues of identity. Yaacov Lozowick reflects upon his experiences while conducting seminars at Yad Vashem for German educators. His experience demonstrates that hidden cultural assumptions about the Holocaust can impede dialogue. Millen and Lozowick's piece is complemented by Matthias Heyl's analysis of issues confronting German educators. Heyl examines how today's teachers, now one or two generations removed from the Holocaust, must confront their own biases and self-deceptions before entering the classroom—whether in Germany, Israel, or North America. These two essays themselves demonstrate the kind of introspection that is a necessary preparation for genuine dialogue. They stand in a kind of dialogic relationship that suggests that all true education begins with the dictum *gnothi seauton,* know thyself.

The second pair of essays by Steven L. Jacobs and Stephen R. Haynes examines issues of religious belief in the post-Holocaust era. Inevitably, the study of the Holocaust leads students to fundamental questions of belief, of justice, and of meaning. Jacobs suggests that the Shoah must alter fundamentally Judaism's concept of God and divine election. He contends that honest answers to such questions require a radical reinterpretation of Jewish tradition and the acknowledgment that the Holocaust has shattered the possibility of naive religious belief. Haynes demonstrates that the effect of the Holocaust on Christian belief is no less radical. A Christian educator, Haynes wrestles with issues the Holocaust raises for Christianity: can the concept of Christendom as the New Israel be redeemed in light of its anti-Semitic prejudice, and is the concept of Christian love tenable despite the legacy of Christian anti-Semitism? His essay suggests that an authentic post-Holocaust Christian theology must engage in a thorough and honest analysis of the Church's history of anti-Semitism while using that analysis to create a moral imperative to reject supersessionist claims.

The section concludes with essays from William E. Seidelman and John T. Pawlikowski. Based on an examination of how Germany's healers not merely failed to prevent but actually made the Holocaust possible, Seidelman argues that ceremonies of commemoration must become part of the education of physicians. He presents a model of professional education that moves beyond the transmission of professional expertise to finding symbols that help professionals understand their fundamental humanity. Pawlikowski also examines the failure of traditional curricula. He, however, focuses on the inadequacy of rational moral systems. He argues not only that the Holocaust demands that we reexamine and revise radically our understanding of faith and ethics, but that we also recognize the need for symbols and forms of faith expression that nurture the ethical life of communities and prepare the way for genuine Christian-Jewish dialogue.

NOTES

1. Sander L. Gilman, *Inscribing the Other* (Lincoln: University of Nebraska Press, 1991), 17.

2. Richard L. Rubenstein, *After Auschwitz: History, Theology, and Contemporary Judaism,* 2nd Edition (Baltimore: Johns Hopkins University Press, 1992), 27.

3. Rubenstein, *After Auschwitz,* 122.

CHAPTER 20

Pitfalls of Memory: Israeli-German

Dialogues on the Shoah

YAACOV LOZOWICK AND ROCHELLE L. MILLEN

There is in contemporary Germany no dearth of individuals who come to Jewish-German dialogue with unclean hands. We do not here refer to those who seek to "master" the past, thus attempting to put the past firmly behind them, nor about those whose amnesia may be occasioned by guilt and shame brought on by true cognizance.[1] Rather, to be more pointed, some Germans who approach the tenuous process of Jewish-German dialogue remain anti-Semites, despite their stated intentions.

This chapter, however, is not about the anti-Semites. It is, rather, an attempt to describe and understand some of the problems which seem repeatedly to arise, precisely when sincere and well-meaning Germans and Israelis attempt to deal together with their respective—and very different—memories of the Shoah.[2]

The descriptions and analyses offered in this paper are the result of the experience gleaned from several years of repeated encounters with groups of Germans who chose to participate in classes, discussions, and seminars held at Yad Vashem, Israel's National Authority for commemorating the memory of the Shoah. While some of these individuals may have found themselves at Yad Vashem unintentionally, brought there as part of a more general tour of Israel, those involved in the more lengthy programs were generally more invested in the process of dialogue. On four separate occasions in 1992 and 1993, Yad Vashem offered seven- to ten-day seminars in German; the participants in these put out substantial sums of their own money in order to participate. Clearly, these were highly motivated individuals. The Israeli participants in the dialogue were German-speakers, generally affiliated with Yad Vashem and also comparatively highly motivated.

A preliminary remark, the significance of which cannot be overrated: Israeli memory of the Shoah fits into an ancient pattern of memory in general. The role of remembering in Jewish culture has been formed over millennia;[3] the way in which Jews in general and Israelis in particular remember the Shoah has very little to do with the way contemporary Germans remember. Nor are Germans the target of these memories: actually, although Jews have repeatedly suffered persecution, the very attempt to hold a dialogue with members of the persecuting nation seems to be a novelty. There should be no surprise in the fact that this dialogue is far from smooth. The tension that arises derives from the very seriousness of the dialogue and its utter complexity, a complexity which may be subsumed under four arenas of discussion: guilt versus responsibility; detachment versus emotions; content, or "whose history is it?"; and lessons or the didactic aspect.

GUILT VERSUS RESPONSIBILITY

Though often undeclared, each side in these dialogues tends to have a different view of the position of contemporary Germans, most of whom are too young to have been perpetrators.[4] The Germans are preoccupied with guilt. Many, perhaps a majority, insist from the onset that they don't bear it. Others actively grapple with it; a minority claim it. None of them seems to notice that their Israeli counterparts rarely demand any of these, preferring instead to talk of responsibility.

The roots of this distinction can probably be traced deep into the historical and cultural conditioning of the two groups. "Guilt" as an inheritable trait is a basic Christian concept—indeed, one which traditionally has been linked to the Jews. It refers to the attribution by Christians of Jewish blood-guilt for the death of Jesus.[5] This concept is foreign to Jews not because they suffered from collective guilt as formulated in Christian theology, but rather because the major interpretation of guilt in Judaism is that it results from the actions of the individual.[6] If one is guilty, fully but solely, for evil which one has perpetrated, then the guilt cannot be inherited.[7] One could point out that each theological approach has its specific advantages and disadvantages. While the disadvantage of inheriting someone else's guilt is clear, the advantage is that one can also find absolution from an external agent:[8] God, perhaps, or possibly the descendants of the victims. However, while being responsible only for one's own actions removes the burden of inherited guilt, the responsibility itself will never disappear, and it demands action and continual self-awareness, not only prayer.[9] Thus, the Germans involved in the Jewish-German seminars at Yad Vashem may be seeking absolution or atonement; the Israelis, in contrast, seem to want actions and commitment to actions in the here and now. That is, the Israelis seek response on a political level, responses deriving from elements of deep soul-searching and the resolve to take a moral stand, such as combating contemporary anti-Semitism or increasing sensitivity to Jewish forms of memory. Absolution brings a kind of closure,[10] while commitment to action is open ended and an everpresent responsibility.

Detachment versus Emotions

While the differing expectations with which each group approaches the dialogue can cause suspicion and misunderstanding, the style of discussion preferred by each group is the source of no end of mischief. In recent years, the Israeli public has seen a succession of Israeli public figures—mayors, generals, national politicians, and comedians—visiting sites of Nazi camps. Many of them have been observed, on prime-time television, with tears on their cheeks. This has never adversely affected their popularity; if anything, it has enhanced it. To an American public, this may sound quite natural. In Germany, however, public display of overt emotions is often frowned upon, unless possibly in clearly defined situations. The true, deeply felt emotions are usually reserved for a small, intimate circle.[11]

For Israelis, discussion of the Shoah includes emotions, although not necessarily tears. Sorrow, a feeling of holiness *(yirat hakodesh)*, desolation, rage: all these and many more arise regularly when dealing with the murder of millions of innocents. These feelings seem natural to most Israelis, who are often puzzled by the ability, common to many Germans, to deal with the subject on a high academic level, devoid of any visible emotion. That this may be a protective shield is a possibility. Once again keeping in mind the limits of generalizations, these behavior patterns have long been observed as part of German national character.[12] Conversely, one supposes some Germans feel their Israeli counterparts may be attempting emotional manipulation. Are Israelis not, after all, trying to arouse that most threatening emotion of guilt?[13]

Lacking systematic and objective evidence, these are, of course, speculations. However, it probably does the Israelis no harm to see the discomfort of the Germans; the Germans, from their perspective, clearly stand to gain from reducing this past to an academic, depersonalized, and intellectual discussion. Yet infuriating as the respective positions often are to the opposite group, each group may overlook the fact that here, also, a divergence of cultural conditioning is present, one which predates the present issue by centuries. Jews have been telling their children about their past for dozens of generations. A central characteristic of the telling has been *"Be'chol dor va-dor,"* "in every generation one must regard oneself as having personally left Egypt." [14] According to this method of remembering, the aim is to feel as if one personally had experienced the event being remembered. The past is not dead, an inert configuration from which we ought to learn whatever lessons, but rather a living memory. Nor should one distance oneself from the past: after all, it is as if these events happened to us. One legacy of this form of memory is that one has emotions about the past, which is a personal event, not a theoretical one. This prescribed structure of historical remembrance and cultural transmission is not inherent in German—indeed European—historical consciousness. [15]

CONTENT OR, WHOSE HISTORY?

We might assume that once the interlocutors learn to overcome their differences in styles, they would then engage in a joint discussion of the historical facts. However, this is generally not the case, as there is rarely much consensus as to what it is that is being discussed.

For Germans, the primary focus of interest is their own history, and the single most important, overarching question is "How could this have been done?" In the search for an answer, Prussian militarism may be discussed, or the aftermath of World War I; one might analyze the failure of modernity, or perhaps the structure of totalitarianism or bureaucracy. The identity of the victims may become blurred; sometimes the victims—consciously or unconsciously—may even be degraded to almost coincidental props, chosen almost accidentally to be the object of an evil force which needed a victim.

Israelis find these deliberations interesting, but often of secondary importance. The primary question for most Israelis is not "How could

this have been done?" but "How could this have been done to us?"
These two small words camouflage a decidedly different perspective. The
discussion might deal with the history of the relations between Jews and
their neighbors, with forms and traditions of anti-Semitism; discussants
might ponder the relevance of Jewish behavior on the non-Jewish population or the inevitability of anti-Jewish sentiments in Western civilization. From a different perspective, one might deal with the multifaceted
issue of Jewish responses to persecution. Could European Jews have
averted the calamity? Should they have reacted somehow otherwise than
they did?

It would be interesting to compare the literature dealing with the
Shoah published in Hebrew with that published in German; noting the
non-overlapping subject matter might be quite instructive.

LESSONS

As previously noted, a primary motivation for Jews dealing with the
Shoah is commemoration. This may not entail the drawing of any
philosophical morals, the very telling of the tale being an end unto itself,
even somehow the repaying of a debt to those who did not survive.[16]
This in itself is a foreign concept to many Germans, who typically
preface any discussion of the past with its justification (e.g., "We must
learn from the past in order that"). However, even once the conversants
get down to discussing the morals to be learned from this past, the gaps
remain.

To most Germans engaged in learning from the Nazi past, it seems
self-evident that the lessons to be learned deal with the bolstering of
democracy and the rights of the individual. Quite simply, had these
elements been more deeply ingrained in pre-Nazi German society, the
whole era might never have come to be. Their Israeli dialogue-partners
have no quarrel with these fine sentiments, only wondering at times why
one needed the Nazi catastrophe to learn them.[17]

Taking their train of thought one step further, many Germans, particularly those more likely to engage in dialogue with Jews, distance themselves from nationalism. What starts as skepticism directed at their own
German national identity can at times evolve into a general negative
feeling towards nationalism of any kind. If the importance of the individual stands above all else, what need be there for nationalism?[18] These

sentiments seem so clear and unassailable that some Germans wonder how they could have been overlooked by any sensible, thinking person.

Finally, many Germans deduce from their understanding of the past a clear code of contemporary political behavior: pacifism. The advantages of going to war seem to be overwhelmingly out-balanced by the disadvantages. The moral dangers of the slippery slope down which anyone who goes to war *must* face (not to mention the mortal dangers): these all seem to have forever banned the waging of war, any war, from the accepted repertoire of human endeavor.

Perhaps the single most important obstacle in Israel-German dialogue to come from the German side is in the expectation that everyone learn these lessons. Undoubtedly, this is sincere; nonetheless, at times the German participants seem unaware of the feelings their words evoke. After all, there can be an element of incongruity when Germans tell Jews how bad the Nazis were and then criticize Israeli nationalism. What seems to the Germans to be an earnest endeavor is heard by the Israelis as a misplaced type of preaching. Neither group may be objectively right, but both feel strongly about their positions.

This makes for further misunderstanding, since the Israelis are no less adamant in their positions than the Germans. Some American Jews seem to regard the Holocaust as a fundamental aspect of their Jewish identity, as if to say: the salient characteristic of Jews is that, had they been there, they too would have been sent to die at Auschwitz.[19] This is probably less true for Israelis, for whom Jewish identity has broader, though not always clearly defined contents. Nevertheless, the memory of the Shoah clearly plays a role in the consolidation of the community identity of the Israelis.

Many European Jews spent the nineteenth century and the first third of the twentieth trying to shed their ancient nationality in favor of a newly adopted one, be it German, French, English, or other.[20] The inroads made by Zionism in the communities of Western Europe were minor because of the incompatibility of this Jewish nationalism with the major trends of the day. The murder of millions of Jews for their ethnic affiliation reversed this trend. Henceforth, although not all Jews committed themselves actively to Zionism, support of Jewish nationalism became the norm.

German-Israeli dialogue, then, is impeded by the diametrically opposed lessons drawn by each side. What for one group is the *NS-Zeit,* the period which proves the need to live without nationality, is for the other the Shoah, the ultimate proof that Jews cannot, and should not, shed their nationality. What for the one is the need to exorcise particularism-run-amok through an overdose of universalism, is for the other a call for a regeneration of particularism, offspring of the failure of universalism.[21]

And where the German position evolves at times into pacifism, so the Israeli one can be transformed into a kind of militarism. The logic that dictates that the lesson of abuse of military power may be the negation of any use of it finds its reflection in the logic of saying that from abject powerlessness one must forever be more powerful.

The wish, uttered from time to time, to see the memories of the two nations grow together seems not to be realistic. Have the Germans among themselves forged a common memory? Have the Israelis? Rather, it seems, we should be striving for a respectful situating of clearly different memories, a situating grounded in understanding and acceptance, rather than in agreement. This, it seems, would already be a considerable improvement over much of the past.[22]

NOTES

1. See Charles S. Maier, *The Unmasterable Past: History, Holocaust, and German National Identity* (Cambridge; Harvard University Press, 1988), esp. chapter 5. Also, Saul Friedlander, "Trauma, Transference and 'Working Through' in Writing the History of the Shoah" in *The Jews in European History: Seven Lectures,* ed. Wolfgang Beck (Cincinnati: Hebrew Union College Press, 1994), 123–42; Manfred Henningsen, "The Politics of Memory: Holocaust and Legitimacy in Post-Nazi Germany" in *Holocaust and Genocide Studies,* Vol. 4, No. l, 15–26; and Jane Kramer, "Letter from Germany: The Politics of Memory," *The New Yorker,* August 14, 1995, 48–65.

2. See Saul Friedlander, ibid., and James E. Young, *The Texture of Memory: Holocaust Memorials and Meaning* (New Haven: Yale University Press, 1993), part I. Also, Dan Bar-On, *Legacy of Silence: Encounters with Children of the Third Reich* (Cambridge: Harvard University Press, 1989).

3. Yosef Haim Yerushalmi, *Zakhor: Jewish History and Jewish Memory* (Seattle: University of Washington Press, 1982) and Cynthia Ozick, "Metaphor and Memory" in *Metaphor and Memory* (New York: Alfred A. Knopf, 1989), 265–83.

4. Jane Kramer, op. cit. 50, states that 75 percent of the current German population was born after World War II. Among the dialogue partners, the proportions are even more one-sided.

5. Matthew 27:25. "And all the people answered, 'His blood be on us and our children.' " This verse has been interpreted for centuries in Christian theol-

ogy as Jewish acknowledgement of the eternal collective guilt of the Jewish people for the death of Jesus.

6. There are many biblical, rabbinic, and later sources which deal with transgression, guilt, repentance, and atonement. A classic source is Maimonides, *Mishneh Torah* (Hebrew), *The Book of Knowledge: Laws of Repentance* (Vilna: 1900). For a contemporary formulation, see Pinchas H. Peli, *On Repentance: In the Thought and Oral Discourses of Rabbi Joseph B. Soloveitchik* (Jerusalem: Oroth Publishing, 1980), trans. from the Hebrew.

7. Of course, when dealing with guilt in the context of any Jewish-Christian dialogue, and even more so Jewish-German dialogue, the specific history can hardly be expected not to compound the complexity. See, for example, Dierk Juelich, "Die Wiederkehr des Verdraengten—Sozialpsychologische Aspekte zur Identitaet der Deutschen nach Auschwitz," in Helmut Schrier and Matthias Heyl, *Das Echo des Holocaust* (Hamburg: R. Kraemer 1992).

8. The process of confession as it evolved in the Catholic Church requires genuine contrition, fervent prayer, and penance. Nonetheless, the power to forgive remains external, within the priest, as he is an agent of God and the Church. This creates a different psychological dynamic (though comparable in some aspects) from that of transgression and repentance in Jewish theology.

9. See Maimonides, op. cit., and Soloveitchik, op. cit.

10. See Friedlander, "Trauma, Transference and 'Working Through' in Writing the History of the Shoah," op. cit., 138. Also Judith Miller, *One, by One, by One: Facing the Holocaust* (Simon and Schuster, 1990), 54–60, and Henningsen, op. cit., 21-22.

11. This is, of course, a broad generalization, one nevertheless supported by substantial sociological and psychological data. Some cultures and groups encourage demonstrativeness; others emphasize restraint and control.

12. This pattern is demonstrated in numerous writings, e.g., Treitschke, "It does not matter what you think but only that you obey" or Nietzsche, "War and courage have done more great things than charity." That Nietzsche was deliberately misappropriated by Nazi ideologues is clearly shown in Weaver Santaniello, *Nietzsche, God, and the Jews: His Critique of Judeo-Christianity in Relation to the Nazi Myth* (Albany: SUNY Press, 1994).

13. An interesting illustration of this was recorded at the site of the former concentration camp of Buchenwald on November 10, 1993. The event was the unveiling of a memorial to the thousands of Jews who perished here, but whose identity had been hidden during forty years of Communist rule. The speeches made by the German public figures, including political figures of some prominence, focused on external issues, and repeatedly used phrases such as "concepts," "educational needs," "programs," and inevitably, "financing." Naftali Lavi, an Israeli survivor of the camp, also a public figure accustomed to ap-

pearing before public audiences, excused himself for speaking in English by referring to his emotional turmoil; only under the cover of this neutral, memory-free language, would he be able to complete his remarks. He was the only speaker to make public reference to personal emotions at an event commemorating ten thousand deaths. Personal emotions and subjective response are likely to arouse guilt, and move beyond the level of abstract conceptualization that keeps feelings at bay. Judith Miller, op. cit., 287, writes in her conclusion: "What fosters memory of the Holocaust? Essentially, any intellectual tool, any mechanism, any tradition that reduces its abstraction."

14. Traditional Haggadah, recited at the Passover Seder. The prooftext for this statement in the Haggadah is Deuteronomy 6:23.

15. The single most important analysis of the Jewish forms of memory is Yosef Hayim Yerushalmi, *Zachor: Jewish History, and Jewish Memory*, op. cit. A poignant example of this memory in operation is Arnold Zable, *Jewels and Ashes* (New York: Harcourt, Brace, 1994).

16. Take for example, the many books written by Jews about various aspects of the Shoah which are dedicated to those who did not survive. Here, a short, random list: Yitzhak Arad, *Ghetto in Flames* (Jerusalem: Yad Vashem, 1980): Eliezer Berkowitz, *With God in Hell* (New York: Sanhedrin, 1979); Elie A. Cohen, *Human Behaviour in the Concentration Camps* (London: Jonathan Cape, 1954); Moshe Standberg, *My Longest Years* (Jerusalem: Yad Vashem, 1968); Elie Wiesel, *Night* (New York: Discus, 1969). See also Gideon Hausner's dramatic opening lines in the trial of Adolf Eichmann, *6,000,000 Accusers* (Jerusalem: Jerusalem Post, 1961), 29.

17. See George L. Mosse, *Nazi Culture* (New York: Schocken: 1981) and his numerous other writings on the rise of fascism and Nazi ideology in German society. Also, Frank Stern, *The Whitewashing of the Yellow Badge: Antisemitism and Philosemitism in Postwar Germany* (Oxford: Pergamon Press, 1992), esp. chapter 6. Studies of the Weimar Republic are also illuminating in this regard.

18. An understandable if naive lament. The literature on nationalism is enormous. See the works of Hans Kohn, as well as George L. Mosse, *Confronting the Nation: Jewish and Western Nationalism* (Hanover: University Press of New England, 1993), esp. chapters 1-7.

19. See Michael Berenbaum, *After Tragedy and Triumph: Modern Jewish Thought and the American Experience* (Cambridge: Cambridge University Press, 1990), part I.

20. See Gershom Scholem, "Jews and Germans" in *On Jews and Judaism in Crisis: Selected Essays* (New York: Schocken Books, 1976), 71–92. Also Jehuda Reinharz and Paul Mendes-Flohr, *The Jew in the Modern World: A Documentary History*, Second Edition (Oxford University Press: 1995), documents in part III.

21. See Sander L. Gilman, "How and Why Study the Other" in *Inscribing the Other* (Lincoln: University of Nebraska Press, 1991), esp. 17, and George Steiner, *Bluebeard's Castle: Some Notes on the Definition of Culture* (New Haven: Yale University Press, 1971), chapters 2 and 3. The Holocaust, Steiner writes on 46, "enacted a suicidal impulse in Western civilization"; and on 30 he puts before us the poignant query, "Why did humanistic traditions and models of conduct prove so fragile a barrier against political bestiality?"

22. In the words of Gershom Scholem, "However sublime it might be to forget, we cannot. Only by remembering a past we can never completely master can we generate hope in the resumption of communication between Germans and Jews, and in the reconciliation of those who have been separated." Scholem, "Jews and Germans," op. cit., 92.

CHAPTER 21

Education after Auschwitz:

Teaching the Holocaust in Germany

MATTHIAS HEYL

In 1966, the German-Jewish philosopher Theodor W. Adorno gave a lecture on education after Auschwitz,[1] twenty-one years after the liberation of the German concentration- and extermination-camp Auschwitz. Anyone writing about education after Auschwitz in Germany must cite Adorno's dictum: "That Auschwitz does not happen again is the primary obligation of all education."[2] Because this phrase has almost become a cliché, people often do not perceive its analytical and critical nucleus and implications. Other Adorno-interpreters add their interpretations to it, rarely reaching a point of understanding that is similar to Adorno's. I intend to discuss some of the issues and dilemmas associated with the term of *education after Auschwitz* in order to gain a better insight into the relationship between this part of history and *German identity after Auschwitz*. You will see that *Adorno's* point of view has influenced my personal perspective.

In Germany, as well as in other places of the world, we are confronted with the issue of defining and deciding[3] what we are to do with the memories connected to what happened in Auschwitz. How do we integrate Auschwitz into our history? What is the *uniqueness* of the Shoah? In the last fifty years, we have had to deal with this question in different contexts. The *Historiker-Streit*[4] or the *Bitburg-fiasco* are just two examples. All the German debates related to the Holocaust are linked by an underlying vehemence. This vehemence shows that German individuals are concerned with the influence of the Shoah on their history, their past and present, and especially on German identity after Auschwitz. What does Auschwitz mean to us? Which interpretations do we accept, and what are we to take from them? Are we facing up to the fact that Auschwitz occurred, although we might not be able to deal with it? Auschwitz challenges ambivalent feelings and emotional resistance. In Germany, we have to face it, with the burden of German history on our shoulders. It is a question we ask ourselves as human beings, educators by profession, who must justify ourselves to our students. As teachers, to provoke and initiate a process of learning, or at least, we want to make it possible for the students, born after Auschwitz, to define their position towards history. But how could we answer their questions credibly, if we are ourselves unable to face the issues? What does the Shoah mean to our existence; what kind of influences does our history have on our present lives and on our identity?

The German writer Klabund says: "Germany, you ought neither to forget the murdered, nor the murderers." Neither the murdered, nor the murderers. This demand remains pertinent. Do not forget! Remembrance. Memory. Memento. Keepsake. Commemoration. To treasure the memory of the victims.[5] However we name it, each term demands that we reflect upon what happened, that we remember the crime that took place, that we remember the perpetrators and their crimes against humanity, and that we remember the victims' fate. Do we fulfill this demand, remembering the murdered and their murderers? Do we make a clear distinction between commemorating the victims and remembering the perpetrators? Do we have separate sorts of remembrance, that allow us to restore the victims' dignity violated in Auschwitz, and that also allow us to regain our dignity, that was forfeited in Auschwitz? Only reflection may lead us to a future, in which we face history that is ours, whether we want it, or not.

As educators we must ask ourselves: *what* do we want to teach, and *how* do we want to do it? These questions have not become less important in the fifty years following the liberation of Auschwitz. We have to declare our position, before the Shoah is *to disappear in common history,* to quote Yossi Klein Halevi.[6]

I shall define more clearly what I mean by *education after Auschwitz,* but allow me first to take a detour. The Israeli historian Moshe Zimmermann, addressing German educators, asked them to imagine a world in which the Holocaust had not taken place, a World War II without the Holocaust. German warfare and the deeds of the Germans and their allies, so Zimmermann said, would suffice to introduce plausibly into the curriculum such subjects as *courage, initiative, emancipation, tolerance, humanity* or even the *concept of civil disobedience.* These aims are all, by the way, aims educators had long *before Auschwitz,* related to the concept of an enlightened, modern curriculum. It would be tempting to suggest that education after Auschwitz demands that we change society and make the world more just. The bitter irony, of course, is that many who were educated to accept humane and tolerant values either died or survived in Auschwitz.

To relate the most common ideas and aims education has had since the era of Enlightenment would trivialize, once again, what happened in Auschwitz, or for what Auschwitz has become a metaphor. Thus, Adorno wanted to justify the concepts of *education, culture, Enlightenment,* and *civilization* after Auschwitz itself. He stated that there was a breakdown of humane values and attitudes. But this *breakdown of civilization as a whole* was not a reason for him to deny the importance of culture for civilization, at all. Adorno reflected on Auschwitz by using the modern methods of analysis he himself criticized. He did not try to solve the problem, but he faced it, pointing out its issues, challenges, and dilemmas. Adorno faced up to the burden of history and delineated the issues, dilemmas, and challenges we face in the post-Holocaust era. In an age when post-Modern thinkers avoid such challenges by regarding history as a kind of quarry that provides raw materials to be exploited and manipulated arbitrarily, Adorno's approach and critical methods suggest a responsible reaction to the issues emerging in the modern era.

Thus, as educators, we must acknowledge that to educate *after, in spite of* and *because of* Auschwitz, we also have to face the very worst dilemmas. There is no way out. We still have to teach, to educate, and to live, in the same way we have to breathe. Auschwitz meant the collapse of all faith in the capacity of civilized society to instill humane values. Educators have yet to come to terms with the enormous significance of Auschwitz for our ideals of education. Hannah Arendt described the breakdown of experience in an interview:

> It was, really, as if we came to the edge of a precipice. Because we thought that everything else could be repaired the way politics can repair everything. But not this! This should not have happened. I do not point out the number of victims. What I mean is the way of industrial creation of corpses and all this—I do not have to name it at all. This should not have happened.[7]

The Jewish historian Dan Diner added:

What took place in Auschwitz is related to the nucleus of civilized certainty, that is a basic need in all interhuman relations and behavior. Bureaucratic manner of an organized and industrial extermination of masses of people, it means a denial of civilization, its way of thinking and behaving rationally that requires anticipatory understanding. . . . Relying on a cultivated social causality that insures the reliability of life and survival was reversed to its opposite: extermination of masses of human beings became a regular, common fact, while survival owed to mere chance.[8]

These experiences, different from all the experiences before Auschwitz, cause Diner to speak of *a breakdown of civilization caused in and by Auschwitz*.[9] The non-Jewish Germans have to admit to this breakdown, and this may be more difficult than for Jewish survivors and their offspring. The memory of the Shoah is divided, for to the non-Jewish Germans, mass murder was neither a common, nor a regular threat, for they were not its intended victims.[10]

Traces of the mentality that made Auschwitz possible also inform the contemporary German sense of identity, as the psychoanalyst Dierk Juelich has shown.[11] We can not escape detecting and explaining its relicts. The Jewish psychoanalyst Sammy Speier, living in Frankfurt, has described the manner of facing history in Germany under the influence of the Shoah. The past of our own parents and grandparents remains exceedingly strange to us, for

After Auschwitz there are no parents and grandparents anymore who would let the children sit on their knees, telling them about their lives in former times. Children need fairy tales, but they also need parents telling about their lives, in order to be able to build up their own relationship towards the past. But the stories their parents would have to tell are no more common stories of war and adventures, but they are stories to be rejected, to be ashamed of, dangerous and awful. The most important stories are not to be told, so the fathers and grandfathers, the mothers and grandmothers, decide to keep silent. What they do not tell causes a kind of emptiness in the lives of their offspring.[12]

I often encounter this emptiness or vacuum in the statements of the members of the German Third Generation. We may ask whether this intergenerational *conspiracy of silence* is always related to the Holocaust. There were also other aspects of the Nazi system that might explain its taboo nature. It has been a painful experience for many of the generation of perpetrators and bystanders that their hopes, expectations, and dreams once linked with their Nazism, failed in the long run. Nazi ideology made them believe that they were superior to everybody else; after the defeat, they acquired an inescapable feeling of immense inferiority. They hid their grief at being defeated, incapable of mourning for their own self-made fate. Alexander and Margarethe Mitscherlich examined this phenomenon in their seminal study *Die Unfähigkeit zu trauern: Grundlagen kollektiven Verhaltens* (The Inability to Mourn: Foundations of Collective Behavior).

However, Auschwitz focuses on a special element in the memories of the generation of perpetrators and bystanders, so they very effectively try to repress the issues it raises. They do not feel that they are harming themselves by doing this, but they are unable to face themselves as individuals or citizens fully participating in social and political life. Thus, it is comprehensible that their offspring, who also define themselves as *children of the perpetrators and bystanders,* feel the enormous repression within the First Generation and its threat for their own integrity and identity. Often they choose to let the sleeping dogs lie and fail to confront the burden of Auschwitz. Maturely facing history would mean to be able to see what happened, and to judge it. This would end the continuation of the attitudes that made Auschwitz possible. This mature way of facing history would help young Germans also discover that maturity is a strength that enables them to be people, competent of deciding what to do with their past, their present lives and future.

In Germany, an *education after Auschwitz* took place that did not enable young people to face their history at all. I am confronted with its efforts every day in my work with students at Hamburg University. "Auschwitz—I cannot hear it, anymore," is a frequent statement among members of the Second or Third Generation. Maybe their teachers emphasized the Holocaust, overdoing it, as the students say. But from my point of view, it is not the extent of speaking about the Holocaust or the intensity of the confrontation, but the way it is done, that threatens young people and leads them to repress their emotions related to it. I know from personal experience, having been educated after Auschwitz, that the attitude a teacher or educator adopts is crucial. Some of my teachers tried to wrestle with their parents, no matter if they were perpetrators or bystanders, while speaking about the Holocaust.

In the most common intergenerational conflict, the teachers tried to derive a better position for themselves, blaming their parents for the past, but not taking the past very seriously. Auschwitz became an instrument within this conflict, and the teachers identified themselves with the victims, thus denying their own personal and biographical links to the past as children of the perpetrators and bystanders. They tried to take over the victims' position from the authentic victims, imagining themselves as avengers. Auschwitz was an argument to them, a justification for ending their dialogue with their parents, instead of asking them seriously what happened. Auschwitz enforced their claim to be superior to their parents' generation, but their rigor helped them to avoid confronting existential issues and dilemmas, arising from the reality of Auschwitz as a historical fact. Thus, Auschwitz was the answer to their parents, not a reason to question and to think about it more seriously. It caused hypocrisy on both sides, which led to continuing the *conspiracy of silence*. Students often get an intuitive impression of this hypocrisy and thus feel detached from a topic, which their teachers misuse for their purposes.

Another attitude I meet is one in which teachers try to pay for the guilt of their parents or their own omissions. Sometimes it is expressed in a very similar manner of dealing with the Holocaust, for they make the classroom courses a permanent examination of the Holocaust. They want to show that they have learned their lessons, that they are able to face it, but they miss the point. No matter which explanation they give — Auschwitz as a result of a capitalistic world, as another highlight of European anti-Semitism, and so forth — they are sure that they are able to give one explanation for it. Their students see the extent of their explanatory attempts, but, intuitively, they also recognize its limits.

A third attitude I find allows teachers to show their emotions in a very fashionable way, trying to provoke their students to feel the same way. Their keyword is *Betroffenheit* (consternation), and they attempt to evoke shock by forcing their students to face the masses of corpses of the victims. In the end, this approach enables them to avoid dealing responsibly with the crimes perpetrated against the victims. To these teachers, it becomes more important to speak about their own feelings, than to speak about the feelings, pain, and dreams of the people who had been killed. Their consternation leads to a rivalry between them and the real victims. The victims' fate has to fade in order to let these teachers be the more *authentic victims* of the Holocaust. Students oppose this, they are accused of behaving as the perpetrators did. The teachers also need this kind of opposition, for it enables them to see themselves as victimized—in this case, their students do the dirty work of their parents. There is no need to grapple with the underlying issues.

All these types of so-called confrontation may be called methods of non-confrontation and repression. They prevent students from understanding the main issues and dilemmas linked to the Holocaust. They do not offer any idea of how to face history. Certainly, I have to point out that these kinds of escapism were not at all the only ways in which the Shoah is dealt with. They are not. Of course, there are teachers who always knew and still know that Auschwitz is part of their own dilemmas, as Germans of the Second Generation, and they cannot find any way to escape. They face the special issues and demands, unable to give an easy explanation for what had happened. They also acknowledge that it still affects German identity and society. On the other hand, I meet teachers who refuse to speak about this period at all and presume that Auschwitz did not exist.

What frightens me the most is that young Germans believe and confess that they have heard enough about it, and they feel able to escape history by rejecting any confrontation with it. Students state that they know enough, so they can turn their face to the future. Their teachers pretend to be able to deal with the legacy of Auschwitz. I want to give another example for this lack of historical consciousness and awareness, an emptiness, as Speier named it, that we still find in Germany—a country, where the Nazis are rarely remembered, as are its Jewish former citizens. While asking students about their knowledge concerning the Jews and Jewry, whether they know any Jews personally, they regularly have to answer negatively. What they do know is derived from a more abstract background. Apparently, Germany is a country without any Jews, although 40,000 Jews are not *no Jews*. The students hesitate to use the term *Jude (Jew)*, for it is a stigmatizing term to them, written in dark characters on a yellow patch. They feel uncertain about what makes a Jew a Jew. Some names they recall, such as Heinz Galinski, Ignatz Bubis, Elie Wiesel, Martin Buber, less often Albert Einstein, Karl Marx, Sigmund Freud, rarely they name Jesus. *Jude* is a synonym for victim to them. They cannot imagine a Jew saying proudly, *I am a Jew,* for they do not know any Jews personally. Jew means to them a religious Jew, for they fear to get too close to the Nazis' definition of the Jews. Jewry— a religious or an ethnic community? A people or a nation? A group that shared a common destiny? What is an atheist Jew? There exists a confusion of terms and concepts. Pseudo-halachic discussions, "a Jew is the child of a Jewish mother." Not to mention the state of Israel! The students endeavor to think sharply, but facing the issues linked to Jewish identity, they have to face ambivalences. Very often the students ask me "How can Jewish individuals live in this country, in Germany, after Auschwitz?" I try to get them to the point where they ask themselves: "How can we, ourselves, live in this country after Auschwitz, with this history we came into." It is an arduous and laborious process to arrive at this question, but it seems to be worth all the work it requires.

Asking the same students whether they know Nazis personally, their answer seems to be the same. They know about history, but they fear relating it to themselves. Movies, T.V. programs, documentaries, let them think that Nazis are tall, fair-haired young people with blue eyes, looking resolutely at the world, a breed of idiotic beings, constantly clicking their heels. This image of a Nazi does not fit into what their grandparents told them or what their grandparents look like. Nazis seem to be either victims of diabolic demagoguery, or inhuman beings, monster-like in a way that does not allow any links to their grandparents, who are infirm, weak, gray-haired, and elderly. Thus, they are captives of the clichés of a Nazi and of *screen memories* or *cover memories*. This way they remain the children of their parents, grandchildren of their grandparents, instead of becoming adults themselves, mature to stand where they are. Listening to their own stories carefully, they feel surprised that Germany is ostensibly a country that has neither Jews, nor Nazis. Both groups seem to have "vanished," to have faded somehow, but they do not know how this has happened.

Then, I usually quote a part of an essay written by Niklas Frank, son of the Generalgouverneur Hans Frank, who "vanished" in 1946; he was sentenced to death because of his prominent participation in the crimes the Nazis committed:

The sound of your neck breaking, it saved me from becoming screwed up. You would have poisoned my brain with all your prattle. The same way as it happened to my fellow-Germans, part of the silent majority of my generation, who were not that lucky to get their father hanged. This makes me feel good being your son. How poor these millions of children are, whose fathers gave the same views, full of craftiness, cowardice, desire to kill and inhumanity, but who were less prominent than you were.[13]

Very often they do not know how to deal with this utterance of a son who tried to find a father who might have a part, that could justify loving him, but the son detected a mere coward, a ridiculous and cruel man, who decided to be one of the perpetrators. One single reaction I often meet: it seems to be disloyal that a son speaks this way about his father, and his accusation seems to be unfair, for it allows no generalization. It takes some time for them to learn where their rejections come from—they try to avoid looking at their grandparents the way Frank looks at his father. They do not know enough about their grandparents to be able to verify or falsify the ideas and fantasies they have while reading Niklas Frank. On the other hand, it is challenging for them to question their parents and grandparents. Many of them say it was the first time they felt motivated to start a discussion.

We come into history by being the children of our parents. *Man is the only living being knowing his grandparents.*[14] From them we derive our historical consciousness. We Germans have our opportunity to decide on which side we are: as perpetrators, bystanders, rescuers, or victims. The Jews had no opportunity to choose.

In Jewish tradition it is said: "Mai de-hawah hawah," what was— was. This is why we have to remember, so that we can leave a world to our offspring that is able to prevent a repetition of Auschwitz. History does not merely repeat itself. The intergenerational problems in Germany, the nation of former perpetrators and bystanders, present a special task for educators and school-teachers. They cannot solve the problem, but they must face it to be able to deal with it. To remember and to commemorate, this is different from a mere rhetorical saying *"Auschwitz—Never Again!"*

Wanting to learn history's lessons, we have to learn first what has happened, and then take a stand. *"You shall not be a perpetrator,"* is one of the unspoken mottos German educators had after Auschwitz. At the same time other people, our European neighbors and also the Israeli society and Jewish community, developed another motto: "You shall not be a victim again!"[15] The Israeli historian Yehuda Bauer gives three commandments as the human imperative of the Holocaust: "Thou shalt not be a victim. Thou shalt not be a perpetrator. Above all, thou shalt not be a bystander."

In my opinion, a major task for any education after Auschwitz is to emphasize the central meaning of identity and choices. If you know who you are, you will be able to identify with someone else temporarily, meeting the human being as well in your neighbor, as in the stranger. I try to let the students know a bit more about Jewish identity, about Jewish life before, during and after the Holocaust, in order to see the former and actual variety of Jewishness and Judaism, so that they can also get a feeling of what they are missing in Germany today. It is similar to a sort of cultural phantom limb pain,[16] as the Polish author Hanna Krall called it. Germans will never be able to say Kaddish;[17] it is not their way to commemorate, but they should know about saying Kaddish. Then they can understand a bit more about this Jewish way of commemorating the dead.[18]

We cannot undo what happened, but we can remember and commemorate. We can and must remember the perpetrators and the circumstances which led to the Holocaust, and remember and commemorate the victims. And we should never forget the suffering the survivors endured, that this trauma and the most different psychological sequelae still exist for both Jewish and German Second and Third Generations. History does not end, and it affects us all. Thus, it is our task to do what we can to keep the crimes of the past from recurring.

NOTES

This chapter began as a lecture for the conference "Teaching the Holocaust: Issues and Dilemmas" at Wittenberg University, October 24–26, 1993. Portions were published before in the German language: M. Heyl, *Von der Notwendig- und Unmöglichkeit einer Erziehung nach Auschwitz,* and M. Heyl, *Anstelle eines Nachworts: Von der dritten Generation gesprochen,* in H. Schreier and M. Heyl, eds., *Das Echo des Holocaust: Pädagogische Aspekte des Erinnerns,* Hamburg 1992, 217–33, and 257–68 [Hamburg 1994, 215–31; 255–66]. See also my articles in H. Schreier and M. Heyl, eds., *Die Gegenwart der Schoah: Zur Aktualität des Mordes an den europäischen Juden,* Hamburg 1994, and the preface to M. Heyl, *Vorwort,* in L. Poliakov, *Der arische Mythos,* Hamburg 1993.

I have to thank Timothy A. Bennett, Helmut Schreier, Carolyn Blume, Zezette and Steven Black (Facing History and Ourselves) and my dear wife and colleague Margit Maronde-Heyl for reading this paper, helping to correct my English and letting it sound less German.

1. This is the literal translation of the German term "Erziehung nach Auschwitz," which is the equivalent for the English term education after the Holocaust or Holocaust education.

2. T. W. Adorno, Erziehung nach Auschwitz, in T. W. Adorno, *Stichworte: Kritische Modelle 2,* Frankfurt 1969, 85.

3. Definition is always a process of deciding.

4. The debate among German historians in the middle of the 1980s.

5. In German, there are only two words for remembrance, memory, keepsake, and commemoration: "Erinnerung" and "Gedenken." A third term is "Vergangenheitsbewältigung," literally to master your past, which is only used while speaking about the problematic attitudes of Germans concerning their Nazi past.

6. Y. K. Halevi, *Who Owns the Memory?* in *The Jerusalem Report,* Jerusalem 1993, February 25, 1993, 28–33; here, 31.

7. A. Reif, ed., *Gespräche mit Hannah Arendt,* 9–40, here, 24. Germans have to face it and they have to face what Hannah Arendt meant while saying "and all this." We have to think about what happened, very clearly.

8. D. Diner, ed., *Zivilisationsbruch: Denken nach Auschwitz,* Frankfurt 1988, 7.

9. *Zivilisationsbruch,* ibid., 9.

10. Listening to the debates taking place within German families, you often hear that the bombing of German cities like Dresden or Hamburg, or the expulsion of German residents from the former German-ruled areas balance Auschwitz. We find in this notion another hint that the Germans did not lose their idea of causality: For they had only one means to explain the effects of World War II to themselves by relating it to the crimes done to the Jews. The threat of being punished for their crimes, afterwards, is also to be read in the secret reports of German *Sicherheitsdienst* (literally, Security Services) on the situation in the *Third Reich.*

11. D. Juelich, "Die Wiederkehr des Verdrängten: Sozialpsychologische Aspekte zur Identität der Deutschen nach Auschwitz," in Schreier/Heyl (1992), 57–71.

12. S. Speier, "Der ges(ch)ichtslose Psychoanalytiker: Die ges(ch)ichtslose Psychoanalyse," in *Psyche* 6/41, June 1987, 481–91, especially 486.

13. N. Frank, *Der Vater: Eine Abrechnung,* München, 1993, 24.

14. Professor Dr. Nathan Peter Levinson, the former Rabbi of the Jewish community in Hamburg, quotes the sociologist Willi Hellpach this way, as written in a letter to me of January 29, 1992.

15. There is a conflict between these statements: the German peace movement stated during the Gulf War that Germany had to refuse any kind of participation in this war, for Germans should no longer participate in wars, thereby giving up solidarity with Israel, that was threatened by the Iraqi government's threats and attacks. If the same Germans would have prevented the German arms and technology that enabled the Iraqi government to attack Israel, this might have made their statement more reasonable—but they did not.

16. H. Krall, "Fantoompijn," in *Vrij Nederland,* Amsterdam 1992, August 15, 1992, 31–35.

17. Famous Jewish liturgical doxology and mourners' prayer (Heb. Ahse, consecration).

18. Survivors very often reacted to my description of the attitudes of the German society connected to the Nazi past by saying: "I can imagine what they feel about their own past, and I can also imagine what German Second and Third Generation feel about their parents' or grandparents' past. You should not blame them." This is when I have to argue with the survivors: I do not want to blame anybody of the Second or Third Generation. What I want to do is to make them understand what the survivors feel or think, while facing history. Too often I find that survivors do care about the feelings of German Second and Third Generation, but they get no (emotionally based) response. One of my main important educational aims is to enable German students to come back to more human terms, to sympathize with their grandparents' victims, to see their faces, and to listen to their stories.

CHAPTER 22

Post-Shoah Jewish Theology:

Identifying the Categories

STEVEN L. JACOBS

I am not Job; I am only Job's son and grandson.

To the memories of Ralph Albert Jacobs (died 1981) and Ella and Leo Jacob (murdered 1941/1942?)

The construction of any post-Shoah Jewish theology has now moved into its second phase after that of its initial exploration and discussion of the role/presence/absence of God during the years 1933–1945: that of identifying the various and appropriate categories now required for a meaningful and relevant theology, one with a *practical* orientation. Such a reformed and reformulated theology will find itself, more likely than not, at variance with the "historically traditional" notion of faith presented by Judaism.

For Jews, the primary categories and questions, and the substance of this chapter, include the following: (1) *God and Covenant:* What understanding of God is now appropriate and what relationship with that God now makes sense after the Shoah? (2) *Prayer:* What meaning do we now attach to that which was formerly understood as the vehicle of communication between the two? Does any concept of God as *Shomea tefillah* ("Hearer of prayer") make sense? (3) *Israel and Zionism:* Does the Jewish responsibility towards Israel now take on a different understanding post-Shoah? Do the philosophy and theology of Zionism—both secular and/or religious—change because of the Shoah?

This essay, then, is a preliminary attempt to tentatively provide answers based on my own thinking and previous writing. It is not to be understood in any way, manner, shape, or form as providing definitive answers to these vexing questions. Its very brevity does, however, represent something of a distillation of my own work in this area for now more than a decade.[1]

GOD AND COVENANT

The "historically traditional" understanding of God as most fully expressed by the Jewish religious tradition is that of a "God-who-acts-in-history," whose caring concern for His Israelite/Jewish progeny led Him to enter into Covenant with them, initially at Sinai, whereby He would protect them throughout all subsequent history—provided they honored Him by both their acceptance of Sacred Scripture and their observance of the "system" of Judaism as set forth in Torah and subsequently interpreted by authoritative spokesmen (i.e., Pharisees, and, later, Rabbis). Though the course of Jewish history has been both difficult and problematic, that understanding—including, all-too-often, self-flagellation on the part of the Jewish People for its own supposed "sins" which merited punishment by other nations as God's "agents"—has held firm until the revelations of the Shoah have called this "truth" into question.

What possible "sins" had the Jewish People—and others—committed which merited such heinous and horrendous punishments? Could any honest religionist, however desirous of affirming a commitment to the Biblical position, truly believe Adolf Hitler, *yimach sh'mo* ("May his name be blotted out!"), his minions and their recruits were doing God's work and serving as God's agents?[2] What role does this "God-who-acts-in-history" perform now when the best evidence available suggests both His absence and His silence?

Better to rethink our understanding of God and realize that the historical understanding of a *limited* Deity, non-omnipotent, non-omniscient, non-omnibenevolent is more in accord with observable and experienced reality than prior belief. Better still to accept the following: that of a Creator God, a *Borei olam*, who in the very act of creation, whether by accident or design, caused the erection of an impenetrable barrier whereby neither God nor humanity could transcend it ever to interact with each other.

Thus, a God incapable or unable to interact with His creation is a God with whom a covenantal relationship makes precious little, if any, sense. That understanding, too, is a casualty of the Shoah. The Jewish

People can no longer imagine, assume or presume to call upon God because of our seeming preexistent relationship as reflected in the Covenant, *B'rith,* to protect us from the horrors of that which we human beings can do and have done to ourselves. God's ultimate failure to save and/or protect the Jewish People during the Shoah invalidates, one, any belief in the efficacy of the Covenant itself, and, two, any claim the Jewish People might otherwise have to call upon God for active involvement, including, but not limited to, intervention and/or rescue.

Better now, realistically and honestly, to perceive "salvation" in human terms, to enter into "Covenants of Dialogue" with all those who would wish to interact with us, whatever their agenda, than to rely falsely on Israel's supposed historic covenant with God. As Michael Berenbaum has written, "The God who was silent then should be ashamed to act now." [3]

Corollary to this, and equally a casualty of the Shoah, is the notion of the Jewish People as the "Elect of God," the "Chosen People of God." Better an understanding of the Jewish People as the "Choosing People of God," a people who glimpsed a reality unlike any the world had heretofore experienced, and who, over the course of the centuries, continue to affirm that reality by their seeming willingness to pay whatever price is exacted from them. The Jewish People are God's witnesses that God exists, or at least existed, however we now choose to understand that God, however our neighbors, for good or ill, now choose to understand that God.

The Shoah shatters forever and all time the easy theological understanding of God as affirmed by countless previous generations of believing Jews. Better to realize the Shoah was in its entirety the work of humanity gone awry, the result of generations of human efforts towards that end, and not the interaction, or lack thereof, of an absentee God.

PRAYER

Logically, therefore, a God with whom humanity cannot interact and cannot enter into Covenant is not a God to be addressed as the recipient of prayer when that notion itself, at least initially, was a plea for action and Divine response, and only secondarily that of thanksgiving, adoration, and acknowledgment. Better to realize now, after the Shoah, that *tefillah* (prayer) will have to become an internal plea, given voice, that

1. the universe does manifest certain harmonies if we are but receptive to them;
2. creation allows us more possibilities for human growth than does destruction;
3. aesthetic appreciation of our world enhances our pleasure at being part of it;
4. the prayerfully poetic words of our predecessors, now reinterpreted since the Shoah, likewise increase the shared yearnings of all humankind for peace and survival;
5. the disciplined gatherings of like-minded groups in celebration and in sorrow can help energize us to confront the challenges of our own day and learn from each other; and
6. lastly, we need not suspend our intellect nor deny historical realities, especially the Shoah, when we engage in what we will continue to call "prayer."

Examples, then, of rethought and rewritten prayers, most appropriately in the aftermath of the Shoah, thanksgiving prayers, are the following, no longer dependent on whether or not there is a Deity "out there" who can hear and/or respond to that which is uttered:

Thank you, God, for initiating a process whereby this universe and I came to be for however long I am to be part of it. Amen.

and

Thank you, God, for endowing me/us with potential yet to be actualized for my own benefit as well as for the benefit of others. Amen.

Also, groups of praying Jews after the Shoah must be even more welcoming than ever before, especially towards those who continue to struggle with "God and the Shoah," and who wish to affirm their rightful and legitimate places as members of the Jewish People. Such invitations need be expressed as follows:

We invite you to be part of what we are trying to achieve and accomplish in the aftermath of the devastation and destruction caused by the Shoah. We are confident and open that your own contributions, too, will be meaningful and significant and received with dignity, respect, and integrity.

Thus, prayer after the Shoah must be (1) preservative of that from the past which continues to be meaningful in all of the ways in which "meaning" can be achieved; (2) adaptive of those forms capable of adaptation because they contain within themselves the seeds and kernels of meaningful expression; and (3) innovative where new realities engender new responsibilities.

ISRAEL AND ZIONISM

Lastly, to be sure, is the complex issue of Israel and Zionism in the post-Shoah world. Four interrelated and interconnected religio-theological issues suggest themselves: (1) the question of *yeridah* (emigration from Israel) versus *aliyah* (immigration to Israel); (2) the question of the power of the Jewish State and its Jewish inhabitants versus those who are not Jews and who do not wish to live under the Israeli flag or be ruled by its governmental apparatus; (3) the role, place, and function of a religious philosophy of Zionism, that is, whether Israel is a central or peripheral focus of religious Judaism; and (4) whether Judaism itself after the Shoah can or must affirm a nationalistic component, or is now, in truth, transnational by definition.

No Jew alive after the Shoah can morally, ethically, or religiously refrain from calling himself/herself a Zionist, regardless of where he/she chooses to live. Indeed, if anything, the reverse is the case: After the Shoah, the destruction of one-third to one-half of all Jews alive during the years 1933–1945, not to mention future births, all Jews have in fact become Zionists by virtue of their continuing Jewish existence and Jewish affirmation.

At the same time, the "saving reality" of post-Shoah Jewish life is its transnational character. One can be a religious Jew anywhere one is free to practice Judaism; and that very freedom leads to diverse interpretations, understandings, and redefinitions, some more and some less inclusive than others.

Thus, (1) *aliyah* to Israel remains a viable option for all those who wish to consider it as such, realizing that those Jews currently experiencing oppression may themselves have little choice once escape becomes possible. However, (2) *yeridah* from Israel, as well as the choice of where to settle once free, must be made without guilt and without the opprobrium of the organized Jewish community. By extension, therefore, realistically, what must ultimately transpire in that tumultuous region is the creation of a separate "Palestinian state" as is presently coming into being for those who wish to live there, guaranteeing at all times the safety and security of the State of Israel, an Israel governed democratically and without Jewish religious coercion.[4]

On the question of Israel as centrally or peripherally meaningful for a religious philosophy of Zionism, it is both. Thus, at times, especially in times of crisis, commitments to Israel may overshadow other Jewish commitments and rise to a place of centrality; at other times, it recedes into a place of peripherality, as other, equally valid parts of religious Judaism assert themselves. Taken together, they form one's religious Judaism, no part more precious or sacred than the whole. Thus, at times, Israel after the Shoah is both central to one's Jewish religious self-identity and self-awareness, and peripheral to one's Jewish religious self-identity and self-awareness.

CONCLUSION

The caustic query "Who died and made you God?" has been answered for some among us by the very deaths of the Six Million, including one hundred fifty members of my own family. Their deaths have forced some among us to confront the constraints of the past and a present and future no longer bound by those religious constraints. Out of such a confrontation and need for a rethought and reformulated post-Shoah Jewish theology may very well come a new synthesis of God, Torah, and Israel, both the People and the Land, and a new relationship beneficial to all humankind.

NOTES

1. A fuller, more complete explication of my understanding of each of these categories, as well as a discussion of Jewish-Christian relations, is to be found in my book *Rethinking Jewish Faith: The Child of a Survivor Responds* (Albany: SUNY Press, 1994).

2. The difficulty of affirming this position is best illustrated in Richard Rubenstein's troubling essay "The Dean and the Chosen People" in his seminal work *After Auschwitz: Radical Theology and Contemporary Judaism* (Indianapolis: The Bobbs-Merrill Company, 1966), 46–58. Reprinted in *After Auschwitz:*

History, Theology, and Contemporary Judaism (Baltimore: The Johns Hopkins University Press, 1992), Second Edition, 3–13.

3. Michael Berenbaum, "In a World without a Redeemer, Redeem!" in Steven L. Jacobs, ed., *Contemporary Jewish Religious Responses to the Shoah* (Lanham: University Press of America, 1993), 30–31.

4. I have put the phrase "Palestinian state" in quotation marks because I am still not at all convinced that "Palestine" is the best term for a state for those native Arabs who do not wish to be governed by the Israelis and whose claims to the Land itself are equally valid and equally of long standing. It is, however, the term already chosen.

CHAPTER 23

Christianity, Anti-Semitism, and

Post-Holocaust Theology: Old

Questions, Changing Paradigms

STEPHEN R. HAYNES

HOLOCAUST EDUCATION AND RELIGION

Among the crucial issues associated with Holocaust Education are the "who" and "how" questions: who should teach the Holocaust, and how should it be taught? At their intersection lies a consideration with implications for many Holocaust educators. If the teacher identifies with a religious tradition that has a role in the Holocaust story, in what ways will this fact influence the pedagogical "how"? This question has arisen often in my own teaching of the Holocaust, since I am a Christian who teaches in a church-related liberal arts college. No doubt many Jewish Holocaust educators would acknowledge that their own religious background and identity affects their teaching of the Shoah.

However, even when the "who" religious identity does not come into play, the "what" of Holocaust Education should be informed by the study of religion. Many Holocaust educators would prefer to overlook this fact. For instance, teachers at public institutions—whether secondary or university-level—are often reluctant to talk explicitly of the Holocaust's religious dimensions lest they be accused of breaching the "wall" that is supposed to separate the realms of church and state. Others, whose training may be fields like European history, political science, international relations, or the history of ideas, are loath to venture into a field of inquiry whose terrain is so unfamiliar and so notorious for its pitfalls.

In this chapter, it will be assumed that the study of religion has a fundamental role to play in Holocaust education, and that this role is as crucial for understanding the Shoah as is a grasp of history, politics, or international relations. Unfortunately, one would not suspect this fact from perusing some of the textbooks that are used widely to educate students about the Holocaust. Most do not pay sufficient attention to the religious dimensions of the encounter between victim and perpetrator in the Holocaust, and some offer a simplistic or distorting picture of this encounter.

A useful example of the problem is to be found in the student edition of Raul Hilberg's groundbreaking *The Destruction of the European Jews* (1961; revised 1985). This popular text refers to the Holocaust's religious background in an introductory chapter entitled "Precedents." Here Hilberg treats the problem of Christian anti-Judaism in a few pages, most of which are devoted to pointing out similarities in the anti-Jewish rhetoric of Martin Luther, nineteenth-century German political anti-Semites and Hitler himself. The brevity of this discussion leaves the distinct impression that Hilberg has included a religious angle on his subject matter mainly out of necessity.

Nevertheless, the table of "Canonical and Nazi Anti-Jewish Measures" that accompanies this discussion is one of the more memorable and arresting aspects of the book. Because Hilberg's table is not accompanied by a nuanced account of the relationship of Nazism and Christianity, the table itself must communicate Hilberg's view of this relationship. The table "says," in effect, that Nazis did to Jews only what Christians had done (or wanted to do) much earlier. Hilberg's table of "Canonical and Nazi Anti-Jewish Measures," in other words, communicates a great deal, albeit inaccurately, about the religious dimensions of the Holocaust; this communication takes on greater import because it is not explicit. Thus, the table provides one example of why it is virtually impossible to avoid a thoughtful treatment of religious belief and practice and teach the Holocaust without distortion.

Nevertheless, the notion that one can do just that persists among students and teachers of the Holocaust. Despite the fact that many pioneers in American Holocaust studies are scholars of religion,[1] and despite evidence that in one segment of higher education about one-third of courses on the Holocaust are taught in departments of religion or theology,[2] the view that Holocaust education can steer happily clear of religious concerns remains widespread. This chapter reviews the recent history of research on the relationship of Christianity and anti-Semitism in an attempt to encourage teachers of the Holocaust to approach the religious dimensions of the Holocaust in an informed manner.

CHANGING PARADIGMS

Concerning the relationship of religious belief and anti-Semitism, the scholarly world is currently plagued by ambivalence. Some recent publications on the subject of anti-Semitism by influential Jewish scholars have played down or ignored religion as a source of anti-Semitic feeling in the modern world.[3] But while a few notable authorities soft-pedal the importance of religious belief for comprehending Jew-hatred, many scholars of Christianity with a special interest in this topic have taken a very different view. In fact, an important trajectory in twentieth-century scholarship on anti-Semitism affirms the centrality of Christian belief, attitude, and practice for understanding Jew-hatred and the Holocaust. This chapter attempts to chart this trajectory and the ways it has altered over the past few decades.

Over the last sixty years or so, scholars seeking to fathom the mystery of anti-Semitism in light of religious belief and practice have tended to share a series of shifting methodological assumptions about Christianity. These provocative commonalties suggest the existence of distinct scholarly paradigms which have developed as ways of grasping the relationship of Christianity and anti-Semitism. In the movement between these paradigms, we discern also a subtle but unmistakable transition in the scholarly view of the relationship between Jew-hatred and Christianity.

THE REFORMIST PARADIGM

The reformist paradigm emerged in the first two-thirds of this century in the work of historians who sought to document the tragic history of Jewish life in Christendom. Works in the reformist paradigm emphasize the persistence of anti-Jewish prejudice in the centuries preceding the Holocaust while searching out points of contact between modern anti-Semitism and the popular anti-Jewish sentiments of earlier ages. Whether the roots of Christian anti-Judaism are discerned in "the conflict of the church and the synagogue," the credulity of the Christian masses in the Middle Ages, or the perennial human need to condemn what is strange, a governing assumption for work in this paradigm is that Christian anti-Judaism possesses historical roots and concomitants that can be located and extirpated.

In the reformist paradigm, anti-Judaism is assumed to be a medieval habit of mind that is bred of intolerance; it is therefore an anachronism in the modern world. Reformist writers assume that xenophobia, paranoid delusion, and the neurotic need for evidence of religious superiority are not characteristics of enlightened societies. Thus, the continued existence of anti-Jewish prejudice is a sign of societal regression resulting from ignorance and insecurity. From this point of view, Christian anti-Judaism, based as it is on the persistence of irrational fears and hatreds, should have disappeared with the rise of modernity. In the literature of the reformist paradigm, Christian anti-Judaism is regarded as a perennial, but alien—and certainly not incorrigible—blight on Christianity. It is assumed that anti-Semitism is essentially foreign to authentic Christianity, and that when its stubborn existence in the history of European Christendom is faithfully documented thoughtful believers will ensure that this irrational prejudice is removed from Christian faith once and for all.

The adjective "reformist" is not meant to suggest that these scholars lack nerve as they approach the problem of anti-Semitism and Christian belief. In many cases, the effects of reformist scholarship have been revolutionary. For instance, beginning in the late 1940s research by the French scholar Jules Isaac inaugurated a new era in the study of the pagan and Christian roots of anti-Semitism.[4] According to John G. Gager, the effect of Isaac's work was twofold:

> 1) to lay the blame for anti-Semitism squarely at the door of Christianity; and 2) to buttress the argument that anti-Semitism, while exclusively a Christian product, results from a misinterpretation by Christians of their own scriptures and founder, and stands in fundamental opposition to the historical origins and basic tenets of Christianity.[5]

But Gager's summary also captures the features of Isaac's work which place it squarely within the reformist paradigm. While not hesitating to assert Christendom's culpability for the existence of anti-Semitism, Isaac viewed Jew-hatred as a tragic corruption of Christian faith in its essence.[6]

Today, Christian theologians and church spokespersons operate within the reformist paradigm whenever they regard anti-Semitism as a corruption of true Christianity or an aberration from faithful Christian behavior. In fact, the majority of Christians who recognize that anti-Semitism is a Christian concern view anti-Judaism as a historical accretion to Christian teaching that is fundamentally opposed to the gospel and correctable by a return to biblical Christianity. This is also the paradigm to which the analyses and affirmations of most official post-Holocaust church statements on Jewish-Christian relations should be assigned.

Ironically, the characteristic of the reformist paradigm which has produced its greatest impact and has made it attractive to many thoughtful Christians is also its major limitation. This is the tendency of its practitioners to assume that Jew-hatred is related to Christian belief only superficially through historical circumstance. This assumption has produced excessive optimism concerning the prospects of overcoming this relation via a heightened level of historical awareness. One encounters this optimism in claims that the existence of contemporary anti-Semitic prejudice is rooted in a failure of Christian love and/or Enlightenment values.

THE RADICAL PARADIGM

Around 1970 a new paradigm for conceiving Christianity's relation to Jew-hatred began to take shape. While a few scholars writing before this time had looked to the New Testament to explain the existence of Christian anti-Judaism, such conclusions received little attention before Rosemary R. Ruether's *Faith and Fratricide* was published in 1974.[7] The response to Ruether's book was profound, and the radical paradigm for interpreting the relationship of Christianity and anti-Semitism became ascendant among serious post-Holocaust scholars by the end of the 1970s. In *Faith and Fratricide,* Ruether contended that Christian anti-Judaism had been fundamental to the early Christian movement's understanding of itself as "true Israel," and of Jesus as the Jewish Messiah. According to Ruether, anti-Judaism was so basic to the Christian self-understanding forged within two decades of Jesus' death that it can rightly be called "the left hand of Christology."

On the other hand, Ruether pointed out that this anti-Jewish development was not at all faithful to the life of the historical figure on whom the church's christological doctrine was based. Ruether located Jesus squarely in the world of first-century Jewish sectarianism and found no evidence of anti-Judaism in Jesus' own teaching or self-understanding. Significantly, however, she did not shy away from evidence that Christian Scripture and basic Christian doctrine were deeply infected with anti-Jewish ideology. In fact, the hallmark of scholarship which has followed Ruether's lead is the acknowledgment that "the basic root of modern antisemitism lies squarely in the Gospels and the rest of the New Testament."[8] Thus, it is not surprising that the major published responses to Ruether's book have focused on the problem of anti-Judaism in the New Testament, despite the fact that only one chapter of *Faith and Fratricide* was concerned directly with this matter.

Ruether was not the only Christian scholar in the 1970s to claim that anti-Judaism was endemic to historic Christian faith.[9] The distinctive element in Ruether's work, however, was her argument that the roots of Christian anti-Judaism were planted in earliest Christianity and could be detected in the New Testament itself. It is this claim that makes *Faith and Fratricide* indispensable for understanding the radical paradigm. And since the mid-1970s this paradigm has proven immensely provocative and influential among scholars concerned with anti-Semitism and Christian origins. Gregory Baum is an example of a prominent post-Holocaust Christian scholar whose mind was changed under Ruether's influence.[10] But the influence has been subtle as well. In 1979, the editor of a collection of articles on the origins of anti-Semitism demonstrated the extent to which the radical paradigm had been adopted when he described the book's contributors as scholars who are convinced that "through careful study, Christians can isolate what genuine forms of anti-Judaism really color the major writings [of the New Testament], and, by examining their historic genesis, neutralize their potential for harm." This, of course, is the radical paradigm's view of the relationship of anti-Semitism and Christian origins in a nutshell. It begins with the acknowledgement that anti-Judaism is woven into the fabric of the Christian story; yet it never relinquishes the hope that scholarship can extricate authentic Christian faith from the New Testament kerygma.

Anyone willing to acknowledge that Christianity is not only historically anti-Jewish but also doctrinally and to some extent textually so shares the guiding assumption of this approach: that anti-Judaism can be detected in some of the earliest expressions of Christian theology, but is not essential to saving faith in Jesus.

A Rejectionist Paradigm?

The radical paradigm emerged in the 1970s as Rosemary Ruether and others convinced their peers that previous studies had not looked carefully enough at the connection between anti-Judaism and the origins of Christianity. If such are the circumstances under which intellectual paradigms change, then recent illuminations of flaws in the radical approach may signal the birth pangs of a new paradigm. I will refer to this paradigm proleptically as "rejectionist."

While the radical paradigm has satisfied post-Holocaust Christian scholars for two decades, a few non-Christian[11] researchers have restlessly continued the quest for anti-Semitism's origins. The work of two scholars in particular—Gavin I. Langmuir and Hyam Maccoby—has had the effect of problematizing radical assumptions. Despite their considerable differences, Langmuir and Maccoby attack reigning scholarly assumptions on two common fronts: (1) the supposed discontinuity between medieval, religious anti-Judaism and modern, racial anti-Semitism, and (2) the alleged existence of a pure essence of Christianity that is discernibly free of anti-Jewish sentiment, but which was subsequently corrupted (by the Church Fathers, by early christological doctrine, by editing of the New Testament, or by the earliest Christian reflection on Jesus' death.)

To refer to the writings of Langmuir and Maccoby as the harbingers of a new paradigm for understanding the relationship of religion and anti-Semitism is not to suggest that a majority of scholars have embraced their views, for they have not. It is simply to claim that these men have produced an insightful body of historical and psychological research which serious students of anti-Semitism cannot ignore. In any case, the term "rejectionist" must be applied to Langmuir and Maccoby in different ways.

Langmuir is most concerned with rejecting facile distinctions between anti-Judaism and anti-Semitism and the unwarranted conclusions of historians who are also Christians. Maccoby does not explicitly question the motives of religious persons who explore the origins of anti-Semitism, but he condemns Jews and Christians alike who offer superficial analyses of anti-Judaism in the interest of interfaith *rapprochement*. Broadly speaking, the Langmuir-Maccoby approach is "rejectionist" in its dogged suspicion of claims that the Christianity which paved the way for Nazism was a tragic distortion of authentic Christian faith, and of attempts to defend Christianity by positing a pristine essence of the gospel that is not anti-Jewish.

Since Ruether and other radicals have acknowledged that religious and racial forms of Jew-hatred are not entirely discontinuous, an explicit emphasis on continuity does not by itself signal the emergence of a new approach for understanding the relationship of Christianity and anti-Semitism.[12] Crucial differences are to be found, rather, in the manner in which the connection between Christian images and anti-Semitism is interpreted: Is Christianity ultimately responsible for the existence of anti-Semitism, or have modern anti-Semites simply utilized Christian images to commend their policies to a populace for whom Christian symbols are still meaningful? To put it another way, can Christian anti-Judaism—the trunk on which other varieties of anti-Semitism have been grafted, according to Jules Isaac—be reformed at its roots, or is a cancerous growth which will always yield a deadly anti-Jewish fruit?

It is in responding to these questions that the "rejectionists" transcend the methodological confines of the radical paradigm. In doing so, they open the possibility that "Christianity" or "Christian faith" may be inherently as well as historically anti-Jewish, thereby seriously problematizing the conclusion that anti-Semitism is a corruption of the Christian gospel. Specific attention to the writings of these putative "rejectionists" will enrich our understanding of the rejectionist challenge.

Gavin I. Langmuir

Langmuir, a medieval historian at Stanford University, describes himself as the nonreligious product of an atheistic family that occasionally attended church.[13] Frustrated by his inability to understand medieval anti-Semitism "historically"—that is, without resorting to the religious categories invoked by medieval writers—Langmuir has undertaken to provide fresh definitions of anti-Judaism, anti-Semitism, religion, and religiosity, and has sought a reapplication of objective historical inquiry to the problem of Jew-hatred.

Langmuir's careful definitions and painstaking historical analyses comprise a serious obstacle for all attempts to speak of anti-Semitism as a nonreligious or postreligious phenomenon. Langmuir is particularly critical of the scholarly tradition which assumes a priori a distinction between religious "anti-Judaism" and racial "anti-Semitism," as if the former were benign and the two easily separable. In fact, by defining German National Socialism as a "physiocentric religion," Langmuir attempts to deliver a *coup de grace* to all endeavors to distinguish between religious and secular forms of Jew-hatred. Ignoring unstudied distinctions between anti-Judaism and anti-Semitism and regarding Nazism in religious terms allows Langmuir to interpret the Holocaust as the most sweeping expression of religious irrationality ever witnessed.[14]

Langmuir's work on anti-Semitism has been preoccupied with locating this hatred's genesis in Western history. Defining anti-Semitism as the hostility aroused by irrational thinking about "Jews," Langmuir concludes that anti-Semitism first appeared in late medieval Europe, specifically in the blood libel tales of the twelfth century. However, despite his rather late date for the commencement of "anti-Semitism," Langmuir is far from accommodating of those who would dissociate Jew-hatred from Christian origins.[15] In fact, Langmuir feels obliged to begin his historical search for anti-Semitism from scratch, as it were, partly because he believes Christian scholars of anti-Semitism have unconsciously abused historical methodology.

This is a problem detailed in Langmuir's review of the historiography of anti-Semitism in chapter two of *History, Religion, and Anti-Semitism.* As we have seen, essential to the radical paradigm is a distinction between, on the one hand, the life and message of Jesus and the early faithful traditions about him, and on the other hand, the way these were corrupted in the developing theology of the Church and in later redactions of the New Testament. But Langmuir casts doubt on this all-important discrimination by contending that Christian scholars who postulate a pure religious essence unaffected by anti-Jewish ideology have not done so as objective historians: "they try to disconnect Jesus and genuine Christianity from anti-Judaism but fail to demonstrate that differentiation in an empirically convincing way."[16] In other words, Langmuir believes apologetic concerns have been a corrupting force in the research on anti-Semitism carried out by Christian scholars.

In *History, Religion, and Antisemitism,* Langmuir explores in some depth the unsuccessful combination of religious faith and historical inquiry that in his view has characterized too many works on anti-Semitism. Langmuir notes that since the end of the last century many attempts to analyze this problem have been "carried out by Christians whose primary concern was the extent of Christian responsibility for contemporary antisemitism." [17] Influenced by Enlightenment ideals and committed to eschewing religious intolerance, early scholars of anti-Semitism wanted to ascertain why Christians had treated Jews in a way they believed contradicted true Christianity. [18]

Langmuir notes that when analyses of religious intolerance and fanaticism proved incapable of comprehending the essence of twentieth-century anti-Semitic passions, historians interested in the origins and nature of Jew-hatred began to distinguish between anti-Judaism and anti-Semitism. [19] This distinction eventually was embraced by Christians who sought in various ways to disculpate Christianity from responsibility for modern Jew-hatred. [20] According to Langmuir, the approach of Christian scholars was guided by the following syllogism: "Intolerance and antisemitism are bad; right religious faith is eternally good; therefore, whatever Christians have done that might be classified as antisemitism was not done out of genuine faith." [21]

In this regard, Langmuir devotes special attention to the work of James Parkes and Rosemary Ruether, scholars I have assigned to the reformist and radical paradigms, respectively. According to Langmuir, despite these thinkers' courage in confronting their own religious tradition's responsibility for the existence of anti-Semitism, both remain blind to the manner in which faith considerations determine their historical conclusions. Langmuir notes how Parkes's argument that Christianity faced ultimate responsibility for modern anti-Semitism would seem to imply that anti-Semitism was a necessary consequence of Christianity. But Parkes resisted this conclusion, Langmuir opines, precisely because he had been moved to condemn anti-Semitism on the basis of his own Christian beliefs. Langmuir cannot disprove Parkes's determination that Christian Jew-hatred is "not an expression of true Christianity but a very ancient deformation that had to be eliminated," but he does allege that the criterion for this judgment is Parkes's own Christian faith. This is "a criterion," of course, which "no objective historian could accept." [22]

Perhaps surprisingly, Langmuir's criticism of Ruether is virtually the same one he levels at Parkes: "As might have been expected from her

Christianity and condemnation of anti-Judaism, Ruether finds no anti-Judaism 'in the teachings of Jesus himself.' "[23] But Langmuir finds a contradiction here. Since Ruether believes anti-Judaism grew up very early after Jesus' death and is found in every writing of the New Testament, it would seem to follow that anti-Judaism is an essential part of Christian faith. Yet, Langmuir continues, both the historical and theological sections of *Faith and Fratricide* imply that Christian anti-Judaism stems not from Jesus or his first-century Jewish revival movement but from the Christology that arose almost immediately after his death. According to Langmuir, because Ruether cannot accept the judgment that anti-Judaism and Christian faith are inseparable she "concludes with a theological argument to enable people to be Christian without being anti-Judaic."[24] Langmuir observes that the arguments of Ruether and the other Christian scholars he discusses "may defend Christian faith after Hitler by changing it; they cannot change its past."[25]

HYAM MACCOBY

A scholar who has ventured even further in consciously undermining the assumptions of the reformist and radical paradigms is Hyam Maccoby. Like Langmuir, Maccoby disputes the claim that religious and secular versions of anti-Semitism can be distinguished qualitatively. But more importantly, he explicitly denies that Christian faith can be extricated from Jew-hatred. Maccoby's view on this matter is summarized in his statement that "anti-Semitism is not merely an extraneous outcome of religious rivalry but forms an essential ingredient in the Christian myth of redemption."[26]

For Maccoby, Christianity's defining characteristic is a "diabolization" of the Jewish people that stems from the mythic role they are forced to play as murderers of a deified Jesus. Maccoby identifies three sources of the Christian anti-Jewish impulse: pre-Christian Gnosticism and its anti-Semitic mythology; a historical schema in which the church replaces Israel as the vehicle of God's promises; and the ancient mystery-cult myth of a god murdered by an evil force or rival god.[27] For Maccoby, Christianity's uniqueness lies "precisely in this amalgamation of gnosticism with mystery religion to form an anti-Semitic myth of unprecedented potency."[28]

Maccoby views the gnostic strain in Christianity as an especially perduring theme, one that is basic for comprehending Christianity's responsibility for the Holocaust. According to Maccoby, the Christian Jew-image most evident in Nazism was "the myth of the Antichrist." This Antichrist myth also represents the apotheosis of the gnostic theme in Christianity.[29] The major point of contact between the Christian story and the Hellenistic mystery-cult tradition Maccoby finds in the Christian "Sacred Executioner" myth, whose central figure is Judas Iscariot. Maccoby notes that analogues to the Judas figure are typical in all religious myths in which a god who offers salvation through death is opposed by an evil power who brings this death about. The decisive difference between the Christian drama of salvation and other ancient myths— Judas's function as an eponymous representative of all Jews—is the very characteristic which lends the Christian myth its deadly power.[30]

Maccoby renders the major lines in his portrait of Christianity in *The Sacred Executioner* (1982). In this book, Maccoby traces the growth and influence of Christianity's Sacred Executioner myth—in the New Testament itself, in the history of the church, and in the modern world. According to Maccoby, the mature Christian portrait of the Jewish people is a picture of the Jews as a collective Sacred Executioner. This portrait is animated by the fantasy that "Jews see in every Christian the lineaments of Jesus himself; they therefore wish to repeat their crime of christ-murder whenever opportunity occurs." The influence of this Sacred Executioner myth, Maccoby claims, is evident in Western history from the book of Acts to the propaganda of the Nazis.[31]

Maccoby does acknowledge some discontinuity between traditional and modern versions of anti-Semitism, but plays down the differences in several important respects. First, he stresses that the racial anti-Semitism of the nineteenth century actually had its background in the medieval Christian notion of the Wandering Jew.[32] Even more potent in the soil of modernity, however, has been the populist millennial myth of the Antichrist. The "paranoiac, dualistic scheme" represented in the Antichrist myth demonstrates for Maccoby that Christianity is inscribed with a plan to completely exterminate Jews. Maccoby views Nazism as a secular millenarian movement with apocalyptic overtones, not unrelated to the Antichrist doctrine "that was always such a persistent thread in the history of Christian thought."[33] In this way, the massacres associated with the Crusades can be regarded as precursors to the Final Solution.[34]

Maccoby pictures Christianity as a religion conceived in blood and

developed out of pagan anti-Jewish materials: a religion which in its
maturity spawned the images and ideologies that have stocked the imaginations of modern anti-Semites. But does this view of Christianity qual-
ify Maccoby as a "rejectionist"? It is interesting to note that unlike
Langmuir, Maccoby lends implicit support to Ruether's "radical" pro-
viso that the church's hedge against anti-Judaism is the Jewishness of
Jesus.[35] However, what Maccoby allows with regard to the Jewishness
of the man Jesus he takes back with his insistence on the non-Jewishness
of Paul, whom Maccoby claims divinized Jesus and mythicized his death
as a cosmic sacrifice for sin. In Maccoby's view, this founder of Christianity was an "uneasy convert" to Judaism whose formative ideas were
not Jewish, but developed under the influence of Gnosticism and mystery
religions in a Hellenistic environment.

Maccoby also appears to step into radical territory when he argues
that secular versions of anti-Semitism should be treated as "rationalizations" (Ruether calls them a "translation") of the Christian myth in
scientific garb.[36] But Maccoby departs clearly from the radical fold when
he contends that modern Jew-hatred is a rationalization of something
fundamental to Christianity, namely, the anti-Semitic Christian myth
first constructed by Paul. For Maccoby, in other words, Jew-hatred is
endemic to Christianity as a religion of salvation. For all their pessimism
about Christianity's historic anti-Judaism, Ruether and the Christian
radicals imply that history could be overcome if the Christian church
returned to its original orientation in the life of Jesus the messianic
prophet of God's kingdom. Maccoby's rejectionism is revealed in his
conviction that "Christian anti-Semitism derives not from some accidental and inessential layer of Christianity, but from its central doctrine and
myth, the crucifixion itself."[37]

TRAITS OF THE "REJECTIONISTS"

Thus, two recurrent themes characterize the work of these admittedly
diverse "rejectionist" scholars. First, Maccoby and Langmuir problema-
tize the belief that Christianity in its uncorrupted essence is free of anti-
Judaism; second, they accuse Christian scholars who have established
the parameters of the reformist and radical paradigms with interested
scholarship and special pleading.[38] But Langmuir and Maccoby distinguish themselves from reformists and radicals not only methodologically

but stylistically as well. In fact, compared with the writings of other scholars who have addressed the question of Christianity's responsibility for anti-Semitism, the works of Langmuir and Maccoby are quite unusual.

For instance, Langmuir writes in the detached, analytic mode of a historian or sociologist who is devoid of empathy for the religions and religiosities he deals with. While identification with a religious community is often foregrounded in work on this topic, Langmuir dismisses the research of respected Christian historians as methodologically flawed and apologetically inspired. While Maccoby's tone is anything but detached, his often provocative and at times shocking prose stands out in another way. Maccoby simply ignores the etiquette that governs interfaith dialogue. It is not just that his portrait of Christian faith is unflattering; Maccoby portrays "Christianity" as a monolithic phenomenon and pays no heed to Christian self-understanding in most of his work. As Jews often have said of Christian writings on Judaism, so Christians might well say of Maccoby's work: "We simply don't recognize ourselves here."

If the rejectionist approach to the problem of anti-Semitism suggested in the work of Langmuir and Maccoby can be said to have governing assumptions, they are these: that Christian attempts to understand the religious roots of anti-Semitism, no matter how ostensibly critical and objective, must be carefully scrutinized for apologetic concerns; that qualitative distinctions between anti-Judaism and anti-Semitism are only apparent; and that there exists no version of Christian faith, regardless of how "authentic" it is alleged to be, that is rescued easily, if at all, from the taint of anti-Semitism. Understandably, scholarly reaction to the challenges thrown up by Langmuir and Maccoby has hearkened back to the assumptions of the reformist and radical paradigms.[39]

A limitation of the rejectionist stance is one which to a lesser degree afflicts the radical paradigm as well: the closer one comes to arguing that anti-Semitism is a necessary concomitant of Christian belief, the more directly one is confronted with a historical contradiction. For if Jew-hatred is at the heart of Christian theology, then one must explain why genocide never was resorted to in the centuries when the church possessed the power and influence to carry it out. Or, to put it another way, if religious hatred was a sufficient condition for the Holocaust, why did it occur only after the rise of secularism in Europe?

This limitation, and the fruitfulness of the radical paradigm for post-Holocaust Christian theology,[40] make it doubtful that Langmuir and Maccoby will ever effect a genuine paradigm change. Nonetheless, these "rejectionists" have already succeeded in posing questions that scholars concerned with the relationship of Christianity and anti-Semitism must consider. In fact, quite apart from their persistent troubling of radical assumptions, Maccoby and Langmuir deserve the attention of Holocaust educators. For in their explorations of the "irrational" (Langmuir) and "mythical" (Maccoby) dimensions of anti-Semitism, these scholars illuminate anew the connection between Jew-hatred and Christianity, while at the same time emphasizing the unique quality of anti-Semitism.

A Non-Rejectionist Approach to Christianity and Anti-Semitism

"Rejectionism" in the Langmuir-Maccoby mold is a force both challenging and disturbing for post-Holocaust Christianity: challenging, because where rejectionist theses are accepted a firmer historical basis will be required for arguments that Jesus and his original movement were free of anti-Judaism; disturbing, because if Christian faith is perceived to be fundamentally and necessarily anti-Jewish, the hope which is so crucial to post-Holocaust theological reflection in the Christian tradition is gravely threatened. In order to be "Christian," post-Holocaust theology must retain the vision of an essential "Christian faith" that is unsullied by anti-Judaism. If the reigning assumption were that such a version of Christian faith never has existed, even in the first century C.E., whence would this animating vision derive?

Despite conflicting assumptions, reformists and radicals share a confidence in the possibility of locating a stratum of Christianity which predates anti-Jewish prejudice. Reformists suppose this pro-Jewish level of Christian belief exists because Christianity is a religion of love and is incompatible with hatred, while radicals assume it can be reached only through sophisticated source and redaction analysis of the New Testament documents. But since it must bear the weight of Christianity's moral viability after the Holocaust, this pro-Jewish layer of Christian faith must be posited, even if only in faith.

As we have seen, the radical paradigm is characterized by a pivotal distinction that is made between the original message of Jesus and the anti-Jewish "Christianity" that developed when in the heat of controversy some of Jesus' followers began preaching a triumphalist or supersessionist version of his life and death. This distinction is crucial, since it allows radicals to admit deep flaws in historic Christian faith at its very heart, without relinquishing the life of faith itself. However, it is precisely this distinction that is called into question by the rejectionists. I wish to chart a future course for post-Holocaust Christian reflection that is informed by the emerging rejectionist challenge but which does not conclude that the Christian tradition is irredeemably anti-Jewish. I will do so by offering a non-rejectionist critique of the radical paradigm; specifically, by addressing the uncritical employment by post-Holocaust Christian theologians of assumptions that are part of the radical program.

Biblical scholars aware of the church's historic anti-Judaism and attuned to contemporary Jewish-Christian relations have placed a new set of concerns on the agenda of responsible biblical research. One of these is the New Testament's putative anti-Semitism. Of course, most studies by Christians interested in the problem of anti-Semitism have entertained the question, "is the New Testament anti-Semitic?" But Christian radicals have faced this question head-on, utilizing the historical-critical method—particularly the insights of source and redaction criticisms—to isolate the sources and editors responsible for corrupting the Christian message in the process of the New Testament's transmission and compilation. A second concern of biblical scholars in the post-Holocaust milieu is the nature of Jesus' relationship with his Jewish contemporaries.

Many of the best Christian biblical scholars have been outspoken regarding their responsibilities vis-à-vis anti-Judaism in the New Testament. For instance, in a recent published symposium on Jewish-Christian relations, New Testament scholar James H. Charlesworth challenges biblical scholars to engage the Jewish-Christian past with passion and insight, warning them "not . . . [to] hide from the tensions, misunderstandings, and fears that continue to separate Jews and Christians." [41] In fact, Charlesworth maintains, "to refuse to participate in the dialogue towards better relations among Jews and Christians is not the mark of an objective biblical scholar; it is a tacit commitment to the impossibility of being scholarly, and an assent to prejudicial methods and warped conclusions." [42]

Charlesworth is only one of a growing number of biblical scholars who encourage and engage in research that balances the integrity of history and the needs of interfaith dialogue. In this connection, he echoes the assumptions of an emerging consensus among scholars of the Bible that "the historical Jesus should be seen as a devout Palestinian Jew who was influenced by the liturgy of the synagogue."[43] Charlesworth even generalizes that "the apparent anti-Judaisms in the New Testament are usually additions to the tradition, and reflect the social hostility between two distinct Jewish groups, especially after 70."[44] While there no doubt are theological considerations operative in Charlesworth's reading of the New Testament, the boundary between history and theology remains intact.

This boundary can be completely obscured, however, when the judgments of biblical scholars such as Charlesworth are appropriated by theologians in their "quests" for a historical Jesus from whom they can fashion a post-Holocaust Christianity. Affirmations of the Jewishness of Jesus and his message are abstracted from the ongoing dialogue of biblical scholars and established as normative principles for understanding Jesus today. Determinations of Jesus' probable historical context become rigid statements about what could and could not have taken place between Jesus and other first-century Jews. Often these statements become theological axioms which are used to define the parameters inside which authentic Christianity can be conceived.

Biblical scholars, even those deeply concerned with anti-Judaism and the origins of Christianity, exhibit discomfort with this process, occasionally reminding each other that "a scholarly historical issue cannot be decided on the basis of the needs of contemporary Jewish-Christian dialogue."[45] Post-Holocaust theologians, however, rarely reveal such caution with the results of historical research. At times, in fact, the distinction between ancient history and contemporary need becomes quite blurred. Examples range from the specific claim of Paul van Buren—that Paul "could never have said" that Jews rejecting the gospel convict themselves as unworthy of everlasting life[46]—to the broader and quite dubious contention of Alice L. and A. Roy Eckardt that there was no conflict between Jesus and the Jews of his day.[47]

The Eckardts defend their conclusion by invoking the historical-critical method of biblical research, in which historical truth is painstakingly sought. They depart from a strict application of this methodology when they contend that Jesus did not claim to be Messiah of Israel. But when the Eckardts generalize that "it is incorrect to say that Jesus stood in opposition to contemporary Judaism, its representatives and its teachers," they display not critical skill, but their interest in exploiting historical research in the interest of theology.[48]

Paul van Buren is more circumspect and more informed in his treatment of the New Testament (which he prefers to call the "Apostolic Writings"). But even in his case, biblical interpretation emerges too transparently from theological presuppositions. Most troublesome is van Buren's tendency to distinguish, sometimes on flimsy historical evidence, between what he confidently calls "early" and "late" witnesses in the Apostolic Writings. Not only does van Buren's methodology reveal an outdated confidence in the ability of historical criticism to identify early and late texts, sources and pericopes with any certainty, it is also conspicuously tautological. Passages that affirm Israel's covenant and are not perceived to be supersessionist are invariably classified as "early," while those open to an anti-Jewish interpretation are always considered "late" and thus less authentic.[49]

It is true that in the past New Testament scholarship has disguised its anti-Jewish biases under a veil of objectivity. For instance, a "criterion of dissimilarity" (from first-century Judaism) has too often been relied upon to determine the authenticity of sayings attributed to Jesus. To its credit, post-Holocaust theology renders support for the sort of biblical scholarship which is sensitive to the moral implications of its research. But this does not justify the implicit substitution of a "criterion of similarity" as the chief interpretive principle for study of the gospels before such a principle is articulated, debated, and accepted by biblical scholars themselves.

While most New Testament scholars now reject a "complete opposition" model for understanding Jesus' relationship to first-century Judaism, they are also unwilling to relinquish the possibility that Jesus encountered resistance from the Jewish leadership of his day. Nor is the admission of such conflict necessarily antithetical to a positive Christian evaluation of Judaism. In fact, since it is indisputable that bitter conflict between "Christians" and "Jews" characterized the Mediterranean world within a generation of Jesus' death, it is not clear what purpose is served by reconstructing a Jesus who was loved by everyone but the Roman governor.

The post-Holocaust theologies of van Buren and the Eckardts reveal a new awareness of the fateful historical effects of biblical interpretation. But their readings of the New Testament are no less tainted by pre-exegetical assumptions than the approaches they seek to replace. For this reason, a more honest approach to the problem of the Bible and Christian origins is the one outlined by Darrell Fasching in *Narrative Theology after Auschwitz*. Fasching too places theology in control of the biblical message, but he does so not surreptitiously or under the guise of historical objectivity. Rather, Fasching allows the Holocaust to establish a stringent hermeneutical control on the biblical material. He observes that the Shoah creates a "new hermeneutical criterion" for reading Scripture, and advocates the acceptance of "a canon within the canon" corresponding to theological necessity:

> the burning children can forge for us a new canon, in which nothing is the word of God that does not teach the irrevocable election and integrity of the Jewish people. By implication, nothing is the word of God that teaches or in any way implies the supersession of Jews by Christians.[50]

In this way, Fasching bypasses the supposedly objective quest for "what really occurred" in the first century, and in doing so also avoids hidden theological assumptions, unarticulated hermeneutical principles, and naive confidence in the historical-critical method.

Clearly, in the endeavor to reconceive Christian origins, post-Holocaust theology and biblical scholarship intersect and inform one another. Unfortunately, however, the historical data collected by biblical scholars in order to address important questions about Jesus, Judaism, and the New Testament are too often transformed by theologians into confident assertions about "what really happened" in the first century. In the mouths of theologians, such assertions reflect unwarranted optimism about the possibility of reconstructing a history encased in layers of tradition and controversy.

Post-Holocaust theology, under the influence of radical assumptions, has applied to the traditions about Jesus, Paul and the rest of early Christianity a "Christian historicism"[51] which it is believed will aid in fashioning a new basis for Christian-Jewish relations. But this Christian historicism establishes an unfortunate precedent: If we indulge the imperialistic tendencies of one group of theologians—as they tell us what the New Testament *really* means, what Jesus' relationship with his fellows *must* have been like, what Paul *could* and *could not* have said,[52] and what the Jews of Jesus' day *could* and *could not* have done—then on what methodological grounds shall we resist those with a less honorable axe to grind when they read Jesus' history from their own perspective?

The intentions underlying this Christian historicism are commendable, and perhaps the events of contemporary history alone lend it a certain moral justification.[53] But post-Holocaust theologians have failed to articulate or defend a moral imperative for embracing tenuous interpretations of history. More often, they write as if they are reading the New Testament in the only sensible and morally defensible way—a hegemonic approach to interpretation not foreign to the Christian tradition they criticize, and conspicuously void of humility. This situation is largely responsible, I think, for the association of post-Holocaust theology with the pitfalls of the radical paradigm outlined by the rejectionists. The life of the radical paradigm will be prolonged, and its role as a catalyst for post-Holocaust theology preserved, if theologians pay closer attention to the limits of historical inquiry, and if they better explain why Christians are morally obligated to read the New Testament in a pro-Jewish way.

NOTES

1. These scholars include Franklin H. Littell, A. Roy and Alice Eckardt, John K. Roth, Richard L. Rubenstein, and Steven T. Katz.

2. This result comes from an extensive survey of Holocaust education at church-related liberal arts colleges taken in 1994. Full survey results will appear in Stephen R. Haynes, *The Holocaust in Christian Education: The Church-Related Liberal Arts College,* forthcoming from Greenwood Press.

3. In 1988, for example, in a brief essay describing the major theories that have arisen since the end of World War II to explain the existence of anti-Semitism, Israeli historian Shmuel Ettinger had little to say about contemporary scholarship on the religious roots of contempt for Jews. He acknowledged that in the Middle Ages anti-Semitic outbreaks often were the result of religious rivalry between Christians and Jews, but maintained that since Christianity has lost much of its cultural influence in Europe since the eighteenth century, Christian prejudice cannot be viewed as a major influence upon anti-Semitism in the modern world. See "Jew Hatred in Its Historical Context" in Shmuel Almog,

ed., *Antisemitism Through the Ages,* trans. Nathan H. Reisner (Oxford: Pergamon, 1988), 1–12.

More recently, in an article appearing in *The New York Review of Books* during the Summer of 1993, Arthur Hertzberg delineated conflicting trends in current research on anti-Semitism. One interpretive divide reported by Hertzberg follows diverging opinions on the relationship of Jew-hatred and Christianity. Hertzberg sided with those for whom historic Christian anti-Judaism is only one source of anti-Jewish sentiment, a source that maintains little explanatory power vis-à-vis contemporary anti-Semitism ("Is Anti-Semitism Declining?" in *The New York Review of Books,* June 24, 1993, 51–57).

4. John G. Gager, *The Origins of Anti-Semitism: Attitudes toward Judaism in Pagan and Christian Antiquity* (New York: Oxford University Press, 1983), 15.

5. Gager, *Origins,* 16.

6. Similarly, in *The Conflict of the Church and the Synagogue,* Parkes's groundbreaking work on Jewish-Christian relations in the first centuries of the common era, James Parkes concluded that Christianity provided the only adequate foundation for anti-Jewish hatred. But by "Christianity" Parkes meant theological conceptions arising in the first three centuries of the Christian era, not the Christian story related in the New Testament. Another influential Christian scholar who should be placed in the reformist tradition is Edward Flannery, whose *The Anguish of the Jews* was first published in 1965. For Flannery, as for Parkes and Isaac, Jew-hatred is the antithesis of authentic Christianity.

7. E.g., A. Roy Eckardt in *Elder and Younger Brothers* (1967) and Alan T. Davies in *Antisemitism and the Christian Mind* (1969).

8. James Parkes, "Preface," in Alan T. Davies, ed., *Antisemitism and the Foundations of Christianity* (New York: Paulist, 1979), xi. It is interesting that Parkes himself apparently came to this view by the end of the 1970s, as his preface to Davies's volume demonstrates. Parkes reveals how his own thinking led him to embrace the radical paradigm when he affirms that the "basic root of modern antisemitism lies squarely on the Gospels and the rest of the New Testament." But Parkes remains on "radical" ground when he adds that Christian scholars must confront the source of Christian anti-Semitism in order to "distill the religious essence from its cultural malformations" ("Preface," xi, xvi).

9. For instance, in 1973 Franklin Littell published what has become his best-known book, *The Crucifixion of the Jews,* in which he asserted that "the cornerstone of Christian Antisemitism is the superseding or displacement myth . . . [which] already rings with a genocidal note." See *The Crucifixion of the Jews,* Rose Reprints (Macon: Mercer University Press, 1986), 2. Later in the decade, Douglas John Hall pursued a similar approach to Christian anti-Judaism, viewing it as a function of triumphalism (see "Rethinking Christ," in

Davies, *Antisemitism and the Foundations of Christianity,* 167–87; and Ruether's response, 230–56. Much of the work of Alice L. and A. Roy Eckardt also shares the assumptions of the radical paradigm.

10. See Baum's introduction to *Faith and Fratricide:* "I was . . . convinced that the anti-Jewish trends in Christianity were peripheral and accidental, not grounded in the New Testament itself but due to later developments, and that it would consequently be fairly easy to purify the preaching of the Church from anti-Jewish bias. Since then, especially under the influence of Rosemary Ruether's writings, I have had to change my mind" (3).

11. Because neither Langmuir nor Maccoby identify themselves as Christians, it may appear that I have switched categories at this point in my analysis and that Christian theologians are now being compared with non-Christian historians. This switch is necessitated, however, by the form in which the attack on the radical paradigm has come.

12. In fact, Maccoby's statement that "the Nazis . . . expressed in racialist terms the concept of the final overcoming of evil that formed the essence of Christian millennarianism" (*The Sacred Executioner: Human Sacrifice and the Legacy of Guilt* [London, Thames and Hudson, 1982], 175) is not qualitatively different from some of Ruether's statements in *Faith and Fratricide.* Indeed, on this point even reformists such as the early Parkes may be indistinguishable from radicals such as Ruether. Scholars in each paradigm have seen modern racial anti-Semitism as a mutation or translation of themes and images that have Christian sources.

13. All Langmuir references are to *History, Religion, and Antisemitism* (Berkeley: University of California Press, 1990), unless otherwise noted.

14. Ibid., 305, 346. The apparent continuity here between Christian and Nazi attitudes toward Jews is somewhat misleading. Langmuir notes that "in contrast with Christian antisemitism, Nazis were obsessed with the alleged physical characteristics of Jews . . . Nazism was a physiocentric religion, not a psychocentric one, and the difference was lethal" (344–45). See Langmuir's discussion of "physiocentric antisemitism" in chapter 16.

15. Langmuir establishes the continuity of medieval and more recent forms of anti-Semitism by describing modern mass movements as "religions." He acknowledges that the advent of modernity brought profound changes to European civilization, but argues that the modern "revolution in religiosity" failed to end religion's influence in Europe. New social and intellectual forces gave rise to xenophobia and an "agnostic anxiety" from which many sought refuge in "physiocentric" religions such as Nazism and dogmatic Marxism. Because it was particularly susceptible to empirical disproof, Langmuir argues, Hitler's religion could be maintained only by massive irrationality.

16. *History, Religion, and Antisemitism,* 40.

17. Ibid., 19.

18. Langmuir discusses the work of Anatole Beaulieu and Count Coudenhove-Kalergi.

19. Langmuir cites the work of Bernard Lazare and Hannah Arendt.

20. Langmuir mentions Jacques Maritain and the Jewish scholar Maurice Samuel in this connection.

21. *History, Religion, and Antisemitism*, 25.

22. Langmuir discovers a similar, though less sophisticated, attempt to disculpate Christianity of responsibility for anti-Semitism in Edward Flannery's *The Anguish of the Jews*. Langmuir comments that Flannery's distinction between anti-Judaism and anti-Semitism "rests so obviously on theological premises and is so unsupported by evidence that no scholar who sought empirical objectivity could be satisfied by it" (*History, Religion, and Antisemitism*, 34).

23. Ibid., 37.

24. *History, Religion, and Antisemitism*, 38.

25. Ibid., 40.

26. See Maccoby's "The Origins of Anti-Semitism" in Randolph L. Braham, ed., *The Origins of the Holocaust: Christian Anti-Semitism* (New York: Columbia University Press, 1986). See also *The Mythmaker: Paul and the Invention of Christianity* (New York: Harper and Row, 1986); *The Sacred Executioner;* and "Theologian of the Holocaust," *Commentary* (December 1982), 33–37.

27. Ironically, a number of Christian scholars also have fixed the origins of anti-Judaism in the pagan world. But Maccoby's version of this argument does not deflect responsibility for anti-Semitism away from the church. For Maccoby, while Christian anti-Semitism was forged from extra-Christian sources, the Christian myth actually intensified and focused pagan anti-Jewish traditions.

28. "The Origins of the Holocaust," 8.

29. *The Sacred Executioner*, 173.

30. See also Maccoby's recent book, *Judas Iscariot and the Myth of Jewish Evil* (New York: The Free Press, 1992).

31. *The Sacred Executioner*, 147.

32. Maccoby contends that a negative version of the Wandering Jew legend — from which the hope of millennial salvation for Jews is conspicuously absent — became a central part of the Nazi Jew-image. This version of the myth gave rise in turn to the image of the Jew as a "rootless cosmopolitan" and nomad, concepts embraced by nineteenth-century anti-Semites and elaborated by Hitler in *Mein Kampf*.

33. *The Sacred Executioner*, 175.

34. "The Nazis thus expressed in racialist terms the concept of the final overcoming of evil that formed the essence of Christian millenarianism. The choice of the Jews as the target arose directly out of centuries of Christian

teaching, which had singled out the Jews as a demonic people dedicated to evil" (*The Sacred Executioner*, 175).

35. Especially in *Revolution in Judea: Jesus and the Jewish Resistance* (London: Ocean Books, 1973). See also *The Sacred Executioner*, 103.

36. "The Origins of the Holocaust," 5.

37. Maccoby, "Theologian of the Holocaust," 36.

38. This is the essence of Maccoby's critique of Lloyd Gaston, John Gager, and Krister Stendahl, Christian interpreters of Paul who wish to mitigate the apostle's apparent anti-Judaism by viewing him in a new critical light. The best Maccoby can say of the Pauline portrait rendered by these scholars is that it "is a picture which . . . has its attractions for many people seeking to solve the problem of Christian antisemitism." See *Paul and Hellenism* (Philadelphia: Trinity Press International, 1991), chapter 6, "The Gaston-Gager-Stendahl Thesis," especially 154.

39. See especially Braham, ed., *The Origins of the Holocaust,* where a variety of Christian scholars I consider "radicals" react quite negatively to Maccoby's claims in "The Origins of Anti-Semitism."

40. On this, see Stephen R. Haynes, "Changing Paradigms: Reformist, Radical, and Rejectionist Approaches to the Relationship Between Christianity and Antisemitism," *Journal of Ecumenical Studies* 32:1 (Winter 1995): 63–88.

41. James H. Charlesworth, "Exploring Opportunities for Rethinking Relations among Jews and Christians," in Charlesworth, ed., *Jews and Christians: Exploring the Past, Present, and Future* (New York: Crossroad, 1990), 35.

42. Ibid., 36.

43. Ibid., 46.

44. Ibid., 53.

45. D. Moody Smith, "Judaism and the Gospel of John," in Charlesworth, ed., *Jews and Christians,* 76–96, 87.

46. *A Theology of the Jewish-Christian Reality, Volume 2: A Christian Theology of the People Israel* (San Francisco: Harper and Row, 1983), 322.

47. See Alice L. and A. Roy Eckardt, *Long Night's Journey into Day: A Revised Retrospective on the Holocaust* (Detroit: Wayne State University Press, 1988).

48. See *Long Night's Journey into Day,* 104–5. The scholarship on which the Eckardts are dependent is that of Haim Cohn and David Flusser.

49. See *A Christian Theology of the People Israel.* See also the article by Robert R. Hann, "Supersessionism, Engraftment, and Jewish-Christian Dialogue: Reflections on the Presbyterian Statement on Jewish-Christian Relations," *Journal of Ecumenical Studies* 27:2 (1990): 327–42, where the author takes to task a recent Presbyterian Church (U.S.A.) statement on Jewish-Christian relations for its insufficiently developed and defended claim that supersessionism is

a second-century theological construct absent from the New Testament documents. Hann argues that supersessionism is very much a part of the New Testament and is found in both early and late first-century texts, including the letters of Paul.

50. Darrell Fasching, *Narrative Theology after Auschwitz: From Alienation to Ethics.* (Minneapolis: Fortress, 1992), 46.

51. "Salient Christian-Jewish Issues of Today: A Christian Exploration," in Charlesworth, ed., *Jews and Christians,* 151–77, 154.

52. Eckardt and Eckardt, *Long Night's Journey into Day,* 129–30.

53. So Charles Vernoff: "recent events have in fact lent additional *moral* reinforcement to the historicizing perspective in its old tension with classical Christian theology's ontological truth claims." In "After the Holocaust: History and Being as Sources of Method within the Emerging Interreligious Hermeneutic," *Journal of Ecumenical Studies* 21:4 (1984): 639–63, 646.

CHAPTER 24

Power, Responsibility, and Abuse in

Medicine: Lessons from Germany

WILLIAM E. SEIDELMAN

The history of medicine in Germany is important because that country is the birthplace of modern medicine and medical science. Germany's medical eminence recently received special emphasis in the United States when the Clinton administration attempted to reform the American health care system along the lines of the German model, a model introduced over a century ago by Bismarck. Early in this century, the American educator Abraham Flexner proposed a new model for medical education in North America, the archetype for which was the German university.[1, 2] It was the German university which merged science, education, and patient care as exemplified by the contemporary system of medical education in the United States and Canada. The vocabulary of medicine today includes the names of many distinguished German clinicians and scientists such as Koch, Virchow, Roentgen, Neisser, Wassermann, Ehrlich, His, Recklinghausen, and Krebs. The ophthalmoscope, laryngoscope, cystoscope, cardiac catherization, and X-ray are all German inventions. It was German science and the German university which accounted for so many Nobel Prizes in the early part of this century. It was to the German university that thousands of physicians journeyed to further their scientific medical training.[3] It was those same German universities and research institutes which played a decisive role in the dehumanization, exploitation, and destruction of human life during the Hitler period.

The story of medicine in Nazi Germany is *not* a story of Germans and Jews or Germans and Gypsies. It is a story of doctors and patients, and medicine and medical science. It is about power and the abuse of power.

319

The modern history of medicine in Germany, in particular the history of medicine following Hitler's ascension, has been marked by denial, distortion, suppression, repression, and oppression. The denials and distortions continue until this very day. Within the German professional and academic community, objective and proper examinations of the record have been met with considerable resistance which has suppressed the truth.[4, 5] This suppression has had a corrosive effect on medical ethics worldwide, as exemplified by the recent scandal involving the World Medical Association where the president-elect for 1993–1994 was a German physician who had been member of the SS and was linked with the Nazi euthanasia program. Ironically, the World Medical Association is the only international medical body responsible for international ethical declarations regarding human experimentation and the treatment of prisoners in custody.

The common impression of the role of medicine in the horrors of the Nazi period is that it was the work of a few evil doctors working in the isolation of the death camps in German-occupied Poland. The corollary is that the majority of the German medical profession was divorced from the nefarious activities of the Nazi regime and that the academic community was not implicated. There is also the myth that the influence of the Nazi era on medicine ended at the Nuremberg war crimes tribunal and that the only enduring legacy is the Nuremberg Code on Human Experimentation which was enunciated to prevent the possibility of similar abuses in medicine. The reality is that members of the German medical profession were not reluctant participants in Hitler's Germany. Of all the occupations in Germany of the day, the medical profession had the largest membership in the Nazi party. Physicians were overrepresented in the (Nazi) party by a ratio of three to one. 45 percent of German physicians were members of the Nazi party, and they tended to join early.[6]

As for Nazi racial policies, they were not thrust upon the German medical profession but were derived in large part from the medical profession itself. The profession found in the Nazi movement a sympathetic ear to its thinking on the ideas of eugenics, race, and degeneration. The Nazi leadership found in medicine a scientifically legitimate vehicle for the achievement of its goal of racial purification. It was a symbiotic relationship.[7] The medical profession of the day did not protest becoming subjugated by the state nor did it protest when the state abrogated the ancient tradition of patient confidentiality. All of this was done in pursuit of the goal of *Volksgesundheit* or population health. A key element of Nazi population health policy was race hygiene. Proctor has written that by 1932 racial hygiene had become scientific orthodoxy in German medicine. The winter semester *before* the Nazi rise to power saw the subject of racial hygiene being taught in twenty-six separate courses of lectures in German medical faculties.[7]

A critical milestone in the process of genetic and racial purification was the July 1933 sterilization law. The law called for the enforced sterilization of people who had, or were considered to be, carriers of conditions which were considered hereditary and undesirable.[8] The sterilization law was formulated by leading genetic experts. The entire German health care system was mobilized to support the sterilization program. Physicians were obligated to report patients with suspected hereditary conditions. The public health care system was transformed into a system of eugenic health centers.[9, 10] The sterilizations were performed in hospitals under general anesthetic. Later, the sterilization of some women was carried out using X-rays.[11, 12] It is estimated that 500,000 people were sterilized under this population health program.

Two years after the enactment of the sterilization law, the German parliament took the next step in its eugenic/race hygiene program and proclaimed the infamous Nuremberg Race Laws which medicalized race. With these laws, race became a medical diagnosis requiring a physical examination. The laws called for a racial tribunal which included physicians as members.[13] The infamous racial laws were formulated in part by a physician, the Munich general practitioner Dr. Gerhard Wagner, who was the Reichsführer of physicians.[14]

The German university and academic and research community played a critical role in the entire enterprise of eugenics and race hygiene including the processes of dehumanization and destruction. During the Third Reich, the German faculties of medicine became the preeminent academic disciplines in all colleges and universities. Kater has documented that between 1933 and 1945, 59 percent of all university and college rectors in Germany were physicians. University rectors were appointed by the Nazis. Membership in the SS helped ensure an academic appointment.[6]

Curriculum changes in medicine during the Hitler period provide a case study of how the subject of racial hygiene was institutionalized by academia. Questions on race hygiene were asked in the state medical examination required for entry into medical practice. By 1936, professorships in race hygiene had been established at ten universities. The subject of racial science was taught in all medical faculties irrespective of whether or not there was an established chair in the field.[7] Race hygiene, however, was more than an abstract concept taught in the classroom. The university institutes of race hygiene became referral centers for expert opinions on people being considered for sterilization under the 1933 law and for disputed cases before the racial tribunals established under the Nuremberg racial laws.[15]

Some professors of medicine played key roles in the implementation of a racial hygiene program of medical murder known as the "euthanasia" campaign. Headquartered at a house in Berlin, the operation assumed its codename, Aktion T-4, after the address at Tiergartenstrasse 4. The T-4 action began in 1940 and continued until late 1941. An itinerant team of "euthanasia experts" traveled to mental institutions to select patients for killing. The ill-fated patients identified for killing were transported to one of six designated killing centers. The victims were conveyed by postal vans.[16]

Upon arrival at the psychiatric hospital/killing center at Hadamar, the hapless victims were led into a basement room that looked like a large shower. The room was in fact a gas chamber disguised as a shower. The infamous gas showers were designed by physicians, many being academics with professorial rank, for the killing of patients entrusted into their care.[17] The basement of Hadamar also contained two autopsy tables where the bodies of the victims were dissected for the removal of organs for research and teaching purposes. The specimens were sent to the medical schools and research institutes. The bodies were disposed by cremation in a coal fired cremation oven in the basement. The ashes were placed in metal urns and mailed to the families with death certificates giving a false cause of death.[17, 18]

Over 70,000 people were killed in this program of medicalized murder. One of the purported benefits of the T-4 campaign was the saving of food which might otherwise have been "wasted" for the feeding of so-called useless lives.[7] The T-4 action could not be kept secret from the public. It was stopped because of public protest, in particular the public remonstrations of Cardinal von Galen of Münster in a sermon given on August 3, 1941. Three weeks later, on August 24, Hitler ordered an end to Aktion T-4. Despite the end of the T-4 campaign, the experienced personnel and equipment of the killing program were not to be wasted.

On January 20, 1942, four months after Hitler's order ending the T-4 action, a number of government officials met for ninety minutes over coffee and cognac at a mansion on the shores of Lake Wannsee in Berlin. The purpose of the gathering was the organization of the Final Solution to the Jewish problem. The meeting was chaired by Reinhard Heydrich, then head of the Gestapo. Of the fourteen people known to have been in attendance at that meeting, seven held doctorates. One of the proposals was for mass sterilization to prevent racial contamination. When that was considered impracticable, the method eventually chosen was mass execution by gas chamber with disposal by cremation.[19, 20] The antecedent medical "euthanasia" program had been the pilot project, a feasibility study, for the process of mass extermination.

The euthanasia apparatus, personnel and equipment, were transferred to Poland where they formed the basis of the largest program of organized mass destruction of human life in recorded history. The medicalization of the destruction process extended to the railroad ramp at Auschwitz, where the unknowing victims were met by a medical selection team responsible for deciding who was fit to be a slave laborer or who was "unworthy of life" and thus selected for killing. The SS physicians chosen for this sardonic duty were required to have a proper license for the practice of medicine with extra training in genetics.[20]

Medicine's role included the exploitation of the victims for medical research. Having been defined as "life without value," the inmates of the concentration camps were considered appropriate subjects for deathly research. Medical science deemed the mass of humanity a unique research opportunity ready for exploitation. While the T-4 action ended in 1941, the killing in the mental hospitals did not. The liquidation of patients continued until the end of the war as a so-called wild campaign where untold thousands died from purposeful starvation or overdose of medication such as barbiturates and opiates.[21]

The relationship of academia and research to the Nazi racial program is best exemplified by a baron, a certain Professor, Dr. Otmar Freiherr von Verschuer. A noted expert on genetics and twin studies, Verschuer was the founding director of the largest institute of genetics and race hygiene of the day at the University of Frankfurt. Housed in a municipal health building, the institute was a center for research and consultation on genetics and eugenics. The staff provided expert opinions for racial consultations under the Nuremberg racial laws and eugenic/genetic consultations for the sterilization courts. The institute was also responsible for the race hygiene curriculum for medical students at the University of Frankfurt.[15, 22]

Verschuer's first assistant at the Frankfurt institute was a Frankfurt medical student who had recently been awarded a Ph.D. in anthropology from the University of Munich: Josef Mengele. Mengele's career continued until the end of the war under the mentorship of his professor, Verschuer. Mengele's professional origins were completely legitimate. In addition to a Ph.D. from the Ludwig-Maximillian University of Munich, Mengele received an M.D. from the Johann Wolfgang Goethe University of Frankfurt. Mengele's research, including his later work in Auschwitz, was done with the personal objective of achieving an academic appointment. Mengele's goal was to become, like Verschuer, a distinguished scientist and, above all, a professor.[23] His prewar anthropological studies on the human jaw were cited in the 1937 edition of *Index Medicus* and in English language medical journals well into the 1970s, long after he was a known war criminal.[24]

In 1942, Mengele's mentor, Verschuer, left Frankfurt to assume the directorate of the prestigious Kaiser-Wilhelm Institute of Anthropology in Berlin-Dahlem. Verschuer in Dahlem applied to the German Research Council for a research grant for twin studies. The grant was awarded after peer review. Verschuer's research assistant for this project was Mengele. The laboratory was the Birkenau death camp at Auschwitz. The research subjects were twins enslaved in Auschwitz. Verschuer, as principal investigator, was required to report to the funding agency on his research. It is known that Mengele in Auschwitz collected specimens from his victims/subjects which were sent to Verschuer's institute in Dahlem. After the war, Verschuer was permitted to resume his career, becoming professor and head of genetics at the University of Münster. His postwar career was distinguished.[20] His work continues to be cited in the genetics literature.[24]

Another professor who continues to be cited in the current literature is Professor Ernst Rüdin. Rüdin was the director of research at the renowned Kaiser Wilhelm Institute of Psychiatry in Munich, an institute established by the famed psychiatrist Emil Kraepelin. One of the authors of the 1933 sterilization law, Rüdin was a principal advocate of the Nazi eugenic program. He was twice honored by Hitler for his eugenic work. Rüdin's early work on the genetics of schizophrenia continues to be cited without any discussion of the consequences of that work and its current relevance as exemplified by Rüdin's professional career.[24, 25]

Professor Julius Hallervorden was a noted neuropathologist who exploited the Nazi program of dehumanization. A director of the famed Kaiser Wilhelm Institute of Brain Research at Berlin-Buch, Hallervorden has been immortalized through the eponym for a congenital neurological condition named after him and his colleague, Dr. Hugo Spatz: Hallervorden-Spatz Disease. Hallervorden is known to have capitalized on the T-4 killing in Brandenburg to acquire brains for his collection in the Kaiser Wilhelm Institute.[26] After the war, Hallervorden explained to American authorities that he knowingly exploited the "euthanasia" program because, "There was wonderful material among those brains, beautiful mental defectives, malformations and early infantile diseases."[27]

After the Soviet occupation of Berlin-Buch, the Kaiser-Wilhelm Institute of Brain Research was moved to Frankfurt. Renamed as a Max-Planck institute, the true origins of parts of its neuropathological collection were revealed in Germany in 1987 and 1988.[26] In 1990, the entire collection from the Hitler period was buried in the Forest Cemetery in Munich. Along with the specimens from the Frankfurt institute were brain specimens from the collection of the Max-Planck Institute of Psychiatry in Munich. Two gravesites were required to accommodate all the specimens, principally glass slides. The smaller collection from the Munich institute weighed one hundred kilos. The brain specimens from the Munich psychiatric institute were derived principally from children murdered at Eglfing-Haar as part of the "wild euthanasia" program which followed the T-4 campaign.[28] The headstone was unveiled at a commemorative ceremony held in May 1990.[29]

In 1988, it was revealed that the Institute of Anatomy at the University of Tübingen had in its collections specimens derived from victims of the Nazis. That revelation, the consequence of a protest by a group of students, resulted in a public outcry which led to a formal investigation. It was subsequently revealed that during the war the institute had received the cadavers of 429 victims of Nazi terror. Some of the victims were Russian and Polish prisoners of war exploited as slave laborers and executed for socializing with German women. They included a fifteen-year-old boy executed for unknown reasons, a twenty-year-old young man executed for fraternizing with a German woman, and two Polish slave-laborers hanged for receiving Christmas parcels from women in the town where they had worked. The names of all those foreign workers executed by the Nazis whose bodies were sent to the anatomy institute are listed in the records of the institute.[30]

The University of Tübingen, because of the demands of a group of students, formed an independent commission of inquiry chaired by a leading lawyer and expert on medical ethics.[31] All suspect specimens or specimens of uncertain origin were buried in a special section of the Tübingen cemetery reserved for the remains of subjects used for the teaching of anatomy. On July 8, 1990, a commemorative ceremony was held. The commemorative address was given by Dr. Jürgen Peiffer, emeritus professor of neuropathology who had studied under Hallervorden.[30, 32]

Professor Peiffer declared, "We must remember that there is a dangerous possibility that we may bury our bad consciences together with these tissue remains, thereby avoiding the necessity of remembering the past at least once every semester, together with our students." Peiffer continued,

> We must ask ourselves why today's ceremony is not the 45th commemoration of the victims of Nazism. Why is this the first solemn hour which brings together University teachers of medicine and representatives of the judiciary in order to remember events which, in the words of Giordano, we have been tempted to suppress through collective denials of guilt. When remembering these victims we have to ask how human beings like ourselves, came to lose—or failed even to develop—a sensitivity for transgressing certain limits that the Christian religion has set out to respect for creation and compassion for those who suffer.

The epitaph on the Tübingen grave reads:

> Displaced, oppressed, maltreated,
> Victims of despotism or blind justice,
> They first found their rest here.
> Science which did not respect
> Their rights and dignity during life
> Sought even to use their bodies after death.
> Be this stone a reminder to the living.[30]

The University of Tübingen is the only institution to have conducted a proper inquiry into this matter with outside experts and a report in the public domain.[31] Serious questions remain about some collections, in particular those of the Institute of Anatomy of the Ludwig-Maximillian University of Munich, the collection of Professor Hermann Voss of the University of Jena, and that of Professor Hermann Stieve of the Charité Hospital in the former East Berlin.

Professor Voss, during his tenure as dean of the Medical Department of the Reich University of Posen (1941–1945), is known to have exploited the bodies of Polish victims of the Gestapo. According to Aly, "Voss developed a booming trade in skeletons and skulls that he sold to Breslau, Leipzig, Vienna, Königsberg, and Hamburg; he received 15–30 RM per skull, or 150 RM per skeleton." In his diary, Voss describes how he enjoyed a postprandial siesta sunning himself on the anatomy institute's "bone whitener" where skeletal human remains were prepared. In Voss's own words, "To my right and left, Polish bones lay bleaching, occasionally giving off a slight snapping sound." In 1994, Aly noted, "These skeletons of Polish resistance fighters are probably still being used today."[33]

After the war, Voss continued his anatomy career in Halle (1948–1952) and Jena (1952–1962), and subsequently, as professor emeritus at the Greifswald anatomical institute. Voss was also the author of a textbook of anatomy which is considered a standard work in the field. From 1952 to 1974, he served as coeditor of Germany's leading journal of anatomy, the *Anatomischer Anzeiger*. In 1954, he established the journal *Acta Histochemica* which he directed until 1980. Voss died in Hamburg in 1987.[33]

Professor Hermann Stieve is known to have used doomed women imprisoned at Ravensbrück concentration camp as subjects for his studies on the effect of psychic trauma on the menstrual cycle. According to Stieve, after studying his first case of a woman sentenced to death (1942) and the effect of the impending execution on her menstrual cycle, he wrote, "Later (1943), I had the opportunity to investigate a large number of such cases. . . . I later had many opportunities to observe the effect of highly agitating events on female sexual organs." A prisoner's execution was timed so as to permit Stieve to perform a gynecological examination on the doomed woman while she was still alive. Upon her execution the "subject's" sexual organs were removed for Stieve's studies. Stieve, whose evil work was well known by his colleagues and inferentially acknowledged in his obituary, was professor at the University of Berlin, which after the war was renamed Humboldt University. He taught and performed his research at Berlin's Charité Hospital. He died in 1952.[33] A bust was sculpted and a lecture hall in the Charité Hospital named in his honor. According to Aly, who wrote in 1994, "The experiments on imprisoned and executed women, hinted at in Stieve's obituary and in his publications, have not been investigated to this day."[33]

Another example of the Nazi legacy in anatomy can be found in the 1989 English-language edition of the anatomical atlas *Pernkopf Anatomy.*[34] The late Austrian anatomist Eduard Pernkopf was the author of this landmark atlas, first published in 1937.[35] The 1943 and 1952 German-language editions included illustrations in which the artists incorporated Nazi icons (swastika and "SS" symbols) into their signatures.[36, 37] Pernkopf, who became dean of medicine at the University of Vienna after the March 1938 *Anschluss,* was an active member of the Nazi party and an avid racist and anti-Semite who openly published his views in the *Wiener Klinische Wochenschrift* (Viennese Medical Weekly) of which he was an editor.[38] The 1989 English-language edition of *Pernkopf Anatomy* includes two paintings from the 1943 edition in which the illustrator Karl Entresser incorporated the "SS" symbol into his signature (volume 2: pages 338 and 339, figures 336 and 337). The 1989 English-language edition also includes illustrations which appear to have been altered in order to remove the swastika from the signature of the artist Erich Lepier and the "SS" symbol which the artist Franz Bratke used for the numbers "44" to indicate the year 1944 (volume 1, pages 240 and 241, figures 293 and 294). The artists who painted the illustrations in Pernkopf's *Anatomy* were employed by the publisher, Urban and Schwarzenberg, who owns the original paintings and continue to publish the work.

The revelations of the medical crimes of the Hitler period, including the "euthanasia" programs, resulted in the trial of twenty-three individuals accused of crimes against humanity, also known as the "medical trial." The judgment of that trial established ten principles for the conduct of human experimentation which are known collectively as the Nuremberg Code. The first and foremost principle of the Nuremberg Code is informed consent.[39] The Nuremberg Code has become the benchmark against which ethical guidelines are measured. The modern discipline of medical ethics had its genesis at Nuremberg in the ashes of medicine from the Hitler period.

A year before the judgment of the Nuremberg medical tribunal, representatives of thirty-two national medical associations from around the world had met in London at the invitation of the British Medical Association to establish the World Medical Association (WMA) in response to the horrors of Nazi medical crimes. One of the first acts of the WMA was to create a modern version of the Hippocratic Oath.[40] The moral challenges raised by medical practices during the Hitler period were recognized. The World Medical Association was the first international organization to address medical ethics. The principle objective of the organization, however, was the advocacy of doctors' not patients' rights.

With headquarters in France, the WMA has been responsible for important declarations on medical ethics, beginning with this modern interpretation of the Hippocratic Oath. The WMA Declarations of Helsinki have become the international code for the conduct of human experimentation. The WMA Declaration of Tokyo deals with the treatment of prisoners in custody. In the WMA Helsinki declarations on human experimentation, the principle of informed consent has been relegated to ninth position.[41] It was felt that the Nuremberg Codes applied to Nazi crimes and the WMA declarations corrected that "error."[42]

Despite its pretence of ethical piety, the WMA is an organization which has been beset by controversies that have crippled its credibility. Its problems have been twofold. First, there have been long-standing concerns over its organizational credence and effectiveness: in other words, over whether it has been worth the money. These have been aggravated by conflicts over dues and voting power. The second problem is the more serious, namely that the WMA is an ethically compromised organization which is no longer a credible leader in the field of medical ethics. In fact, the WMA continues to be haunted by the legacy of the Nazi period.[43, 44, 45]

In October 1992 at its annual world meeting at the luxurious Spanish resort of Marbella, the WMA selected as its president-elect Professor Dr. Hans Joachim Sewering of Dachau, Germany. An announcement of Dr. Sewering's WMA appointment was carried in the October 1992 issue of the official journal of the German physicians' chamber, *Deutsches Ärzteblatt*. The German medical journal took note of the fact that

Dr. Sewering was a past president of the German Federal Chamber of Physicians and had been the representative of the German Chamber to the WMA since 1958 and a member of the Council of the WMA since 1966. The 1992 announcement of Dr. Sewering's WMA appointment omitted mention of his membership in the SS terror organization (#143,000) and the Nazi party (#1,858,805).[46, 43]

The announcement also omitted the fact, reported in Germany in a national publication in 1978, that the same Dr. Sewering had been linked to the death of a fourteen-year-old mentally handicapped girl killed in the "wild" euthanasia program. That child, Babette Fröwis, was sent on Sewering's order from the Schönbrunn Hospital where Sewering practiced, to the notorious killing center at Eglfing-Haar where children were being killed by starvation, neglect, and poisoning. Schönbrunn is an institution for handicapped children near the town of Dachau which is operated by a Catholic women's order. The order transferring Babette Fröwis from Schönbrunn to Eglfing-Haar had been signed by Dr. Sewering on Tuesday, October 26, 1943. In that transfer order, Dr. Sewering wrote that he considered Babette to be "no longer suitable for Schönbrunn; she will be sent to Eglfing-Haar, the healing institution responsible for her." Babette Fröwis died three weeks later. The probable cause of her death was murder by poisoning with an overdose of barbiturate.[47] While Sewering's tarnished history was well known in Germany, it did not become widely known outside Germany until January of 1993.[48]

The first and, for a while, the sole German physician to publicly protest the outrage of Sewering's WMA appointment was Professor Michael Kochen of the University of Göttingen. In 1992, Kochen was one of the few, if not the only Jewish physician to hold a professorship in a German medical school. On January 22, 1993, a group of German physicians publicly joined with Kochen to publish in three leading German newspapers a protest against Sewering's appointment to the World Medical Association position. Signed by about one hundred German doctors, the statement included documentation on Sewering's nefarious past.[49]

In response to the outcry, Sewering acknowledged his membership in the Nazi party. With regard to his membership in the SS, Sewering minimized his participation by suggesting that he only belonged to the Reiter SS, a ceremonial SS riding organization. As for the links with the euthanasia program, Sewering initially claimed that the euthanasia campaign ended in 1941, two years before he worked at Schönbrunn. He also claimed that nothing was done at Schönbrunn without the authority of the nuns and that the fateful document would only have been signed with the full agreement of the nuns. According to an interview given to the Dachau edition of the Munich newspaper *Die Süddeutche Zeitung für den Landkreis,* Sewering implied that the sisters of Schönbrunn did not know the fate awaiting patients transferred to Eglfing-Haar and that they, and by implication he, Sewering, had acted in good faith.[50]

That day following Sewering's published interview in the Bavarian newspaper, officials of the Schönbrunn institution, with the authorization of the Archbishop of Munich, issued a statement disclaiming Sewering's denial. The Schönbrunn statement was based on an examination of institutional documents and the testimony of four nursing sisters still living at the institution who had been there during the war. The facts as revealed by the Schönbrunn officials are:

- Between January, 1943 and June, 1945, 444 patients were starved to death in "hunger houses" at Eglfing-Haar.
- Between 1940 and 1944 there was a planned transfer out of patients from Schönbrunn and the sisters knew that the children were to be destroyed as "unworthy life" as part of the "euthanasia" killings.
- Between 1940 and 1944, 909 children from Schönbrunn were "transferred out."
- In 1943, 203 children from Schönbrunn were sent to Eglfing-Haar, 179 three days before Christmas.
- The sisters would not have authorized or approved the transfer of these children to a place where they would be killed.
- The sisters did whatever was in their means to protect the victims from planned destruction but were powerless to prevent the forceful removal of people.
- Five decades after the event, the four surviving sisters continue to be tormented by their memories of what happened.

The Schönbrunn officials issued the statement of "clarification," "in the interest of the memories of the criminally killed people, of the self-sacrificing and courageous sisters and fellow workers in Schönbrunn during the National Socialist times. It is also necessary in the interest of the currently active women of the order, fellow workers, the handicapped, and their relatives."[51]

The following day, January 23, 1993, the Federal Chamber of Physicians of Germany issued a press release announcing that Dr. Sewering was stepping aside from the World Medical Association office. According to this statement from the Chamber, Sewering said, "After I spent 25 years building up this world organization of doctors, including 20 years as its treasurer, it is now my duty to protect the World Medical Association from severe damage that could result from the threats of the Jewish World Congress." In the same press release, the president of the German Physicians' Chamber, Dr. Karsten Vilmar, issued a statement of support for Dr. Sewering.[52] No mention was made of the allegations against Sewering or the murdered children of Schönbrunn and Eglfing-Haar.

In April 1993, the Council of the World Medical Association met in Turkey at the Istanbul Hilton. At that meeting, Dr. Vilmar issued an official statement of support for Dr. Sewering. At the Istanbul meeting, the WMA Council was addressed by a close friend of Sewering, the WMA Executive Treasurer, Adolf Hällmayr. In defending his friend, Hällmayr suggested that Sewering "had been swept along by the Nazi movement in Germany," that SS membership was compulsory for medical students, and that Sewering, at the time, "was not aware of the full consequences of his action." As for Babette Fröwis, Hällmayr made the following statement:

> With regard to the papers (Sewering) signed transferring a 14-year-old, epileptic girl to a Nazi euthanasia clinic near Dachau, the policy was that when disabled people became aggressive, they became dangerous and were no longer allowed to live in the convent.[53]

Sixty years since Hitler came to power, fifty-five years after the start of the euthanasia programs and fifty years after the murder of Babette Fröwis, the death of an innocent handicapped girl in the Nazi terror state was justified with the assertion that disabled people who are aggressive are dangerous!

Sewering's career is a rueful example of the sequelae of five decades of denial and suppression by the German medical establishment. He is the third postwar president of the Federal Chamber to have been a member of the SS or the SA. The current, and fourth, president of the chamber,

Dr. Karsten Vilmar, is too young to have been implicated in any way in the Nazi era.

The Federal Chamber of Physicians of Germany has a dishonorable reputation for turning a blind eye to the physicians who participated in the programs of medical murder. The Federal Chamber permitted doctors associated with the "euthanasia" programs to continue to practice medicine while facing accusations of having murdered thousands of patients, accusations which were proven in court. In 1987, a German medical student criticized the Federal Chamber of Physicians for permitting the euthanasia doctors to continue to practice. In response to the student, the President of the Federal Chamber of Physicians, Dr. Karsten Vilmar, replied, "your letter and the questions and conclusions contained therein give rise to the suspicion that the history and knowledge of the chief principles of our democracy have escaped you . . . since you, too, are calling for the persecution of those doctors without due recourse to the law." [54]

One year earlier, in 1986, Dr. Vilmar and the Federal Chamber of Physicians did not await the niceties of due process of law before they took action against a German physician. That person was Dr. Hartmut Hanauske-Abel, an emergency room physician from Mainz. Hanauske-Abel's offense was authorship of an article entitled "From Nazi Holocaust to Nuclear Holocaust: A Lesson to Learn?" published in the *Lancet* in August 1986. [55] In that article, Hanauske-Abel described the role of the medical profession during the Third Reich and raised questions about the social responsibility of physicians in the nuclear age. Whereas in the case of the euthanasia doctors, the Federal Chamber of Physicians would not act after forty years, in Hanauske-Abel's case they acted within a matter of days. Three weeks after the publication of the *Lancet* paper, Hanauske-Abel's license to practice medicine was suspended. Vilmar publicly rebuked Hanauske-Abel and the Federal Chamber vigorously sought to keep him from practicing medicine in Germany. In contradistinction to the death doctors, Hanauske-Abel was excommunicated from medical practice in Germany and has become a professional nonperson in that country. He is now practicing medicine in the United States. [5]

The World Medical Association at its April 1993 meeting did introduce new guidelines concerning the ethical qualifications of candidates for the office of president of that organization. At that meeting, the

WMA elected a new treasurer to replace Dr. Sewering. That person is Sewering's colleague and advocate, Dr. Karsten Vilmar.

Sewering and Vilmar's appointments to the WMA position of treasurer are not surprising given the close relationship between the WMA and the Federal Chamber. The German doctors' organization is the keeper of both the press and the purse of the world body. The journal of the WMA is published in Cologne by a subsidiary organization of the Federal Chamber. The publication office for the WMA is in the headquarters of the German medical organization. The editorial staff of the WMA journal are principally associated with the German medical organization. The WMA bank is the same bank as the German doctor's group. The Federal Chamber is the second largest contributor, after the AMA, to the WMA treasury.[44, 45] The WMA position of treasurer has traditionally been held by a representative from Germany.

If Sewering had become president of the WMA, he would not have had the distinction of being the first SS alumnus to have held that office. That honor was held by Dr. Ernst Fromm (WMA President, 1973–74), who was an alumnus of both the SA and the SS. Formerly a "brown shirt," Fromm switched to Himmler's "black shirt" after the Röhm purge. Dr. Fromm preceded Sewering as both President of the German medical chamber and Treasurer of the World Medical Association.[56, 57]

The Sewering episode illustrates that the world medical community cannot divorce itself from the tragedies of the Hitler era and the continuing legacy. Medicine cannot escape by saying the evils of the Nazi era were the work of a few demons working in isolation from the mainstream. Medicine cannot claim ignorance of the reality and ignore the growing body of evidence which documents the critical role medicine played in the development of the entire process of destruction. As Professor Herbert Hochhauser has pointed out, the first victims were patients in the mental hospitals in Germany who were murdered by doctors and nurses.[58] Holocaust scholarship and education requires an examination of the relationship between doctors and patients and the power of medicine.

A proper recounting of the medical origins of the Holocaust ultimately will depend upon the sense of responsibility and accountability of the German medical profession, including the academic and scientific community. Given current symptoms and signs, the prognosis for such a response is poor. The evidence is to be found in the discussions within

Germany on the subject of euthanasia which continues to bring back memories of the medical murders of the Nazi era. Kochen has noted that the problem of euthanasia is addressed by avoidance. While emphasizing that it must never happen again, the German attitude is also that one should not talk about it. According to Kochen "collective forgetfulness" is used as a defense against the threat of "collective guilt." But as he has emphasized, "it is not . . . a question of guilt but of *collective responsibility* for the historical development in one's own country." [59]

Rather than collective responsibility, the response of the leadership of the German medical profession is best characterized as one of collective irresponsibility. This response is illustrated by the absence of a formal requirement for the teaching of ethics in the medical curriculum in Germany today. The teaching of medical ethics or modern German medical history in German medical schools today is the exception rather than the rule. In 1991, during a visit to Germany, this deficit was pointed out to officials of the federal government who replied that the curriculum was determined by the universities and not by the government. When university officials were asked, they said that the curriculum was determined by an Approbation Order of the federal government. When the problem was pointed out to federal government officials, they convened an interministerial meeting at the German Foreign Office to consider the issue. According to a summary report of that meeting, the conclusion was, "There is no immediate need to change successful and established practice." [60]

This question was also posed to the Federal Chamber. With respect to the teaching of medical ethics in German medical schools, an official of the Federal Chamber, Prof. Fuchs, stated:

> At the medical faculties in the Federal Republic of Germany "medical ethics" belongs for many years to the curriculum. A uniform structure for the representation of this discipline of instruction is neither sensible nor expected: there are, especially in the most recent times, chairs for medical ethics, special departments or interdisciplinary work groups.
>
> With the 7th Amendment of the Physicians Regulation of 1989, ethical aspects of medical activities have been taken up in the examination material for the first part of the medical examination. The German Ärztetag in 1991 demanded a stronger consideration of

medical ethics in the study of medicine. All groups which are working on the reforms of the study of medicine are anticipating the establishment of medical ethics in their model curricula.[61]

The report from the Federal Chamber was written the same week that the official representative of the Federal Chamber of Physicians of Germany to the WMA, SS alumnus Prof. Dr. Hans Joachim Sewering, was elected president-elect of the international body responsible for world leadership in the field of medical ethics.

Despite the ethical vacuity of the Federal Chamber, that organization is now extending its hegemony from the World Medical Association to encompass medical education in Europe. The Secretariat for the European Academy for Medical Training *(Europäische Akademie für Ärztliche Fortbildung: EAMF)* is the Federal Chamber of Physicians of Germany. The president of that organization is Dr. Karsten Vilmar. This organization for medical education in Europe takes on added importance given the establishment of the European Community.

A further example of the ethical vacuum created by "collective forgetfulness" is illustrated by the controversy concerning pathoanatomical specimens derived from victims of the Nazis. When Professor Arthur Caplan and I proposed a special international commemoration to deal with the universal ethical challenges, officials obfuscated. When discrepancies were identified concerning some collections, more obfuscation. When suggestions were proposed, in private not public, more evasion. To paraphrase Kochen, the suffering of the victims as exemplified by such specimens will again cry out from the shelves and laboratories of institutions which have yet to properly examine their collections.[62]

The only institution that dealt with the anatomical specimens issue effectively through a formal inquiry with outside experts and a published report was the University of Tübingen. The Federal Chamber of Physicians has failed to recognize or acknowledge the role medicine played in the development of the process of destruction. It has failed to consider the role it played in the greatest program of mass murder in recorded human history. In so doing, it has destroyed any pretence of ethical credibility and may have irreparably damaged the one international organization which was intended to restore credibility to medicine in ethical matters.

While the world is challenging the medical profession and medical science to consider the ethical questions arising from critical issues such as the end of life, or abortion, or genetic selection, or the human genome project, we need to ask ourselves why it is it that the German medical profession continues to hide from its own history? How is it that the German medical profession would tolerate the murderers of the Hitler era? Why, in the case of the Sewering affair, does the German medical profession four decades after the end of the Nazi state continue to promote the old lies of an international Jewish conspiracy or the aggressiveness and dangerousness of the mentally handicapped? Why do German physicians and the German public continue to tolerate such irresponsible behavior? I would suggest that the reason can be found in the role that German medicine played in the destruction of the Jews.

There are two aspects to this. The first is German medicine's purposeful avoidance of culpability for the process of organized destruction of human life during the Hitler regime. Medicine played key roles in selection for enforced sterilization, selection on the basis of a clinical racial diagnosis, and selection for death. Medicine played a critical role in rationalizing, developing, legitimizing, and operationalizing the processes of destruction in the medical murders of the euthanasia programs: As Professor Gisela Bock has written, "the most systematic, scientific, bureaucratic, industrialized, anonymous and therefore the must dehumanizing, anti-human form of killing."[63] The mass destruction of the Jews arose in medicine and the destructive impact of the Final Solution was magnified by the role of medicine. The doctors made it possible. The doctors made it acceptable. The doctors had the power.

The other aspect of this is that in destroying the Jews, German medicine destroyed its conscience. By removing from its midst the influence of its Jewish colleagues, German medicine created an ethical vacuum that has yet to be filled. The Sewering affair, the absence of teaching of medical ethics in the German medical schools, the pathoanatomical specimens episode, are all indications of the continuing ethical vacuum. The constitution of the Federal Republic notwithstanding, the basic value system of Judaism is the preservation of human life. It may not be perfect or without its problems and challenges, but the Jewish presence in medicine involves advocacy for human dignity and human life. It involves not theological teaching nor preaching nor religious injunction but the presence of peers and colleagues people whose personal and professional value system was influenced by those values. The German medical profession played a key role in destroying that presence, that conscience. When a few brave individuals have dared ask the question in public, the Federal Chamber has resorted to humiliation or, as in the case of Dr. Hanauske-Abel, professional persecution. It is quite apparent from the Sewering affair that the consequences of that vacuum continue.

The shame of Sewering was initially decried by only one person in the entire German medical community who was then, quite possibly, the only Jewish physician holding a professorship in all of German medical academia.

CONCLUSION

Given the critical role that German medicine has played in the evolution of modern medical science, the world medical community requires that the German medical community undertake a proper examination of its own history in order that we might better understand, not just how German doctors behave, but how all doctors behave. If the preeminent domain of medical science could become captive to evil, then any domain is vulnerable. In this complex age of biotechnology and the risk of a new eugenics, the world medical community requires a proper pathological examination of medicine in Germany before, during and since the Hitler era.

The World Medical Association must consider the implications of the Sewering affair and its impact on the credibility of the medical profession worldwide. The WMA must now address its own victimization. It could begin by helping establish a new ethical spirit which recognizes that physicians are mortal human beings who can err.[64] This new ethical spirit should begin with a commemoration to the victims of medical abuse, those human beings like the 909 children from Schönbrunn and the hundreds killed at Eglfing-Haar, whose bodies, souls and lives were exploited by medical science and sacrificed in pursuit of a politically defined "higher" good.

Given the pathetic lesson of the Sewering affair, the World Medical Association should help physicians around the world light a candle in commemoration of those who, like the martyred children, suffered in the name of medical science. Medical schools and medical organizations should set aside a time when students and faculty collectively commemorate the tragedies of the past and affirm their humanity, vulnerability, and responsibility for human life and dignity. This can be done by preparing a moment, an hour, perhaps even a day, when doctors confront their own humanity and obligations together. It would be an occasion when physicians and medical scientists recognize and acknowledge their own fallibility, to themselves, to their colleagues, to their students, to the community, and to the human beings they serve and who, in turn, place their trust in them.

That is the challenge to the profession, to the past, to the future, and to the memory of the murdered children of Schönbrunn and Eglfing-Haar.

ACKNOWLEDGMENTS

A number of people have, directly or indirectly, assisted in aspects of this work over the years. They include Professor Michael Kater of York University (Toronto, Canada), Professor Nahum Spinner of McMaster University, Professor Michael Kochen of the University of Göttingen, Professor Michael Weingarten of the University of Tel-Aviv, Professor Velvl Green of Ben-Gurion University of the Negev, Professor Arthur Caplan formerly of the University of Minnesota, Professor Herbert Hochhauser of Kent State University, Professor Michael Grodin of Boston University, and Dr. Michael Franzblau of San Francisco. Professor Howard Israel of Columbia University and Professor Gerhard Aumüller of the University of Marburg are responsible for having identified the Nazi icons in the Pernkopf anatomical illustrations.

This work could not have occurred without the support of my former colleagues at McMaster University and the North Hamilton Community Health Center. It had its genesis in the Program for the History of Medicine under my good friend and colleague, Dr. Charles Roland, the Jason Hannah Professor of the History of Medicine at McMaster.

My wife Racheline and three children Aviva, Ayëla, and Rhona, have been constant in their support for this work despite its many distractions. Over the years, they have helped me with my writing and presentations on this theme. When I first undertook this journey Rhona was just learning how to read and write. In the intervening years she has become an adviser and editor and helped in the preparation of the original paper.

The opinions expressed are entirely my own and in no way reflect those of the above. The facts speak for themselves.

Notes

1. Flexner, A. *I Remember.* New York: Simon and Schuster, 1940.

2. Wheatley, W. *The Politics of Philanthropy.* Madison: University of Wisconsin Press, 1988.

3. Bonner, T. N. *American Doctors and German Universities.* Lincoln: University of Nebraska, 1963.

4. Kater, M. in G. Aly, P. Chroust, and C. Pross, eds., *Cleansing the Fatherland: Nazi Medicine and Racial Hygiene.* Baltimore: Johns Hopkins University Press, 1994.

5. Pross, C. in G. Aly, P. Chroust, and C. Pross.

6. Kater, M. *Doctors under Hitler.* Chapel Hill: University of North Carolina Press, 1989.

7. Proctor, R. *Racial Hygiene.* Cambridge, Mass.: Harvard University Press, 1988.

8. Reichsausschuss für Volksgesundheitsdienst. *Law for the Prevention of Hereditarily Diseased Offspring* (approved translation of the *Gesetz zur Verhütung erbkranken Nachwuchses*). Berlin, 1935. Archives du Centre de Documentation Juive Contemporaine, Paris. Document B.15.076.

9. *JAMA* 109:15 (1937): 1212.

10. *JAMA* 111:7 (1938): 638–39.

11. *JAMA* 106:18 (1936): 1582–83.

12. *JAMA* 113:20 (1939): 1823–24.

13. *JAMA* 106:14 (1936): 1214–15.

14. Bracher, K. D. *The German Dictatorship: The Origins, Structure, and Effects of National Socialism.* New York: Praeger, 1970.

15. *JAMA* 105:13 (1935): 1051–53.

16. Burleigh, M., and W. Wippermann. *The Racial State: Germany 1933–1945.* Cambridge: Cambridge University Press, 1991.

17. *"Verlegt nach Hadamar": Die Geschichte einer NS-"Euthanasie"-Anstalt.* Eine Ausstellung des Landeswohlfahrtsverbandes Hessen, Historische Schriftenreihe des Landeswohlfahrtsverbandes Hessen, Kataloge Band 2. Kassel: Eigenverlag des LWV Hessen, 1991.

18. Hadamar today functions as both a psychiatric hospital and a memorial and documentation center on the "euthanasia" program. The memorial and documentation center are maintained by the Landeswohlfahrtsverband Hessen. The original gas chamber/shower remains relatively intact.

19. Davidowicz, L., ed. *A Holocaust Reader.* New York: Behrman House, 1976.

20. Müller-Hill, B. *Murderous Science: Elimination by Scientific Selection of Jews, Gypsies, and Others, Germany 1933- 1945.* Oxford: Oxford University Press, 1988.

21. Weindling, P. *Health, Race, and German Politics between National Unification and Nazism, 1870–1945.* Cambridge: Cambridge University Press, 1989.

22. The original building which housed Verschuer's Frankfurt institute remains standing today. Presently owned by an electrical company, it is a short distance from the Faculty of Medicine of the Johann Wolfgang Goethe University of Frankfurt.

23. Lifton, R. J. *The Nazi Doctors: Medical Killing and the Psychology of Genocide.* New York: Basic Books, 1986.

24. Seidelman, W. Mengele Medicus: Medicine's Nazi heritage. *Milbank Quarterly* 66:2 (1988): 221–39.

25. Seidelman, W. Lessons from eugenic history. *Nature* 337 (26 Jan. 1989): 300.

26. Shevell, M. Racial hygiene, active euthanasia, and Julius Hallervorden. *Neurology* 42 (1992): 2214–19.

27. Alexander, L. *Neuropathology and Neurophysiology, including Electroencephalography, in Wartime Germany.* Combined Intelligence Objectives Sub-Committee G-2 Division SHAEF (rear) APO 413. Washington, D.C.: National Archives. Document No. l-170.

28. Personal Communication. Prof. G. Kreutzberg. Munich: Max-Plank Institute of Psychiatry, 20 March 1991.

29. Dickman, S. Memorial ceremony to be held. *Nature* 345 (17 May 1990): 192

30. Peiffer, J. Neuropathology in the Third Reich: Memorial to those victims of National-Socialist atrocities in Germany who were used by medical science. *Brain Pathology* 1 (1991): 125–31.

31. *Berichte der Kommission zur Überprüfung der Präparatesammlungen in den medizinischen Einrichtungen der Universität Tübingen im Hinblick auf Opfer des Nationalsozialismus.* Herausgegeben vom Präsidenten der Eberhard-Karls-Universität Tübingen. Abdruck—auch auszugweise—nur mit Genehmigung des Herausgebers. 1990.

32. Dickman, S. Graves desecrated. *Nature* 346 (26 July 1990): 306.

33. Aly, G., P. Chroust, and C. Pross. *Cleansing the Fatherland: Nazi Medicine and Racial Hygiene.* Baltimore: Johns Hopkins University Press, 1994.

34. Platzer, W., ed. *Pernkopf Anatomy: Atlas of Topographic and Applied Human Anatomy.* Volumes I and II. Baltimore and Munich: Urban and Schwarzenberg, 1989.

35. Williams, D. J. The history of Eduard Pernkopf's *Topographische Anatomie des Menschen. Journal of Biocommunication* 15 (Spring 1988): 2–12.

36. Pernkopf, E. *Topographische Anatomie des Menschen: Lehrbuch und Atlas der regionär-stratigraphischen Präparation.* Berlin and Vienna: Urban and Schwarzenberg, 1943. For the signature of Erich Lepier with swastika see: II Band: Erst Hälfte: Tafel 2 Abb. 13, Tafel 33 Abb. 14, Tafel 14 Abb. 25, Tafel 15

Abb. 26, Tafel 16 Abb. 27, Tafel 17 Abb. 28, Tafel 18 Abb. 29, Tafel 32 Abb. 43, Page 351 Abb. 108, and Tafel 65 Abb. 94. For the signature of Karl Entresser with "SS" symbol see: II Band: Zweite Hälfte: Tafel 102 Abb. 188, Tafel 103 Abb. 189.

37. Pernkopf, E. *Topographische Anatomie des Menschen: Lehrbuch und Atlas der regionär-stratigraphischen Präparation.* Vienna and Innsbruck: Urban and Schwarzenberg, 1952. For the signature of Franz Bratke with "SS" symbol see: III Band: Tafel 9 Abb. 14, and Tafel 10 Abb. 15.

38. Weissmann, G. *They All Laughed at Christopher Columbus: Tales of Medicine and the Art of Discovery.* New York: Times Books, 1987.

39. Perley, S., S. Fluss, Z. Bankowski, F. Simon. The Nuremberg Code: An international overview. In G. Annas and M. Grodin, *The Nazi Doctors and the Nuremberg Code: Human Rights in Human Experimentation.* New York: Oxford University Press, 1992.

40. *World Medical Association Bulletin* 1:1 (April 1949): 1–20.

41. Katz, J. The consent principle of the Nuremberg Code: Its significance then and now. In Annas and Grodin.

42. Fatturosso, V., ed. Biomedical science and the dilemma of human experimentation, CIOMS Round Table Conference, Paris: *CIOMS* (1967): 9. As cited in: Refsauge, W., The place for international standards in conducting research on humans: Proceedings of the international conference on the role of the individual and the community in the research, development, and use of biologicals. Supplement 2 to the *Bulletin of the World Health Organization* 55 (1977): 133–39.

43. Beck, W. The World Medical Association and South Africa. *The Lancet,* 24 June 1989, 1441–42.

44. Beck, W. The World Medical Association serves Apartheid. *Int. J. Hlth. Services* 20:1 (1990): 185–91.

45. Richards, T. The World Medical Association: Can hope triumph over experience? *BMJ* 308 (1994): 262–66.

46. *Deutsches Ärzteblatt* 89 (30 Oct. 1992): C-2072.

47. *Der Spiegel,* 19 June 1978, 84–88.

48. Whitney, C. R. Top German doctor admits SS past. *New York Times,* 16 Jan. 1993, 3.

49. "Deutsche Ärzte protestieren." *Die Zeit,* 22 Jan. 1993, 22.

50. *The Washington Post,* 24 January 1993, A20.

51. *Die Pressestelle des Ordinariates München meldet: Stellungnahme der Leitung der Behinderteneinrichtung Schönbrunn zu Aeusserungen von Professor Sewering in einem Interview mit den Lokalnachrichten der "Süddeutschen Zeitung" für den Landkreis Dachau.* Schönbrunn (Dachau). 22 Jan. 1993.

52. *Pressestelle der deutschen Ärzteschaft.* Cologne: 23 Jan. 1993.

53. "Professor Sewering's resignation from WMA President-Elect." *World Medical Journal* 39:2 (1993): 22–23.

54. Klee, E. "Turning the tap on was no big deal."—The gassing doctors during the Nazi period and afterwards. In Benz, W., and B. Distel, eds. *Dachau Review* 2: *History of Nazi Concentration Camps Studies, Reports, Documents.* Vol. 2. Brussels: Comité International de Dachau, 1990. 46–66.

55. Hanauske-Abel, H. From Nazi holocaust to nuclear holocaust: A lesson to learn? *The Lancet* (2 Aug. 1986): 271–73.

56. The 27th World Medical Assembly. *World Medical Journal* 21:1 (1973): 4–9.

57. Kater, M. The burden of the past: Problems of a modern historiography of physicians and medicine in Nazi Germany. *German Studies Review* 10:1 (1987): 31–56.

58. Hochhauser, H. Comments made at "Holocaust and biomedical ethics: The contemporary use of Nazi data." Ninth Annual Holocaust Conference. Kent State University. March 20–21, 1990.

59. Kochen, M. Euthanasia in Germany. Paper presented at the German Historical Institute and Goethe Institute in Washington, D.C., conference on "Medicine in Nineteenth- and Twentieth-Century Germany: Ethics, Politics, and Law." Washington, D.C., 1–4 Dec. 1993.

60. Medical ethics in Germany: Summary of an inter-ministerial meeting at the German Foreign Office on 19 Aug. 1991. Auswärtiges Amt. Der Leiter der Kulturabteilung. Bonn.

61. C. Fuchs. Medizinische Präparate von NS-Opfern/medizinische Ethik als Gegenstand des universitären Studiums. Ihr Schreiben vom 8. Nov. 1991 und vom 27. Aug. 1992, Unsere Zwischennachricht vom 19. Nov. 1991. Bonn: An das Auswärtige Amt. Herrn Dr. von Treskow, 5 Oct. 1992.

62. Correspondence between W. Seidelman and officials of the Office of the Federal Chancellor of Germany (L. Stavenhagen), the German Foreign Office (B. Witte and R. von Treskow), the Max-Planck Society (W. Hasenclever), and the Institute of Anatomy of Ludwig-Maximillian University of Munich (R. Putz). Files of Prof. W. Seidelman. Toronto: University of Toronto, 1989–1993.

63. Bock, G. Sterilization and "euthanasia," 1933–1945. Paper presented at the German Historical Institute and Goethe Institute in Washington, D.C., conference on "Medicine in Nineteenth- and Twentieth-Century Germany: Ethics, Politics, and Law." Washington, D.C., 1–4 Dec. 1993.

64. McIntyre, N., and L. Popper. The critical attitude in medicine: The need for a new ethics. *BMJ* 287 (1983): 1919–23.

CHAPTER 25

The Holocaust: Its Impact on

Christian Thought and Ethics

JOHN T. PAWLIKOWSKI

In this chapter, I aim to confront some of the overriding theological challenges posed by the Holocaust, which we are gradually coming to recognize as an epochal event in the history of Western society, including the Western churches, but with decided implications for the future of all humanity. It is truly an "orienting experience" for contemporary human existence, to speak in the words of Irving Greenberg. We shall probe the Holocaust's impact on our sense of God and ethics as well as related theological issues. But as we undertake this necessary task of theological and social analysis we must never let our minds and hearts stray very far from the memory of the six million Jews, including one million children, who were annihilated simply because they were Jews, nor of the up to five million Poles, Rom people (Gypsies), Gays, mentally and physically incapacitated, and others who joined them in victimhood as part of the Nazi effort to purify humanity.

Christians must likewise never lose sight of the fact that the Holocaust continues to strain Christian credibility. While contemporary scholarship has adequately documented that the Holocaust was primarily parented by currents within certain modern secular philosophies and by social theories which at their core were often also profoundly anti-Christian, little doubt remains that classical Christian teaching and preaching constituted an indispensable seedbed for the success of the Nazi effort.

Even a scholar such as the late Uriel Tal, who argued strongly for the predominance of secular (and anti-Christian) anti-Semitism in the genesis of Nazism, continued to underscore the pivotal contribution of the Christian tradition. He insisted that Nazi racial anti-Semitism was not

344

totally original when subjected to careful analysis. Rather traditional Christian stereotypes of Jews and Judaism were clothed in new pseudo-scientific jargon and applied to specific historical realities of the period. In summation, Tal says that "racial anti-Semitism and the subsequent Nazi movement were not the result of mass hysteria or the work of single propagandists. The racial anti-Semites, despite their antagonism toward traditional Christianity, learned much from it, and succeeded in producing a well-prepared, systematic ideology with a logic of its own that reached its culmination in the Third Reich." [1]

Christianity cannot equivocate regarding its responsibility for the spread of Nazism if it is to enter authentically the continuing debate about the broader theological implications of the Holocaust. Achieving such authenticity clearly will involve a commitment to the full and final purge of all remaining anti-Semitism from its theological statements, catechetical teachings, and liturgical expression. The churches likewise must be willing to submit their World War II record to a thorough scrutiny by respected scholars. Ultimately, they cannot avoid confronting the question a fellow inmate posed to Alexandre Donat, author of *The Holocaust Kingdom:* "How can Christianity survive the discovery that after a thousand years of its being Europe's official religion, Europe remains pagan at heart?" [2]

In the final analysis, the Holocaust represented the beginning of a new era in human self-awareness and human possibility over which hung the specter of either unprecedented destruction or unparalleled hope. With the rise of Nazism, the mass extermination of human life in a guiltless fashion became thinkable and technologically feasible. The door was now ajar for an era when dispassionate torture and the murder of millions could become not merely the act of a crazed despot, not just a desire for national security, not merely an irrational outbreak of xeno-phobic fear, but a calculated effort to reshape history supported by intellectual argumentation from the best and brightest minds in a society. It was an attempt, Emil Fackenheim has said, to wipe out the "divine image" in history. "The murder camp," Fackenheim insists, "was not an accidental by-product of the Nazi Empire. It was its essence." [3]

The fundamental challenge of the Holocaust lies in our altered percep-tion of the relationship between God and humanity and its implications for the basis of moral behavior. What emerges as a central reality from the study of the Holocaust is the Nazi effort to create the "superperson," to develop a truly liberated humanity, to be shared in only by a select group, namely, the Aryan race. This new humanity would be released from the moral restraints previously imposed by religious beliefs and would be capable of exerting virtually unlimited power in the shaping of the world and its inhabitants. In a somewhat indirect, though still powerful, way the Nazis had proclaimed the death of God as a guiding force in the governance of the universe.

In pursuit of their objective, the Nazis became convinced that all the "dregs of humanity" had to be eliminated or at least their influence on culture and human development significantly curtailed. The Jews fell into this "dregs" category first and foremost. They were classified as "vermin." The Nazis could not imagine even a minimally useful role for Jews in the new society to which they hoped to give birth. In addition, there existed a "sacral" mandate for persecuting Jews which did not obtain for any of the other victim groups. Nonetheless, new research is beginning to suggest a closer affinity between Jews and Poles, Gypsies, and mentally and physically impaired in particular than many have acknowledged previously. Evidence has now surfaced that Hitler entertained the idea of total extermination, not mere subjugation, of Poles, for example, at some future date.[4] But the mass extermination of Jews became a reality and we should never blur the distinction between fact and possibility. Nonetheless, the extermination or subjugation of the other victim groups under the rubric of humankind's purification assumes important theological significance. Regrettably the non-Jewish victims are generally ignored in the emerging theological reflections on the Holocaust whether by Christian or by Jewish scholars.[5]

Uriel Tal captured as well as anyone the basic theological challenge presented by the Holocaust. In his understanding the so-called Final Solution had as its ultimate objective the total transformation of human values. Its stated intent was liberating humanity from all previous moral ideals and codes. When the liberating process was complete, humanity once and for all would be rescued from the imprisonment of a God concept and its related notions of moral responsibility, redemption, sin, and revelation. Nazi ideology sought to transform theological ideas into exclusively anthropological and political concepts. In Tal's interpretation of the Holocaust for the Nazis, "God becomes man in a political sense as a member of the Aryan race whose highest representative on earth is the Führer."[6]

Tal's research led him to conclude that this new Nazi consciousness emerged only gradually in the decades following World War I. Its roots, however, were somewhat earlier. It was undeniably related to the general process of social secularization that had been transforming Germany since the latter part of the nineteenth century. Its philosophic parents included the deists, the French encyclopedists, Feuerbach, the Young Hegelians, and the evolutionary thinkers in concert with the developing corps of scientists who through their many new discoveries were creating the impression that a triumphant material civilization was on the verge of dawning in Western Europe. In the end, Tal argued, "these intellectual and social movements struck a responsive chord in a rebellious genera-tion, altered the traditional views of God, man, and society, and ulti-mately led to the pseudo-religious, pseudomessianic movement of Na-zism." [7]

The principal theological problem raised by the Holocaust is how humankind properly appropriates the genuine sense of human liberation that lay at the heart of Nazi ideology without surrendering its soul to massive evil. However horrendous their legacy, the Nazis were percep-tive in at least one respect. They astutely recognized that basic changes were underway in human consciousness. The impact of the new science and technology, with its underlying assumption of freedom, was begin-ning to provide the human community on a mass scale with a Prometh-ean-type experience of escape from prior moral chains. People were starting to realize, however dimly, an enhanced sense of dignity and autonomy far more extensive than most of Western Christian theology had previously conceded. Traditional theological concepts that had shaped much of the Christian moral perspective, notions such as divine punishment, hell, divine wrath, and providence, were losing some of the hold they had exercised over moral decision making since biblical times. Christian theology had tended to accentuate the omnipotence of God which in turn intensified the impotence of the human person and the rather inconsequential role played by the human community in main-taining the sustainability of the earth. The Nazis totally rejected this previous relationship. In fact, they were literally trying to turn it on its head.

Michael Ryan has emphasized this direction of Nazism in his theologi-cal analysis of Hitler's *Mein Kampf*. For Ryan, the most striking aspect of the "salvation history" found in this volume is Hitler's willingness to confine humanity in an absolute way to the limits of time. In the Hitlerian perspective, humankind must resign itself to the conditions of finitude. But this resignation is accompanied by the assertion of all-pervasive power for itself within those conditions. The end result of all this was the self-deification of Hitler who proclaimed himself the new "Savior" of the German nation. It is this Hitlerian mind-set that allows us, in Ryan's judgment, to term *Mein Kampf* a "theological" treatise. In the final analysis, in Ryan's words, Hitler's worldview "amounted to the deliberate decision on the part of mass man to live within the limits of finitude without either the moral restraints or the hopes of traditional religion—in this case, Christianity." [8]

The challenge facing theology after the Holocaust is to discover a way whereby the new sense of human freedom that is continuing to dawn might be affirmed but channeled into purposes constructive rather than destructive for the future course of creation. The understanding of the God-human relationship must be significantly altered in light of the Holocaust. The intensified sense of power and human enhancement that the Nazis championed as a novum of our age needs to be acknowledged as a crucial and inescapable element in the ongoing process of humanity's salvation. There is simply no reversing the consciousness of a profound readjustment in the nature of the divine-human relationship.

The mere repetition of biblical images and precepts will prove insufficient as a response to the Holocaust. Contemporary humanity perceives itself in a far more liberated condition relative to divine power and authority than the authors of the biblical texts could ever imagine. There exists today an awareness of dimensions of the Genesis notion of co-creatorship which the biblical world could never fathom. As the late moral philosopher Hans Jonas reminded us, we constitute the first generation with the responsibility for ensuring the future of all forms of life in the universe. No previous generation has in its grasp the possibilities for massive destructive power that are open to us. In the past, nature had sufficient recuperative powers to heal whatever wounds humanity's capitulation to evil might inflict. This is no longer the case, at least not to the same extent. That is why, while it is important to consider the Holocaust separately so as to properly illustrate its profound distinctiveness as a historical and theological event, it is also necessary to establish a link with the other shattering experience of World War II—Hiroshima. In one sense the two events are of a significantly different order; but, in another, as concrete expressions of the newly discovered power of humanity to destroy, they remain profoundly intertwined.

The question at hand is whether post-Holocaust theology can develop an expression of God and religion which will help prevent the newly recognized creative power of humanity from being transformed into the destructive force unveiled in all its ugliness during the Nazi era. Put another way, can post-Holocaust humanity discover a relationship with God which will provide warrants for the use of its vast new power to shape itself and the creation it has inherited? This fundamental issue has been basically ignored by most Christian theologians until now.

Reflections on the divine-human encounter in light of the Holocaust have emerged in the last decade or so as one of the central theological discussions in Judaism. Unfortunately, as David Tracy has regretted, no corresponding development has occurred within Christian theological circles. Few Church theologians, says Tracy, are focusing on the ultimate religious question for all believers, including Christians—the problem of God—which, as Schleiermacher perceptively insisted, can never be treated as one among many doctrines but must pervade all other statements of belief. In this regard, Tracy is convinced that "Jewish theology, in its reflections on the reality of God since the *Tremendum* of the Holocaust, has led the way for all serious theological reflection." [9]

Theological discussion about God in light of the Holocaust has generated a variety of viewpoints among Jewish Scholars. It is impossible in this presentation to treat them individually in any comprehensive fashion. [10]

The basic division among Jewish scholars has come over the question of how central a role the Holocaust should assume in the contemporary reconstruction of Jewish belief. Most Orthodox Jewish scholars have tended to downplay the Holocaust as a major turning point in the understanding of the divine-human relationship. While they remain acutely sensitive that the annihilation of six million innocent men, women, and children has traumatized the Jewish people, they hold fast to the belief that this experience ultimately still can be incorporated into classical religious categories of evil.

David Hartman, though hardly a centrist figure in Orthodox Jewry, remains an articulate, creative spokesperson for this point of view. He opts for the contemporary renewal of traditional covenantal religion, rather than the Holocaust, as central to the generation of the faith commitment required to guarantee Jewish survival. Adopting a position similar to that advocated by the leading Christian ethicist James Gustafson about humankind's inability to know what God ultimately intends for creation, Hartman stresses the development of a new faithfulness to Torah observance as the only way of assuring communal survival and a measure of meaning in a frequently chaotic world. The Holocaust was certainly a part of this chaos, and its continued remembrance is vital, but in no way should it provide the basis for contemporary belief. For Hartman, "Auschwitz, like all Jewish suffering of the past, must be absorbed and understood within the normative framework of Sinai." Jews will mourn forever the memory of the victims, but they "will build a healthy new society because of the memory of Sinai." [11]

A few Reform Jewish scholars such as Eugene Borowitz have likewise deemphasized the Holocaust as a theological issue in favor of the more traditional concern in Reform Judaism with the problem of how belief in God is to be reconciled with the enhanced awareness of human autonomy that is characteristic of modernity. Recently Borowitz has modified his position to a significant extent, to the point where he can now be described as standing about midway between Hartman and the Holocaust theologians.

This is especially evident in his new volume, *Renewing the Covenant: A Theology for the Postmodern Jew.*[12] Working out of a framework of what he terms "relational revelation" that is rooted both in Reform Judaism's classic concern with individual human autonomy and Orthodox's Judaism more communal emphasis on covenantal faithfulness, Borowitz now maintains that in a postmodern age we need to adopt "a more realistic view of our human capacities and a determination not to confuse the junior with the senior partner" in describing the God-human relationship. One of the principal realities that has made such a reassessment necessary is the experience of the Holocaust. But having issued this sober warning, Borowitz goes on to argue that the person in covenant with God today must claim a more active role in the relationship than was the case with the biblical-rabbinic Jew for whom God was far more dominant. "This consciousness of ongoing intimacy with God," he says, "precedes, undergirds, and interfuses all the Jewish self's other relationships. It ties us to God's other partners for more than pragmatic or utilitarian reasons." [13]

Among those Jewish scholars who have argued for major theological reinterpretation of the divine-human relationship in response to the Holocaust, the names of Richard Rubenstein, Emil Fackenheim, Arthur Cohen, and Irving Greenberg stand out. In this chapter, I can only briefly sketch each of their positions.

Rubenstein's volume *After Auschwitz*[14] caused a great stir in Jewish circles when it first appeared. Its boldly stated claim that the Holocaust had buried any possibility of continued belief in a covenantal God of history and that, in place of traditional faith, Jews must now turn to a creed of "paganism" which defines human existence as wholly and totally an earthly existence shook the foundations of Judaism. When the dust had settled somewhat, the prevailing opinion was that Rubenstein had gone much too far, a point that he himself seemingly acknowledges (at least implicitly) in some of his more recent writings.

Today Rubenstein's position seems somewhat closer to a mystical approach to God. The cosmos is no longer as cold, silent, and unfeeling a reality as he projected in *After Auschwitz*. As John Roth presumably writes in the volume co-authored by Rubenstein and himself, "Today, Rubenstein would balance the elements of creativeness and love in the cosmos somewhat more evenly with those of destruction and hate than he was prepared to do in 1966. What has not changed is his affirmation of a view of God quite different from the mainstream view of biblical and rabbinic Judaism and his rejection of the notion that the Jews are in any sense a people either chosen or rejected by God."[15]

Whatever else may be said in judgment about Rubenstein's initial or more refined perspective, he is credited by a number of fellow scholars with at least one major contribution. Steven T. Katz, who rejects Rubenstein's original summons to "paganism," is a case in point. He considers Rubenstein "absolutely correct" in his judgment that classical categories of evil no longer are convincing relative to the God-human relationship when confronted by the immensity of the Holocaust.[16]

Fackenheim, Cohen, and Greenberg, in their approaches to the post-Holocaust divine reality, stop far short of Rubenstein's total rejection of a covenantal God. But, despite some significant differences among them, they speak with a unified voice regarding the need for a major restatement of this relationship in light of the Holocaust.

In his numerous writings, but especially in the volume *The Jewish Return into History*,[17] Emil Fackenheim states his conviction that the image of God was destroyed during the Holocaust. Our task today, a mandate incumbent in a special way upon the survivors of the Holo-caust, is to restore the divine image, but in a way that conveys a sense of a new curtailment of God's power in comparison with past images.

Arthur Cohen picked up on this same theme, but used more philo-sophically oriented language to make his point. In *The Tremendum: A Theological Interpretation of the Holocaust,*[18] Cohen pointedly rejected the continued viability of any image of God as the Strategist of human history. A post-Holocaust God can legitimately be perceived (and must be so perceived if radical evil is to remain in check) as

> the mystery of our futurity, always our posse never our acts. If we can begin to see God less as an interferer whose insertion is welcome (when it accords with our needs) and more as the immensity whose reality is our prefiguration, whose speech and silence are metaphors for our language and distortion, whose plenitude and unfolding and the hope of our futurity, we shall have won a sense of a God whom we may love and honor, but whom we no longer fear and from whom we no longer demand.[19]

Turning now to Irving Greenberg, we find that his language about the effects of the Holocaust on the divine image are not as blunt as those of Fackenheim, but he shares the conviction that a major readjustment is required of our statement of the force of the covenantal obligations upon humanity in light of the Holocaust. "The Nazis," he says, "unleashed all-out violence against the covenant." Their program for the Final Solution involved a total assault on Jewish life and values. For Greenberg, "the degree of success of this attack constitutes a fundamen-tal contradiction to the covenant of life and redemption."[20]

The reality of the Nazi fury forces a thorough reconsideration of the nature of moral obligation upon the contemporary Jewish community and seemingly by implication upon all those other believers (Christian and Muslim) who in some way regard the Sinai covenant as foundational for their faith expression. For this covenant has called Jews as witnesses to the world for God and for a final perfection. "In light of the Holo-caust," insists Greenberg,

> it is obvious that this role opened the Jews to a murderous fury from which there was no escape. Yet the Divine could not or would not save them from this fate. Therefore, morally speaking, God

must repent of the covenant, i.e., do *teshuvah* for having given his chosen people a task that was unbearably cruel and dangerous without having provided for their protection. Morally speaking, then, God can have no claims on the Jews by dint of the covenant.[21]

The end result of any serious reflection on the Sinai covenant in light of the Holocaust experience, as Greenberg sees it, is simply the disappearance of any "commanded" dimension on the part of God. "Covenantally speaking, one cannot *order* another to step forward to die."[22] Any understanding of covenantal obligation must now be voluntary: "One cannot *order* another to go on a suicide mission. Out of shared values, one can only ask for volunteers. . . . No divine punishment can enforce the covenant, for there is no risked punishment so terrible that it can match the punishment risked by continuing faithfulness to the covenant."[23]

The voluntary nature of the post-Holocaust covenantal relationship unquestionably heightens human responsibility in the eyes of Greenberg: "If after the Temple's destruction, Israel moved from junior participant to true partner in the covenant, then after the Holocaust, the Jewish people is called upon to become the senior partner in action. In effect, God was saying to humans: you stop the Holocaust. You bring the redemption. You act to ensure that it will never again occur. I will be with you totally in whatever happens, but you must do it."[24]

My basic response to the post-Holocaust reflections of Fackenheim, Cohen, and especially Greenberg is that, despite some reservations, they provide the basic parameters within which we need to understand the God-humanity relationship today and its connections with the foundations for contemporary morality.

There is also some reason to show a measure of sympathy for the stance of Hartman. No post-Holocaust faith expression can totally divorce itself from the covenantal experience and promises. And to the extent that Hartman means to direct his remarks against those in the Jewish community who would use the Holocaust as a basis for the development of a chauvinistic nationalism in the midst of the current Israeli-Palestinian-Arab conflict, he deserves applause. Yet, in the final analysis, Hartman's position falls short because of his inability to grasp that the reality of the Holocaust no longer allows us to speak of covenantal faith in the same way as did the biblical or rabbinic traditions.

The Holocaust was not merely the most extreme example of the classical theological problem of evil. It has burst asunder the traditional position. To confine our response to the Holocaust to the renewal of covenantal faith as Hartman prescribes would be to endanger human survival. For we would remain unprepared to deal with the magnitude of the power and consequent responsibility that has come into the hands of humanity. And failure on the part of humankind to recognize these new post-Holocaust realities may allow this power to pass once again into the hands of a new class of Nazis.

Borowitz's position, as presented in his recent writings, seems to be moving to a point that brings it close to that of the Holocaust theologians. While I would still fault him for not giving sufficient attention to the full impact of the Holocaust and its unique dimensions, nonetheless I find his thought important in moderating some of the excessive stress on human initiative after the Holocaust that is characteristic of most of the Holocaust theologians.

Clearly, the Holocaust theologians have made us conscious of the greatly enhanced role of the human community in preserving human history from further eruptions of radical evil akin to Nazism. This is the supreme moral challenge of the post-Holocaust era. Humanity now finds itself facing the realization that "future" is no longer something God will guarantee. Survival, whether for the People Israel or humanity at large, is now more than ever a human proposition. In their differing ways Fackenheim, Cohen, and Greenberg have made this fact abundantly clear. And we need to be profoundly grateful for that. They have confronted us with the post-Holocaust reality that any simplistic belief in an interventionist God of history was buried in the ashes of Nazi Germany. Preventing massive human destruction is now far more evidently than before a burden primarily incumbent upon the human community. We must learn to save ourselves from future instances of holocaust, nuclear, ecological, or otherwise. We are summoned to answer "right now" to D. H. Lawrence's plea, "God of Justice, when wilt Thou teach them to save themselves?"[25] We no longer have the luxury, and in fact it would be the height of human irresponsibility after the Holocaust to imagine that God will do it in response to simple petitions of prayer. Perhaps because of the freedom God has granted humanity, he cannot do it. It might be added here that a fruitful source in our search for a post-Holocaust vision of God that would strengthen the human role in the process of salvation might be the Jewish mystical literature with its notion of divine self-constriction in the act of creation.

Despite my gratitude to Fackenheim, Cohen, and Greenberg, their prescriptions for God-belief after the Holocaust to me fall short in the final analysis. They would appear to leave humanity too much to its own whims after the Holocaust. Here is where Borowitz's recent writings provide a useful balance. The Holocaust theologians have not explored adequately whether God continues to play a significant role after the Holocaust in the development of a moral ethos within humanity that can restrain radical evil. The role they have in fact assigned to God is not potent enough.

The post-Holocaust theological vision must be one that recognizes both the new creative possibilities inherent in the human condition as well as the utter necessity for this creative potential to be brought under the sway of an encounter with the living and judging God. Only such an encounter will direct the use of this creative potential away from the destruction represented by Nazism. We need to find a way of articulating a notion of a transcendent God which can counterbalance the potential for evil that remains very much a live possibility in the contemporary human situation. In other words, we shall have to recover a fresh sense of transcendence to accompany our heightened sense of human responsibility after the Holocaust. This is something basically absent from the reflections of Fackenheim, Cohen, and Greenberg.

Men and women will once more need to experience contact with a personal power beyond themselves, a power that heals the destructive tendencies still lurking within humanity. The newly liberated person, to be able to work consistently for the creation of a just and sustainable society, must begin to sense a judgment upon human endeavors that goes beyond mere human judgment. Such a sense of judgment is missing in Fackenheim's emphasis on human restoration of the divine image, in Cohen's language about God as our "posse," and in Greenberg's notion of the voluntary covenant, as valid as each notion is in itself.

The Holocaust has shattered all simplistic notions of a "commanding God." On this point Fackenheim, Cohen, and Greenberg are perfectly correct. Such a "commanding" God can no longer be the touchstone of ethical behavior. But the Holocaust has also exposed humanity's desperate need to restore a relationship with a "compelling" God, *compelling* because we have experienced through symbolic encounter with this God a healing, a strengthening, an affirming that buries any need to assert our humanity through the destructive, even deadly, use of human power. This sense of a compelling Parent God who has gifted humanity, whose vulnerability for the Christian has been shown in the Cross, is the meaningful foundation for any adequate moral ethos after the Holocaust.

Some have suggested that "compelling" may be too strong a replacement adjective for "commanding" in speaking about the post-Holocaust God. Perhaps they are right. Perhaps "compelling" does tip the scales too much back towards a pre-Holocaust vision of divine reality. These critics have offered the alternative of speaking about a "God to whom we are drawn" which admittedly is more cumbersome than "compelling." This inherent and enduring "drawing" power of God would substitute for pre-Holocaust models which emphasized God's "imposition" upon humanity.

At this point, the "compelling" vocabulary seems preferable. But whatever image eventually wins the day, the basic point must be made that post-Holocaust humanity needs to rediscover a permanent relationship with God who remains a direct source of strength and influence in the conduct of human affairs.

In speaking of the need to rediscover a "compelling" God, I believe I am close to the stage Elie Wiesel has reached as he has probed the depth of the Holocaust these many years. Despite the remaining ambiguities, despite the apparent divine failures in covenantal responsibility from God's side, atheism is not the answer for contemporary humanity according to Wiesel. After we have exhausted ourselves in protesting against God's non-intervention during this period of night, we still are unable to let God go away permanently. Any attempt, Wiesel insists, to make the Holocaust "fit" into a divine plan, any belief that somehow we can imagine a universe congruent with it, renders God a moral monster and the universe a nightmare beyond endurance. But, as theologian Robert McAfee Brown has put it,

> for Wiesel and for many others the issue will not go away. He must contest with God, concerning the moral outrage that somehow seems to be within the divine plan. How can one affirm a God whose "divine plan" could include such barbarity? For Wiesel, the true "contemporary" is not the modern skeptic, but the ancient Job,

the one who dares to ask questions of God, even though Wiesel feels that Job gave in a little too quickly at the end.[26]

Wiesel hints that after all is said and done the Holocaust may reveal that divine and human liberation are very much intertwined and that, despite continuing tension, both God and humanity yearn for each other as a result. In consequence of this linkage, Wiesel is prepared to say that human acts of justice and compassion help to liberate God, to restore the divine image as Fackenheim has phrased it. Job, says Wiesel, "did not suffer in vain; thanks to him, we know that it is given to man to transform divine injustice into human justice and compassion."[27] But they also show the need for God's continuing presence, for the human person who claims total freedom from God will not likely pursue such a ministry of justice and compassion for very long. So the human person is also liberated from the corrupting desire to cut all ties to the Creator.

At this point, the inevitable question must be posed. How can this "compelling God" serve as the ground of contemporary morality? Strange as it may seem, the Holocaust provides us with some assistance in responding to this question. For if the Holocaust reveals one permanent quality of human life, it is the enduring presence of, the continuing human need for, symbolic affirmation and communication. What Reinhold Niebuhr called the vitalistic side of humanity has not been permanently obliterated. But increasingly in the West it has been relegated almost exclusively to the realm of play and recreation. The Enlightenment and its aftermath caused a bifurcation in Western humanity which has catapulted reason to a place of overwhelming dominance in the self-definition of the person. All other human dimensions tend to be relegated to an inferior position. In this setting, ethics has become too exclusively rational a discipline and far too dominated by the scientific mentality. The liberals in Germany were powerless in fighting Nazism, not because they did not care, but because they naively assumed that the masses would respond to mere rational moral argumentation. The Nazis were far more perceptive in recognizing the centrality of the vitalistic in human life.

Recovery of abiding contact with the personal Creator God first revealed in the Hebrew Scriptures is as indispensable a starting point for social ethics in the post-Holocaust era as recognition of our enhanced co-creational responsibility for the world. The two go hand-in-hand.

Any attempt to construct a social ethic for our age by merely *assuming* the continued reality of this divine presence, however, will not succeed. Neither will efforts built around natural law, Kantian rational consistency models, or psychoanalysis provide the requisite moral grounding. The kind of post-Holocaust relationship between God and humanity pivotal for the development of social morality in our time will come only through divine-human encounter in worship and prayer. The failure of nearly all contemporary forms of social ethics to deal constructively with the role of symbols, especially liturgical symbols, in fostering social morality, to recognize how crucial they are for overcoming the prevailing one-dimensionality infecting Western society has left us with an increasingly barren public morality.[28]

In this discussion, I have chosen to focus on what I regard as the fundamental theological issues facing us in the postmodern world that the Holocaust has had a major hand in shaping. There are other important questions, theological and ethical, which also need addressing. I shall mention only a few of them at this point as I bring my remarks to a close.

Certainly there will be need for Christological restatement relative to the Jewish-Christian relationship. While it is not possible to discuss the various proposals brought forward by Christian theologians such as Paul van Buren, Franz Mussner, Peter von der Osten-Sacken, myself, and others, one reality is crystal clear. In light of the Holocaust and the indisputable contribution religiously based anti-Semitism made to its popular acceptance, the church's moral integrity will not allow it to retain the classical supersessionist models of the relationship which have their roots in the patristic period. In the words of Johannes Metz, "Christian theology after Auschwitz must stress anew the Jewish dimension in Christian beliefs and must overcome the forced blocking-out of the Jewish heritage within Christianity."[29] It will also prove necessary to reexamine Christological statements, particularly those relating to the Incarnation, in light of the new understandings about the God-humanity relationship which have begun to emerge among Jewish and Christian theologians reflecting on the Holocaust experience.[30]

Other more specific questions will also demand our attention. What is the relationship between Jewish denigration throughout the ages and patriarchal tendencies within Christianity, something Elisabeth Schussler-Fiorenza has addressed?[31] How might we understand the connection between Holocaust theology and a liberation theology, a theme Rebecca Chopp has probed?[32] How does the study of the Holocaust help us to understand better the development of what Robert Jay Lifton has termed the "genocidal mentality"?[33] What do we learn from the Holocaust regarding the relationship between religion and public culture, particularly from the Nazi public rallies?[34] Finally, what does the Holocaust teach about the need for a critical dimension in authentic faith expression, a dimension Darrell Fasching has begun to explore?[35]

The centrality of the issues discussed above gives ample evidence of the Holocaust's continuing relevance for theology in our time. The event was the child of many of the forces most influential in the shaping of contemporary Western culture. And these forces are alive in nearly every part of the world, making the Holocaust something far more than a Western phenomenon even though that was its actual locale. Any faith perspective that believes it can avoid the issues raised by the Holocaust or summarily dispense with them is opening itself up to self-destruction. Both Christians and Jews for their own well-being, for their mutual enrichment, for the safety and sustainability of creation, must continue to wrestle with them even though we may never penetrate the veil of darkness that covers the event.

NOTES

1. Uriel Tal, *Christians and Jews in Germany: Religion, Politics, and Ideology in the Second Reich 1870–1914* (Ithaca, NY: Cornell University Press, 1975), 305.

2. Alexandre Donat, *The Holocaust Kingdom* (New York: Holt, Reinhart, and Winston, 1965), 230–31.

3. Emil Fackenheim, *The Jewish Return into History* (New York: Schocken Books, 1978), 246.

4. On Polish extermination under the Nazis, see Eugeniusz Duraczynski, *Wojna i Okupacja: Wrzesien 1939-Kwiecien 1943* (Warsaw: Wiedza Powszechna, 1974), 17; Nora Levin, *The Holocaust: The Destruction of European Jewry 1933–1945* (New York: Schocken, 1973), 163, 193; Leon Poliakov, *Harvest of Hate: The Nazi Program for the Destruction of the Jews of Europe* (New York: Holocaust Library, 1979), 263; Janusaz Gumkowski and Kazimierz Leszczynski, *Poland under Nazi Occupation* (Warsaw: Polonia Publishing House, 1961), 59; and Karol Pospieszalski, *Polska pod Niemieckim Prawem* (Posnán: Wyoawnictwo Instytutu Zachodniego, 1946), 189.

5. On non-Jewish victims, see Bohdan Wytwycky, *The Other Holocaust: Many Circles of Hell* (Washington, DC: The Novak Report, 1980); Frank Rector, *The Nazi Extermination of Homosexuals* (New York: Stein and Day, 1981); Richard S. Lukas, *Forgotten Holocaust: The Poles under German Occupation, 1939–1944* (Lexington, KY: University Press of Kentucky, 1986); Gabrielle Tyrnauer, "The Gypsy Awakening," *Reform Judaism* 14:3 (Spring 1986): 6–8; Richard Plant, *The Pink Triangle: The Nazi War against Homosexuals* (New York: Henry Holt, 1986); Ian Hancock, *The Parish Syndrome* (Ann Arbor, MI: Karoma Publishers, 1987).

6. Uriel Tal, "Forms of Pseudo-Religion in the German *Kulturbereich* Prior to the Holocaust," *Immanuel* 3 (Winter 1973–74): 69.

7. Uriel Tal, *Christians and Jews in Germany,* 302–3.

8. Michael Ryan, "Hitler's Challenge to the Churches: A Theological-Political Analysis of *Mein Kampf*" in Franklin H. Littell and Hubert G. Locke, eds., *The German Church Struggle and the Holocaust* (Detroit: Wayne State University Press, 1974), 160–61.

9. David Tracy, "Religious Values after the Holocaust: A Catholic View" in Abraham J. Peck, ed., *Jews and Christians after the Holocaust* (Philadelphia: Fortress, 1982), 101.

10. For a fuller presentation of recent Jewish perspectives, see my essays, "Christian Ethics and the Holocaust: A Dialogue with Post-Auschwitz Judaism," *Theological Studies* 49:4 (December 1988): 649–69, and "The *Shoah:* Its Challenges for Religious and Secular Ethics," *Holocaust and Genocide Studies: An International Journal* 3:4 (1988): 443–54.

11. David Hartman, "New Jewish Religious Voices II: Auschwitz or Sinai," *The Ecumenist* 21:1 (November/December 1982): 8.

12. Eugene Borowitz, *Renewing the Covenant: A Theology for the Postmodern Jew* (Philadelphia: The Jewish Publication Society, 5752/1991).

13. Eugene Borowitz, *Renewing the Covenant,* 289.

14. Richard Rubenstein, *After Auschwitz* (Indianapolis: Bobbs-Merrill, 1966). Also see "Some Perspectives on Religious Faith after Auschwitz" in Littell and Locke, eds., *The German Church Struggle,* 256–68.

15. Richard L. Rubenstein and John K. Roth, *Approaches to Auschwitz: The Holocaust and Its Legacy* (Atlanta: John Knox Press, 1987), 311–12.

16. Steven T. Katz, *Post-Holocaust Dialogues: Critical Studies in Modern Jewish Thought* (New York: New York University Press, 1983), 176.

17. Emil Fackenheim, *The Jewish Return into History* (New York: Schocken, 1978).

18. Arthur Cohen, *The Tremendum: A Theological Interpretation of the Holocaust* (New York: Crossroad, 1981).

19. Cohen, *The Tremendum,* 97.

20. Irving Greenberg, "The Voluntary Covenant," *Perspectives I* (New York: National Jewish Resource Center, 1982), 14.

21. Greenberg, "The Voluntary Covenant," 15.

22. Greenberg, "The Voluntary Covenant," 15.

23. Greenberg, "The Voluntary Covenant," 16.

24. Greenberg, "The Voluntary Covenant," 17–18.

25. D. H. Lawrence, *Selected Poems* (London: Penguin, 1967), 144.

26. Robert McAfee Brown, "The Holocaust as Problem in Moral Choice," in Harry Cargas, ed., *When God and Man Failed: Non-Jewish Views of the Holocaust* (New York: Macmillan, 1981), 94.

27. Elie Wiesel, *Messengers of God* (New York: Random House, 1976), 235.

28. See my essay, "Worship after the Holocaust: An Ethician's Reflections" in Kathleen Hughes, R.S.C.J., and Mark R. Francis, C.S.V., eds., *Living No Longer for Ourselves: Liturgy and Justice in the Nineties* (Collegeville, MN: The Liturgical Press, 1991), 52–67.

29. Johannes Metz, "Facing the Jews: Christian Theology after Auschwitz," in Elisabeth Schussler-Fiorenza and David Tracy, eds., *The Holocaust as Interruption: Concillium* (October 1984) (Edinburgh: T. and T. Clark, 1984), 31.

30. See my essay, "The Holocaust and Contemporary Christology," in Schussler-Fiorenza and Tracy, eds., *The Holocaust,* 43–49.

31. Elisabeth Schussler-Fiorenza and David Tracy, "The Holocaust as Interruption and the Christian Return to History" in Schussler-Fiorenza and Tracy, eds., *The Holocaust,* 86.

32. Rebecca Chopp, "The Interruption of the Forgotten" in Schussler-Fiorenza and Tracy, eds., *The Holocaust,* 20.

33. See Robert Jay Lifton and Eric Markusen, *The Genocidal Mentality: Nazi Holocaust and Nuclear Threat* (New York: Basic Books, 1990).

34. See my essays, "The Holocaust: Its Implications for the Church and Society Problematic" in Richard W. Rousseau, S.J., ed., *Christianity and Judaism: The Deepening Dialogue* (Scranton, PA: Ridge Row Press, 1983), 95–106, and "The Holocaust: Its Implications for Public Morality" in Franklin H. Littell, Irene G. Shur, and Claude R. Foster, Jr., eds., *The Holocaust: IN ANSWER* (Westchester, PA: Sylvan Publishers, 1988), 287–97.

35. Darrell J. Fasching, *Narrative Theology after Auschwitz: From Alienation to Ethics* (Minneapolis, MN: Fortress, 1992).

INDEX